ECONOMICS

The Historical, Religious & Contemporary Perspectives: A Treatise

Nabil M. Mustapha

authorHOUSE®

AuthorHouse™ UK Ltd.
500 Avebury Boulevard
Central Milton Keynes, MK9 2BE
www.authorhouse.co.uk
Phone: 08001974150

This book is a work of non-fiction. Unless otherwise noted, the author
and the publisher make no explicit guarantees as to the accuracy of

http://www.nabil.mustapha.com

First published by AuthorHouse 6/15/2009

ISBN: 978-1-4389-4983-3 (sc)

Printed in the United States of America
Bloomington, Indiana

THIS BOOK IS DEDICATED TO MY PARENTS, WHO TAUGHT ME THE LOVE OF HUMANKIND, AND THE VALUE OF ENDEAVOUR

IT IS ALSO DEDICATED TO MY WIFE LAILA, FOR CREATING THE HOME ENVIRONMENT THAT ENABLED ME TO SPEND THE HOURS ON THIS WORK

Table of Contents

FOREWORD

The reader will no doubt wonder why a surgeon would find the urge to put together his thoughts on the subject of economics. The answer may lie in the fact that there is a always the desire in perhaps everyone to engage in a subject, a hobby, or any other pursuit in order to satisfy two major purposes. The first is the need for some diversionary activity to stretch one's ability in art, craft, sport or intellectuality. The second is perhaps just an interest or curiosity that takes hold on, and encourages the individual, to take on the challenge.

Economics fascinated me since boyhood, and my attraction to it was on account of the continuing internal struggle anyone feels between the dream of wealth and the need to uphold the human values. The lure of wealth is ever-present, and to respond to this lure regardless of any care for those around is neither easy nor meritorious, unless, of course, one appreciates the consequences of such action. One immediately thinks of religion as a check on one's thoughts and actions, and no doubt that it is a powerful influence. I was however, so enchanted by the thoughts of eminent economists who intellectualised this need to consider the good of the others and to do so as a necessity for the prosperity of the individual as well as the community. The cast was thus set in my mind that here is one line of thought that could satisfy my interest in history, in religion and in a subject (economics) where these avenues of knowledge can converge.

With this mindset, I found myself attracted to reading about economics, until a moment of time when I felt that reading about it was not enough. I had to put thought into word. I had to satisfy myself, however, that whatever approach I made to write about this subject had to be in a way that would not challenge the dedicated well versed economists. I had to create my own environment on the subject, indeed, my "comfort zone". My approach had to be that of a non-purist economic one. I found that the more I read economics the more I developed respect not only for the subject, but even more so for the economists themselves. I will never cease to admire the different approaches the various economists take in presenting their thoughts. Their intellectuality can, indeed, be awesome. I had to ensure that I do not become a fake pretender.

I aim this work at the reader who may be almost exactly in the same position as I am; the reader who would like to know something about economics but is scared away by the complexities and the jargon. There will be the reader who would appreciate the context within which economics can be a humanities subject rather than a quantum and mathematics one. Furthermore, I hope that I have presented the usefulness of religion along the ages, and the relevance of what I considered to be economic principles within the various scriptures to the times of their revelation and the needs of the people on the receiving end of these scriptures. While concentrating on the three major religions, Judaism, Christianity and Islam, I have added those principles of the more recent Religion, the Bahá'í Faith, to which I adhere. Other religions, particularly Buddhism, Hinduism and Sikhism will also contain useful scriptures and teachings of an economic nature. I have developed a most deep respect for their scriptures, and the civilisations they have established at their time. But to include these Faiths would lengthen the work quite appreciably and add little to what I believe is one of the common threads that one finds in all Divinely Inspired Faiths. I wish to mention very clearly that in this I mean to testify to the value of these Faiths, and aver my belief, and that of the Bahá'í Faith, that Divine Revelations have so much in common, and that any perceived differences are only minor and only meant to address the exigencies of the time of revelation and the particular needs of the people at the time.

With regards to my knowledge of history, I add my sincere deference to the history academicians who have given us so much insight into the past. To them we owe the passing down of the wisdom of those who preceded us from time immemorial. While the world is in need of wisdoms relevant to our times, it would be very unwise to dismiss time honoured wisdoms of the past. Many of these are timeless verities, and it is to the historians that credit must be due for passing them on throughout the ages.

In conclusion, I would beg the reader to credit me for only one thing. That I may have triggered off a fresh, and indeed a freshman's, thinking on a subject that people may shy away from, and maybe also that I have shown that the subject of religion can be approached with an unbiased wish and will to see the nuggets of wisdom, and how some of them are practical applications for our everyday life.

I have put the work together in the form of a treatise rather than a book. Perhaps this is to fit in with my limitations, as I hope that a treatise may not be so demanding in format and layout. It is the subject matter that I hope will be deemed useful.

Nabil M. Mustapha
M.B B.Ch. MRCS, LRCP, FRCS

PART I

INTRODUCTION

Economics is one of those subjects that people tend to shy away from on the assumption that it is a speciality better left to the experts.

Moreover, people tend to equate economics with *making money*, and therefore is the domain of bankers, investment specialists, merchants, shopkeepers and the like. On a more ordinary level of thinking, people relate economics to the art or ability of *saving*.

Yet, the origin of the word economics is the Greek word *"Oikonomia"* meaning the problem of organising the *"oikos"* or household. In other words, it is the art of housekeeping and household budgeting[1]. Naturally, the term has expanding along the ages, in accordance, as will be clear later, with the development of society, and the increase in complexity of its affairs. Nevertheless, economics is still the art or science of organising the "house keeping" affairs of the family, community, state, or, as is increasingly necessary nowadays, the world.

It is easy to think of economics as a science, obeying certain laws and conforming to recognised patterns. It is also easy to think of it as an arm of politics and affairs of the state. It is, however, less easy to think of economics as a response to moral and ethical issues. But this will become more apparent later.

And finally, it may appear almost unthinkable that economic principles, some quite profound and lasting, are, in fact, enshrined in religious teachings. It is customary to look at the texts in major religions as utterances of spiritual values, and perhaps historical anecdotes. Yet, it will become apparent from even a not too deep study of some religious teachings that these teachings had enunciated some of the economic principles taken now a days for granted. Even more interesting, is the fact that these economics principles had evolved with progressive religions so as to "up-grade" them in keeping with the development of society, and with it the more complex and sophisticated needs. The binding of these principles of economics within a spiritual context may be an aspect of both religion and economics that has perhaps, and if so, sadly, been missed by both economists and ecclesiastics.

A conclusion, therefore, is that economics is essentially a "*Social science*"[2], and it is accepted that, as such, it is one of the youngest of the social sciences, probably about 200 years old.

In the early days:

The evolution of humankind over the ages started from the recognised very simple beginnings, when people subsisted on the vegetation around them. The essential requirement was that of "*survival*". And that was essentially individual, and so long as the vegetation and fruit were available, man and woman had almost equal access to it. Even with the development of hunting, the order of the day was that of instant consumption[3] , with hardly any time lag between the time the effort was put in and the availability of the material for consumption and subsistence.

The difference here is that with hunting, there appeared some differences between man and woman, in that the man had the greater strength and developed the prowess required to turn him into the "procurer". This factor may also have ushered in the beginnings of the *"family"* unit and with it the man's role of heading, providing for and protecting the family. Following such a development in the structure of the primitive beginnings of *"Society"* the needs began to develop further from mere subsistence to that of subsistence plus *"shelter"*. Fishing became an added tool, although probably it was a later discovery, and may not have altered the primitive structure of life. It is only when the age of *"shepherding"* followed by the age of *"agriculture""* and then *"commerce"*, did the economic activity start to develop so as to provide the basis of, and explain the need for, law and government[4].

Government as such took much longer to develop, as will be seen later. But with the next step of development of society, that of the tribal formations, the beginnings of some "laws" can be seen to emerge. There appeared the traditions governing relationships between individuals, in the time honoured "neighbourliness" fashion which is so well emphasized in Biblical texts, as well as those attempting to harmonize relationships within the family, be it the immediate or the extended.

It can be seen that these laws and traditions demonstrated, as they set in, the first relationships with recognised religion particularly apparent in the Judaic laws and the tribes of Israel.

Next it was trade. This became an important aspect to satisfy early needs that were not met locally, and to enhance prosperity through the exchange of goods and services across land and, as for example with the Phoenicians, the sea.

The earliest civilisations, particularly those of ancient Egypt and ancient China demonstrated a remarkable ability to create unified structures over large expanses of territory, and multitudes of peoples very varied in language, tradition, and circumstance. A strong central ruling authority acted not despotically, but rather as a rallying and centripetal force, commanding respect, deference, and loyalty. With this there appeared the need to establish some laws that would regulate these relationships, whether in between the subjects, or between the subjects and their rulers. Once again, the interaction of these civilisations with religion can be seen, most noticeably with Moses and Egypt, and with Confucius and China.

It is a long gap between these stages in the social structural development of Humanity and the beginnings of *"nationhood"* which perhaps had its beginnings in the Roman state, but came into its own with the establishment of Islam throughout a large swathe of the recognised world of the time. Laws had to be enacted to govern these societies, and by then the religious influences, particularly Christianity and Islam, were easily apparent, though not necessarily always quite fitting with the needs of the time, or that the teachings were interpreted intelligently and befittingly enough.

The political systems that followed drew their authority from the relevant religions, but the socio-economics thoughts and doctrines that began to take shape reflected an inquiring attitude of thoughtful people of the time, and the gradual emergence from the grip of established authoritarian rule, mainly those of feudalism and established religious churches and leaderships.

Philosophy, Politics or Ethics?

It is difficult to differentiate the early economic thoughts from those of the philosophers, the political theorists, and the ethicists of the time. The earliest amalgam of all three can easily be seen in the thoughts of the renowned Greek Philosophers, most notably, in this respect, Plato and Aristotle. Both derived their thoughts and inspirations from the Father of them all, Socrates (469 BC-399 BC), who tragically had to end his life by drinking hemlock after the Athenian court ordered his execution, on the grounds of heresy, plotting against the state, twisting of the minds of youth and indeed, atheism. This tragedy affected his friend and pupil Plato (c. 428-c.348 B.C.) so much that he decided with some friends to take refuge elsewhere. They spend time in a cave, then visited the south of Italy before deciding to return to Athens in the year 387 BC. Thereafter, Plato took up his master's baton and established his "school" (the *"Academy"*) in the garden of *"Academus"* on the outskirts of the City[5] .

In his book, the *"The Republic"*, Plato expressed his opinions on society and politics, and formulated his project for the establishment of an ideal or "utopian" social structure. This work remained for a long time, and, in particular during the renaissance, a source of inspiration and a reference. But to understand the background and backdrop within which Plato developed his thoughts, it is necessary to appreciate three points: 1- That Plato was an aristocrat, and was thus defending with all his intellect and literary flair the interests of the aristocracy in Athens, and its efforts to bolster slavery and a stable state. This will prepare the road to the division of labour according to the situation that was beginning to take shape noticeably at the time. 2- That Plato formulated his ideas and philosophies under the influence of the social and political chaos that has swept Athens as a result of its decline in the face of the Spartans. 3- That he was influenced by the social and economic evolution that was under way in the Greek society, and with it the accompanying competition and strife between the different strata of the population with their contradictory and competing interests

Indeed, the contrast between the slaves and their lords was so apparent that it created in the Athenian society an arena of bitter struggle at the same time as the evolution that was taking place, whereby society was changing from a tribal self sufficient order, with authority totally in the hands of the kings and clerics of the day, to an agrarian society.

This latter was being built on an aristocratic land ownership coming into being but denying any opportunity for the working peasants or a share for them in the land.[6]

Plato therefore set out to lay down what he believed to be the firm foundations of a strong society, with the division of labour between its various factions as the basis. Indeed, he felt that a strong and stable society will be one where there is a distinct and clearly cut partition between the factions. That the ideal society is one where the ruling elite composed of rulers/philosophers would rule with the assistance of a posse of military personnel. In this way the state will be defended from external dangers, and from internal strife. As for peasantry, artisanship, and other menial labour, these were not fit to be undertaken by Athenians, but by slaves and prisoners of war.

It is interesting that Plato had come to realise that there can be three reasons why division of labour is necessary: **1-** That no one person is able to satisfy all his varied needs, particularly because these needs were becoming more complex and were changing from mere necessities to some luxury. **2-** That people differ in their abilities and natural talents. and **3-** That he was appalled at the tendency of the ruling elite to indulge in extravagance to the detriment of their duty to safeguard and rule.

In his book "The Republic" Plato states: "Should they (Guardians of the state) ever acquire homes or lands or moneys of their own, they become housekeepers and husbandmen instead of guardians, enemies and tyrants instead of allies of the other citizens." In other words, Plato favoured a pure communistic ethic for those on the top.[7] He thus postulated that levelling down of the ruling (or governing) class, denying them the luxury of land ownership, and forcing them to live communally and simply will in the long run reduce their appetite for extravagance and exploitation, leading them to direct their attention to their real role of administering the affairs of state.

Plato's thoughts may have been accepted at the time, but for subsequent thinkers, these thoughts were unacceptable. Indeed, it was Plato's renowned pupil, Aristotle, who was vociferous in his criticism, in particular with regards the "communistic" sides to Plato's "Utopian Republic", and especially the denying of opportunity for the ruling elite to acquire and own land and property and thus constitute themselves into independent "families".

Aristotle (384-322 BC) believed that communal property will never benefit from the care and attention that private property will have. In addition, he postulated that it is in the nature of man to be ostentatious with his private acquisitions. He is quoted saying: "How immeasurably greater is the pleasure, when a man feels a thing to be his own, for the love of self is a feeling implanted by nature and not given to vain...no one, when men have all things in common, will any longer set an example of liberality or do any liberal action; for liberality consists in the use which is made of property

In relation to the governing class, Aristotle thought that they should have the right to form "families", which are, after all, the basis upon which villages and cities are composed. A State is in turn a collection of cities. This was, it will be remembered, the age of the "City States", as exemplified by Athens, Sparta, Corinth and Rome.

Aristotle went to the extent of postulating that this division between the ruling elite and the working class is indeed a natural phenomenon inherent in people, whereby all those who can only do menial work cannot, by nature, be Hellenic. He states: "It is clear, then, that some men are by nature free, and others are slaves, and that for these latter slavery is both expedient and right"[8]. And again: " The lower sort are by nature slaves, and it is better for them as for all inferiors that they should be under the rule of a master...indeed the use made of slaves and animals is not very different"[9]. The status quo, in his opinion therefore, is there to stay, and is not confined to a time or a place. In this context, his view was that the great "moral superiority" is ascribed to farming, and his ethical justification for the state of slavery (the "lower sort") is in fact an example of the ethical (acceptable or otherwise) intonation in his ideas.

In developing these thoughts, Aristotle also postulated that such family units will need to interact economically in order to satisfy their inherent necessities. These interactions he called *"Oikos"*, which in plain language, as mentioned above, will translate as "family housekeeping", although technically it signifies "economic productivity". It follows therefore that the family can barter or exchange surplus goods and services, provided this is not undertaken with profit as the motive. He made a distinction between this type of interaction, and another which he called "Chremastia" *(or Chrematistiké)*, where there is a profit motive (the acquisitive system)[10]. However, while accepting that production is legitimate as it reflects a person's natural effort, trade profit is unnatural, and can only be considered cheating and theft. It is thus immoral. Aristotle then adds that: "The most hated sort (of moneymaking), and with the greatest reason, is usury...for money is meant to be used in exchange, but not to increase at interest"[11].

Aristotle in this way made a distinction between acquiring or exchanging a product for necessary use, and exchanging a product simply for profit, coining the two terms: "the use value", and the "exchange value".

PART II

THE BEGINNINGS OF THE LEGAL FRAMEWORK FOR AN ECONOMIC SYSTEM:

The Roman Era:

It would seem that Rome had a much greater opportunity, and indeed, a need, to study and develop a more sophisticated economic system than that of Athens. Rome was larger. It was the all important centre for Italy, and it was the hub of an expanding Empire. This is a far cry from the "City State" that Athens was. Moreover, Rome was not operating on a self-sufficiency basis.

Significantly, money was recognized as a means of measuring value, and exchange. Silver was the preferred metal, as it was in Athens. Coinage had acquired a tendering status through the official stamps that indicated its weight, and therefore value. The Romans had no misgivings about the use of money, and so it gradually replaced barter. Trade between the various "Provinces" within the Roman Empire was growing, and extended throughout most of the European territories, Anatolia, North Africa and some Asiatic Arab states.

The reason for the paucity of thought by the Romans on economic matters is the subject of debate and discussion. A satisfactory answer is difficult to find. It may, however, be their belief, as in Athens, that economics is not such a creative subject fit for thinkers and philosophers to apply themselves to.[12]

Nevertheless, there was one major contribution that the Romans are credited for. That is the indirect benefit to economics in the political and legal structure that they established. The so-called "Roman Laws" fell mainly into three categories:

1- <u>The Civil law</u>: Which applied to the Romans exclusively.
2- <u>The Peoples law</u>: dealing with all other subjects.
3- <u>The Natural law</u>: covering natural resources and livestock

Thus, within these laws, this one major Roman contribution, that ostensibly was outside the conventional boundary of economics, and may have escaped the more conventional economic discussion, and yet, nevertheless, very useful, was the role of private property within the Roman law. The Romans supported without any restrictions the right to private property, and to entering into individual legal contracts. An essential reason for this has been the greater development of society in the Roman Empire, whereby there were more than the Athenian two classes of the population. In Rome, there was the third class of "soldiers" who had to be given privileges in reward for their effort, sacrifice, and loyalty. The higher echelons of the military, the "Commanders" were, moreover the elite of society, with direct access to the Emperor of the time and his entourage. Their recompense had to be commensurate with their value and achievement. Property, no less, was an important ingredient in this recognition, as it entailed not only wealth, but also a compliment of "servants", slaves and other helpers i.e. all the trappings of prestige and status.

This situation must have been one of the reasons for the emergence of the early Christian ethos and the economic "Deism" thoughts in

Mediaeval Europe, which are more in tune with the Greek thoughts than those of the Romans. Aristotle had an effect on these early Christian Churches despite the recognized value of the "liberal" theories of "Individualism".

The Basic Concepts In Economics

The basic and historic origin of economics, as mentioned above, is the function of "house-keeping". In its primitive form, it was essentially the labour, based on the individual, and perhaps the family, as well as the use of available natural resources. All this was to satisfy the immediate needs of subsistence, and perhaps shelter. With the development of people's lifestyles, the needs, as expected, started to increase and become varied. People were able to manipulate natural resources better, and in this way, individual expertise started to show differentiation and specialization, much like the primordial cells of the foetus differentiating with its organic growth in order to perform specialized tasks within distinct organ systems.

Economic thinking began to address the task of putting labour and natural resources to best use. This meant the interlocking of specialized functions, and with the increasing needs and increasing categories of needs, certain "standards" emerged, to enable people to measure what they would consider as their "greater" or "more important" needs, and distinguish these from the "lesser" or "less important" ones, bearing in mind, however, that such standards can differ from one person to the other, or, indeed, for the same person from time to time. "Economizing" thus began to imply the thought process of *measurement* of needs as well as to establish a *hierarchy* of needs and therefore of labour. An *"Order"* had to develop, and any such order required a measure of *"Liberty"*. The two had to be in balance, as liberty without order is physically impossible, and order without liberty is intolerable. The balance can provide a state of *"Harmony"*, and while most people would recognize a natural tendency to harmony, there is, nevertheless a need to "influence" the many variables that could play a part in producing or spoiling harmony.

At this juncture, one could consider briefly the question as to why history is important when considering the economic needs of the present? Economic ideas, as mentioned previously, are a product of their time and place. Political economy or economics has been described by Alfred Marshall, of the University of Cambridge, (also recognized as the economic "God-father" of J.M. Keynes), as "a study of mankind in the ordinary business of life"[13]. Moreover, economics is obsessed with the future, and by now it is accepted that the future will always retain compelling aspects of what exists now. At the same time, every new development is bound to make us think again about some old familiar text in the history of economics. The present is thus to a great extent a product of the past. and so, while we should not be "Ancestor worshippers" we also should not be arrogant towards thoughts and writers of the past.

Economic science, can thus be looked at as different from other sciences in that there is no inevitable advance from the lesser to the greater certainty, and is not a strict intellectual development from error to truth, but rather as a progression that advances through incremental additions to thought and knowledge[14].

This is the aspect of economics that is essentially related to the social and political development and structure, with the emphasis on such attributes and principles as justice, fairness, equal opportunity and other ethical and moral issues. The mathematical, statistical, forecasting, and other aspects of applied economics is the domain of the experts, and relates predominantly to day to day financial, budgetary, and similar needs of modern society. It is beyond the subject matter of this work.

Economics Of The Middle Ages

The "Middle Ages" is generally understood to be the period between the demise of the Roman Empire as a result of the conquests of the Germanic tribes in the fifth century AD up to the fifteenth century. During this thousand year period there was very poor evidence of economic thought[15] In spite of growing markets, people merely grew, made or killed what they ate or wore, giving a proportion to a hierarchy of lords and masters who provided protection. The essence of the new order lay in the class division between the landowners and the serfs. Transformation occurred gradually as a result of the drying up of the source of slavery which was mainly in the extensive territories of the Roman Empire[16]. It was more practical therefore for the owners of large swathes of property, i.e. land overlords of the church, kings, great noblemen, gentry of higher or lower degree, or rich tenant-farmers, to let in the workers as share-croppers or tenants. Products and services were, however, surrendered not sold. The use of money became less necessary, and therefore reduced in significance because large estates were able to be relatively self sufficient, and produce enough surplus to satisfy the needs of local or regional markets. People were reconciled to this order as a de facto situation and because they thought of it as the *Divine* wish. The laws governing relationships on this basis were consolidated, and the (Catholic) Church transformed into a formal establishment based on a Spiritual and Temporal authority. The Church, taking its power from a vast land ownership that made it the largest feudal organisation of its time, used this status to fill the void left by the demise of the Roman order in laying down a new foundation of temporal laws based on moral and ecclesiastic principles.

An essential feature of the Church's attitude at the time was to instil into people the need to disregard any material hardship in this world and to accept the class differences as inevitable. In circumstances like these, it is easy to imagine that thinking about economic matters will be irrelevant. Life in this world was but a preparation for the worlds to come. *"Deism"*, with its emphasis on Nature, the Divine Creation, and Man as an instrument to maintain or destroy order was the dominant basis of thought at the time. Authority and Liberty were looked at in terms of the importance and need to maintain order and avoid "Chaos". Indeed the Deists were bereft of real thinkers at the time, and so resorted to classical and time-honoured Athenian philosophies, mainly of Aristotle.

The "Deists" were unable to unravel the Teachings of the New Testament in terms of their "economic" content. They were thus content with reconciling any differences between what they saw as moral and spiritual teachings with the exigencies of the time. Having developed very large endowments and assets, the Church was content to act as part of the established order, and that meant being a custodian of these large holdings with their complement of workers, whether they happened to be those in some religious habit (monks, nuns, priests etc.), or lay workers. These latter would probably be content with the feeling that they are serving the Church and thus, indirectly, God.

Whether the Church was aware of another development not too far from its established domain or not, may be difficult to ascertain. But Islam, which originated in the Arabian Peninsula in the sixth Century AD, was beginning to spread very close to Europe and indeed into Europe, while becoming a displacing force around the Christian Holy places in Palestine and other parts of the middle and near East. Islam was not only to become a flourishing wave of religious fervour and conversion, but also a formidable political and socio-economic civilisation with an evolving Spiritual ideology that blended itself into a Temporal and Religious Order, based on the idea of "Nationhood". It will be fair to consider this phase in religious and political evolution as the beginning of the transformation, at least in the Islamic part of the world, from the order of Feudalism or City Statehood, into that of Nationhood. This Nationhood was based on the two distinct but complementary meanings of the Arabic word *"Umma"*. A nation was described as an Umma in territorial terms, and hence the "United Nations" in Arabic is translated as "Al Ummam (plural for Umma) Al Mottaheda". In a more encompassing context, the whole of the Islamic World at whatever time in history is described as **"Ummat'u'l Islam" (the "Nation of Islam")**. It took the rest of the world some time to wake up to this formidable shaping up of a great chunk of the world, which even at those mediaeval times was beginning to open up known and not so known territories, ranging from the African shores of the Atlantic to the far off Eastern Territories of what is now Indonesia, China, and the Indian Sub-continent together with the sprinkling of Islands in the surrounding seas.

No such developing civilisation can be without adequate supporting economic principles. Basic principles can be found in the Teachings of the Qur'an. These, however, were elaborated upon by early Islamic Scholars, foremost among whom was "Ibn Khaldun". This subject will be discussed further in a section dealing with the Religious Teachings in the Mosaic, Christian and Islamic Scriptures.

Evolving Economics In The Christian World:

The Crusades

The Interaction between the Christian World and the Islamic World would have started on mutual respect and acceptance were it not for the circumstances that led to the "Crusades". One of the effects of these crusades was that the Christian World, in its need to finance the expeditions, had to reconsider the economic structure. No longer was it enough to maintain a local, self sufficient economy based on barter and exchange of services. The need for tangible exchangeable assets became obvious, especially in dealing with the territories the Crusaders had to traverse to reach their destinations. Money and precious metals had to be used, minted or otherwise. Soldiers had to be paid, and even local arms craftsmen had to be remunerated. Trade was beginning to be accepted as a "legitimate" means of earning. This was a departure from the philosophies of Aristotle and the moral teachings of Christianity, both having looked at trade as being a rather immoral act.

In the spirit of these changes, new thoughts emerged which were to further give moral and ethical credibility to these changes. Salient among these new philosophies were those of Saint Thomas Aquinas or Saint Thomas of Aquina (1225-1274 AD). An Italian born citizen of France, he became conscious of the need to instil moral values within the processes of trade. He condemned the " profiteer, the predator, the exploiter, and the unduly grasping seller or buyer. In "Saint Thomas Aquinas, *Summa Theologica*, Question 77" he is quoted as saying:..."I answer that it is wholly sinful to practice fraud for the express purpose of selling a thing for more than its just price...to sell dearer or to buy cheaper than a thing is worth is in itself unjust and unlawful.."[17].

Inevitable discussions and opinions then had to start addressing how to determine the "just" price. Thoughts ranged from "leaving it to the market", to "decide on a market price". That was deemed not enough. There appeared, scantily but exiguously, the thought that there is a need for a "higher order" of justice than that of the market. While this, as recorded by the eminent economist J.K. Galbraith[18] provided a legislative "minimum" wage or "a fair price to the producer", it could also have been a manifestation of the inner workings of these, essentially spiritual thinkers/philosophers, that such a higher order has to be based upon spirituality and religious teachings. The questions extended from fair price to such matters as the controlled rent, and then more deeply into what St Thomas affirmed as the need for honesty. Declaring any defect on a good on offer for sale, or not selling if knowing of a defect, for example, except when the defect is seen, such as in a one eyed horse.

St Thomas also condemned interest. He affirmed that there are two kinds of exchanges: **1**- Natural and necessary (praiseworthy) and **2**- Money for money (condemned). As such professional traders—brokers, scalpers, speculators, middlemen, etc.. joined money lenders in moral oblique, i.e. those who are abusers and therefore ill spoken of.

Early monetarist thought

The emergence or re-emergence of money as a necessary means for pricing and exchange, meant that there also emerged the need to establish certain rules. Conditions had changed from those where trade was from one person to another on a limited scale, such as trading a horse or a head of cattle from one person to the other, to merchandise between groups of traders. Where crafts in particular were concerned, the formation of "Guilds" became necessary. Their job was to regulate their respective trade, quality of workmanship, price, and wages. In the process, these guilds formulated high standards of agreeable social observances, and wielded political influence.

There was a sea change within a relatively short time of about one hundred years, during which another spiritual philosopher, Nicole ORESME(1320-1382), the Bishop of Liscieux (France), ushered in what is probably the first *"Monetarist"* thoughts[19]. The need to do away with the uncertainties and awkward tedium of having to weigh metals to give them value was addressed by Oresme in his *Traictie de la Premiere Invention des Monnoies"* which showed how coins can be fixed in weight and reliable in purity. The metals used were silver, gold and copper. Moreover, he put the responsibility of coinage squarely on the Princes i.e. the Government. What was also important was that the Prince had a duty to safeguard the debasement of the coinage metal, the consequences of which would be: "who would trust a prince who should diminish the weight or fineness of money bearing his stamp".

To put further moral and ethical qualities to transactions involving money, he further said: "There are three ways, in my opinion, in which one can make profits from money., aside from its natural use. The first of these is the art of exchange, the custody of or trafficking in money, the second is usury, and the third is the altering of money. The first is base, the second is bad, and the third is even worse."

Thus, although Oresme may have announced the importance of reliable and "good" money, it rested with Sir Thomas GRESHAM the great Elizabethan merchant, financier diplomat, and one of the founders of the Royal Exchange to announce his *immutable law* that "Bad money drives out good". It is now taken for granted that anyone would be more interested in keeping and dealing in currency that is of reliable value, and in those days it meant that the quality, weight, and, in certain cases the correct proportion of gold and silver, were correct and reliable.

PART III

RELIGION AND ECONOMICS

It can be seen from the above historical summary, that the progress of economic thought was slow, hesitant, and relying heavily on the thoughts of such original thinkers as Plato and Aristotle on the one hand, and the Church on the other. It can be argued that much of the stimulus to the thoughts of the ancient Greeks has been provided, directly or indirectly, by Jewish Scriptures, particularly with regards to the practical applications of the laws of the Torah and other Scriptures[20]. The (predominantly Catholic) Church and its leaders were content in maintaining a status quo as explained, in which the main element was that man's life in this world is but a prelude to the vastly more important and everlasting life thereafter, and that therefore material matters are to be subsumed in favour of acceptance of basic well-being with endurance, patience, and the drawing on the power of prayer and worship. A colourful description in narrative form of the cross-roads of spiritual thinking can be found in John BUNYON's *The Pilgrim's Progress"*, which is an expression of the sort of thoughts that have emerged within the *Puritanism"* and *"Non-Conformism"* that swept Europe and its Christianity around the seventeenth Century and defied attempts towards *"Restoration"* such as that tried by Charles II in 1660[21]. There was certainly fresh thinking in religious matters, and in the relationships between Religion and the practicalities of everyday life.

Christianity had been the established Religion in Europe, based predominantly on the Papal and Vatican Authority in Rome. But with a gathering and ever-loudening chorus of *"Protesting"* voices. This was epitomized by the withdrawal of King Henry VIII from under the "umbrella" of the Pope and the establishment of the Church of England as a separate independent identity, albeit, at least nominally, within overall Catholicism. While the reason for this "separation" or "Divorce" (the words used advisedly) may not have been quite "altruistic", the separation became consolidated and can be described as the next major schism that has affected Christianity, the first being the separation of the "Orthodox" Church based at Constantinople from that of the Catholic Papal Seat in Rome.

Subsequent developments in Economics were, therefore, very much less influenced by Spirituality or the opinion of the Churches and its Leaders. We see *"Mercantilism"* developing as a "system", or indeed "non-system", and maintaining its place for about three hundred years. Thereafter we witness the emergence of the "Father of Modern Economics" Adam Smith, followed by the other economic thinkers who together dominated the so-called "Classical Era" of Economics. These, and later developments, will be discussed in more detail later.

But what were the teachings of Christianity that can be considered pertaining to economic thought? The Spiritual background was undoubtedly, as noted above, well tapped into. And people are in the habit of reading the Scriptures as Scriptures; noting their spiritual and moral content. They may perhaps also look at the narrative or anecdotal events mentioned with a view of relating them to other historical happenings, contemporary or otherwise.

Nevertheless, Christ and His Disciples, in many of their Teachings had announced principles that have stood the test of time as lasting verities with distinct economic messages.

But before searching for these teachings in the New Testament, it is just as important to consider similar relationships between the Scriptures in the Old Testament and Economics.

While Judaism lasted for about two thousand years in the "Land of Israel" with all its colourful, nay sometimes chequered, history, any economic or organisational framework was essentially rather parochial, and based on the "Tribes of Israel", no matter how extended these became in number or "Diaspora". Christianity, however, had the benefit of extending and spreading its wings over a much wider sphere, taking in peoples of infinitely varying ethnic and geographical backgrounds. However, in terms of economic thought development, it is noted as shown above that a full millennium and three quarters had provided little more than the limited spiritual and moral backdrop for whatever "system" was in place. This is not to be belittled or under-estimated. For the world was not equipped or ready for any major departure from the relative stability of the systems at the time. Certainly not until the impact of several other factors and developments came into play, These were essentially the great explorations, the momentous advances in Science and Technology, leading to greater inter-action between far off places in the world, and the discovery of means of Communication previously undreamed of. The effect of all this was the evolution of the "Social Status" of Humankind resulting from its increasing ability to deal them with and harness Nature and the Plant and Animal Kingdoms.

Considering the various religions in more detail, it is probably more instructive to deal with them in reverse order of revelation. Islam and Judaism have many similarities. Christianity slots in neatly providing some "adjustments", "refinements" and a greater emphasis on "spirituality" and the transcendence above the material aspects of life.

Islam

Islam was mentioned briefly above. By the end of the XVII Century, it had been around for a little more than a millennium, and had passed through several stages, some noted for their eminence and advance relative to its surrounds, but others, regrettably showing degradation and fractionation. The Teachings of the Qur'an were much more specific in announcing recognized principles of economics. These Teachings have had an effect on the social and administrative (or organisational) framework of life under Islam. But the information available about the economic history of the Arabian Land is to this day too limited for any reasonable "scientific" deductions to be made. Certainly, there is nothing that could act as a base for defining the "Economic System" prevailing since the dawn of the Mohammedan Message to the collapse of the Arab Islamic Rule and the beginning of the Ottoman hegemony[22]. When compared with the available history of the corresponding period in Europe, the Middle Ages, what is found in the Islamic Communities of the time does not exceed a few general points. This is thought to be due to the neglect of this important angle of Arabic Islamic life by Arab historians who concentrated rather on the political and military aspects, particularly because of the political strife that dominated Islamic society in the latter years of the governance of the "Early Caliphs" *(Al Khulafa' al Rashideen)*.

The void thus presented by Islamic scholars and Islamic governance provided the "Classical Economic Thinkers" of Europe the opportunity for greater prominence than would have probably been the case had the Islamic historians and thinkers given the economic teachings of Islam and their development more attention.

This neglect on the part of history should not, however, detract from the fact that the relationships between individuals in the Arabic Islamic Society were quite deeply affected and regulated. To understand these influences one must understand the sources of Arabic Islam. This is essentially the "Shari'a" Law, or Islamic Jurisprudence. Understanding and implementation of these (Shari'a) laws went through several epochs in succession, each with its own characteristics. Starting from inception and establishment of the laws, it goes on to building and extension of the implementation of these laws, and thereafter on to branching out and flourish and finally settling into concrete thinking and imitation[23].

Phase one (inception & establishment): Spans a period of twenty two years approximately, starting with the advent of Islam and ending with the passing away of the Prophet Mohammed in the year 11 A.H.(After Hejira, which is the historic landmark upon which the Islamic calendar is formulated). In this phase, the Qur'an was revealed and with it the *"Shari'a"* (Islamic Religious Laws). In addition, much value is drawn from the extensive utterances attributed to the Prophet Mohammed, which were not considered direct Revelation and therefore were not included in the Qur'anic Text. Nevertheless, the so-called "authenticated" ones, are accepted as detail and wisdom worthy of inclusion as authoritative and illuminating Teachings. This is known as the *"Hadith"*. A third element of the "total" Islamic understanding is the anecdotal experiences recorded of the life of the Prophet Mohammed *("Sunnatu'l Rassoul and "Al-Seerah" Al Nabawiah),* All three add up to a fairly full understanding of the thrust and detail of the Mohammedan Dispensation.

23

Phase two (Extension & Implementation): Is the period to the early second century of Islam, during which the Moslems of the Arabian Peninsula expanded enormously, opening up territories and converting peoples to Islam. Islam was thus exposed to conditions and circumstances totally different from those prevailing in Arabia where life was simpler and much less complex. Moslem legislators faced aspects of life for which no provision was available in the Qur'an or Hadith. The Caliphs and their *"Companions"* thus provided the fourth element or source of the Islamic Jurisprudence as acceptable extensions of the understanding of "Shari'a" This was a period of intense study and discourse, and a period when the method of theological thought had taken shape, and its general rules laid down.

Phase three (Branching out & flourish): This spanned the period between the early second century and until the middle of the fourth century of Islam. During this period, known as the "Abbasid" era, Islamic Shari'a reached a state of maturity, fullness and flourish. The Abbasids based their rule on the laws of Islam. It was a period of prosperity and landmark in the history of the "Islamic Nation", and an important phase in the development of Islamic Theology and Law. As a result there was a closeness between the *Theologians, Al 'Ulama'* (who were raised to prominence) and the Rulers, and an effective address regarding matters of state and life in general. Not only were laws laid to deal with events and occurrences, but indeed, some were laid down to deal with possible or predictable eventualities. The expansion of knowledge and thought in this era also resulted in the appearance of theological sects and branching schools of thought.

Phase four (Concrete thought & Imitation): This was the period from the fourth century onwards. It was characterised by stagnation of thought and mere imitation. Theologian lost their "independent" thinking ability and the philosophical agility displayed by their predecessors. They became followers, not leaders of thought.

Life in the ARABIAN PENINSULA before ISLAM:

To understand the impact of Islam on the Arabian Peninsula, which naturally was the initial part of the world to be affected, it is useful to outline in brief the prevailing conditions of life in that society beforehand. The main areas of settlement were the three important "townships" of Mecca, Medina and Ta'if. Mecca was the most renowned, and was a place of pilgrimage even before it gained its paramount Pilgrim Status after Islam. Apart from these three places, life was nomadic, primitive and disparate. The pilgrimage season brought with it in Mecca a seasonal trade. It was an important trade and barter event and, while coinciding with the (*Pagan*) pilgrimage, actually went further than just satisfying the needs of the Pilgrims who came from far and wide.

However, the most noted of *"fairs"* or market events was held over a period of four months a year close to Ta'if, the famous market of *"Okaz"*. While most of the merchandise was from within the Arabian Peninsula, it was certainly not limited to that. Trade routes were extended, and camel caravans, some comprising up to one thousand camels, plied their way to and from the southern reaches of the Peninsula, to Syria, Egypt, and Ethiopia, and through the northern reaches and the Arabian Gulf reaching as far as the Indian subcontinent. Activity was not restricted to trade of goods, but also involved "trading" of poetry, horsemanship and other showmanships, and perhaps some "politics"[24],[25]

It was an elaborate situation by comparison with the surrounding parts of the world, and the mainspring to this trade activity was the large tribe of *"Quoraysh"* which dominated Mecca and had a wide range of overall support roles. They provided the "logistic" support, guarded the trade routes and caravans, provided the guides, and arranged two main annual trips, one to Syria in summer, and the other to Yemen in winter. Indeed, the word "Quoraysh" is derived from the Arabic word *money* or the gathering of money. This commerce generated immense wealth, and this was used to finance all sorts of activities including warfare. The extent of such expenditure can be gauged from that used to provide for one battle alone (the arch-battle of Badr). This was one the major confrontations between Mohammed and the early Moslems, who had fled Quraysh and Mecca, but were still facing the onslaught of their kith and kin in Quraysh, Mecca, and other tribes united in their determination to extinguish this new and threatening "creed". 50,000 Dinars were required, as well as 2500 head of camel accompanied by 300 guards[26]. In spite of this, they were facing a force three times their size, approximately one thousand men strong.

In Summary : Life in the Arabian Peninsula before Islam, was in the main simple and nomadic with contrasting centres where life relied heavily on commercial activity.

Economic Aspects Of The Islamic Law:

The early days of Islam were characterized by fast and furious developments. Judaism took time even to reach "the promised Land", and then required several generations to be under the suzerainty of various kings, and was guided by a number of Prophets. Christianity effectively took about three hundred years before being established as a result of the declaration of Emperor Constantine. Islam, however, took hold within about one hundred years. The notion of "nationhood" was mentioned above, but the establishment of the Shari'a and the development of "government" took shape, after the initial principles laid down, in particular during the time of Al Khulafa' Al Rashideen, and again mainly during the Abbasid times. The spirit of the law was slower to be appreciated, and the rich academic toil only appeared much later, particularly in Andalusia and North Africa, where a vast innovative array of thought and method were produced. More of this later.

The salient features of the economic principles in Islam can therefore be summarized as follows:

Ownership: This was a subject of intense study, and many angles and aspects were discussed in detail. The initial premise is derived from the Qur'an which states clearly that *"God alone is the "owner" of all that is on Earth and in Heaven, and in between"*[27]. and also: *"He possesses what is in the Heavens and on Earth and underneath"*[28]. This was interpreted by Al-Zamakhshary (1075-1145 A.D.), a widely respected scholar also known as *"Jar Allah"* i.e. the neighbour of God, as indicating that any possession people have are indeed God's alone. He is the Creator and Mankind is the custodian thereof, "enfranchised" to make use of it and enjoy all the benefits, but clearly duty bound to entrust its "Heritage" for the generations to come. It is therefore incumbent upon anyone laying claim to property or ownership to use it for personal gain, but only within limits, and in complete regard to the common good and the benefit of others[29],[30],[31],[32],[33],[34]

The indication, therefore, is that ownership should:

1- Not be a reason to allow a person to exploit another by virtue of any privilege or power endowed.

2- Not lead to amassing of wealth and denying wealth to others.

3- Ensure that the welfare of the community or individuals is regarded when spending.

4- Ensure that any wealth surplus to one's needs is directed towards the common good which has a right to such resources.

In Short; Ownership carries social responsibility which is accepted *voluntarily* and in the spirit of the moral and spiritual qualities expected in a Moslem. Seen from another angle, it can be considered *obligatory* in view of the fact that any (declared) Moslem has, by definition, accepted the Laws and Spiritual Teachings of Islam.

Whether the question was that of ownership (of land, livestock or otherwise), or whether it is that of permanent or temporary rent was a subject of intense study, particularly with regards to the benefits accruing to the individual or to the community. The importance lay in the manner in which situations are considered and in relation to expressions over the real meaning of ownership. Scholars maintained the discussions and further developments in the understanding of ownership and property in Islam took shape. In particular:

1- That it is incumbent on the "ruler" to safeguard the welfare of the community. This could entail the possibility of re-possessing any property if the "owner" fails to respect the obligations to the public. An occasion arose when the Caliph Omar Ibn Al-Khattab admonished Belal Ibn Harith Al-Mazni, who was given a large land by the Prophet Mohammed, saying: *"The Prophet, peace and prayers be upon Him, has not given you this land for you to withhold it from the people, but He gave it for you to work it. So take what you can cope with and return the rest".*

2- That the Caliph Omar Ibn Al-Khattab has also taken a land in "Rabda", a place near Al-Medina into public ownership for the benefit of the "poor". He even prohibited the livestock of the rich people to come near that land announcing such high ideals as: *"If the rich man's livestock perishes, he can resort to his money. If the poor man's livestock perishes, he will come to me suffering and holding his children, requesting gold and silver, and*

I cannot turn them back...So cultivating (the land), now, is easier than spending gold and silver later.."[35]

3- The same applied to other ownerships such as produce, and natural resources, and the natural elements. These were considered essential and thus should be available to the public. Water, pasture and fire are the rights of all. Some also added salt[36]. Indeed, according to Imam Al-Shafe'i, a major Theologian and originator of one of the four main Sunni sects, natural resources "such as (fossil) fuel, sulphur, gems and stone are not to be sequestrated for the benefit of any one person, and no ruler is to withhold it for himself or the privileged ones...as this will be unjust"

Factors of production in Islamic Theology: There has been some discussion as to the essentials of these factors. The consensus is that they comprise of *Capital and Labour*, whereby Capital can be as generally understood, or it can be in the form of tangible assets such as land. It follows that Capital must fulfil two conditions: 1- it can be owned or acquired, and 2- it has to be useful. Therefore elements like water and sunshine cannot be considered capital. Spoiled food also cannot be considered capital because it is of no use. Capital being that which is acquired or owned and useful is, however, at variance with the generally held view that Capital is valued according to its use and rarity.

But there was another opinion held. And that is that the factors are not capital and labour, but *Labour and Nature*, whereby labour utilises what nature provides, and any tools, land, etc. Man uses, are but means to enhance the yield and value of natural resources[37].

In considering the first concept, therefore, any profit is to be shared by the provider of capital and the provider of labour. Profit can be claimed by the owner of capital in return for "managerial or organisational" effort, and this can apply to different situations such as land, factory, trading unit and so on.

<u>**Wages**</u>: Islam has lauded labour and work, and has not relegated it to meniality and low class. Indeed as an example, a Hadith says *"You have not eaten anything more delicious than what you have earned"*. Moreover, in another Hadith, Mohammed raises the value of work to that of worship in saying:*" Sins that will not be forgiven by prayers, pilgrimage or "Umra", will be forgiven through toil and worry in securing livelihood"*[38]

As such, labour deserves its recompense. Another Hadith says:" Give the labourer his wage *before his sweat dries up"*. And again: *"God says: three people I shall not be on their side at the end of the world: A man who gives and then bites back, a man who sold on behalf and embezzled the money, and a man who took on a labourer who fulfilled the work, and then did not pay him"*.

As such, there came the need to decide what constitutes a "just" wage. In general terms, the principles can be gleaned from the following Verse in the Qur'an:" Fill the measure, and be not of those who minish: Weigh with exact balance: And defraud not men in their substance, and do no wrong on the earth by deeds of licence."[39] It is therefore a matter of conscience, and it is left to the beneficiary to decide justly the value of the labour provided.

<u>**Profit**</u>: Islam accepts the principle of profit, in contradistinction to the prevailing Christian doctrines of the time. This is more understandable considering the status of trade and commerce in the Arabian peninsula and surrounding regions at the time, and indeed the fact that the Prophet Mohammed himself started his life in trade. In verse 15 of Sura El-Mulk(The Kingdom) it is said:" It is He who has made the world level for thee: traverse then its broad sides, and eat of what He hath provided.". The Prophet conceded that "nine tenth

of my Nation's bounty is from trade", and again: "Nine tenths of my nation's bounty is in buying and selling".

The merchant in Islam, therefore, is raised to a high social status. However, as expected, the Qur'an has stipulated the principle of moderation and non exploitation. In the Surat Al-Nessa'(Women), verse 28, the Qur'an says: "O believers! devour not each other's substance in mutual frivolities*(gambling and usury)*; unless there be a trafficking among you by your own consent *(the arabic word used here is "trade")*, i.e. there must be trade with mutual acceptance between people. The inference is that there should be no monopolistic attitudes, greed or the quest for money to satisfy matters of passion and squander.

Islamic theologians were unable to define further the meaning of just profit in the same way as they were unable to define the just wage. They could only say that the owner of capital has the right to a profit but has also to accept a loss. If the labourer has been in partnership with the owner of capital on the basis of his labour only, then any loss in the business should be accepted by the owner of capital alone, on the basis that the labourer has suffered a loss in his livelihood and work as a result. In any case, Islamic theology states that such agreements have to be on the basis of shared profit and not on the basis of wage only, otherwise it will be *"usury"*

Rent: Islamic theologians agreed that a person can toil his land and benefit from the produce and proceeds of sale, being thus rent and profit. But there has been differences in opinion with regards to renting land to others. Some scholars believed that this is against Islamic law, because renting out is a contract for the sale of a facility. A contract of a facility should in the law be well defined and capable of being fulfilled, i.e. quantifiable and precise. Naturally this is not the case with arable land. A fixed rental regardless of the value of return to the tenant is also considered against the spirit of the Law, and was banned. Islamic

Scholars, notably Al-Rei' Bin Hazm (943-1064 AD) and Jaber Bin Abdullah quote the Prophet saying:" Whoever owned a land should cultivate it, or his brother should cultivate it, but should not rent it out for one third or one fourth or for an agreed amount of food[40]. Bin Hazm's opinion on this matter, therefore, is that: " It is not lawful as a basic principle to rent out land; neither for tilling, nor for planting *(presumably trees, my italics)*, nor for building upon, and not for any other thing; not for a finite period, be it long or short, nor for an infinite period; not for dinars, nor dirhams, nor anything at all."

Other Theologians, perhaps the majority, while agreeing that renting out land is in fact a contract of sale of the facility, and as such is illegitimate, were able to sanction this on the grounds that the population is in need of it. In the author's opinion (Dr Adnan Abbass Ali)[41], Bin Hazm's scholarly opinion is nearest to the spirit of Islam, as their are numerous Hadiths that indicate total rejection of any "unearned" income, that is income which has not been worked for. As an example, the Hadith that says:*"The most honourable earning is that which a man earns from the work of his arms"*.

Thus there is no "land aristocracy" within the spirit of Islam. The motto: "The land is for who cultivates it" is nearest to the spirit of Islamic justice, and anyone should only own what he is capable of cultivating himself. An example of this is what was mentioned previously, when Omar implemented the Prophet's wish to take back some land given to Belal Bin Al-Harith Al-Mazni with the edict::" Look at what you can cope with and hold it. What you cannot cope with, push it back to us so that we can distribute it between the Muslims."

Usury: Usury or interest on capital is clearly prohibited in Islam, and anybody profiting from this is promised the severest of consequences. The Qur'an says:*" They who swallow down usury, shall arise in the resurrection only as he ariseth whom Satan hath infected by* *his touch. This for that they say ,"selling is only the like of usury.:"* and yet God hath allowed selling, and forbidden usury...but they who return to usury, shall be given over to the fire; and therein shall they abide for ever. God will bring usury to nought. O believers! fear God and abandon your remaining usury, if ye are indeed believers. But if ye do it not, then hearken for war on the part of God and His Apostle: yet if ye repent, ye shall have the principal of your money"[42].

Taking interest of any kind on capital is thus prohibited, whether in money or in kind, whether in production or consumption. The reason can be deduced from the previous paragraphs. That is that in Islam, earning should be through work. If there is a surplus of earning because of this work, this surplus should not be used to generate "unearned" income. Certainly the "money-lenders" are considered the enemies of society.

Another aspect is that of compassion and regulation in debt. The same "sura" verse 283 says: *"O ye who believe! when ye contract a debt (payable) at a fixed date, write it down, and let the notary faithfully note between you.."* It goes on to say if there is no notary available, then there should be witnesses, although noting it down is preferred, and the note should specify the date the debt is due to be returned. On the other hand, and here is the balancing aspect typical of many religious teachings, verse 280 says:" If anyone find difficulty in discharging , then let there be a delay until it is easy for him: but if ye remit it as alms it will be better for you, if ye know it"

Monopoly: In the same spirit, Islam forbids monopolisation. The Hadith says: "Whoever monopolises is wrong", and again: "The procurer is promised bounties, but the monopoliser is accursed". The Prophet goes to the extent that the hoarder or monopoliser should be rejected from within the ranks of the Muslims: "Whoever hoards food for more than forty days, he is absolved of God and God is absolved of him".(A Hadith)[43]

The Scholars, in trying to implement this principle which they found to be comparable to that of usury, on the grounds that the sole purpose of hoarding is to await scarcity and therefore higher price, were at some difficulty as to whether this should be considered in relation to food only, or to other items as well. Some considered regulating prices, but the Hadith says: "Do not price, for only God can price"[44]. Others were of the view that the rulers can interfere with the pricing, especially if it relates to hoarding or monopolising and if it in the interest of the public.

Care And Social Security In Islam

Islam has provided detailed arrangements for care and social security, and the method to counteract poverty and unfair distribution is based on five societal affairs:

1- Islam looks upon uneven or unfair distribution of wealth in society not in isolation, but as part of the overall structure and order of life and society in general.

2- Islam accepts that the poor have a right to the rich people's wealth to the extent that this is needed, especially that wealth is considered effectively belonging to God, and that people are but custodians thereof. The Prophet is quoted saying:" Wherever the inhabitants of a courtyard spend the night with a hungry person in their midst, those will forfeit the Blessing of God and His Prophet".

3- Islam gives the right of the poor to the rich people's wealth through two channels:

A- The Voluntary Contributions Channel: being part of their belief in Islam. The Prophet is quoted saying: "He who sleeps fully fed and his neighbour is hungry, is not one of us".

B- The Obligatory Channel: This is enshrined in the system whereby wealth is all the time being re-distributed so as not to be amassed. Laws and exhortations relating to tribute, tax, seasonal contributions, offerings etc.. all aim at assuring this continuing process of re-distribution.

4- That the Muslim should demonstrate in deed and in words, complete obedience to the system of care and social security.

5- Islam has laid down the grounds and means that would ensure the giving of taxes and its use in spending on the poor and needy.[45]

The "State" in Islam therefore has the duty of ensuring as good a standard of living as possible to its population through two essential processes: Initially by enabling the individual to work and earn, and creating the opportunity to do so. Where the person is unable to earn or the "State" has failed to provide avenues of work, the second process comes in, and that is finding the funds to provide for that person's needs.

There are two doctrinal principles that govern this socio-economic programme: One is the communal care, and the other is the right of society to the public resources of the "State". The first is expected to provide the basics for the individual, and the second is expected to cover wider needs and higher level of life, as far as its resources can afford.

Islam has linked caring with the concept of "brotherhood" within Islam, so that any taxation is not only considered an indication of superior income, but is also a practical expression of this "brotherhood" in caring for others.

The theoretical background to all this is that in Islam, the public is entitled to the sources of wealth, and that natural resources are the property of the whole and not certain factions.

Some scholars have stipulated that the duty of the Muslim "State" is not only towards the Muslims, but indeed to all factions under its jurisdiction. All should be provided for from the "Central Treasury" according to need.

Implementation And Development Of Post-apostolic Islam

The implementation of any set of economic principles requires a framework within which it can take root, develop, and hopefully flourish. Within a religious framework, it can be seen from the above brief description of Christian thought that there appeared a fairly spontaneous assault on "time-honoured" doctrines which protected the landed establishments, and provided "spiritual" succour to the lower social strata of society. It remained for Islam to provide a more coherent framework for implementation of the distinctly more elaborate sets of economic principles and doctrines. Such a system would have had to be based on the orderly passing on of Authority from the Prophet, and the retaining of a coherent and united early Muslim Community that prevails upon its members to observe the Teachings in spirit and in practise.

Alas! The succession to the Prophet Mohammed was not apparent and was not clearly indicated by Him. It thus became problematic even on the day of His Ascension on 8 June 632 AD

Details of the way in which the Muslims managed to choose their first four Caliphs (*Al Khulafa' Al Rashideen)* is not the subject of this work. What is important is the meaning of the word "Caliph", the Arabic version being "Khalifa". Linguistically this is "a cross between two things". The assumption is that it signifies that the Religious (Inspired Revelation) responsibility of the Apostle has ended, and what remains is the "Temporal" responsibility which He would have delegated to one of the Muslims. The inference is that the "government" led by the Caliph will be temporal but ruling within the precepts and understandings of religion, and using the principle of consultation known as *"Al Shura"*[46]. The followers, or public, were to relate to the "rulers" in accordance with the Qur'anic verse 59 of Surat Al-Nessa'(Women), Verse 59 :"O ye who believe! obey God and obey the Apostle, and those among you invested with authority." .

The first of the four "Initial Caliphs", Abu Bakr Al-Siddique, during His brief two year Caliphate established a principle by asking the people to: "Obey me as long as I obeyed God and His Apostle, but should I disobey God and His Apostle, then there will be no obedience due to me from you". In this manner the leadership of the "State" is the "Governing Authority" within the religious framework. The "State" here means the "Umma". The Characteristics of the "Ummatu'l Islam" was identified very early on by the Prophet who recognized in the first year of the Hejira that there was a need for a "Constitution" which defines the relationships between the various factions of the newly developed Muslim entourage or "society": He announced the following principles:

1- The Muslims-all are one nation distinct from the rest of the people. Belonging to this nation (Umma) takes precedence over belonging to the tribe, and is a level above it.

2- The Islamic "State" is an expression of this "Nation" ("Umma") of Islam. Obedience to it is obligatory. They would go to war if

war breaks out, and will observe peace if it makes peace. They
will observe all treaties and documents laid down.

3- They will therefore boycott Quraysh as it is the enemy of this
State. They will not deal with it or with its allies, and this will
apply to trading with it.

4- They are as one against whoever is unjust to them or who
harbours malice or antagonism, regardless of any relationship
or blood. The believer who kills another believer like him
with intent should be punished except if the guardians of the
deceased relinquish their right.

5- If the Muslims differ in matter, they should refer to the book of
God and His Prophet, peace and meditation be upon Him.

6- There should be security and order within Medina, and it
should be considered as Holy as Mecca.

7- As for the Jews, they should have the freedom to remain within
their religion, and their security, and their people's safeguarded.
If one of them becomes a Muslim, he is to have all the rights
of the Muslim as well as the duties. In case of war, the Muslims
and the Jews will fight together, and each will spend on the war
according to their turn.

This, then, was the "political" framework for the Muslims. It appears,
and certainly is, parochial, particularly when it relates to Quraysh so
intimately. It also means that the Caliph takes on the temporal authority
bestowed upon the Apostle, but not the *"Inspirational"* one, and that
this authority carries with it obedience conditional to adherence to
God, His Apostle and the Teachings. And finally, there is the principle
of "Shura" or "Consultation with the followers."[47]

These conditions and circumstances never realistically materialised
during or following the era of the Four Initial Caliphs. Indeed, the

second of the four, Omar Ibn Al-Khattab was stabbed to death in the tenth year of His Caliphate, the third, Othman Ibn 'Affan, while lasting twelve years, was assassinated by mutineers in A.D 656. These mutineers became known as "AL-Khawarij, or outsiders. They believed that anyone could lead the Muslims, and therefore would not submit to the Caliph Omar Ibn Al-Khattab. This schism affected the ascension of the last of the Four Initial Caliphs, Ali Ibn Abu Talib, whose accession was disputed by Mu'awwiyah the then governor of Damascus[48]. He was then also assassinated while about to pray in the mosque of Kufa, in Iraq, in the year 40 A.H. These last two assassinations inaugurated the process of schism and divisions in Islam, so early on in the Dispensation, not only because of the Al-Khawarij dissidents , but also because of the very major schism that resulted and has its effects to this day. That major schism is the division of Islam into the "Sunnies" and the "Shi'ites". This schism remained a cause of severe and deep sectarianism, with more than just the occasional violent eruptions throughout the history of Islam. While it started with the above mentioned groups of apostate tribes, and renegade sectors of the growing "Nation" of Islam, the more serious division into the Shi'ites was based on the fervent belief of those who thought that the right of succession, nay some would go to the extent the it is the right to "Apostlehood", was due to Ali Ibn Abu Talib, and the Sunni's who believe otherwise.

As to implementing the basic economic principles described above, that again did not materialize following the death of the Prophet Mohammed. Al Medina is said to have, by virtue of its prominent status as the champion and protector of Islam, acquired enormous wealth, turning a lot of its people to materialism. Some acquired mansions and estates, while many, mainly the Bedouins outside the city, remained in abject poverty.

Nevertheless, this did not prevent new Scholars looking at the principles enshrined in the Qur'an and other Scriptures from further scholarly elaboration and working out practical applications in every day life, very much in line with the thinking that permeated Europe at the time of the beginning of emergence from the staid periods described above. Two most noted Scholars deserve mention, both because of their thoughts , and the fact that both were related to the Arabs of Andalusia, the parents and extended family of one (Ibn Khaldun) having moved to Tunisia in the mid thirteenth Century AD, making him effectively a Tunisian Arab.

Bin Hazm AL-DHAHIRI: 943-1064 AD

Bin Hazm lived in Andalusia and was very well versed in Religion. His treatise "The Right of the Poor" outlined his ideas on combating poverty based on the principle that Islam "rejects" poverty. As such, his starting point is the poor man, whom he thinks ought to fight for his rights with the ruler and demand his rightful standard of living. His principles are thus summarized :

1- It is everyone's right to demand a decent standard of living.
2- The State alone should accept this social responsibility.
3- If the "Zakat" (or Tribute, an annual 6% of income, residual assets, savings etc.. that should be given by every Muslim to the "Common Treasury") is not enough to cover the cost of providing for the poor, then the Ruler should impose more tribute on the rich, as there is no upper limit in Islam to the rights of the poor on the rich.
4- Bin Hazm laid on the minimum standard required for a decent living, aimed at satisfying the need for food, clothing and shelter.

Among the many texts he relied on, two are most representative for this brief note: 1- The Prophet quoted as saying:" And to parents benevolence, as well to those who are related, the orphans and the disadvantaged". 2- The Caliph Ali Ibn Abu Talib is quote as saying:" God has imposed on the rich from their wealth the amount that will suffice the poor. If they go hungry or are without clothes, then they too go without. It is God's duty to judge them at the end of time and to mete the punishment to them." [49]

Ibn Khaldun: 1332-1406

Ibn Khaldun was an original thinker with a wide range of interests. He was "both a *faylasuf* and a *qadi*,(i.e. a philosopher and a judge) a combination more common in Andalusia and the Maghrib than anywhere else in Islamdom. In his *Muqaddimah* (the introduction or *"Prolegomania"* to his multivolume world history) he used his training in *falsafa* (philosophy) to discern patterns in history...establishing careful standards of evidence...explaining things as cycles of nature and inevitable stages...and the unavoidable instability of all pre-modern Muslim dynasties, caused by their lack of the regularized patterns of succession that were beginning to develop in European dynasties[50]

Beginning with the premise that knowledge is complex and specialized, there is, therefore a need to use different "tools" for different studies, in the same way that we need ears to hear, but for seeing we need eyes, and so on. On another subject, he realized that there are essentially two aspects to Human thought: the spiritual which cannot be approached logically, but only through the Inspirational Powers given to Man through the Divinely Chosen Prophets and divinely enlightened souls, and the temporal "sciences" that required enquiring minds. Of these avenues of thought, there are those Natural studies that people can strive to elucidate through their own efforts individually, generally analysing society and the relationships within it, developing theories and providing the bases for them. And others that are built up through handing over of knowledge and experience producing evolving "rules and regulations", and laws to govern society, and these give little allowance for askance and debate.

Ibn Khaldun took up the various subjects of thought current at the time and gave them his own insight. For example, as mentioned above, he realized that History is all important. But it should not be just a narrative of incidences and historical occurrences. He postulated that in studying it, one can discern the patterns whereby societies shape and evolve. In this way, not only can these studies be analytical, but also they can predict some of the changes expected in future: "For I have created in history a book...Where I have demonstrated the reasons and factors in the development of civilisation...and what every civilisation in a particular state or nation offers...the existing status and the expected".[51]

Ibn Khaldun may have inaugurated "Philosophical Sociology" in his part of the world, and indeed probably preceded similar organized and studied thoughts in Europe. He realized that "society" is not a static structure that maintained its structure rigidly in spite of differences in location or time, but is a "living creature" which starts small, grows, flourishes and matures, and then goes into decline. All this, in his view, is within an "order" and not just casual. History therefore assists us in providing the medium through which we can see the present and in it the seeds of the future.

He believed that economics was the essential medium, but additional influences were to be seen in behavioural, legal, political and religious attitudes and others. Economics, however, was in his view the most important factor. To demonstrate this point, Ibn Khaldun referred to Plato's aphorism that Man is "by nature civilised". It is his opinion that while Plato made this statement with the social dimension being the underlying meaning, i.e. that Man is civilised because he is a Social being, Ibn Khaldun thinks that Man is by nature civilised because of his need and desire to survive. This is only achieved through subsistence, and therefore the social instinct is driven by the need to "pull together". As Nature has given animals different qualities and strengths, some of them specific and exceed man's ability to compete with, man has collectively developed the two most important faculties that animals lack: The brain (intelligence) and the hand. With these, Man further developed "tools, implements and weapons". In all this endeavour, there is a need for humankind to co-operate. He thus in this context, analysed the dynamics of group relationships and showed how group-feelings, *al-'Asabiyya*, give rise to the ascent of a new civilisation and political power and how, later on, its diffusion into a more general civilization invites the advent of a still new *'Asabiyya* in its pristine form. He identified an almost rhythmic repetition of rise and fall in human civilization, and analysed factors contributing to it. His contribution to history is marked by the fact that, unlike most earlier writers interpreting history largely in a political context, he emphasised environmental, sociological, psychological and economic factors governing the apparent events. This revolutionised the science of history and also laid the foundation of *Umraniyat* (Sociology)[52].

Ibn Khaldun and the social and economic evolution:

Ibn Khaldun sees society as essentially two tiered: the *"manual"* and the *"civil"*. The former being the lower and the latter being the higher level within the evolutionary process in society: "Any differences in the social status along the generations are related to their particular stratum of livelihood..." Thus: "The co-operation and working together of the *(manual)* class in relation to their livelihood, residence, and other needs, are only within the limits required to satisfy their survival and basic needs, with no surplus to spare.."

As for the "Higher Tier", that of the *"Civil"* lifestyle, theirs is a productive and varied life, well developed, and at a higher level. They are the members of society who demand and cherish the luxuries and good things in life, always eager for more and always able to maintain the appearances of the "good life". They would usually be "industrialists" or merchants, and their incomes and profits allows this lifestyle. He goes on to say: "The rough life of the manuals is the springboard for the luxurious life of the civil...and the civil situation originates from the manual one, which in itself is the original." _

Ibn Khaldun believed that the transfer from the lower to the upper stages or echelons occurs mainly because of the migration to the cities. The increase in population, which in turn leads to increased specialization of labour, increased production, increased surplus provides the basis for material progress. The common factor in all this is the increased co-operation between people. Thus: "Any one individual is not independent in acquiring his livelihood needs. So they are all co-operating within their overall structure for that. The goods that are produced by any one faction will, in fact, suffice many multiples of their number. For example, the production of Corn (Wheat) is not just for the person who produced it, but rather for six or ten others: the ironsmith, the carpenter who works the tools, the cattle keeper, and the person who tills the land, etc.. all have joined in and therefore earned the reward of their labour....thus producing surplus, leading to acquisition of luxuries and making produce available for other countries*(an early indication of the idea of export...the author's italics)*... the result is increased all round prosperity..."

Ibn Khaldun's thoughts on Economics

Ibn Khaldun may have preceded Sir William Petty, Adam Smith, and Ricardo in presenting the idea that labour is the basis for value. Thus:" The benefits and earnings are all or mostly the value of human labour". His mention of "mostly" is in recognition of natural elements such as air and water. He recognised that the amount of labour increases the value proportionately.

He mentions four ways through which acquisition can occur: 1- Taking from someone else's hands through power or through a recognized "law", and this is called "Tribute". 2- Acquiring a wild animal or a product of the sea, and this is called "hunting". 3- Acquiring trees or agricultural produce, and this is called "peasantry or farming", or 4- Through manufacture or other forms of enterprise such as storing, selling, bartering etc.. and this is called "Trade" or "Mercantilism". To summarize:" Acquisition can be through Ruling (tribute or tax), trade, agriculture or industry."

However, he differentiated between productive(or natural) labour, which adds value, and the non-productive(or unnatural) labour such as the tax or tributes recovered by rulers, who must not take part in trade or transactions otherwise the temptation to interfere and skew the markets in their favour will be irresistible. Moreover, should the rulers squeeze out more from the people in taxes, there will be less profit left, and there will be a tendency for the people to allow for these taxes in there prices. This inevitably leads to less prosperity and more inflation, and a reduced incentive for people to work and produce more.

Ibn Khaldun and the role of the Rulers

Ibn Khaldun recognized three main needs and sources of assistance for the ruler: The Soldier, the Pen and the Revenue. While not coining the term Tax (a rather more recently recognized term), he did talk of "tribute" which can be exacted on tradesmen in proportion to the value of their products. "Where the Ruler is adhering to religion the needs will be minimum, as the expenditures will be minimum.. but then the needs and expenditures increase, particularly when more affluence and luxury is entertained, leading to greater and greater pressures on the people to finance this. He quoted the early Islamic Ruler Taher Ibn Al-Hussein (AD 775-882) who advised his son Abdullah when handing him the powers for the rule over Egypt;" To be careful with the charge, ..and not to be extravagant, ...and to be fair and just, ...and not to overburden the people"

Ibn Khaldun was aware of the role of the rulers in generating commercial activity and prosperity by way of spending from their revenue on the people, and that on the contrary, should they accumulate or amass their wealth, the result will be a downturn in the economy with less money going round.

Ibn Khaldun describes the stages that every civilization passes from the turmoil of the inception of political entities, through the stability of the "middle period," to the "senility" and decline. Where the pursuit of luxury and ease in a society dominates this results in the eventual death of the dynasty. His parallel of the life of a society and with the life of an individual is a concept that is thought provoking[53],[54].

Application Of Economics In Islam

The above principles, whether those enshrined in Qur'anic Laws, accepted as verifiable Hadith or "Seera", or indeed as postulated by the early Islamic philosophers, hardly had a chance to be implemented or indeed tested in a "state-like" manner. The early Caliphs, as mentioned above, had been accepted as the "temporal" standard bearers after Mohammed. In addition, they assumed the roles of : *"Amir El Mo'mineen"*, i.e. the "foremost believer or follower"(of Mohammed and

Islam) as well as the *"Imam"* which is the significant role of leading the Congregation of Muslims to Prayers. These roles were established as early as the first Caliph, Omar Ibn Al-Khattab. Together with the "Consultative Body" of trusted and wise entourage, the *"Shura"*, some delegated functions were given to some prominent people such as Abu Bakr Al-Siddique which could have been described as comparable to that of the function of a *"Vizier"* or "Minister". The term "Vizier" however was coined for the first time during the Ummayad rule approximately from the sixth Islamic decade onwards[55].

There was the need to organize the *"military"*, and to create a *"Judiciary"*. The need to keep some records became also necessary, and this gave great importance to the cabal of *"Scribes"* that emerged. Budgeting was very primitive in the early stages as the expenditures were extremely limited. Extravagance and possibly decadence necessitated more access to income for the rulers, and hence the system of "Tax" or "Tribute" *("Jibaya")* had to be developed. In later stages, this tax was called *"Al Kharaj"* a word derived from the Aramaic *"Choregia"* which actually means tax.

In spite of all this , however, it is difficult to identify a system of economics based on the Laws as described above, or indeed as elaborated by such thinkers as Ibn Khaldun.

A resurgence of Islamic fervour in recent decades, generated a growing call for a return to Islamic Laws including economics. But the examples of so-called "Islamic States" that came into being failed as yet to demonstrate an ability to adopt the Laws as revealed in the Qur'an and to disregard the current trends in International economics. Politicians and Muslim Scholars and Institutions are quite active at present throughout the Islamic World in trying to fit in Islamic principles to modern economics.

Further Thoughts On Christianity And Economics

In considering the historical sequence, it would have been appropriate to have discussed Christianity and such Christian doctrines as may reflect economic principles. These could have been dealt with in the previous section on the middle ages. However, discussing Islam first provides a means of relating economics aspects of religions and for them to be understood and appreciated in context rather than in isolation. Thus, by moving back in the history of religion and looking in a little more detail into the relevant texts of the New Testament outlining some economic principles, the attempt is not just to go backwards in time, but to show the development of Divine Religious themes, which, it is hoped, will demonstrate that the Christian Teachings managed on the one hand to "refine" the early Teachings of Judaism, and on the other to provide the right "spiritual" template upon which the Teachings of Islam managed to build a more comprehensive and organised "system" of economics; one that was aimed at laying adequate foundations for a just and equitable society, governed by well defined laws. That must have been the purpose and intention of these religious principles. Their implementation, however, was rather short of expectations..

With this in mind, the salient teachings in Christianity will be discussed, followed by those of Judaism.

No matter how difficult it may be to lay a coherent and logical order to the Biblical Teachings that have an economic message, it will help to understand the thrust of the message reasonably well by the spiritual and moral orientation that can be gleaned with that most significant of Jesus Christ's wisdoms as inspired in the "sermon on the mount". [56]

GOD AND MA'-MON: In Matthew chapter 6, vs 24-34: " *No man can serve two masters: for either he will hate the one, and love the other; or else he will hold to the one and despise the other. Ye cannot serve God and mam'-mon. Therefore I say unto you, Take no thought for your* *life, what ye shall eat, or what ye shall drink; nor yet for your body, what ye shall put on. Is not the life more than meat, and the body than raiment? Behold the fowls of the air, for they sow not, neither do they reap, nor gather into barns; yet your heavenly Father feedeth them. Are ye not much better than they? Which of you by taking thought can add one cubit unto his stature? And why take ye thought for raiment? Consider the lilies of the field, how they grow; they toil not, neither do they spin; And yet I say unto you, That even Solomon in all his glory was not arrayed like one of these. Wherefore, if God so clothe the grass of the field, which to-day is, and to-morrow is cast into the oven, shall he not much more clothe you, O ye of little faith? Therefore take no thought, saying, What shall we eat? or, What shall we drink? or wherewithal shall we be clothed? (For all these things do the Gentiles seek:) for your heavenly Father knoweth that ye have need for all these things. But seek ye first the kingdom of God, and his righteousness; and all these things shall be added unto you. Take therefore no thought for the morrow: for the morrow shall take thought for the things of itself. Sufficient unto the day is the evil thereof".*

There are several messages here: 1- That people have to be single minded in their faith in God. 2- That they have to shun all the attitudes of the "gentiles" (i.e. the contemporary non Jews, implying non-believers). 3- Christ gave the three examples that reflect the three essentials of society's needs of the time: eating, drinking and clothing. He called upon the believers to adopt the stature of the content and not abase oneself as the "gentiles" would. God will provide even more than Solomon was provided for. This is the way to attain general health and well being.

This theme is bolstered by earlier passages from the same sermon (vs. 19-21): " *Lay not up for yourselves treasures upon earth, where moth and rust doth corrupt, and where thieves break through and steal: But lay up for yourselves treasures in heaven, where neither moth nor rust doth corrupt, and where thieves do not break through nor steal. For where your treasure is, there will your heart be also"*. The message here is twofold: 1- Condemnation of hoarding (echoed as mentioned previously in Islamic doctrine) and 2- Allowing people's thought not to be distracted by worldly and material matters. This is also echoed in the Qur'an ("The Cave" verse 46): *"Wealth and children are the adornment of this present life: but good works which are lasting are better in the sight of thy Lord as to recompense, and better as to hope"*. And also in "The Poets" verse 88:*" The day when neither wealth nor children shall avail, save to him who shall come to God with a sound heart"*.

Here again, it is noticeable how the theme is re-iterated with minor variations between the two religions. It is thus worth noting Christ's well quoted Utterance, following the sorrowful dismissal of the rich man who has done all the good deeds, but could not accept that he had also to relinquish his wealth for the poor before he could have eternal life. This is the quote in Matthew 19, verse 23/24: *"Verily I say unto you, That a rich man shall hardly enter into the kingdom of heaven. And again I say unto you, It is easier for a camel to go through the eye of a needle, than for a rich man to enter the kingdom of God"*.

This then is the spiritual template which Christ would wish as the base that would govern society's attitude and behaviour. And to a great extent, as was mentioned in the above sections of this work, this explains the way society seems to have settled down, especially in Medieval Europe, whereby acceptance of the ordinary person for his or her lot in life was reconcilable on the understanding that what is required in this world is the constant endeavour towards securing the "kingdom of heaven" in the afterlife, coupled with the confidence that what one lacked in worldly privileges will be more than compensated for there-after.

It would, however, be wrong to assume that Christ limited His Teachings to these purely spiritual exhortations. Indeed, He was "worldly-wise" enough not to fall into trap of the spies sent by the chief (Jewish) priests to ensnare him in some words that would incriminate Him in the eyes of the authorities of the time. These "spies" asked Jesus (Luke 20, verses 22-24): *"Is it lawful for us to give tribute unto Caesar, or no? But he perceived their craftiness, and said unto them, Why tempt ye me? Shew me a penny. Whose image and superscription hath it? They answered and said, Caesar's. And he said unto them, Render therefore unto Caesar the things which be Caesar's, and unto God the things which be God's"*. Thus Christ not only managed to thwart the cunning of those people, but in the process laid down two important principles: 1- That it is the right of the governing authority to receive "tribute" from its subjects, being a necessary requisite for the conduct of the affairs of State, and 2- that the head of Caesar represents that authority and should be respected. In the context of the prevailing sentiments of resentment of the Roman yolk that is known to have been significant among the Jews of Palestine in those days, Jesus saw it fit to reduce as many sources of turmoil as possible. It was not His mission to incite insurrection, but rather to give hope and a new understanding of the verities of old. Indeed, it could even be surmised that had the Jews (and early Christians) adhered to the advice to *"render unto God the things which be God's)* the spiritual and moral gain would have created a greater force of moral strength, and a greater source of comfort. It would conceivably have been also a source of tranquillity on the part of the "occupiers" who would reciprocate by providing greater rights concomitant with the greater the security they feel and perceive.

Enterprise, confidence and trade: Christ managed to establish very important economic principles of a practical nature, which sadly seem to have been overlooked by the early Christians and indeed the ecclesiastical leaders. In Matthew 25, verses 14-30 we have the following story: *"For the kingdom of heaven is as a man travelling into a far country, who called his own servants, and delivered unto them his goods. And unto one he gave five talents, to another two, and to another one; to every man according to his several ability; and straightway took his journey. Then he that had received the five talents went and traded with the same, and made them other five talents. And likewise he that had received two, he also gained other two. But he that had received one went and digged the earth, and hid his lord's money. After a long time the lord of those servants cometh, and reckoneth with them. And so he that had received five talents came and brought other five talents, saying, Lord, thou deliverdst unto me five talents: behold, I have gained beside them five talents more. His lord said unto him, Well done, thou good and faithful servant: thou hast been faithful over a few things, I will make thee ruler over many things: enter thou into the joy of thy lord. He also that had received two talents came and said, Lord, thou deliverdst unto me two talents: behold, I have gained two other talents beside them. His lord said unto him, Well done, good and faithful servant; thou hast been faithful over a few things , I will make thee ruler over many things: enter thou into the joy of thy lord. Then he which had received the one talent came and said, Lord, I knew thee that thou art an hard man, reaping where thou hast not sown, and gathering where thou hast not strawed: and I was afraid, and went and hid thy talent in the earth: lo, there thou hast that is thine, His lord answered and said unto him, thou wicked and slothful servant, thou knewest that I reap where I sow not , and gather where I have not strawed : Thou oughtest therefore to have put my money to the exchangers, and then at my coming I should have received my own with usury. Take therefore the talent from him, and give it unto him which hath ten talents. For unto every one that hath shall be given, and he shall have abundance; but from him that hath not shall be taken away even that which he hath. And cast ye the unprofitable servant into outer darkness".*

There is no doubt that this story is meant predominantly in the spiritual sense, in that one reaps in the afterlife what one sows in this life. But it would be wrong to ignore the economic message that: 1- It is important to put one's talents to good and fruitful use. The parable describes two aspects of these talents: the money aspect and the "ability" aspect: "to every man according to his several abilities" . Multiplying the money or ability is a good thing, spiritually and materially. 2- The man who was given one talent turned out to be slothful, i.e. lazy and not inclined to work. He failed even to undertake the rather passive "investment" procedure of giving the talent to the exchangers, preferring to keep the talent stagnant inside the earth. 3- There appears to be a tacit acceptance on the part of Christ that there are circumstances when usury, i.e. interest is acceptable.

In another version of this theme, described in Luke 19, verses 12-26, the noblemen before going *"into a far country to receive for himself a kingdom, and to return...called his ten servants and delivered them ten pounds and said unto them, Occupy till I come...*On returning, *"he commanded these servants to be called unto him, to whom he had given the money, that he might know how much every man had gained by trading. Then came the first, saying, Lord, thy pound hath gained ten pounds. And he said unto him, Well, thou good servant: because thou hast been faithful in a very little, have thou authority over ten cities...* the second, who made five pounds was given authority over five cities, and the hapless man who laid the pound in a napkin was given the same treatment mentioned in the previous version, including the admonition of *"Wherefore thou gavest not my money to the bank, that at my coming I might have required mine own with usury"...*

Once again, it is important to stress that these stories or parables had as their main objective the spiritual message; that if one's spiritual and moral standing in small affairs or situations is in keeping with God's wishes, then God will compensate that person accordingly, if not in this world, then at least in the world to come. But the "worldly" message that is of economic significance is undeniably that of Christ's appreciation of the value of trade and, to a lesser extent, the more "passive" enhancement of the value of money through banking and interest, especially if it is for a good cause. Naturally, Christ was averse to exploitation, and these principles of trade and usury must be combined with the other Teachings of Christ which emphasize kindness, love, care for one another and overall social justice.

In support of the above concept of safe keeping and good management of entrusted material, and trustworthiness, Christ in another reference: Luke 16, verse 10-12 says: *"He that is faithful in that which is least is faithful also in the much: and he that is unjust in the least is unjust also in the much. If therefore ye have not been faithful in the unrighteous mammon, who will commit to your trust the true riches? And if ye have not been faithful in that which is another man's, who shall give you that which is your own?"* Once again, one has to appreciate the spiritual connotation in this wisdom. But its value in maintaining a healthy economic climate of trust and faithfulness is unmistakable.

The excerpts from the "New Testament" presented here are in no way meant to be comprehensive. Rather they are meant to give salient features of doctrines that are of relevance to the economic inter-actions within society, and to act as examples of how such teachings could be looked at from different angles, and given more than one interpretation, all interpretations being complementary and not contradictory.

The application of these teachings within the Christian world has, as mentioned in the previous sections, depended on the interpretations that society and the clergy managed to put together at various stages. Thus, "The principle social attitude perpetuated by Christianity supported the equality of all mankind. All being children of God, all were, in consequence, equals in the brotherhood of man. In keeping with this instruction was an inevitable suspicion of wealth as a differentiation between brothers, a source of some unequal power, prestige and enjoyment. By slight extension, there was also a sense of the superior virtue of the poor."[57] Moreover, "Christ, addressing Himself to the labourers of His time, proclaimed for the first time the worthiness both in the material and the spiritual sense of all work"[58].

Again, Christian doctrine strongly condemned the extraction of interest, although it later "adjusted " to economic need. " When money lending was not in relation to investing in machinery or equipment, but rather to satisfy various urgent personal needs, to permit present extravagance or to repair extravagance of the past, the ethical question was that interest is not viewed as a production cost, but rather as something the more favoured charge the less fortunate or the less wise." When it became compellingly evident that the one who borrowed money *made* money out of doing so and should, in all justice, share some of the return with the original lender--did it (interest) become reputable. Very important early Christian "money-lenders"--the *Fuggers, Imhofs and Welsers*-appeared in Europe. However, doubts as to the righteousness of money lending was never expunged, as for example is seen in the term "loan sharks" that is still in use. "[59] .

It is of note that, while, as mentioned previously, formal expressions of economic ideas in the scholarly and priestly thought of the one thousand years that followed the dissolution of the Roman Empire was hard to find, it will become apparent that at least some later economists, including the eminent Adam Smith actually evolved their economic thoughts through the moral, ethical, and philosophical routes with distinct theological undertones and overtones.

The development of economic thought and practice within the Christian world in the last three centuries or so, while gradually becoming more and more distant from religious, especially Christian, doctrine, has, to this day, been punctuated with calls from Christian leaders, including the present Pope Paul and the Archbishop of Canterbury, George Carey and his predecessor, to take heed of the rapidly consuming wave of materialism, and the increasing divide between the rich and the poor. These calls are, however, only in the nature of their "pastoral" role on a level commensurate with their status, i.e. more world wide in case of the Pope and the Archbishop, and at a more congregational level with others.

Judaism And Economics

The "Old testament" is, as is well known, a much bigger tome than the "New Testament". Moreover, Judaic Doctrine can be found in other traditions, mainly the "Talmud". It is thus beyond the scope of this work to delve too deep in all these sources in an attempt to extract everything that can be considered of relevance to economic principles and thought. Some examples, all well known, will illustrate certain of these principles.

Indeed, the first encounter will be found in the Book of Genesis, and is the well known story of Joseph and the Pharaoh's dream (Genesis 41) which can be summarized as follows: Pharaoh dreamt that he had stood by the river," *and behold there came out of the river seven kine (cows) fatfleshed and well favoured; and they fed in the meadow: And behold, seven other kine came after them, poor and very ill favoured and leanfleshed, such as I never saw in all the land of Egypt for badness: And the lean and the ill favoured kine did eat up the first seven fat kine...And*

I saw in my dream, and, behold, seven ears came up in one stalk, full and good: And, behold, seven ears withered, thin, and blasted with the east wind, sprung up after them: And the thin ears devoured the seven good ears...And Joseph said unto Pharaoh, The dream of Pharaoh is one: God hath shewed Pharaoh what he is about to do. The seven good kine are seven years ; and the seven good ears are seven years...And the seven thin and ill favoured kine that came after them are seven years, and the seven empty ears ...shall be seven years of famine...Behold, there come seven years of great plenty throughout all the land of Egypt: And there shall arise after them seven years of famine...Now therefore let Pharaoh look out a man discreet and wise and set him over the land of Egypt...to take up the fifth part of the land of Egypt in the seven plenteous years....and lay up corn...for store to the land of Egypt; that the land perish not through the famine..." Joseph was given this task. Pharaoh "set him over the land of Egypt", and when these prophesies were fulfilled, Joseph was raised to the highest level and was given a high priest's daughter to marry.

The moral of this story in economic terms is that it appears to be the first time that the principle of storing in bumper harvests to provide for lesser yielding seasons has been established. This is different from individual hoarding which is condemned as we have seen in Christianity and Islam, because here it is a policy implemented by the ruler for the benefit of **All** the people. Moreover, as we can read later in this chapter that: *"All the countries came into Egypt to Joseph to buy corn because the famine was so sore in all lands"*, and in the next chapter (42) of Genesis, we read the story of Jacob, the father of Joseph who, not aware that his son is so flourishing in Egypt, had sent his other sons to buy corn, and the story goes on.

An incidental moral could also be deduced, in the recognition by Pharaoh of the value of wisdom, honesty and sincerity, an astute act from a ruler who can appreciate these qualities and recompense the subject accordingly.

The Ten Commandments: The ten commandments are recognised as the basis upon which all religious and moral principles are built. They are time honoured verities that are not disputed by any religious follower or indeed any non-religious person. Whether they are followed and adhered to or not is obviously a very individual behaviour.

Announced in the book of Exodus chapter 20, these commandments are preceded by one important statute which has became as much a hallmark of Judaism as for example circumcision is: this is the statute of the *Sabbath:* " *Remember the Sabbath day, to keep it holy. Six days shalt thou labour, and do all thy work: But the seventh day is the Sabbath of the Lord thy God: in it thou shall not do any work, nor thy son, nor thy daughter, nor thy manservant, nor thy maidservant, nor thy cattle, nor thy stranger that is within thy gates."(vs.8-10)*

The spiritual and religious connotation in this statute is recognised. The economic effect may, however, be less evident. But the rejuvenating effect of a day's break in the weekly cycle, with its ability to "re-charge" the batteries of people, allow the benefits of family life to come to the fore, and create a healthy social environment for the community, all must be a factor that can be appreciated. The person's productivity is enhanced, and because it was, and hopefully still is, expected that people will use this break to achieve spiritual and social renewal within the family or otherwise, the overall effect on the economy must be beneficial. One can even say that in the present state of society, where leisure is appreciated even more than previously, and where work can be more demanding of one's time, mental and/or physical effort, as well as the emotional investment required in stressful working conditions, and where, at least in affluent societies, people's financial status is so satisfactory, more attention should and could be given to the total well being of the individual and the family. A "day off" for leisure, with or without prayer and contemplation (depending on one's personal disposition) is, for most people, certainly of benefit. A day off, while certainly good in the past, is probably of more value to-day. On economic grounds, moreover, it can be said that the leisure industry is now so well developed in most countries, and so well made use of, that a day off once a week, is almost essential to keep this particular industry alive and flourishing.

It is interesting to note the different emphasis that Christ put on this concept of the Sabbath. In Mark chapter 2, vs.23-28 there is the first indication that Christ sanctioned the breaking of the Sabbath under certain conditions. Thus: *"And it came to pass, that he went through the corn fields on the Sabbath day; and his disciples began, as they went to pluck the ears of corn. And the Pharisee said unto him, Behold, why do they on the Sabbath day that which is not lawful? And he said unto them, Have ye never read what David did, when he had need, and was an hungered, he, and they that were with him? How he went into the house of God in the days of A-bi-a-thar the high priest, and did eat the shewbread, which is not lawful to eat but for the priests, and gave also to them that were with him? And he said unto them, the Sabbath was made for man, and not man for the Sabbath: Therefore the Son of man is Lord also of the Sabbath."*

In this way Christ gave legitimacy to work of essential nature on the Sabbath, and also gave himself the right and authority to change a law of the Old Testament. Furthermore, in the next chapter(3, vs 1-4) Christ undertakes yet a further act to challenge the rigidity about observance of the Sabbath. Thus: *"And he entered again into the synagogue; and there was a man with a withered hand. And they watched him, whether he would heal him on the Sabbath day; that they might accuse him. And he said unto the man which had the withered hand, Stand forth. And he said unto them, Is it lawful to do good on the Sabbath days or to do evil? to save life, or to kill? But they held their peace. And when he had looked around about on them with anger, being grieved for the hardness of their hearts, he saith unto the man, Stretch forth thy hand. And he stretched it out: and his hand was restored whole as the other".*

The consequences of this and the reaction of the Jews can be seen in St John chapter 5, vs. 16-18: *"And therefore did the Jews persecute Jesus, which had made him* (the sick man) *whole, and sought to slay him, because he had done these things on the Sabbath day".*

The importance of not withholding good deeds on the Sabbath is demonstrated in this episode. But the principle of the one day of rest in the week and its value in the weekly rythm of life, is held, even by Christ. Moreover, Christ gave man the opportunity to use judgement when He said: *"the Sabbath was made for man, and not man for the Sabbath".*

The organizational and moral principles in the ten Commandments: The ten commandments offer further teachings and messages which have an effect in organising society, and which also carry a direct economic significance. The obvious one is: *1-"Thou shalt not steal"* But there are others: *2-"Thou shalt not bear false witness" 3-"Thou shalt not covet thy neighbour's house...nor his manservant, nor his maidservant, nor his ox, nor his ass, nor anything that is thy neighbour's".* These messages against greed, untrustworthiness, covetousness, jealousy and licentiousness are messages against all that exercises a very negative effect on trade, economic behaviour, and the sanity and preservation of a society that, in God's intention, should feel secure and thus able to attain its total potential for advance and prosperity.

These commandments furthermore are, later in the same book, bolstered by laws governing theft, trespassing and other misdemeanours or violations. An additional statute worth noting appears in Exodus ch. 23, vs 8 which says: *"And thou shalt take no gift: for the gift blindest the wise, and perverteth the words of the righteous".* This can easily be translated in modern parlance as taking of bribes, which would certainly have the undesirable effects mentioned. While these violations are all integrally established in every legal system in every country, it is important to note their origin in the scriptures. Naturally, the meaning of theft can be stretched to any extent, and while these laws were made even more strict in Islam, there is a discrepancy between how sometimes minor thefts are treated (perhaps harshly) and some more serious thefts such as major embezzlement or fraud are either passed over or dealt with relatively leniently. The moral and spiritual framework within which these principles should be observed is, indeed, an aspect that is ignored or, to say the least, overlooked, certainly in the present age, but probably as long as history.

Other laws of a socio-economic nature can be found in Leviticus. Among all the laws and ordinances that have been given to Moses, regarding such matters as behaviour, marriage, offerings, the following would be noted in chapter 18 vs 9,: *"And when ye reap the harvest of your land, thou shalt not wholly reap the corners of thy field, neither shalt thou gather the gleanings of thy harvest. And thou shalt not glean thy vineyards, neither shalt thou gather every grape of thy vineyard; thou shalt leave them for the poor and stranger: I am the lord your God. Ye shall not steal, neither deal falsely, neither lie one to another. And ye shall not swear by my name falsely...Thou shall not defraud thy neighbour, nor rob him: the wages of him that is hired shall not abide with thee all night until the morning."*

In these passages, the importance of honesty, trustworthiness, and truthfulness is well stressed. But in addition, there is the concept of leaving some harvest or produce in the land to be available to others and especially the poor. Just as importantly, is the ordinance that wages should not be delayed, a principle re-iterated in the teachings attributed to the Prophet Mohammed, in Islam, as mentioned in the relevant section, that is that a labourer's wage should be paid **before** his sweat is dried. Thus: *"nor rob him: the wages of him that is hired shall not abide with thee all night until the morning."*

Again, and certainly not exhaustively, the laws regarding the tithes, and releases seen in Deuteronomy chapter 14 vs. 22-25: *Thou shalt truly tithe* (tenth part) *all the increase of thy seed, that the field bringeth forth year by year...the tithe of thy corn, of thy wine, and of thine oil, and the firstlings of thy herds and of thy flocks...And if the way be too long for thee, so that thou art not able to carry it; or if the place be too far from thee... thou shalt turn it into money...and thou shalt bestow that money...for whatsoever thou desireth; and thou shalt eat there before the Lord thy God, and thou shalt rejoice, thou and thine household...And at the end of three years thou shalt bring forth all the tithe of thine increase the same year, and shalt lay it up within thy gates....and the stranger, and the fatherless, and the widow, which are within thy gates, shall come, and shall eat and be satisfied; that the Lord may bless thee in all the work of thine hand which thou doest".*

In Chapter 15, vs 1&2 another law is given by which: *"After the seventh year, thou shalt make a release...Every creditor that lendeth aught unto his neighbour shall release it; he shall not exact it of his neighbour, or of his brother, because it is called the Lord's release".*

The above passages show the extent to which people must look after each, and that a debt, if not redeemed after seven years must be "released". The balance to this is in Verse 4 which states: *"Save when there shall be no poor among you".* a situation that appears to have been envisaged in that book which, significantly is the fifth and last of the books that are attributed to Moses himself.

No account of this nature will be complete without a quote on "usury". In Deuteronomy chapter 23, verse 19 the ordinance is clear: *"Thou shalt not lend upon usury to thy brother; usury of money, usury of victuals* (i.e. food or provisions)*, usury of anything that is lent upon usury. Unto a stranger thou mayest lend upon usury; but unto thy brother thou shalt not lend upon usury..."*

The mention of brother in this context probably refers to anyone belonging to the "Children of Israel".

In Conclusion

It can be seen from the brief outline of the three major religions that valuable principles of economic nature have been formulated in religious texts, many of which have become time honoured verities taken for granted by people, and with most, without the appreciation of the fact that their origin lies in the Revered Books. Whether one believes that Religion has or had a role in structuring life and human endeavour along the ages, there appears no doubt that within any structure in society or law are included valuable religious principles combining the need for equity and fairness, with wisdom as the core method in achieving this. If implemented, the main aim of religion which is to create a sound basis for a rewarding life in this world, in addition to any thoughts on the individual's preparation for the life thereafter, will not be jeopardized. Economics, underpinned in the religious context with the "spiritual" element of "belief" would act as a "designer" method capable of preventing schisms and social class discrimination within society, particularly because of the "promise" of compliance in deed and in spirit.

Human frailty may have resulted in the loss of valuable opportunities, some irreplaceable, in achieving these desired aims. It is a very interesting exercise to think what would have been the course of history had these principles been applied, or had the rulers, especially those who assumed religious as well as temporal authority, tried, fervently, to implement even some of these principles.

PART IV

PRE-ADAMITE ECONOMICS

The period before the emergence of the so-called "Classicist Economists", starting with Adam Smith, who is widely recognised as the "Father of Modern Economics", spanned approximately three hundred years roughly from the latter half of the fifteenth century. During this period and especially during the initial transitional phase, traditional thoughts were influenced by the original Greek philosophers, and the Christian Churches. Adam Smith, commenting later on, noted that "The different progress of opulence in different ages and nations has given occasion to two different systems of political economy, with regards to enriching the people: *the system of commerce or mercantile system*", and *"the system of agriculture"*[60]. The former later became known as *"Mercantilism"*.

A combination of changes in State and Society appears to have been the underlying stimulus, whereby, on the one hand the ambitions of the non landed non privileged people led them to enhance their social and economic status by acquiring the skills of trading, and on the other hand, the statesmen, civil servants, and financial and business leaders of the time saw the need to strengthen the foundations of statehood and national wealth without actually formulating a policy or system as such. There were thus several important factors that producing these changes:

Firstly: There was a noticeable migration of the overburdened underprivileged classes from the rural feudal regions to the cities in an attempt to unshackle themselves and release their energies.

Secondly: The appearance of important "Merchant Towns", notably Venice, Florence, Bruges and then Antwerp, Amsterdam, London and others. In these towns or cities, trade was a respected pursuit, society having rid itself from the "stigma". Indeed, the big merchant activity generated big advances in parallel with the increased wealth. Thus the flourishing culture, art and architecture that was generated greatly exceeded what the feudal landlords were able to foster and encourage.

Thirdly: The tremendous opportunities opened up by the successful voyages of discovery of the time, mainly those of Columbus to America (1492) and Vasco da Gama to India (1497), and subsequent further discoveries by others from Spain, Portugal, France, Holland and England. This exposed the Europeans to exotic produce as well as previously unfamiliar traditions, cultures, and commercial opportunity. Enormous wealth began to flow, particularly to Spain where galleons loaded with silver, gold and other precious goods arrived continually, and further territorial acquisitions allowed Spanish settlers to establish colonies and expand trade. At the same time, particularly with the British, several large trading companies developed, such as the British East India Company (1600-1874), the Dutch East India Company (1602), the French East India Company (1664), Gentlemen Adventurers (1670), and others which, though essentially commercial organisations, actually spearheaded not only large trade and flow of people, but indeed acted as the substrate for eventual colonializations.

Fourthly: The emergence of novel Christian thought that challenged traditional attitudes. Salient among those thinkers was Calvin (1564-

1509), who found it permissible for people to go into financial loans paying or receiving interest provided such loans are used to develop agriculture, trade or industry. He also decided that work of any kind is to be respected.

Fifthly: The release of vast wealth belonging to the Church, particularly the Catholic Church, which was estimated to own fully a third of all wealth in England with endowments and gifts flowing in all the time. Changes resulting from Reformation led to a re- distribution of some of this wealth, and as a result, more efficient use of the released resources.

Mercantilism

It is difficult to note definite ideas about mercantilism as none were apparent. But in a somewhat coherent way, several general principles were articulated by different people: Antoine de Monchretien (1576-1621) in France, Antonio Serra (precise dates unknown) in Italy, Philipp W. von Hornick (1638-1712) in Austria, Johannn Joachim Becher (1635-1682) in Germany and Thomas Mun (1571-1641) in England. They were basically people with significant political influence and spoke very much for the merchants of the time. By far, the most prominent of the theorists mentioned was T. Mun who had definite ideas on the importance of maintaining a positive balance of trade as noted in his important work: *" England's Treasure by Forraign Trade or the Ballance of our Forraign Trade is the Rule of our Treasure"* published in 1664, after his death. He was an employee of the East India Company.

The essential features of Mercantilism, can be summarized as follows:[61]

1- Gold Bullion and treasure of every kind is the essence of wealth.

2- Regulation of foreign trade to produce the inflow of gold and silver.

3- Promotion of industry by encouragement of cheap raw material imports.

4- Protective duties on imported manufactured goods.

5- Encouragement of exports, particularly finished goods.

6- An emphasis on population growth, keeping wages low.

Within the above general principles, there was much discussion as to what really constitutes wealth. For example, Mun and Johne Locke observed that "The wealth of a country consists, not in its gold and silver only, but in land, houses, and consumable goods of all different kinds." However, they seem to have lost their thoughts on anything other than gold and silver, although some redress may have come from William Petty who concluded that "The quantity of money (in England) comprised less than 3% of total property; and in his *Taxes and Contributions*" (1662) he opposed the indefinite accumulation of bullion by appealing to what he called the "needs-of-trade doctrine "about the quantity of money: "There is a certain proportion requisite to drive the trade of a Nation, more or less than which would prejudice the same"

Mercantilists believed that money is "the life of commerce", "the vital spirit of trade" which "like muck" as Francis Bacon put it, "is not good except it be spread".

Mercantilism in Europe during the 16th and 17th century developed differently in different countries in Europe according to prevailing circumstances: In Germany, there was very little interest in balance of payment, foreign trade etc. as they favoured putting more effort to establish their administrative and strong central political system. The three foremost countries (and systems) prevailing therefore were:[62]

Spain: The Mineral System:

With the vast acquisitions of territory in America and the continual stream of bullion loaded galleons, Spain depended almost exclusively on this source of wealth, and relied on the amassing of gold, silver and other metals. There was no need to develop industry, commercial enterprise etc.as happened in France and England. All bullion export was prohibited, and all profit gained by the Spanish was to be repatriated.

This wealth led to extravagance, consumerism, and more seriously, provided the finance for the successive wars that Spain engaged in. Luxury goods were exported from England and France, at inflated prices, and it was not long before this enormous wealth was squandered[63].

France: The Industrial System:

France followed Spain in developing its system of Mercantilism. Having no access to colonies and sources of mineral wealth, and not wishing to be dependent on the uncertainties of agriculture as the main source of wealth, France became aware of the need to establish an industrial base to trade. Credit for the theory and application of this system goes to the most famous French Mercantilist, Colbert (1619-1683)[64] who as Statesman reaching the position of Finance Minister in the French Government, was able to lay the detailed foundations of this "French" system. His policy advocated and actually implemented the direct involvement of the state in directing the country towards developing industry, through state subsidies, prevention of skilled labour from leaving France, and importing skills from other countries. Exports were facilitated, and monopolistic activities encouraged. These measures later extended to what amounted to central planning and detailed directions as to what should be produced and the means of production. All this led to the gradual loss of personal initiative and risk taking and was an obvious drawback in the system.

England: The Trade and Finance System:

Mercantilism was also developed in England, but the system developed aimed at changing the country's reliance on agriculture and increasing its reliance on industry. Towards this aim, the state discouraged foreign merchants to work in England, and concentrated on certain industries, particularly textiles which had readily available markets in the colonies. New markets were opened up. Merchants were encouraged when Gresham established the London Stock Market in 1568, and with it the Insurance services. They were further encouraged when the historic law worked out by Cromwell and passed in 1651 stipulated that all merchandise to and from England are to be transported by British ships or ships belonging to the country that produced the goods, and that these ships' crews are to be three quarters British. Wages were reduced to enhance competition, and tax exemptions and other subsidies were allowed. Significantly also, interest rates were reduced to allow cheaper loans.

The evolution of Mercantilism:

With Mercantilism, as mentioned above, the emphasis was on amassing of money. It is not clear whether the leading mercantilists were differentiating between "money" and "capital" and therefore wealth. However, the pre-occupation with trade and surplus meant that there must have been awareness of a "Specie-flow mechanism", "specie" being a term that could be understood as meaning either money or capital. Thus, a balance of payments must mean "credits" and "deficits", and a country can earn foreign exchange by either: 1- visible commodity exports, 2- invisible exports of services, 3- exports of precious metals or 4- imports of capital, either in the form of foreign investments at home, profits on its foreign investments abroad, or loans granted by foreigners. The opposite applies, and in all this the balancing factor is the flow of money, or the import or export of capital[65].

This development in the thought process within Mercantilism led inevitably to the quantification of money appreciation of the "Quantity of Money", first by the Frenchman Jean Bodin (1596-1530)[66] who realized the inflationary effect of increased flow of money into France and with it the reduced purchasing power. In his *"Reponse aux paradoxes de Malestroit"*, published by Bodin in 1569, he gives the first elaborate explanation of the revolution in prices in the sixteenth century.[67] He ascribes the the rise in prices... to five causes: the abundance of gold and silver, the practice of monopolies, scarcity caused in part by export, then luxury of the king and the great lords, and the debasement of the coin. Of these, he states, the first is the most important.

Later, this aspect was more elaborately considered by the Scotsman John Law (1629-1671), who considered that the key to the economic evolution and advance is the availability of money in sufficient quantity. This will allow investment, employing of labour and general flourish of economic activity.

Law[68] then postulated that the value of money need not depend only on precious metal. Indeed he viewed paper money as being preferred because of the following reasons:

1- Minting of coins is costly, while printing money is cheap.
2- Precious metal used in coins can also be used for other purposes as in manufacture.
3- The value of minted money is dependent on the underlying value of the precious metal, and this is changeable.

According to Law, paper money can be valued according to the underlying cover of property and land which is of known value and is likely to appreciate. The increased availability of money will lead to lower interest rates, and therefore greater economic activity and production.

Under these circumstances, there was a need to regulate the exchange rates of currency, and to take it from the hands of individual money traders. The "Royal Exchange" was therefore established in London and given the role of fixing the exchange rate for the "Pound Sterling".

Nevertheless, paper money was considered to have a value only by virtue of the trust the people have in it. No trust means refusal to accept.

In addition to the views of John Law, it is useful to summarize the thoughts of other salient economists of the time:

Sir William PETTY (1623-1687): Born to a poor textile worker in Hampshire, England, he took up menial jobs selling and then as a seaman. He later managed to study medicine and become a Professor of Anatomy, and subsequently became a rich property owner. This career gave him opportunities to come in touch with eminent scientists and men of literature in France and England, and especially in Oxford.

His main and quite important contribution was to introduce scientific analytical and statistical methods to verify economic theory. In his *"political Arithmetick"* he laid down concepts of number, weight and measure, all adding up to the beginnings of statistics in economics. The applications aimed predominantly at overcoming the deists' evaluation of value and fair price on the basis of conscience and morality, and also the mercantilists' evaluation. This latter was based on the cost of labour according to the need to provide the labourer with the food and his family needs. Instead, Petty[69] analysed the value of goods according to the "political price" i.e. market price, and the "natural price" which is its natural value. Thus the value can be measured by the amount of time spent in production. As an example, if the time taken to extract an amount of silver is the same as that taken in producing a quantity of wheat, then the value of this quantity of silver is equal to that of the quantity of wheat. If the silver mine is rich enough to provide double the amount within the same time, then the value of the same amount of wheat will command double the initial amount of silver. Thus "equal amounts of labour time in producing different commodities impart equal values to them". However, Petty added the economic theory that "labour is the father and land is the mother" of value. The discrepancy here is that he did not manage to differentiate between the "utility value" and the "exchange value" as these were postulated later.

Sir Petty also applied his thoughts on the value of labour in terms of food required, and also the value of property which he worked out in terms of the rental return over the period of years this land is expected to yield its produce. Other factors such as the nearness of the plot of land to the city where the produce will be sold (the nearer, the more valuable, because the cost of transport is not added). In monetary matters, Petty was able to differentiate between money and capital, and the fact that the circulating money represents only a small proportion (not exceeding 1%) of the total wealth of Britain. While stating that economic prosperity is not reliant on the actual quantity of money, he explains this through his idea of the "Velocity of Circulation" i.e. the number times an amount of money is exchanged[70],[71].

John LOCKE(1622-1704): Another English born (near Bristol) and eminent economist who also studied medicine and natural sciences in Oxford, Locke became the doctor and secretary, and later the friend of Count Shaftesbury, grandfather to the famous philosopher bearing the same name. He had to leave England and live in France and Holland having been accused of colluding with the Count against the state, and returned after the 1688 peasant revolt. He was then greatly appreciated and even given good state posts. He was respected and noted for his love for fact, a strong personality, as well as good character and patriotism.

In his political views, Locke was a "liberal" in that he accepted that the ruler is party to the "contract" whereby the individuals agree to live under his protection (the "social contract"), provided the ruler lives up to the spirit and letter of the constitution and laws agreed upon. Locke demanded the separation of the Executive, Legislative, and Judicial arms of authority.

Locke's theory of labour and value is to be seen in this social context Thus, the value of land is related to the amount of work needed to make it produce. In this way, he was only concerned with the utility value, not having appreciated the exchange value. The person's ability to own and work his land is part of Man's ownership of himself. Therefore, he has the right to what he produces and the right to use his abilities as he wishes. Limitations imposed by nature are but the balances which prevent excessive ownership and allow good distribution of produce. God, Locke thought, did not intend to let the land to remain barren, but that it should be the property of the energetic worker, not lazy people. Life was quiet and people were modest in their demands before the appearance of money. With money, people became able to use the proceeds of excessive produce and higher prices in order to acquire more, amass more, and control more through larger land ownership.

Locke accepted that money has a dual value: 1- Its ability to generate interest, i.e. an income similar to that generated by land in the form of rent, and 2- Its value as a means of exchange.

In his "Volume of Trade" he states that the supply of goods versus the demand for them regulate prices. Prices are also a function of the amount of money in circulation within a period of time[72].

Sir Dudley NORTH (1640-1691): North's main importance in economic thought is the result of his belief in free trade. His view is that the "world is one, and international trade is a matter of mutual, not unilateral benefit"[73]. He viewed trade as essentially the exchange of surpluses, and so it is not necessarily only in precious metals, and it is not necessary for the state to limit or regulate it. North demanded the free trade internally within the country and not only between nations, because any form of exchange is of general and not only bilateral benefit. Prices and interest rates should be left to market forces and the effects of supply and demand. Interest rates will fall where there is economic prosperity.

North "also seems to have been the first to suggest that capital—which he called "stock"—is a separate factor of production and that profit is the income that accrues to it. He understood that only by being employed either for loans or as business capital could money earn a revenue, not by being kept in the form of money"[74],

Richard CANTILLON(1680-1734): Irish born but living for some time in Paris, Cantillon is the nearest rival to Adam Smith and considered a co-founder of economics. While not a "Physiocrat", he had an effect on Francois Quesnay. Yet he was a Classicist and thus quite near to Adam Smith who actually mentions him in his "Wealth of Nations". His original Treatise was the first of its kind by an Irish-born British banker and international financier. This book, the *"Essai"* was first published more than twenty years after his death at the hands of assassins.

The main thrust of his theory is "that the sole ultimate source of all wealth is land. Labour only transforms this natural wealth".[75] Wealth in his views had a psychological content in that it is an expression of food, means of comfort and happiness in one's every day life. Based on this, Cantillon differentiated between the value or price of a commodity and the market price. "*Market price* is in his view the *Intrinsic price* (value) plus the land and labour (i.e. *cost of production*)" Thus the value or price of a commodity is the function of the cost of labour and the cost of raw material.

As to the value of labour, Cantillon believed that this lies in the area of land required to satisfy the needs for subsistence for the labourer, and this in turn is related to the "cultural standard" reached in the particular society, there being a difference between the cost as assessed for men or for women, the former needing twice as much so as to satisfy the needs of two children each, allowing, according to studies revealed a the time, for the fact that half the children die before they reach 17 years age.

Cantillon also believed that wages will respond to the forces of supply and demand, and that the chances are that the population will grow (like mice if food becomes plentiful !!), and this will help lower wage demands (a glimpse of the classicists' views to come, perhaps).

Cantillon believed in precious metals as the basis for money, not concurring with Locke's views that the value of money is "notional" and depends on people's acceptance of such value. He believed money had a real value, based again on the cost of producing the metal, i.e. the value of the land plus the labour to mine and purify the precious metal, all within the price allowed by the market. The quantity of money required will be in accordance with the needs of society. Cantillon further evolves this theory so that for the first time it is recognised that it is not only the amount of money in circulation that decides its purchasing power, but in addition there is the factor the *speed* with which it circulates. Again, he was among the first to appreciate that changes in income can influence the amount of money in circulation.

Regarding the economic cycle, Cantillon seems to have prepared the way for Quesnay later on in seeing society as composed of three classes: Land owners, Agricultural workers and land tenants, and finally, Artisans and Merchants. He assumed that half the population lives in the country and the other half in the cities. In this way, land tenants should pay one third of the income from their produce to the land owners as rental, and spend one sixth of the other two thirds to purchase what they need from the cities. As the land owners will also spend their rental income in the cities, this means that the cities will receive a full half of the land proceeds in return for what they sell in goods and services to the land owners and tenants. This makes the land owners the only class that is totally free within the economic hierarchy, as they can decide on their spending pattern, and upon their decisions the economic cycle revolves. Cantillon was very conscious of the value of the human input into the land which would be arid without the labour to cultivate it. Labour is therefore a source of production and increased labour is an important factor in the improvement of the quality of labour as well as the creation of wealth[76],[77].

David HUME (1711-1776): Born twelve years before his very good friend Adam Smith, and having studied law, he apparently had known of Cantillon's work although it had not yet surfaced., particularly during his travels in France, and the fact that the *"Essai"* was originally published in French. However, Hume should take also great credit for his own work. He had become deeply interested in philosophy and had also studied history profusely. His thoughts had great impact on the history of philosophy, political economics, and political science. He assumed important state positions in the British government based in France, Vienna and Turin (Italy). He took part in the peace talks in Versaille, and was British Foreign Under-Secretary during 1767 to 1768.

Hume's' important statement, which became a cornerstone in the political economics of the classical school later on, is that everything available in the world can be obtained through work, and that our needs are the only driving force for us to work. He believed in precious metal as the basis of the wealth of the state, and that foreign trade is the means of obtaining it. Work is therefore the only sources of wealth. He may have exaggerated on this point to the extent that he was noted to say that land which is very fertile will not be a source of increased wealth as there will be little incentive for work on it.

Hume agreed with Locke that money represents goods and labour and is a means of measuring and comparing these. The value of money in any transaction is decided upon by the relationship of the amount of money and the amount of goods in exchange. This means that changes in the amount of money in circulation must be accompanied by corresponding changes in price of goods. He emphasizes that it is the money *in circulation* that affects prices, not necessarily the absolute amount of money available in the country. Stored money will have no effect on either prices or the value of money. A slow but constant increase in the quantity of money in circulation is advisable in order to provide a perpetual stimulant to business activity, because of the increase in price. He recognized, however, that this does not occur immediately, but after a lag period of time. This interim period of increased money in circulation will be used to increase productivity, and increase the need for labour, although it was assumed that workers will not dream of demanding an increase in their wages. Thus, according to Hume, permanent prosperity can be achieved through inflation, what Adam Smith later called *"Profit inflation"* which occurs at the expense of labour wages.

Regarding interest rates, Hume was of the opinion that economic prosperity will lead to their lowering, and vice versa. He disagreed with the demands of the merchants for the intervention of the state in deciding these rates, as they will depend on the supply and demand of money, as well as the level of profit. Thus lower profits encourage acceptance of lower returns on money, while higher interest rates will discourage merchants from selling cheap when they can get higher returns on their money.

In foreign trade, Hume believed that prosperity in one country will lead to prosperity in others. It is wrong therefore to envy those countries that are prosperous (in those days, Spain in particular). His theory of self regulating international trade assumes that imports lead to loss of money, which in turn reduces prices. This stops further importing, and may even turn the situation to exporting, bringing the money back. Thus, while Spain acquired riches from its colonies in America, there was a temporary reduction in interest rates, greater consumption, and squandering of wealth. The beneficiaries were Britain and France who attracted these riches by offering luxury goods, turned these riches into productivity and commercial activity, and thus in turn enjoyed lowering of interest rates and economic prosperity.

It is therefore wrong for countries to assume that they can all have a positive balance of trade all the time[78].

PHYSIOCRACY: A French experiment

A number of factors in France lead to the evolution of Colbert's version of Mercantilism (sometimes actually called *"Colbertisme"*), the most important of which was the powerful interest and mystique for agriculture that has, and still does, prevail in French society. French agricultural produce, notably fruit, wine and cheeses, have always enjoyed admiration, prestige, and indeed a "personality". The French Government was less enthusiastic about the model of Mercantilism that prevailed in its neighbouring England. In addition, the remaining feudal classes in France were still enjoying some independence and a lavish way of life, which Louis XIV was keen to subdue or even destroy. There was a system of enforced labour, the *"Corvee"*, a form of serfdom to the feudal lords and the state. The French aristocracy surrounding successive kings (Louis XIV, XV, and XVI) were, according to Christopher Hill (New Statesman, July 20,1984, p. 23, quoted in 6, p. 47), unable to adapt to the commercial society as the English aristocracy did.

Jean Batiste Colbert, 1619-1683) was appointed as Comptroller General of Finances to France at the time of Louis XIV. The latter had squandered much wealth on wars and on extravagances such as the Castle at "Versaille" outside Paris. Colbert decided that there is a need to accumulate wealth to pay for all this, and his doctrine enshrined the concept that the wealth and the economy should serve the state and not the opposite.

Further factors added to the urge to re-think aspects of philosophy, politics, and social economics. On the one hand, there was the spirit of the "Enlightenment" lead by such famed philosophers as Voltaire and Rousseau mainly, in addition to others such as Diderot and Condorcet. They all noting the need for reforms in society and politics. On the other hand, there were the new scientific discoveries, mainly those of Copernicus(1473-1543), and Gallileo(1564-1642), concerning the universe which challenged established Christian beliefs, William Harvey discovering the human body's circulation in 1628, and Isaac Newton's(1642-1727) discovering the natural laws of gravity, all made it difficult for the Deists and those still relying on the time honoured philosophies of Aristotle and Plato, to remain credible.

Reduced credibility of Christian doctrines led to the adoption of alternative "gods", and what better, with the new discoveries explaining the magnificence of nature, is it than to go to nature, and a more natural way of life. Rousseau's many ideas included those that defined natural man as virtuous and humane and essentially equal, but is spoiled and vitiated through education and urbanisation.

Within this atmosphere, it was unsurprising that a group of people who called themselves *"Les Economistes"* worked towards asserting the rules of nature in an economic system which Adam Smith, who visited Paris and Versailles in 1765 later called *"The Agricultural System".* Significantly, he praised the system "with all its imperfections. as perhaps the nearest approximation to the truth that has yet been published upon the subject of Political Economy"

The neglect of industry and agriculture that was the legacy of "Colbertism", the war of the Spanish Succession, and the magnificence of the Versailles court placed a severe burden upon taxable capacity, and the land tax, being the chief source of revenue, was steadily increasing. Colbert worked to create a favourable balance of trade and increase France's colonial holdings. Historians of mercantilism consider Colbert a key figure.

The Seven Year War with England, however, from which France emerged defeated, deprived of Canada and her Oriental possessions, and reduced to a second rate power in Europe, all added towards setting the stage for a "back-to-nature" movement, a return to rustic simplicity, together with envious glances across the Channel to the successful smallholdings that emerged from the large feudal systems as a result of the "agricultural revolution" in England[79].

The three leading Physiocrats:

Physiocracy is associated with the name of Francois QUESNAY (1694-1774). But the term physiocracy probably is associated with the name of Pierre Samuel du Pont de Nemour(1739-1817) who collected and edited some of Quesnay's work under the title *"La Physiocratie".* Du Pont was suspected of counterrevolutionary tendencies during the

French revolution, went into hiding in France, and in 1800 emigrated to the United States with his sons and developed a small powder industry in Delaware, which later grew into the well known industrial giant "Du Pont".

Another leading figure was Anne Robert Jacques TURGOT (1727-1781) who reached high public service positions in France, including that of comptroller general and minister of finance under Louis XVI. He had studied Divinity at the Sorbonne University, but thereafter lost interest in this subject. While not totally unfaithful to mercantilism, he sought to initiate a minor revolution in an attempt to pre-empt what he saw as a major revolution coming in France. His support of rigid economy in royal and other public expenditures, tax reform, free trade in grain within France, the abolition of public sinecures and monopolies, the toleration of Protestants and the proposed abolition of the *Corvee* all were issues that united against him a most impressive array of vested interests, ranging from landlords and aristocrats to jobholders with varying claims on public revenue; from grain speculators and priests, on to Marie Antoinette herself. Hurt by the effects of a crop failure, he was sacked in May 1776.[80] His sacking was apparently not a result of conviction on behalf of the king, and was lamented by many including Voltaire.

Francois QUESNAY (1694-1774)[81]: Quesnay is recognised as the leading architect of Physiocracy. Surprisingly he came into economics at the age of 62, and after a very successful career as a physician. He reached the position of physician to Madame Pompadour, living in the Versailles Palace, and later on, in 1755, he was even appointed physician to Louis XV himself. He had written on the practice of bleeding, the nature and handling of gangrene and fevers, and at an early age had become the secretary of the Academy of Surgery in Paris. His publication, the ***"Tableau Economique"***, in 1758, while composed only of a few pages, was his crowning achievement as well as that of the physiocratic school. It was, however not its centrepiece since not all the conclusions of the physiocrats can be deduced from it. Indeed, having been mentioned by Adam Smith, and subsequently forgotten, it was rediscovered by Karl Marx in the middle of the nineteenth century. There were apparently several copies, but the fourth, discovered in 1894 is probably the best representative one. It is presented with a zigzag diagram illustrating the circular flow (of money) which describes the expenditure of one landlord, and uses this as a representative of the whole theory.

The Physiocrats' Doctrine:

The first and central commitment of the Physiocrats was to the concept of the natural law (*"Le droit naturel"*). In this they saw the essential rule in economic and social behaviour, whereby freedom of trade, selling and buying, and existence and protection of property, all are best left to the natural laws. People's wisdom, they thought, is on the side of leaving things to work out on their own in accordance with natural motivations and constraints. Governments and legislations are tolerable only if they are consistent with, or an extension of, natural law. Asked what he would do if he were king, Quesnay replied:*"Nothing"*. Upon further questioning, he answered:*"The Law"* (presumably the *natural Law)*, and then provided the motto: *"Laissey Faire, Laissey Passer"* The extent to which this concept was believed in varied, as it could apply in a "theological" i.e. social, sense as well as to legislation and the dynamics of economics.

The practical economic side to the doctrine was the theory that all wealth originated from agriculture, and none in any other industry, or in trade or an occupation. Thus merchants only bought and sold, adding nothing to value, and manufacturing merely added the effect of labour to the products of the soil; "To increase the number of cobblers...there must first be an increase in the number of cow hides".[82] Agriculture is therefore the only real source of what they termed the ***"produit net" (net product)***. In their view, therefore, Agriculture is the "productive" work and trade and manufacture is "sterile" as it does not produce a net increase. Simplistically, they looked at the fact that one can put one seed in the ground, and this will produce twenty. In the Physiocrat theory there is the "Circular flow of Goods", and Quesnay originated the tradition of regarding capital as consisting of a **series of "advances"**: First, there is fixed capital in the form of ***"Original advance"***--livestock, buildings, and implements--interest on which at 10% is included as depreciation (Amortisation). Second, there is a fixed capital in the form of ***"landlord's advances"***--drainage, fencing, and other permanent land improvements. Last, there is working capital under the title of ***"annual advances"***--the wages of agricultural labour, seeds, and other recurring annual expenditures.

The process of circulation is as follows: Taking an assumed figure of five thousand as the gross value added by agriculture, three thousands of this will constitute costs of production incurred in cultivation. Farmers use two fifths of their own output for working capital; one fifth is sold to the "sterile" artisans in exchange for goods required to replace worn out fixed capital. Since farmers receive only "wages of management"-- in their views it is land that is productive, not the labour--the remainder goes to land owners as rent. The landowners in turn exchange half of their two thousand revenue for manufactured articles, while the "sterile" artisans purchase two thousand worth of raw materials and foodstuffs from the agricultural sector. The whole process may be conceived of in real terms, with three fifths of output entering into circulation, or, as Quesnay suggested, it may equally well be pictured in money terms. At the beginning of the process, the farmers are in possession of the entire money stock of the economy (2 thousand). They pay this to landowners to purchase "rental services", who in turn spend it on foodstuffs and fabricated commodities. The farmers now spend the 1 thousand just received to replace fixed capital, and the artisans spend their total receipts of 2 thousand on agricultural products. At the end, the farmers have received 3 thousands and spend 1; they are back to where they started. The net effect of the sterile sector is nil, and the 2 thousand of money is paid at once to landowners as a new cycle of production begins.

The *tableau* as conceived by Quesnay involves a one-period income-spending lag: landowners spend the previous period's rent, while the artisans always retain 1 thousand of the last period's receipts for spending in the following period. Presumably, Quesnay was thinking of output as identical with the annual harvest, the whole of which is consumed in the following 12 months.[83]

Closely related to the notion of the *produit net* was the physiocrats' class structure. In this there was: first, the landlords or proprietors, who guided, supervised, or otherwise presided over agricultural production. To them the produit net ultimately accrued and on them fell the social and political responsibilities of the community and the state. Next, there was the productive class, members of which did the husbandry and worked the soil; it was after their reward was paid that the produit net went to the proprietors. Finally, sharply lower in status, there were the merchants, manufacturers and artisans--the unproductive classes.

Agriculture was thus the source of all wealth not only of the state, but also of all the citizens. It followed that tax, which can only be levied on the beneficiaries of the (ultimate) wealth or net product, cannot be levied on others who do not create wealth. The sterile sector is simply assumed to possess fixed capital but no provision is made for replacement. Competition is supposed to reduce the value of output of this sector to the sum of the wages of workers and managers. The same argument in theory should apply to land rental, but this seems to have been overlooked. This "single tax" concept, i.e. directly taxing only those incomes that ultimately bear net profit was supposed to minimize collection costs, and it was estimated by Quesnay as being about one third of the "net product"[84].

Wages in the Physiocrats' thinking were to be assessed according to the basic needs of the worker, as there is no added value accruing form his work. When it comes to interest rates, it was more difficult for them to work that out, as in theory it is only land that can give a net product. Capital cannot, and so it should not, accrue interest. This was a difficult area in which they got themselves into a muddle, and which they tried to resolve unsuccessfully by assuming that capital is an expression of the amortisation and risk taking.

In foreign trade, the Physiocrats were not very clear in their views. They were unhappy about the Mercantilists' keenness on surplus in foreign trade because, they thought, this will lead to flow of money outwards, and with free trade there will inevitably be the temptation to greater imports. The result will be higher prices in the country, and further loss of money outwards until a state of equilibrium occurs between the amount of money available and the volume of goods on offer. They were only in favour of free trade if it leads to export of excess grain, because this will help cover some of the cost of production and thus more net proceeds (or internal surplus).Other aspects of foreign trade are by necessity acceptable in allowing the purchase of goods not producible locally. But this was considered to be to the detriment of the people, as exchange will be for items of comparable value, and there will not be any net benefit to the wealth of the nation. This ambiguous position was essentially because they were unable to differentiate between ***"Physical productivity"*** (the proportion of cost to rent in quantitative measure) and ***"Work created productivity"*** (the proportion of cost to rent measured in value).

In general therefore, the Physiocrats were effectively in favour of the prevailing capitalist system based on landowners, encouragement and support of the state to these landowners, and glancing sideways at England where successful small land holdings were proving their worth, perhaps encouraging such small holdings(farms) in France as they were likely to add to the overall wealth creation. Their thoughts may have been close to other contemporary economists such as J.B. Say's, who published his "Law of Markets"(essentially a physiocratic critique of Mercantilism) and Mercier de La Riviere who wrote *"L'ordre naturel et essentiel"*(1767). This latter work was cited by Adam Smith as giving "the most distinct and best connected account of physiocracy", One remark in it that "no one is a buyer without being at the same time a seller" is only a small step from Quesnay's "all that is bought is sold, and all that is sold is bought" and also close to Say's "products are paid for by products"[85].

These and similar thoughts were picked up by Malthus later when he stated that the balanced spending by landlords on luxury goods is a factor that maintains the circular flow and therefore economic prosperity. A few years ahead, and it can be seen as a train of thought which developed via Malthus and through Ricardo, ending up in a full scale attack on capitalism by Marx. The fate of physiocracy may have been decided by the French Revolution which swept away all these vested interests in French society. But its rigidity and insistence on one system, albeit, in their views, a complete interlocking system, will probably not have survived more that the quarter of a century that it did. It is worth noting Alexander Gray's comment:"(It was) in its time the crowning achievement of Quesnay and the Physiocratic school, now perhaps better reduced to an embarrassing footnote...It may be doubted whether it will ever be anything but a vast simplification"[86].

PART V

THE CLASSICAL SCHOOL OF ECONOMICS

The label "Classical" was first coined by Karl Marx[87], and since then has become the accepted reference to a period of development of economic thought on a more scientific and structured basis. While the immediate thought would go to Adam Smith as the initiator of this trend, to be followed by David Ricardo and Thomas Malthus, it is arguable that many of Smith's and his contemporary economists' thoughts have their echoes in similar thoughts expressed by Say, Mill, J. H. Von Thuenen and others. whose contributions elaborated on the theories mainly of Smith and Ricardo. Their most significant contribution was the comprehensive outlook on the subject, not relying on simple observations, and in trying to fathom the factors and "laws" that influence and affect the capitalist society surrounding and in which they found themselves.

Their thoughts coincided with the beginning of what Arnold Toynbee termed the "Industrial revolution", the beginnings of which he considered to be the first lighting of the great Carron works in Scotland in 1760. This was followed by major inventions and mechanisations, such as Kay's flying shuttle, Hargreaves' spinning jenny, Compton's mule, and Arkwright's water frame, all of which revolutionized the spinning industry all through the 1780's, and in addition, the momentous invention of the steam engine by James Watts which helped drive all these machines. However, in spite of the fact that Smith lived through some of these developments, he failed to recognize their significance and to anticipate or appreciate that such a revolution was taking place. The thrust of his and contemporary economists' theories, therefore, was in relation to labour, wages and agriculture rather than industry.

Smith was able, however, to identify the ills of his society within the way labour is used. What appears to be the most famous "factory" was the *"pin factory"* described by Smith. In it "one man draws out the wire, another straightens it, a third cuts it, a fourth points it, a fifth grinds it at the top for receiving the head; to make the head requires two or three distinct operations; to put it on is a peculiar business, to whiten the pin is another; it is even a trade by itself to put it into the paper."[88] If one man was to undertake all these tasks, he would, according to Smith produce 20 pins per day. If, however, twenty men divide these tasks between them, they can collectively produce 48,000 pins per day, a 240-fold increase in output.

Prominent Economists Of The Classical Era
Adam Smith

As mentioned previously, it is generally accepted that Smith is the "father of economics". He was the first academic economist, and his thoughts will find resonance and empathy with philosophers, sociologists, ethicists, moralists, and practically all shades of political economists, from the conservatives, liberals, through to radicals and marxists. The reasons can be found on two main aspects: 1- The way his career developed, and 2- The breadth and depth of his thoughts, and the much higher degree of systematic thinking he brought to economics, than was hitherto witnessed.

Adam Smith was born on 5 June 1723, in Kirkcaldy on the Fife coast of Scotland. His father, also named Adam, was a lawyer and civil servant (actually a Scottish Advocate and Comptroller of Customs). Adam Smith the father was married to his first wife Lilias Drummond and had one son from her, named Hugh. Sadly she died when Hugh was eight years old. The father then married Margaret Douglas in 1720, and Adam the son was their first child. The father died before Adam's birth, and Adam was brought up by his mother on her own. This lead inevitably to the development of a strong relationship between Adam and his mother. Whether this explains the fact that Adam Smith the son never got married is not clear, although it is known that he has indeed fallen in love at least twice[89].

Adam attended the school in Kirkcaldy and then went to the University of Glasgow at the age of fourteen, a little older than usual in that time, and subsequently to Balliol College, Oxford. He was interested in mathematics and natural philosophy (meaning physics), and although he wrote an essay on the history of astronomy (while in Oxford), it appeared that these subjects were not his real intent. While at Glasgow, he was very strongly influenced by Francis Hutcheson, the professor of Moral Philosophy with his lectures on ethics, jurisprudence and economics. He went to Oxford with a "Snell Exhibition", a scholarship given to talented students, allowing them to study whatever they wished. He was also able to make good use of the extensive library at Balliol, read Greek and Latin classics as well as French literature and was particularly interested in the writings of David Hume.

From Oxford Smith moved back to Kirkcaldy, living again with his mother. He was given the opportunity to deliver a series of public lectures in Edinburgh for the next three years, not as part of any University course. he lectured initially on rhetoric and **belles-lettres**, and then delivered another series on civil law. The impression was very favourable, and when the Chair of Logic at the Glasgow University became vacant at the end of 1750, he was immediately offered the job, accepted it and was in post in 1751. It so happened that at that time the professor of Moral Philosophy was taken seriously ill, and Smith found himself taking over part of that course in addition to his basic subjects of rhetoric and *belles-lettres,* enabling him to develop his lectures into the field of "natural jurisprudence and politics". In November of that year (1751), the professor of Moral Philosophy died, and Smith succeeded him. He then lectured extensively on law, government and economics apparently with clarity, originality, greater coherence, and a sharp awareness of areas of difficulty. He also proved a very caring professor, taking interest in his students, their health and well being[90]

Although Smith gave lecture on theology, there is virtually nothing that is known about their content. He may have "considered the proofs of the being and attributes of God, and those principles of the human mind upon which religion was founded." He talked of divinities as originally the object of religious fear and conceived to resemble human beings in their sentiments and passions. Together with this, he developed views on ethics, and these he formed after a study of its history starting with the philosophy of Plato to that of his contemporaries, Hutcheson and Hume. These thoughts were put in his first book *"The Theory of Moral sentiment"*, the first of his big works, published in 1759. In his lectures on ethics, Smith considered the subjects of "justice" in the context of a history of law and government, and then developed his themes on "expediency", in which he considered economics as forming the central feature of the workings of society and which in turn explains the history of changes in the law. This latter theme is the basis of Smith's main work: *"An Inquiry into the Nature and Causes of the Wealth of Nations"*, usually abbreviated and better known as *"The Wealth of Nations"*, his most illustrious book. It was published in 1776.

In ideological terms, therefore, Smith's thoughts can be compared with present day "Humanism", but the liberalism is also a reflection of other thinkers at the time. In his travels he met Voltaire whom he visited in his residence just outside Geneva and admired in particular his championing of the cause of justice. He also met eminent people in France, including Quesnay and Turgot. His thoughts, moreover, owed much to Montesquieu.

In Glasgow, Smith had the opportunity to meet the merchants of the city, especially those in the thriving tobacco trade. He was a regular attendant at the Political Economy Club which was founded by Andrew Cochrane, a leading merchant and banker, to "inquire into the nature and principles of trade in all its branches". Smith acknowledged a debt to Cochrane in his book *Wealth of Nations*. His acquaintance with other prominent merchants in Glasgow gave him a feel at the real world of trade and commerce, with mercantilism being the underlying trend. His ideas of free trade must have been alien to those merchants, but he seemed to manage to sway and convert many of them.

Smith's next turn in his career was quite different. he resigned his University post in 1763 to take up an offer as the tutor to the Duke of Buccleuch , having been lured to this by a good financial incentive as well as the opportunity to travel within Europe. He had begun writing a second book while in Glasgow, which mainly dealt with "general principles of law and government", but this apparently never went beyond a short draft. On leaving Scotland, Smith and the Duke spent some time in Paris, Geneva and the south of France, and then settled in Toulouse for eighteen months. During this time his interest and thoughts on economics were becoming prominent, and he began his second book, *"The wealth of Nations"* in earnest. Inevitably, he also came in contact with the Physiocrats, Quesnay, as mentioned earlier, and also Dupont de Nemours. He was swayed away from mercantilism, and appreciated the value of the Physiocrats' thoughts to the extent that he wrote in the *Wealth of Nations* that their "is, perhaps, the nearest approximation to the truth that has yet been published upon the subject of political economy". However, Smith cannot be considered either a mercantilist or a physiocrat. While imbibing from both schools, he developed his own ideas[91].

Smith developed good friendship with Quesnay, and when the Duke fell ill, and later the Duke's brother Hew, who was with them in France also fell ill, he asked Quesnay's help as a physician. The Duke recovered, but Hew died. This made them decide to leave France, returning to London with Hew's body in 1766, and a few months later, Smith returned to his mother's home in Kirckaldy where he remained till 1773, all the time working with little interruption on his book. He then took his manuscript and moved to London, where he had the opportunity to consort with fellow Scots at the British Coffee house, and with distinguished literary people at the Literary Club. He also developed a relationship with Benjamin Franklin who helped with revisions of the chapters of the book, as well as give him valuable information about America, adding to the information about France that he had obtained from his friends there[92]. Eventually the book appeared on 9 March 1776. The book was an instant and resounding success. Its appearance coincided with the publication of another masterpiece by the same publisher a few weeks earlier: Gibbon's *Decline and Fall of the Roman Empire,* the two publications thus signalling an era of literary richness and deep thought. Soon afterwards, Smith's very good friend David Hume died, and in eulogizing him, Smith was criticized and branded as an atheist, because he described Hume "as approaching as near to the idea of a perfectly wise and virtuous man, as perhaps the nature of human frailty will permit". Conventional Christians were shocked at the suggestion of an atheist being described as near perfect, but this probably reflected Smith's own atheistic inclinations.

The final phase of Smith's career came in 1777 when he applied for and was granted an appointment as Commissioner of Customs in Edinburgh. He took a fine house, and brought his mother and his cousin over from Kirkcaldy to stay with him. In this new post, Smith was able to put into practice some of his ideas, especially on free trade which influenced government policies. New forms on taxation based on recommendations by Smith were issued in 1777/1778, policies towards America were discussed, and free trade was granted to Ireland in 1779. *Wealth of Nations* was revised and reprinted, and was translated into German, French, Danish, and Italian.

In his latter years Smith was working on several other books on philosophy (probably including the sciences), the history of philosophy, and the theory and history of law and government, but they were not published. Indeed on his request, the manuscripts were destroyed except for some pieces of work which were published after his death as *Essays on Philosophical Subjects*.

Adam Smith died in 1790, and is buried in Canongate in Edinburgh with a suitable epitaph.

The Thoughts Of Adam Smith

Smith's thoughts ranged very widely, and to a great extent reflected the three main stages of his career. While initially thinking along the grounds of general principles of ethics, he then goes on to look at the economic implications of at least some, if not all, of the ethical considerations that he espoused. He eventually, and in part at least because of his exposure to the way economic principles seemed to shape political and government programmes, went into the practicalities of the ethical, and, more importantly, the economic principles and their application to government.

He was influenced, as has been shown above, initially by his main mentor, Professor Hutcheson, and by his friend and colleague David Hume, and thereafter by a large variety of exposures to people of literary, philosophical, and more practically, merchants, traders, and shapers of government policies such as Quesnay in France.

In all this journey of thought and achievement, Smith was able to relate to history and to look at the way history seems to direct the changes in the laws that govern society and the country. There are echoes in this from previous thinkers, and although Smith was influenced more by the Greek and other European classical thought, it is conceivable that he may have come across the thoughts of the Islamic scholar Ibn Khaldun. The latter's theory about the way history can be shaped, nay even determined and predicted, by society's behaviour is one strand that can be discerned in Smith's thoughts. Another strand is Ibn Khaldun's thoughts on the differing talents and abilities of people, and the need therefore to specialize and capitalize on these abilities in order to obtain the best out of the individual and thus maximize the benefit to society.

Thus, in tracing Smith's thought development, it will be seen to start with the Academic philosophical approach of his early university appointment, culminating in the appearance of his first book *The Theory of Moral Sentiment*. This part of his career dealt with Ethics and Morals. The next stage takes Smith into the core of economic thought, and the fact that it took seventeen years after that for his second book, *The Wealth of Nations* to appear is an indication of how deeply he thought of the subject, and how much revision and re-revision took place.

In the last part of his working career, when he was actually in government, and while managing to influence government policy on some matters, Smith's thoughts seemed to have been directed in their relation to that ultimate application of all his theories, and that is law and government. Interestingly, as mentioned above, towards the end of his life, Smith "spent many months on producing an enlarged version of his book, *The Theory of Moral Sentiments*. He also talked of being engaged on two other works, one "a sort of philosophical history" and the other "a sort of theory and history of law and government"[93].

Ethics[94]

Adam Smith was influenced essentially by the *"Enlightenment"* that was current at the time, and which had the effect of altering one's perception of religious creeds and thoughts so as to move away from strict interpretation of the texts or strict adherence to dogma. His thoughts, therefore, while revealing echoes of religious language and feelings, tended to look at "nature" as the source of human behaviour and social interaction. Human conduct, in Smith's views revolves around three pairs of motives:**1**- Self-love and sympathy; **2**- The desire to be free and a sense of propriety; and **3**- The habit of labour and the propensity to deal and barter or exchange things. In his views, these natural sentiments acted as checks and balances on one another, and supported a social order of natural harmonies. He was unwilling to accept that "man's position in the hierarchy was fixed at birth... The difference between a philosopher and a street porter, for example, seems to arise not from nature, as from habit, custom and education."[95]

With the natural balance of human motives mentioned above, each person when left to pursue his own personal interest or advantage, unconsciously promotes the common good, as if ***"led by an invisible hand to promote an end which was no part of his intention"***[96]. Conversely, in his statement:" I have never known much good done by those who affected to trade for the public good", he implies that the effect of the individual in promoting, not by design, the good for society, is the essential factor operating in society.

Smith was very interested in the concept of *"Sympathy"* as an emotion that dominates moral judgement. It is with this tool that one approves or disapproves, decided whether an act is right or wrong depending on whether the person making the judgement identifies with the action and accepts that this would be his or her action or thought under similar circumstances. In addition, with the same concept of sympathy, one judges an action's merit or demerit, deserving praise or blame, reward or punishment. Sympathy thus creates a "social bond". At times it is synonymous with *"Compassion"*. Thus sympathy of this kind promotes a sense of responsibility to share the burdens of others, and also generates a feeling of satisfaction and pleasure in a person when there is approval of his/her action, or a sense of discomfort when there is disapproval. These interactions tend eventually to modulate one's reactions and emotions and also create an environment that encourages the person to "conform" to society's "norms".

Smith develops this concept further in perhaps the subtlest and most original of his ethical thoughts: that of the *"Impartial Spectator"*. Thus, while it is possible to think about how we judge others, what about the way we judge ourselves? According to Smith, one approves or disapproves of one's own action by imagining himself in the role of a spectator. In this way, one can judge whether in this position (of a spectator) he or she would have approved or disapproved the same action done by someone else[97]. These judgements of conscious will in this way initially reflect the judgement of society, with one assuming to be a mirror of this society. In this way, Smith further postulates, society becomes the important influence on one's conduct and behaviour, inasmuch as if an individual *"grew up to manhood in some solitary place, without any communication with his own species, he could no more think of his own character, of the propriety or demerit of his own sentiments and conduct, of the beauty or deformity of his own mind, than of the beauty or deformity of his own face...as there is no mirror to present them to his view..."* In another statement in his book on Moral Sentiments (pages 128-130), Smith uses some biblical ideas and phrases as in: *"The all-wise Author of Nature has, in this manner, taught man to respect the sentiments and judgements of his brethren...He has made man, if I may say so, the immediate judge of mankind, and has in this respect, as in many others, created him after his own image, and appointed him viceregent. upon earth, to superintend the behaviour of his brethren"*. Using this language and these thoughts indicates Smith's attitude towards Christianity, whereby it is known that, being a product of the Enlightenment, as mentioned above, he had some reservations but not excessive scepticism. He was probably a "deist", considering that observable nature afforded sufficient reason for believing in the existence of God. Indeed, in the same spirit, it is possible to think that Smith is ready to say that the general rules are "justly" regarded as laws of God, and the accumulation of our experiences add up to generalizations which society then calls "rules and principles". Moral judgement is thus intended by God to direct our lives, and moral actions tend, as a whole, to promote general happiness, and this is the end intended by God. With "Utilitarianism" (a term coined by Jeremy Bentham) becoming prominent in the eighteenth century, Smith had to consider it, but he argued that the thought of utility has a subordinate role in the formation of moral judgement. Our approval arises first from sympathy with the motive of the agent and secondly from sympathy with the gratitude of the beneficiary. However, Smith[98], rather than labour "Utilitarianism", actually, believes that "justice is enshrined in the fact that the "Author" of nature...has endowed *(man)* with an immediate and instinctive approbation of that very application which is most proper to attain it."

Economics

As mentioned previously, Adam Smith's thoughts on economics are derived from his second big work, *The Wealth of Nations*. This is one of those books that are frequently quoted, but, as with the Bible, the Qur'an or such works as Karl Marx's *Das Kapital*, not necessarily read in full. The book is in five parts covering 19 main topics which encompass practically every aspect of the subject of economics that could be dealt with at the time.

Two major features and three essentials can be identified: The two main features and the two essentials are: **1-** An economic system or model with an analysis of the nature and workings of the forces that motivate the system, and **2-** The recommendation for policies by which the state can further economic progress and prosperity for its people, in general with a *laissez-faire* attitude. The **third essential** is an explanation of income distribution, wages, profit, rent, and the determination of prices, as an interaction between these forces. The process, according to Smith, is most successful when left to natural forces and the role of *self interest*. Thus, on the one hand, as he asserts (in chapter 2 of book 1), public good comes out of the effect of individual competitive pursuits :*"It is not from the benevolence of the butcher, the brewer, or the baker that we expect our dinner, but from their regard to their own interest. We address ourselves, not to their humanity, but to their self love."* And on the other hand, he also asserts (in chapter 2 of book 4), that the individual :*"Is in this, as in many other cases, led by an invisible hand to promote an end which was no part of his intention"* . This statement about the invisible hand can be taken as an act of faith on his part, or just as a metaphor. But it certainly fits in with his concept of freedom of action and enterprise. More significantly, it is a bold statement that overturns the general thought up to that time that self- enrichment and self interest is contrary to the spirit of the Scriptures, arguing that it is such pursuit that will ultimately benefit society.

In his economic model, Smith evolves his thoughts in a journey of search for the ultimate source of wealth, taking him from the narrow aspects of trade and exchange (as with the mercantilists) to the wider agricultural productivity (as with the physiocrats), and through to the thoughts of Cantillon and Petty. He reaches the conclusion that labour, in its wider sense, is the source that supplies the nation *"with all the necessaries and conveniences of life which it annually consumes"*. Smith also considered wealth in its wider sense of useful material objects, resulting from labour in general. Thus, the wealth of a nation will depend on two conditions: first, the degree of productivity of labour producing that wealth, and second, the amount of useful, i.e. productive, labour employed. These represent the quantitative and qualitative understanding of labour. Smith in this respect was still considering labour in the traditional social setting. It was rather removed from the technical aspects of labour that appeared with the early mechanisations taking place at the time, but which perhaps went unnoticed by him. However, he recognised the value of the specialization in labour in increasing productivity. He describes what must be the most famous factory: *"The pin factory"*. Ten men working in a small pin factory, sharing between them about eighteen simple operations, can make about 50,000 pins a day. If one man had to do all these operations by himself, and without the benefit of special machines, which are themselves the result of the division of labour, he could probably make little more than one pin a day[99].

Division of Labour

As mentioned above, Smith, even in **book I** of the "Wealth of Nations" states that the source of wealth is the division of labour. His initial thoughts were essentially based on the social aspects of this division, with the economic system being an intricate one based on the vast inter-relationships interwoven by the specialised producers, and held together by the price system. In this way wealth is produced in a society, and this will even be reflected in international trade. In his **book V**, Smith develops this idea further, so as to include the value of tools and machinery which can in their own way lead to specialization so that different enterprises can produce specialized, even single, products. This must be a reflection of the influence of the budding mechanization that was taking place around him, especially as the inventions in mechanization were mostly thought out by the workers themselves, with subsequent help from the engineers and technicians. He has indicated in his Glasgow lectures that he had visited a number of modern factories.

The philosophical concept in this is made clear by him when he describes all the different activities that go into a simple item such as a coat. Here, there is the shepherd, the wool sorter, the shipment, the wool- comber, the dyer, the spinner, the weaver, the tailor and so on. In other words, the great benefit of having even a simple and necessary item as a coat is a result of so many specialized and essential people working separately, each serving his own purpose, but ultimately enabling the production of this one item. The same example can be replicated in practically all other aspects of life. But the other philosophical concept, this time with a more definite economic ingredient, is his notion that such division of labour producing this wealth can be seen in the difference not only between the *"very meanest person in a civilized country...compared with the extravagant luxury of the great"*...but that *"perhaps the accommodation of a European Prince does not always so much exceed that of an industrious and frugal peasant, as the accommodation of the latter exceeds that of many an African king, the absolute masters of the lives and liberties of ten thousand naked savages"*[100]. The point driven here is that, whereas the European prince who lives in a productive society but may have very little or no jurisdiction over other people, actually lives in greater opulence than the African chief who lives in a static society and has so much jurisdiction over people. The difference lies in the combined effort of labour, with mutual dependence and resultant economic growth, and one's use of the produce surplus of his labour to exchange for surplus from another labour. The needs of people will thus be satisfied, and the whole cycle will act as an incentive for everyone to excel further in his abilities and productivity. The propensity to exchange, and the quantity of exchange determines the size of the market, and in this way it can be understood that the market is bigger in towns and cities than in rural areas.

However, the number of people alone is not the only factor, because another determinant is communication and the opening up of markets, and the increased potential of buyers and sellers. This is Smith's entry into the international trade arena, and his awareness of the historical importance of trade routes, especially seas and inland waterways. The downside of this division of labour recognised by Smith in his book V, part 3 is that specialization will deprive workers of their *"intellectual, social and martial virtues"*. Repetitive work and simple operations creates a situation where a man *"has no occasion to exert his understanding...becomes stupid and ignorant"*. This was especially apparent in communities where children of 7 or 8 years are made to do menial work, living in *"despicable"* conditions. These children miss out on education, and end up only with *"riot and debauchery... so it may very justly be said that the people who cloth the whole world are in rags themselves"*. These points have indeed been picked up by Hegel and Marx later on, and set the scene for their theory on the "alienation of labour". Smith covered this agonising thought with his plea that *"For a very small expence the publick can facilitate, can encourage, and can even impose upon almost the whole body of the people, the necessity of acquiring those most essential parts of education".*

This may be one aspect of social life where Smith was not comfortable with his *"laissez-faire".*

The economic System

Smith' economic model relies on the value of exchange. While barter is the primitive method, money was by then well established to act as a medium for determining value and exchange. But since money is the recognized medium, the complexity of determining value has to be worked out, and ways of measuring and giving a cause for the value of an item have become important. One essential is need. A person will be prepared to pay a sum of money for something he needs. But while everyone needs water, a prevalent natural element, it is available and cheap. On the other end of the scale, one will have very little real need for a diamond. But because of scarcity and labour required for its production, it is expensive. Smith therefore draws a distinction between the *"real"* price, or the value, of a commodity and its ***"nominal"*** price (in money). In other words, there is the "use value" and the "exchange value". This concept was later on expanded upon by Ricardo.

Apart from this concept of need, Smith describes **three main factors that determine price:** profit or rent, labour, and capital, and the **three groups of people to benefit** are the land owners, workers, and providers of capital. Derived from this concept is Smith's distinction between what he termed as the *"natural"* price of a commodity, which essentially is that price that covers no more or no less, the cost of production at average *"natural"* rates of wages, profit, and rent, and the ***"market"*** price which at any one time can be above or below the natural price and depends on supply and demand. The effect of price will eventually determine whether a greater or lesser need is required, and therefore the movement of capital and labour in the direction of greater or lesser supply.

In defining the factors of profit, rent, wages and capital, Smith gives examples of more complex evaluations than the simplistic ones commonly known. For example, the profit of the owner of a farm or factory is not necessarily related to the amount of work undertaken, but indeed to the capital provided and the risk factor involved. Again, with rent, there can be no actual work done or risk taken for such a return. A landlord in Smith's views can *"like all other men, love to reap where they never sowed."* Again some items derive their price from labour and profit alone, and independent of rent, such as sea fish. Furthermore, a farmer can own land, and invest capital on it, or have other people sharing the enterprise.

A result of all these examples shows up in Smith's comparison of the natural price with the "Centre of Gravity", a "scientific" approach in keeping with contemporary discoveries. Thus "The natural price is, therefore, as it were, the central price, to which all commodities are continually gravitating". In addition to the forces of supply and demand mentioned above, another factor comes into play, that of **competition**, and this can exert a dampening effect on prices, at least initially. But this effect can be offset by workers walking out of the low price labour *(The "disutility" factor)* to a higher one, or capital flowing out of reduced price enterprises to higher rewarding ones. A state of equilibrium may result at some stage. However, in a developing economy, which in his days meant Britain and America, the demand for workers will hike up wages. This compares with stagnant economies or even declining economies (China and Bengal respectively in his days), where wages will drop. Smith tried to postulate on a standard of "real value" to reflect in turn the value of labour with regard to the standard of living enjoyed as a result of labour. Thus the value of labour therefore needs to be measured, and here Smith found difficulty in determining whether the measure is in the "labour commanded by a product" and the labour "embodied" in the product, i.e. the balance between its utility or disutility value. Which means that a product can command more price for less work in some circumstance, and this will be a basis for increased wealth or welfare of the workers in that field. Hence the rising standards in a developing economy, and the tendency for wages in the declining economies to decline and in the long run reach just subsistence level. In this way he shows his interest and concern to explain economic progress and the *"creation of wealth"*.

Smith, in common with contemporary thinkers, looked at the two main economies of his time (Britain and the United States of America), and came to the conclusion that return on agricultural products will tend to rise in the course of economic progress because of limited growth potential, whereas those commanded by manufactured goods will fall. This aspect of Smith's thought could easily be missed as it came under the heading of "digression" in book I, chapter 11, but it is significant.

Smith recognized other factors in relation to wages, such as that disagreeable work commands higher wages, as will work that requires long and arduous training, irregular and insecure work, and work that commands a high degree of trust, such as goldsmiths, doctors, lawyers. Dangerous work or work that carries an improbability of success also come into these categories, so that in general, Smith considers that there is an equilibrium between the unattractiveness of work and the attraction of monetary reward, where one kind of work is more unattractive than another, the attraction of a higher level of pay produces a balance.

Capital and Income: Smith considers capital as the mainspring of economic progress. He looks at capital as either "fixed", that used to buy machines, tools, buildings, and any spend on improvements, and "circulating", which is the money generated in buying and selling. However, Smith added to the "fixed" capital the human element, the capitalist value of "the acquired and useful habits of all members of society", the "human capital". As "circulating" capital is replenished by produced or vendible commodities, it follows that: " What is annually saved is as regularly consumed as what is annually spent, and nearly in the same time too; but by a different set of people." Savings therefore, used in things like purchase of land and human consumption may be "unproductive", whereas savings used as "investments" to increase future capacity will generate more income and create wealth.

Smith talked about gross and net income, echoing to some extent the thoughts of the Physiocrats before him, but with the concept beginning to appear as a foreshadow of the present concept of "gross national product" and "net national product".

This leads him to discuss "banking", the function of which, in his views, is to protect the value of precious metal. In a trading situation, paper money will be presented to exchange for gold. It therefore, *"never can exceed the value of the gold and silver of which it supplies the place".* This is of added importance in view of his argument in favour of free trade.

Smith's Political Economy

D.D. Raphael[101] aptly starts this subject quoting "Wealth of Nations" ,p.428, with Smith's definition: *"political economy, considered as a branch of the science of a statesman or legislator, proposes two distinct objects; first, to provide a plentiful revenue or subsistence for the people, or more properly to enable them to provide such a revenue or subsistence for themselves; and secondly, to supply the state or commonwealth with a revenue sufficient for the publick services. it proposes to enrich both the people and the sovereign"*

Smith advocates the avoidance of profligacy both with individuals and with the state. But the State needs on the one hand a programme of taxation for public finance, and on the other hand is duty bound to take over the role of presiding over responsibilities that either cannot be undertaken by the individual, or fall within the sphere of public, rather than individual interest. His idea of taxation is that it should be certain (clearly known to the taxpayer), convenient (with regards to time and method of collection) and economical to assess and raise (avoiding wasteful administration). It must also be just (*"not to kill the goose that lays the eggs by being a disincentive to work an industry, and by ruining evaders with stiff penalties, and proportional"*). The subjects of every state ought to contribute towards the support of the government, as nearly as possible, in proportion to their respective abilities, that is in proportion to the revenue which they respectively enjoy under the protection of the state"[102]. The State's *"three duties of great importance"* are: **1-** The provision of military security; **2-** The administration of justice; and **3-** *"The duty of erecting and maintaining certain public works and certain public institutions, which it cannot ever be for the interest of any individual, or small number of individuals, to erect and maintain; because the profit could neither repay the expense to any individual or small number of individuals, though it may frequently do much more than repay it to a great society".*

It is worth noting that within the considerations of these public services, there appeared the dilemma of how to remunerate public servants, especially the military, judges etc .as these, at least at that time, would not have been under the influence of market forces as in industry, agriculture and so on.

To conclude this summary on Adam Smith.

it is seen that, a great philosopher, economist and statesman as he is, the greater detail with which he was discussed, in one respect is only a very brief summary, and in another respect a warranted, though modest effort to outline the breadth of his thoughts and the depth of his analyses. He has laid the foundations of economics, using scientific method of analyses and inquisitiveness, but was all the time conscious of the moral and ethical framework within which the subject of economics must be withheld. The discussion of the subsequent great economists will be found to be all the time falling under one shadow or another of Smith's thoughts, and the greater space given to Smith here will no doubt be rewarded with the brevity with which some other economists will be discussed. The next set of great, though perhaps controversial, economic thoughts are those of Robert Malthus, also belonging to the "classical era".

Thomas Robert Malthus 1776-1834[103]

Robert Malthus was born in the town of Rookery in Surrey, England, into a well to do family (probably with some aristocratic pretensions), on 13 February 1776, the second son and sixth child of Daniel Malthus. His father had an intellectual, though scattered attitude, and his enthusiasm covered science, foreign literature, and botany. However, he was very fond of Jean-Jacques Rousseau, Godwin and Condorcet, all essentially optimists, with liberal and socialist leaning. They were perhaps a little utopian in their outlook and in their confidence in the future of Humanity and the resources required for the prosperity of Humankind.

Father and son were reputed to engage in frequent discussions, the son opposing his father's optimism. It is interesting that Robert's father arranged for his son's initial education to be by a clergy friend of his, but at the age of 16, he sent him to the "Dissenting Academy of Warrington" to be under Gilbert Wakefield who had resigned from the Church of England and became a leading and controversial figure in the Unitarian movement. This reflects the father's mind and thoughts, who shared Condorcet's optimism about the future, but who also probably followed the trend of "Dissension" that was current at the time. This was coupled with his belief in the perfectibility of the human race and the possibility of achieving an age in which reason and equality prevailed, with the result that the world can be happy and prosperous.

Robert then went to Cambridge where he studied mathematics, but was thereafter ordained to be a priest in spite of speech difficulty resulting from a cleft palate (defect of the "roof" of the mouth). He took up the post of a curate near his family home in Surrey, and lived with his parents and two unmarried sisters for about 10 years. But during this period he was elected to a non-residential Fellowship at Jesus College, Cambridge. He thus combined an academic and a rural life.

It was, however, not long before Malthus became aware of the misery surrounding him in many of the people to whom he ministered. This made him look at the given wisdoms of the time, and especially of the optimistic views of his father and his illustrious friends, and began to question the belief in the benevolent deity and how this could be squared with the existence of widespread poverty and misery. Any loose connecting of such misery to sin did not carry much weight with him. He continually tried to consider these aspects of the life surrounding him with the combined approach of the moralist's viewpoint and the scientist's objectivity. In all this he expressed his views which clashed with other eminent thinkers of the time, and in particular Ricardo who was his personal friend, but academic challenger.

Indeed, Malthus was so conscious of his controversial views, that his first published work (after an abortive attempt to produce a political pamphlet entitled *"The Crisis, a View of the Present State of Great Britain, by a friend of the Constitution" in 1796)* appeared in 1798, anonymously, to avoid identifying himself with it, under the title: *"An Essay on the Principle of Population (1798) as it affects the future Improvement of Society, with Remarks on the Speculation of Mr Godwin, M. Condorcet, and other Writers".* While appearing to be a humble (domestic) dispute with his father's ideas, this work gave Robert fame and identified him with the ideas and subject matter of this work. It also made it necessary for him to delve deeper into the subject, investigating the historical and demographic facts that would give his thoughts a more thorough impact. This entailed travels to Scandinavia, France and Switzerland, and as a result of added information, he produced his second work in 1803, which was effectively a revised version of his first work, and was subtitled differently thus: *"Essay on the Principles of Population. A View of Its Past and Present effects on Human Happiness, with an Inquiry into our prospects respecting the Future Removal of the Evils which it Occasions".*

In the same year, Malthus became Rector of Walesby in Lincolnshire, a permanent living from which he drew an income for life. This enabled him to marry in 1804, at the age of 38. Whether this late marriage was intentional and based on his beliefs, or a result of circumstances, is not clear. He had three children.

In 1805, another important landmark in his career was attained: His appointment as a Professor of History and Political Economy at the east India Company's College in Hertfordshire, a significant appointment as it was the first of its kind, and could be considered the first post as a "professional" economist.[104]

In discussing Malthus' theories and doctrines, it must be realized that there were two other prominent and contemporary economists with distinctly different approaches who, with the considerable effect of Adam Smith, together all contributed to the "Classical" school.

In addition to Ricardo, mention should be made (again and in this context) of Jean Baptiste Say (1766-1832), who, was a businessman, concerned in a pioneering way with life insurance, and subsequently becoming a professor at the College de France. Ricardo will be further discussed later, but in the meantime it is necessary here to re-iterate Say's main contribution, known as "Say's Law", which is essentially, that *"Out of the production of goods came an effective (that is to say, actually expended) aggregate of demand sufficient to purchase the total supply of goods. No more, no less. There could, in consequence, be no such thing as overproduction in the economic system...and there can never, accordingly be a shortage of demand, the obvious counterpart of overproduction"*[105]. In fact, Malthus doubted this theory, but it survived until the 20th Century, when J.M. Keynes managed to show that there *could* be (as in the "great depression") a general shortage of demand.

Malthus' Doctrines:

Malthus' initial entry into the field of discourse on economic matters was in the spirit of the on-going discussions at the time. These discussions were triggered off by the state of affairs in France after the Napoleonic wars, the upheaval of the French revolution, and the fact that people in England cannot help but reflect on events across the Channel, and compare the two situations. The debate was aroused mainly by Burke's : *"Reflections on the Revolution in France"* in which he denounced the abstract thinkers who brought so much trouble to their country, and the threat that the same can occur in Britain. Malthus and Burke therefore shared some "conservative" views about society and the preservation of the "status quo". Malthus, however, also looked at the two main laws in England that affect society and reflecting political economics: The "Poor Laws" and the "Corn Laws".

Malthus gave the world two expressions which have endured: The word *"Malthusian"* and the expression *"The population explosion"*. It is his thoughts on the population in relationship to nature's resources and human "behaviour" that are central to his doctrines. They reflect his pessimism or worry about the future. He spoke of himself as one who "ardently wished" he could believe in the kind of optimism of "speculative philosophers" like the Marquis de Condorcet or William Godwin who entertained dreams of unlimited improvements for humanity. Such dreams he could not, with his regard for scientific truth, share.

The population explosion

In his first essay, Malthus, having noted a vast increase in the population of England during the last decade of the eighteenth century, especially when compared with the little or no increase in the population during the whole of the previous century, presented in his "principle of population" three propositions: **1-** That the population cannot increase without the means of subsistence. **2-** That the population invariably increases when the means of subsistence are available, and **3-** That the "superior power of population cannot be checked without producing misery or vice".

His reasoning was based on several factors:

1- That the "passion between the sexes" is so strong that Humanity has a propensity to procreate.

2- That the conditions which allow or disallow the people to indulge in procreation is the abundance or scarcity of food and other means for livelihood. People will marry and produce children if they are confident that there are the means to sustain them.

3- That while this propensity to procreation is unlimited, the means of production and the natural resources are by contrast limited. He formulated that the population will tend to increase, if conditions allow, geometrically, i.e. 2-4-8-16-32 etc.. while the means of subsistence will only increase in arithmetical progression, i.e. 1-2-3-4 etc.

4- That in order to avoid the serious effects of this discrepancy there will be a need to look at either limiting the growth capacity of people or limit the means of subsistence to force them to reduce procreation.

5- That the checks which Malthus considered, however, were either to restrain population growth through reducing marriage or increasing the age of marriage, or perhaps reducing the number of births. These are, in his views, the "preventative" measures of "moral restraint" as distinct from "vice", where such things as abortion, infanticide, prostitution and other "unnatural" attempts are in evidence. These latter would probably work by accommodating the constant passion between the sexes while avoiding the consequences. At the other end of this proposition are the "positive" checks inherent in such occurrences or tragedies as war, pestilence and famine, plague or disease, and these will inevitably be accompanied by "misery" and "vice".

Described in another way, Malthus' propositions can be stated as follows: **1-** Man's biological capacity to produce exceeds his physical capacity to increase the food supply. **2-** Either the preventative or positive checks are always in operation to hold back the super fecundity of reproduction; and **3-** The ultimate check to reproduction capacity lie in the limitation of food supply.

These two checks (the preventative and the limitation of food supply), had, in Malthus' views, to fall mainly on the great mass of people at the bottom of society's pyramid, because even in those days, the family size was larger in the lower, poorer class than the richer. He worried that these lower classes will survive at the expense of the richer, presumably more productive, classes. He implied a doubling of the world population every twenty five years, and took note of figures of population growth in the United States that gave credence to this. But while not considering that the increase in the States was partly due to immigration, he appreciated that the same may not apply to Europe. He did, however, worry about countries in Africa, the Far East and other parts of the world. He was also concerned about neighbouring Ireland, where he noted that the success of the potato as a crop that gives good yields and uses small areas of land, has led to the encouragement of marriages at early ages, and to large families. He worried "that the population (there) is pushed much beyond the industry and present resources of the country".

Malthus used "inductive verification" for his theories, as his statistical investigations were inconclusive, partly because of lack of good statistics at the time. But he accepted in the Preface to the second edition of the *Essay* that "any errors in the facts and calculations which have been produced in the course of the work...will not materially affect the general scope of the reasoning".[106]

Malthus had thrown doubt about Say's law, arguing that workers will tend to reduce themselves to poverty as a result of their fecundity, thus reducing their ability to buy and consume. Overproduction will result, and even the affluent people such as landlords, industrialists, and merchants, will be too busy to pay enough attention to increasing their consumption. Some consumption, however, will be accounted for by non-productive members of society, such as doctors, judges, and the military. Malthus made a distinction between productive and non-productive occupations. It remained for Ricardo to counteract Malthus' criticism of Say, arguing that the flow of income from the production of goods did indeed create its own sufficient demand[107].

Malthus was harsh enough to postulate that handouts to the poor, whether charitable or through state intervention as in the "poor Laws" (guaranteeing a minimum level of support to all whose income fell short of that necessary to support them and their families during periods of food scarcity and high prices) will only serve to encourage the poor to procreate and become lazy, thereby exacerbating the problem. This made people think of Malthus as one who converted Smith's "Wealth of Nations" to "Poverty of Nations", and his pessimistic and gloomy thoughts may, with the added effects of Ricardo's doctrines, have contributed to the branding of economists by Thomas Carlyle in 1889, as the "Respectable Professors of the Dismal Sciences".[108]

Malthus addressed some of his thoughts to the Christian moralist issues. While not accepting contraception, he advocated marriages at older ages. He called for longer periods of celibacy. This, he said, would ease relationships between the sexes, and establish "kindred dispositions" before marriage, and on the whole balance between the good and evil flowing from any action, rather than just the motive of the action itself. He considered moral restraint as the solution "dictated by the light of nature, and expressly enjoined in revealed religion"[109] .

Malthus' views were modified in his second essay on the Population, particularly taking into account criticisms of his contemporaries. As a political economist, he expressed views on many aspects of relevance to his time. He was critical of the government keeping large armies. His views were sympathetic to the Physiocrats, on the premise that investment in agriculture resulted in benefit for all, while investment in industry will benefit the few. He considered that investment in agriculture will enhance production, but accepted the principle of "diminishing return" In his later versions and writings he seemed to withdraw this criticism of industry and commerce. He did not believe it was possible or desirable for a "large landed nation" such as Britain to import foodstuffs, as this will increase the price of food and paying for it through income from trade or industry will in the long run become difficult when the country faces competition from newly industrialized countries.

He was in favour of retaining the "Corn Laws" (Importation Act 1815, putting tariffs on imported corn so as to protect the locally produced crop) as he assumed that an increased production is to be expected up to a limit, after which, production will level off or drop. There was in his views therefore the need to protect the price of home produced corn (wheat) when there is glut, by restricting importation. But with scarcity, the hardship has to be accepted, arguing that the higher price and scarcity will on the one hand provide the workers with more money to buy "luxury" items, but on the other hand will act as restraint to population growth.

A subject current at the time was that of defining rent, a subject left in an ambivalent state by Smith, but on which Malthus had distinctive and original position. He defined rent as the return to landowners after the cost of production had been met. This was particularly important to maintain the level of prosperity for the landowners because of what he described as the "bounty of Nature", or the "Bountiful gift of Providence", whereby land will yield more to labour than was necessary to support those working on it. However, on the principle of diminishing return and the fact that available land was finite, more and more will have to be spent to extract produce from the land available. With time, less fertile land will have to be cultivated and again the cost will rise.

In Malthus' views, therefore, the landowner and capitalist must be safeguarded so as to maintain the level of investment required to keep up the production levels. This, again, was an aspect of his leaning towards the aristocracy and the status quo. Rising rent was a kind of barometer of progress and lower rents a prelude to regression. In this way it can be said that Malthus treated rent in the same way as Smith and others had treated interest earlier, and Ricardo was to treat profits later.

In conclusion: It is seen that there are various aspects to Robert Malthus, who can be seen as the population theorist and the political economist, as well as the moralist and the social scientist. His predictions could be understood given the demographic state of society at the time and the prevailing knowledge, the political upheavals sweeping Europe as a result of the Napoleonic wars, and his affinity to the ruling class and conservatism in spite of not being an aristocrat himself.

His thoughts started as rather harsh, but were later softened, and one can see areas of religious thought as well as some of his mathematics background in the formulation of his doctrines. It was, however, not long before his predictions were totally lost as a result of the application of science and technology which proved that production not only can keep up with the increase in population, but that it is production that can increase geometrically and not population. That increase was evident even at his time, and the population "explosion" did not materialize even before modern day contraception.

David Ricardo 1772-1823

Ricardo, a contemporary, as noted above, of Malthus, and is the younger friend who actually eclipsed him.[110] He shared the general backdrop of the condition prevailing in Britain at the time, and has, in his own right, left the world of economic thought with lasting legacies, and such terms as "The Ricardo's System" or "the Ricardian

Effect" are part of the common parlance used by various authors. His prose style was formal, and his method analytical in a scientific, although not academic, manner. While described as a systematizer, he has a tendency to be theoretical and inductive, using observations and abstract reasoning to reach conclusions. His thoughts would formalize the main classical analyses, putting his fundamental proposition in the form of a model.

He was very conscious of the social and general economic upheavals that followed on the Napoleonic wars, and the surge of industrialization which Smith appears to have missed out on. The situation with Britain after Napoleon was different from that of France and other countries in Europe, mainly because there was less destruction within Britain, but also because of the advance of technology and mechanization, the exploitation of the formidable and versatile power of steam and the abundant supply of coal and iron ore. On the other side of the coin, there was a tendency for the continent to be reticent in providing Britain with agriculture products, especially corn (wheat). This did cause some hardship because of scarcity and high price. It may have benefited a small proportion of the population, to wit, the burgeoning capitalist/landowners, particularly because the small landowner was unable to compete. The socio-economic result of this situation was uneven distribution of wealth, and hardship for the lower echelons of society.

The life of David Ricardo[111],[112]

Born in London, of a Jewish father who had moved to England from Holland, his ancestors had moved from Spain to Holland to escape the persecutions of other religions by the Catholic Church during the "Inquisition". David worked with his father at the London stock Exchange from the age of fourteen, having only finished school.

Seven years later, David married a Christian (Quaker), and then himself converted to the Christian Anglican Religion. This strained the family relationship, and David struck out on his own, and managed by the age of forty to become a millionaire, amassing a big fortune from banking and trading in securities. He actually managed to be counted among the richest 100 in England. He then gradually reduced his finance activities, and acquired large land holdings and in 1819 negotiated a seat in the British Parliament, from one of the sitting peers. He earned praise from all around him, not least from Malthus who once observed: "He (Ricardo) is now become, by his talent and industry, a considerable landholder; and a more honourable and excellent man, a man who for the qualities of his head and heart more entirely deserves what he has earned, or employs it better, I could not point out in the whole circle of landholders...."

Ricardo's System

Ricardo read and wrote extensively, not only on economic matters, and in a work like this one can only present, as accurately as possible, a simplified resumé of his ideas. Essentially, Ricardo took Smith's postulates, modified and explained many of them, but in his thinking manner, he removed the anecdotes and assumptions. The results were a more coherent and hard core postulates.

The following facts are useful in understanding his method and thoughts: **1-** Economic growth must sooner or later peter out owing to scarcity of natural resources[113]. **2-** The bare outline of the system can be grasped by supposing that the whole economy consists of a giant farm engaged in producing wheat by applying homogeneous doses of "capital-and-labour" to a fixed supply of land subject to diminishing returns. **3-** The demand for wheat is perfectly inelastic, determined simply by the needs of whatever population size dealt with. **4-** In determining the value or price of a product, the first factor must be its usefulness, i.e. its utility. Thus, if a commodity has no use, it will be assumed to have no value, and on the other hand, if it is vital, but freely available, such as the air we breathe, it cannot be priced because an individual can only consume of it his need and no more. In this respect, Ricardo also assumed that land originally fell into this category. Thus, it (land) was freely available until the early landlords laid hands on it, initially grabbing the most fertile plots, and thereafter the less and less fertile.

In developing his theories, Ricardo was not just interested in *the wealth of nations* as Smith was, but indeed in the *distribution of the wealth* in a nation and the laws that govern this distribution, and the relative income or wealth of the different classes in society. As a basic fact, where there is only subsistence produce, there will be (especially according to Malthus) no population growth. This subsistence only level is the situation where labour is just enough to extract from the fixed (natural) asset of land the necessary produce. Ricardo put it in another way, by describing wages as "that price which is necessary to enable the labourers, one with another, to subsist and to perpetuate their race, without either increase or diminution" This is his "Iron Law of Wages". But as labour tends to produce more than subsistence amount, especially from good land, it follows that the excess value of this produce will accrue to the landowner. In this way, rent is calculated as the total product minus the marginal product of capital-and-labour (which Ricardo accounted as one unit), and the return to the landlord (considered as rent) will be "that portion of the produce of the earth, which is paid to the landlord for the use of the original and indestructible powers of soil".

It will be seen that the owner of the good (fertile) land, will profit more than the owner of a less fertile land. The benefit (or profit) to the owner of the more fertile land will eventually increase as the pressure of the growth of population increases demand, and with time even less and less fertile land used up will not be sufficient. In all this the wealthy landowner is not only benefiting from the workers in his land, but even from the toils of the workers in other land, and herein lies exploitation. In Ricardo's views: "The rise of rent is always the *effect* of the increasing wealth of the country, and the difficulty of providing food for its augmented population." This fact has been ceased upon by later figures especially Karl Marx. The "Iron Law of Wages, assumed that those who worked were meant to remain at subsistence level, although this level can be modified so as to provide not only the worker's necessities, but also "conveniences that become essentials to him from habit". In modern language this equates with "standard of living". In this way Ricardo developed the thought further to describe the fact that with increased investment, demand will also increase, and therefore wages, and therefore standard of living. But as this will also lead to increase in the population, the number of labourers will increase and the "equilibrium" will be altered so that wages are at a lower "natural price", or even below it. The Iron law meant that allowing for the fact that "like all other contracts, wages should be left to the fair and free competition of the market, and should never be controlled by the interference of the legislature", misery is inevitable as it is governed by this economic law that cannot be contravened[114].

Ricardo's ideas show a tendency to utilitarianism, more so in his political views than his economic doctrines. This may be the effect of his close friendship to Jeremy Bentham, the salient utilitarian of that time, and whom he knew through James Mill. In his *"Essay on The Influence of a Low Price of Corn (1815)"*, Ricardo postulated on the theory which later became known as the "Corn Model". In this theory, he considers the production of wheat in the agricultural sector as the basis for calculating the value of other sectors' (mainly manufacturing industry) product. Thus, in considering the wage-goods industry of agriculture producing corn, and the profits-rent cloth production of the manufacturing industry as being both in equilibrium, and as the cost of cloth produced is a factor of the cost of wheat consumed in its production, the price of cloth will therefore rise or fall according to the rise and fall of the price of wheat. Thus, while admitting that the economy consists of two sectors, the profit is determined exactly as it would be in one sector. This theory is, however, criticised on the basis that the cost of production often includes a waiting time during which the cost of capital will have to be taken into account. This, in other words, means interest on capital, and this has been expanded later on in the "Austrian Theory" of capital.

The Ricardo Effect

In keeping with his pre-occupation with distribution, Ricardo assumed that the purchasing power of money over all goods and services, as measured by the average level of prices in the economy, is constant. It follows that distribution is a matter of dividing a given real national income among landlords, capitalists, and labourers. Rent, being an intramarginal surplus, does not enter into the determination of prices.

Ricardo, however, recognised that there are variations. For example, the value of a commodity will differ according to its utility value. This may determine the price, but need not explain the value. This utility value is also determined by the exchange value of the commodity. Rare items, therefore, such as works of art, are therefore not valued simply according to its labour content. But as such, commodities are small in comparison to the total economy, which relies on expandable products, and so they may be disregarded. This leaves the value considerations to be looked at only in relation to the "big" issues. In this respect, Ricardo deviates from Smith's theory that:

Smith: value of commodity = amount of labour = value of labour

Ricardo: value of a commodity = amount of labour, but the amount of labour is greater than the value of labour.

It follows that higher wages need not lead to higher price if the amount of labour is the same, because of the effect of competition which will not allow the possessors of capital to increase the price. In this way Ricardo reaches the conclusion that the value of commodities is only determined by the inherent labour needed in its production, and, all other factors being equal, these values are absorbed and distributed over the nation as a whole according to the economic laws prevailing in any society.

But, he noted, labour varies in intensity and skill, and this must be reflected in assessing the value of labour in the production of a commodity. This neatly leads to the next conclusion, and that is that the "exchange" value of a commodity is also determined by these factors, and the value that the market puts on such labour, and ultimately to the forces of supply and demand. Ricardo assumed that differentials between wages are constant, which is obviously not always the case. He also failed to allow for the value of tools and machines in the production of the commodity. Capital-and-labour, as mentioned above, are thus one, and together are the overriding factor determining value. Ricardo give the following example:

	Capital cost (fixed	Labour	Total Cost	Total Profit	Average Interest	Price	Exchange value
Article "A"	75	25	100	20	20%	120	"A":"B"
Article "B"	25	75	100	20	20%	120	100:100
	100	100	200	40	20%	240	

With Wage rise of 20%

	Capital cost (fixed	Labour	Total Cost	Total Profit	Average Interest	Price	Exchange value
Article "A"	75	30	105	9.5	9.1%	114.5	"A":"B"
Article "B"	25	90	115	10.5	9.1%	125	109.6:100
	100	120	220	20	9.1%	240	

Therefore machine produced articles will cost less than labour intensive articles. But Ricardo compared any commodity production with that of wheat, and over an annual cycle. Differences, he postulated will average out. This was his idea of the "Invariable measure of "value. As an example, this assumed that the production of a bushel of wheat (valued at $1) requires the same amount of capital and labour as that required to produce an amount of gold designated as worth $1. Changes in the ratio of wages to profit will average out over the annual

125

cycle when the total is worked out over the annual cycle and with the economy as a whole.

Foreign Trade:

Ricardo believed in free trade, that competition is paramount, and that foreign trade increases a country's "riches". Real income will always be higher with free trade than without. As the "value" of the national product is, according to him, the same for a closed economy as for an open one, foreign trade will therefore not affect wage rates or the rates of profit.

He recognised three types of goods: **1-** Home produced goods for home consumption, such as cloth, shoes, corn and hats. **2-** Home produced goods for export; and **3-** Imported luxuries such as wine. He devised the "Law of Comparative Cost" distinguishing between national and international trade. He gives the example of two countries (Britain and Portugal) producing two similar product (cloth and wine) by labour alone, making the relative price simply the reciprocals of unit labour requirements. If Portugal can produce the two products more cheaply but the difference is "equal" (cloth: England 100, Portugal 90, and wine: England 88, Portugal 80, ratio: Pw/Pc 0.88 and 0.88) there is no incentive for trade. In the same example using the figures: 100/60,90/60: Pw/Pc=0.6 and 0.88, the difference is "absolute", and both countries have an incentive to trade cloth from England and wine from Portugal. A third example is where the figures are:100/120 and 90/80, Pw/Pc=1.2 &0.88. In this there is a "Comparative" advantage in wine since the cost difference for wine is relatively greater than that for cloth: 120/80>100/90. This has been put in simple algebraic form thus:

Equal Cost-differences: Wp/We=Cp /Ce where W=wine, C=cloth, e=England and p=Portugal

Absolute cost-differences: Wp/We>1>Cp/Ce   Comparative cost-differences: Wp/We<Cp/Ce<1

It is clearly to Portugal's advantage to send wine to England, where a unit of it commands 1.2 units of cloth, as long as 1 unit of wine can be traded with England for more than 0.88 units of cloth. It is to England's advantage to specialize in cloth if less than 1.2 units of cloth must be given for 1 unit of wine. Hence the comparative cost doctrine states the upper and lower limits within which exchange can take place between countries to their mutual benefit. If 1 unit of British cloth were exchanged for 1.2 units of Portuguese wine, all gains from trade would go to Portugal. If instead the ratio were 1:8/9=1:0.88, all gains would go to England. Ricardo assumes a terms of trade of 1:1. England produces cloth with 100 man-hours and receives 1 unit of wine, which would have cost her 120 man-hours to produce at home, and Portugal obtains cloth for 80 man-hours which would have cost her 90 man-hours to produce at home. The point Ricardo makes is that the conditions that make international trade possible are quite different from the conditions under which domestic trade will arise. If England and Portugal are two regions in the same country, all capital and labour would migrate to Portugal and both goods would be produced there. Within a nation, trade between two places requires an absolute difference in costs but a comparative difference is a sufficient condition for the existence of international trade[115].

Ricardo appreciated the implications of this theory to the question of the balance of payments between countries, which David Hume termed "the natural distribution of specie", and the international price and wage levels. Importing countries will have to ship gold to purchase goods if other commodities are not available to exchange, but this will lead to higher hourly wage rates in terms of gold in the importing countries because people will buy these commodities more cheaply from domestic suppliers until these hourly gold wages (and prices) rise sufficiently to redress the trade advantage. With the added effect of competition, an equilibrium will result, and Ricardo insists that there will be no need for governments to intervene as the mercantilists believed. There are echoes here of Hume's views, and also those of Nassau Senior who coined the memorable phrase: Relative price levels between countries are determined by differences in the *cost of obtaining gold*: the greater the efficiency of labour in the export industries of a country possessing no gold mines and the less the expense of conveying gold, the lower will be the cost of obtaining precious metals and the higher will be the level of average wages and prices relative to countries exporting gold bullion. Therefore, an overall disadvantage in productivity in a particular country relative to the rest of the world need not prevent her from participating in international trade; There is always a rate of exchange that would permit her to export those goods in which she had the least comparative disadvantage, while importing those in which she had the greatest disadvantage.

Monetary Views:

Ricardo was essentially a "metalist", believing that the quantity of money in the long run is governed by the cost of production of gold. As Britain at that time and following the Napoleonic wars was off the gold standard, the paper currently was accepted as reflecting the cost of both "specie" and paper, although in the long run it was recognised that the real cost will be that of the "specie" money only, i.e. the bullion and other underlying value supporting the circulating money.

Ricardo expressed views on the machinery question and on taxation, but these will be discussed in more detail in the final version of this work.

In summarizing the effect of Ricardo on economic thought, it is important to note that while his theories were criticized by many contemporary and subsequent economists, and more importantly that his theories were taken so seriously by Karl Marx later on, he managed to offer the world a method of analysis and postulating based on hard facts rather than sweeping generalizations. In this way, his legacy has endured.

Other Classicists

This section will not be complete without mention of other economists who have contributed well to the classical doctrines during the nineteenth century, including Say, John Stuart Mills, Jevons, the German school, the Austrian Theory of capital and interest, and Marshall. This will be dealt with later as it is important at this juncture to discuss the ideas of Karl Marx, and J M Keynes, and then to describe some Baha'i Teachings in context.

Karl Marx (1818-83) & Marxism

Born in Trier at the head of the Moselle Valley in Germany, Marx's father was Trier's leading lawyer, an officer of the high court and a member of an old Jewish family, who converted to Protestantism at about the time of the birth of Karl. This placed Karl within the elite society and enabled him to marry Jenny von Westphalen, the daughter of Baron Ludwig von Westaphlen. This was rather an ironic and an unlikely setting for the revolutionary dissenting thoughts that were subsequently to emanate from Marx.

Karl grew up at a time when the concept of "socialism" started appearing in reaction to the capitalism and industrialism that had become the dominant socio-economic state in Europe at the time. He was, however, influenced in a significant way by the thoughts of Georg Wilhelm Friedrich HEGEL (1770-1831), to which he was exposed when he moved from Bonn to Berlin to study law[116]. The strong and lively "Hegelian" debates captured Karl's imagination, and made him change from law to philosophy, as well as identify himself with the "Young Hegelians" who sought to transform Hegelian orthodoxy into a radical social doctrine. The essential Hegelian thoughts in this respect were the belief that economic, social, and political life is in a process of constant transformation, and as one structure assumes authority or eminence, it is soon challenged by another, and so on. Thus, in the same way that the industrialists challenged and replaced in eminence the landed bourgeoisie, so should the workmen whom the industrialists have amassed for their own capitalist benefit in turn challenge and replace their masters.

Marx failed to secure a university post as a philosopher because the Hegelian left was proscribed by government. The death of his father made it necessary for him to earn his living. This he did by taking up journalism, writing in a newly founded anti-government journal in Cologne, the *Rheinische Zeitung*, and subsequently becoming its editor. The journal, however, was banned by the government in 1843, as Marx's articles ranged in sedition from inciting people to collect dead wood from forests regarded by some as private property, assailing royalty, and encouraging a secular approach to the problems of divorce, to mention but a few of his dissident thoughts. Marx set off for Paris where he assisted in editing another journal, but also came in contact with European leftists including Friedrich ENGELS. In 1845 the French government expelled him in response to protests from the

Prussian authorities, and in 1849 he went into exile to London, but had managed during this period to draft with Engels the *"Communist Manifesto"*. Thereafter, he spent most of his time in the British Museum library devouring the literature, and earning a living through journalism, sustained predominantly by the American paper *The New York Tribune*, parent of the present *New York Herald Tribune*. It is interesting to note that this is a republican paper. He was, however, living under very poor conditions, hardly able to afford food and health care to his family, in spite of some help from Engels, who had a family textile business in Manchester. Only later in his life did he apparently find means, from Engels and elsewhere to attain a decent standard of living. But he managed to put together his major contribution to economic thought and theory: the three volumes of *"DAS KAPITAL"*. It is appropriate to state that by his efforts, Karl not only shaped economic thought and doctrine, but has actually shaped a large chunk of society, as well as world history, a fact that has to be accepted whether one agrees or disagrees with his thoughts. It is also now clear, in the light of the recent developments in the communist world, that the effects on history may not have been all that beneficial, but no one can doubt his effect on the course of history.

Marxian Economics

Marx addressed himself to the classical tradition of economic thought. On the one hand, he derived some thought from Ricardo's ideas that the inequality of distribution of power (of the capitalist industrialist) leads to inequality in distribution of income, and on the other hand he wrote to demolish Malthus' theory that the members of the working class had only themselves to blame for their poverty and misery. Thus in his book "Capital" vol. 1, pp 692-3 there is the following passage: " *The labouring population...produces, along with the accumulation of capital produced by it, the means by which itself is made relatively superfluous, is turned into a relative surplus population, and it does this in an always increasing extent. This is a law of population peculiar to the capitalist mode of production; and in fact every historic mode of production has its own special laws of population, historically valid within its limits alone. An abstract law of population exists for plants and animals only, and only in so far as man has not interfered with them."*[117] Marx was aware of the power of government to further the interests of corporate or business power. He refined the classicists' theories that labour wages will reduce as more workers are available, and those paid at marginal wage levels actually add value to capital and profit instead of accruing the added value to themselves. This, Marx notes is the law of diminishing return, being part of the law of production as given by nature, as distinct from the laws of distribution which are given by man, by man made arrangements which need not be adhered or surrendered to.

Marx did not at all question the productive achievements of the capitalist system, and in page 9 of The Communist Manifesto, he writes: *"During its rule of scarce one hundred years, (it) has created more massive and more colossal productive forces than have all preceding generations together... It has created enormous cities, has greatly increased the urban population as compared with the rural, and has thus rescued a considerable part of the population from the idiocy of rural life.... The cheap prices of its commodities are the heavy artillery with which it batters down all Chinese walls".*[118] Workers were reminded that the *first* object of their revolutionary attention should not be to the great capitalists who were the source of this productive power, but rather *"the remnants of absolute monarchy, the landowners, the non-industrial bourgeois, the petty bourgeoisie"* who are the enemies of capitalist power and achievement. He thus directed his attack at the weak underbelly of society, those struggling to maintain their diminishing status with the advance of industrialism and productive enterprises. This explains to some extent the flourish of Communism in such feudal societies as those that existed in Russia, China, and more recently Cuba and some third world countries.

However, Marx saw in the capitalist society a situation where collective and co-operative endeavours are necessary because of the complexity of the means of production and the reliance of workers not on their simple tools, but rather on complex machinery. Tensions therefore will inevitably arise, leading to collapse of capitalism. In its place, a socialist arrangement with harmony, rather than strife will emerge. Class groupings in his view should be reduced from three (capitalists, landlords, and labourers) to two: capitalists and owners being one genus, and labourers as the other, but both should have legally recognised rights to property. Furthermore, Marx, regarded labour (along Ricardian lines) as the productive element and the value adding elements for a product as well as a commodity. The wage therefore should reflect the time and effort of labour, the training of labour, and the "subsistence" needs of labour, not just for the produced item, but also for the reproduction and the possibility of replacement in the next generation, taking into account the input of unskilled labour. His illustration for this was the fact that with the introduction of power looms, the production of the machine, and thus the value added, was twice that of a manual labourer. Nevertheless, the manual labourer with only half the production and therefore the value added is still subsistence. He recognised the value of technology, and was not sentimental in appraising the fact that advances are there to stay and to add value. He accepted that exchange values for commodities were to be expressed in terms, *"because all commodities, as values, are realized human labours, and therefore commensurable, that their values can be measured by one and the same special commodity, and the latter converted into the common measure of their value, i.e. into money.*"[119]

Labourers are capable, according to Marx, of producing the subsistence requirements by putting an amount of work, and this may be sufficient for them. But capitalists would demand extra work to enhance profit, through surplus production. Exploitation can result, although increased wages can, in his view, be regarded as "variable capital", harping back to the Classicists' theory of capital being of two types, fixed and circulating. Three important ratios were devised around this analysis: *s/v, being "rate of surplus value" or "rate of exploitation", c/v being the two components of capital (the "organic composition of capital")* and *s/v+c being the "rate of profit".*

Machinery, he contended, enabled the capitalists to exercise greater control over the workers, enabled them to employ women and children who would command less wages, and allowed a reduction in cost of commodities and extraction of raw material. The industrial segment of the economy might be the dynamic engine of change. But the mere growth of capitalism will tend to homogenize conditions of production throughout the economy. He states: *"In the sphere of agriculture, modern industry has a more revolutionary effect than elsewhere, for this reason, that it annihilates the peasant, that bulwark of the old society, and replaces him by the wage labourer. Thus the desire for social change, and the class antagonisms are brought to the same level in the country as in the towns. The irrational, old fashioned methods of agriculture are replaced by scientific ones."*[120]. Thus there is no distinction between the capitalist and the landlord, both being able to exploit the workers and extract surplus value, and this in turn permitted *"Accumulation"* which he abhorred as it represented according to him the relentless drive to exploit, introduce labour-saving innovations, more accumulation and ultimately *"accumulation for accumulation's sake, production for production's sake".* It is the capitalist system rather than the individual capitalist that he really blamed. Increased mechanisation will result in loss of job opportunities for the unskilled workers, will create a competitive state where only the fittest (of both labourers and capitalists) will survive, leading to greater centralisation and concentration of the ownership of the means of production, and will march hand in hand with increasing misery and inequality.

Marx's Theory of Crisis

Marx forecast for capitalism was an inevitable and violent collapse. The reason he gave for this relies on the premise that in a stable state, equilibrium between production and consumption is maintained by both processes occurring without resorting to either net surplus (saving) or net investment. But this is not to happen. There will be the desire to achieve net gain, and to produce luxury commodities to satisfy the needs of those who can afford them and would want them. This creates an intricate situation where the equilibrium can be difficult to sustain, as factors such as variability in acquisition, in durability, and in replacement requirements will operate. Accumulation of unwanted stocks, price cutting and so on will result in what Marx terms as *"realization"* crisis. In this analysis of chronic instability of capitalism one can read the beginning of the theory of business cycle which is part of present day economic analysis. His scenario showed aspects of the unfolding of the system: *"Along with the constantly diminishing number of magnates of capital, who usurp and monopolize all advantages of this process of transformation, grows the mass of misery, oppression, slavery, degradation, exploitation; but with this too grows the revolt of the working class, a class always increasing in numbers, and disciplined, united, organized by the very mechanism of the process of capitalist production itself. The monopoly of capital becomes a fetter upon the mode of production, which has sprung up and flourished along with, and under it. Centralization of the means of production and socialization of labour at last reach a point where they become incompatible with their capitalist integument. This integument is burst asunder. The knell of capitalist private property sounds. The expropriators are expropriated.[121]"*

"The social tensions bred by capitalism were too intense for the transition to be accomplished peacefully. Revolution was an essential part of the Marxian theory of crisis. The violent overthrow of the capitalist order, however, cannot be explained on technical economic grounds. Marx's view of the dynamics of history was an essential prop to this conclusion.[122]"

The March Of Marxism

It is not the purpose of this treatise to delve into the historical sequence of events that led to the evolution of the Marxist theories within political movements and ideologies. It is relevant to state that Lenin's main contribution to this evolution was the fact that, but for colonialism and the exploitation of the colonized countries, the process of disintegration of capitalism would have occurred very early on. Colonialism, in his views merely postponed that collapse. In addition, Stalin's contribution was to interpret the Marxist/Leninist thoughts into the development of heavy industry, and a severely centralized government, system, and planning of the means of production, distribution and outlets for consumption. There appeared to have been no rational theoretical basis for this development in the thoughts and doctrines of Karl Marx.

The Communist take over in Russia as a result of the October 1917 revolution had its seeds in the terrible misery experienced by the peasant and poor working class, before, but more significantly so, during the 1914-1917 War. It is this war which, among other things, necessitated the mass movement of the peasantry into the cities and towns, giving them insight into a life they were ignorant of. No less a reason, was the severe discrepancies between the elite classes and the destitute masses who had their eyes opened to the repulsive inequalities and oppression. As mentioned above, other countries, notably China, had similar conditions with similar outcomes after the World War II.

While Communism expanded after the war, the ideology took root in many emerging countries, some maintaining their democratic political system but adopting socialist/communist economic doctrine, such as India and Pakistan, but the majority resorted to outright dictatorships incorporating communist economic regimes, albeit termed by the rulers as "socialism".

Again it will be noted that the twentieth century witnessed the seeds of two world wars, and innumerable episodes of strife throughout the world, all resulting from socio-economic disequilibrium with the common feature of inequality of opportunity, whether on the scale of conditions between nations, or the lesser scale of conditions between factions within a nation. For a while, notably the early 1950's, communism had reached significant heights, and the world was in danger of almost a complete take over by that system. Such sophisticated societies as France and Italy, and to a lesser degree, Britain, were witnessing real pressures from its communist parties and revolutionary groups. In Britain a strong and active Communist Party became the focus of concern of the post war British governments. Capitalism had its upheavals, with financial crashes, depressions, and social evidence of discontent that were at times severe enough to express themselves as national strikes, even though they did not reach levels of revolution. The social and economic order was severely disrupted by these events, and the disruption was heightened in its starkest manner during the two world wars. It is only in recent years, that a call and a sincere desire for a "New World Order" appeared on the thoughts and lips of politicians, statesmen and leaders of thought.

The counter-balance to Communism, and the realization that government has a leading role in providing the best conditions for the realization of the aspirations of the masses of population, as well as creating the right economic climate for flourish of wealth creation and prosperity, became the subject of many economists as well as politicians, but salient among these was John Maynard KEYNES.

PART VI

EARLY TWENTIETH CENTURY ECONOMISTS

John Maynard Keynes (1883-1946)

J.M. Keynes is arguably the most eminent of the twentieth century economists, whose influence and economic systems pervaded most of the developed countries in one shade or another. He is the product and mover of the "Neo-Classical" school of economic thought, influenced by his teacher, Professor Alfred Marshall of Cambridge University, as well as the other salient Neo-Classical economists and systems of the time, mainly J.S.Mill, Menger, Jevons, Wicksteed, Walras, Wicksell and J.B. Clark. The Swiss and the Austrian schools of thought were being developed and adopted, with the concepts of "Utility" and "Marginalism" the accepted theories. Economics started to be taken seriously in the USA, and although no real original thoughts were developed there, discussions were ardent and widespread. The main concern in the States was the preservation of private capital and the individual holdings as these constituted the prevalent economic base at the turn of the century and a little into it. Allowing a little digression, it is useful to make mention of the work of Böhm-Bawerk (1851-1914)[123] in the late nineteenth century, on capital and interest. The "Theory of Interest" formed the basis of the Austrian School, and essentially demonstrated the value of allowing capital to perform more efficiently and more productively if the time between capital expenditure and accruing of profit was bridged financially on the basis of interest bearing transactions. As production could be on a round about way in some instances, such financial bridging will be for longer or shorter periods as the case requires, assuming the round about ways can increase the value of the ultimate product/s, making payment of interest a positive enhancement factor.

Socialism and welfare were discussed, and reform of the capitalist system, essentially for its preservation, became the important consideration. Three eminent scholars came to Britain from Nowosielitza near Czernovitz in Austria (later part of Romania) strongly urging the need for an alternative to capitalism's self destruction. They were Nicholas Kaldor, later Lord Kaldor (1908-1986), Thomas Balogh, later Lord Balogh(1905-1985), and Eric Roll (1907-2005), later Lord Roll of Ipsden. The first assisted in the preparation of the Beveridge report, for social and health care, the second advised British Labour governments and later became an advocate of "Monetarism". Incomes and Prices policies were advocated, means of counteracting unemployment, idle production capacity and inflation addressed, and the third, Lord Roll committed the largest part of his life to government service, international economic policy and was a leading negotiator for the "Marshall Plan", the Common Market" and in general steered the British Government towards milder economic policymaking. They were in retreat from right wing fascist regimes. But others, notably, von Mises, von Hayek, Machlup, Haberler, and Schumpeter, found their way to the USA from "Socialist" working class orientated nations such as Austria and Germany to promulgate their classical purist orthodox economics based on the premise that any deviation from orthodoxy will inevitably lead to socialism.

The social and economic environment in which Keynes found himself was thus vibrant and changing rapidly. He was born into a world which assumed peace, prosperity and progress to be the natural order of things, and lived long enough to see all these expectations toppled. When he grew up, Britain was the centre of a mighty Empire; in the last months of his life he was handing round the begging bowl in Washington. His life spanned not just the collapse of the British power, but the growing enfeeblement of the British economy. It spanned the passage from certainty to uncertainty, from the perfumed gardens of his youth to the jungle of his mature years, where monsters prowled. In addition, his was the time when society was emerging from the strictures of the Victorian mores and attitudes, veering away from Christianity in an age of "neo-Enlightenment", conducting one's life in the pure light of reason. Experiments were the order of the day, in science, art and philosophy, rather than in economics and politics. The first World War changed many things, and after the war a state of chaos appeared to develop, and Keynes began to mature in his thoughts. He is quoted as saying to Virginia Woolf in 1934: "That our generation -yours & mine...owed a great deal to our fathers' religion. And the young...who are brought up without it, will never get so much out of life. They're trivial, like dogs in their lusts. We had the best of both worlds..."

Keynes's fundamental insight was that *we do not know--cannot calculate--what the future will bring. In such a world, money provides psychological security against uncertainty.* This will appear later in discussing his work on *Probability,* which indicates the philosophical drive of his economics. But Keynes moved from "classical" to "Keynesian" economics in parallel with the larger transitions in politics, international affairs, science, philosophy, and aesthetics through which he lived[124].

The life of J.M. KEYNES

Keynes was born on 5 June 1883 in Cambridge, the eldest of three children of a well off academic family. His father was a Fellow of Pembroke College, Cambridge, as a philosopher and an economist, later to become the Registry of the University (that is the chief administrative officer). His mother was the daughter of a congregational minister father and a schoolmistress mother who also was devoted to women's education. The upbringing was religiously non-conformist, and socially Victorian. The family setup therefore was a mixture of intellectuality, and social conscience. Their circle of friends included foremost philosophers and economist such as Alfred Marshall, Herbert Foxwell, Henry Sidgwick, W.E. Johnston and James Ward.

Keynes himself went to Eton and then Cambridge University. He never "rebelled" against his parents, and accepted without question the high value his father and mother placed on academic excellence. He judged his own life, and others', by intellectual and aesthetic criteria. Later, he became part of the so-called "Bloomsbury group" in London. At school he was outstanding in a wide variety of subjects and activities, but particularly Mathematics, classics and history. He also realized early on that cleverness, and not only intelligence or ability, were the route to success and dealing with adults.

At Kings College, Cambridge, which he joined in 1902, he gave up mathematics, and became more interested in philosophy, but he also became the president of the Cambridge University Union, played bridge, and in 1905 joined the Civil Service (India Office) as a junior clerk. Within two years, he understood the finances of the Indian Government so well, that he was appointed, in 1913, member of the Royal Commission on Indian Finance and Currency. At that time, he showed more interest in his theory concerning "probability" *(Treatise on Probability, 1921)* which was to form subsequently an integral part of his economic thoughts.

He submitted a dissertation which earned him a fellowship at kings College, Cambridge in 1909, leading to the rest of his career in Academic life. This was a time of changing and shifting values in Victorian England, with doubts being cast on religious tenets, and social mores. Keynes developed atheistic ideas, and was attracted to the thoughts of the philosopher G.E. Moore, whose thoughts provided justification for the break from the social and sexual codes of his parents. Support and succour was at the same time provided by the "Bloomsbury" group of close friends, male and female, whose association in London, away from the strictures of the outside society, was the setting within which this group could indulge in their "non-conformist" pursuits away from the glare and scrutiny. His relationship was for quite some time male oriented, and not until 1918, did he find the woman who would attract him enough, and signal the reorganization of his personal life. He met the Russian ballerina Lydia Lopokova in London, wooed her over several of her visits to London for performances, and eventually they got married on 4 August 1924. This gave him emotional stability, and as he had earned good money in the meantime, he was able to buy a farmhouse in Sussex, where they spent their vacations, and where he was able to write his two major works: *A Treatise on Money* and *The General Theory of Employment, Interest, and Money.*

Keynes' Professional Progress

Keynes' career was remarkable for the exposure to momentous international events at a very young age. Keynes was a contemporary of very eminent World-Stage personalities, notably Stalin (born 1879), Mussolini (born 1883) and Hitler (Born 1889). He was thrown "at the deep end" at the age of 31 when the 1914-18 war broke out. Having acquired good knowledge of the working of finance and Central Banking from his days in the Indian Civil service, he played a leading part in averting the collapse of the gold standard in the banking crisis of 1914. In 1915 he joined the British Government Treasury, where he remained until 1919. In 1917 he became head of a new "A" division. He achieved a high reputation for competence and resourcefulness, on the one hand in taking to Whitehall, and on the other in managing Britain's external finance, distributing proceeds of loans and sale of securities to cover needed imports and overseas expenditures. He even assisted and guided Russia and France on these matters. However, while achieving a very high reputation, he internally harboured serious reservations about the war, and unease in his conscience. He argued against the deployment of armies, conscription, and loss of life, preferring that Britain would use her foreign earnings to subsidize her allies, mainly Russia, in their war efforts. This view clashed with that of the then British Prime Minister, Lloyd George, who believed in the "knockout blow".

Nevertheless, Keynes acquired during the war the exquisite credentials that would make him an obvious choice to serve with the British delegation to the Paris Peace Conference in 1919, where he was to be in the company, at the age of 36, of such eminent people as Lloyd George, Georges Clemenceau, and Woodrow Wilson, and to be involved in that great challenge and tremendous task of working towards the establishment of world peace, now that the war has ended.

He was aware of the financial dependence on the USA as a result of the depletion of Britain's assets because of the war effort, and realized the implication that this can have in creating a sort of financial hegemony by the USA over Britain. His opinion of the proceedings and results of that Paris Conference and the treaty of Versailles was offered in his treatise, *The Economic Consequences of the Peace*, published in December

1919. In it he described the Paris mood as vengeful, myopic, and deeply unrealistic. He described Wilson as the "blind and deaf Don Quixote", Clemenceau as having "one illusion--France, and one disillusion---mankind". As for Lloyd George, Keynes described him in a passage that was deleted at the last minute, as "that goat-footed bard, this half human visitor to our age from the hag-ridden magic and enchanted woods of Celtic antiquity".

It was the reparation clauses that invited Keynes' professional condemnation. Germany could not, he held, meets the amounts contemplated out of any conceivable export earnings. The effort and resulting trade and financial dislocation would penalize not only the defeated enemy but all of Europe as well. ...In consequence, Germany ceased to be seen as the punished aggressor and can, instead, to thought of as the victim[125]. He predicted the destruction of the pre-war prosperity of Continental Europe, and a war of vengeance by Germany. He was of the view that all Inter-ally war debts should be cancelled, leaving a limited liability for reparation to be paid for in modest annual instalments to Belgium and France. He called for the loans by the USA to Europe to be used to finance European Industry, stabilize currencies, and pay for essential foods, rather than just to repay war debts. In this way Keynes managed to influence public opinion in Europe and lessen or eliminate the effects of the war propaganda machine, and, most significantly, bring economics to the forefront of public opinion and discourse. These facts were taken into consideration after World War II, as the Allies refrained from repeating the mistake of imposing severe penalties on Germany.

After the war, Keynes returned to Cambridge University, but rather on a part time basis. He had outgrown his pre-war status, and became, among other things, Chairman of the *New Statesman and Nation*, Chairman of the National Mutual Assurance Company, member of the

Government Committee of Enquiry into Finance and Industry, and bursar of King's College, Cambridge. He speculated in currencies and commodities, but was not initially successful. With help from friends he managed subsequently to alter his investment policy and included stocks and shares, managing finally to acquire net assets of £411,238 in 1919, worth many millions at current value.

In between the two world wars, the world went through very significant changes, both in mood and in social, political, and economic structures. Falling moral standards, failing religious influence, political upheavals. The epitome of these upheavals at the time were the rise of Communism in Russia, mainly as a direct suffering of the masses during World War I and then the appearance of Nazism in Germany as a result of the rise of Hitler on the back of the general disgruntlement of the German people from the burden imposed on them as predicted by Keynes. In addition, the world witnessed economic upheavals in the financial and business sectors and these led eventually to the great depression of the early 30's. All this created situations far removed from the relative stability that the then advanced world (essentially the USA and Western Europe) had been accustomed to prior to the war.

In Britain, Keynes clashed with the then Chancellor of the exchequer, Winston Churchill, over the issue, in 1925, of the return to the gold standard, the £/$ parity, and the resulting overvaluation of the pound. The reduced competitiveness of British trade, high interest rates, inflation, and rampant unemployment that followed was attributed by Keynes to monetary mismanagement, particularly the failure of the government to raise interest rates soon enough and high enough. There followed a long and bitter strike in the coal-fields, followed by a general strike in 1926, which at least had the effect of achieving wage reductions.

In 1923, Keynes, in his *A Tract on Monetary Reform* presented his views on monetary "regime" as he named it, rejecting the high value of currency as indicating a strong currency. Indeed, he thought it was the opposite. Moreover, a domestic currency fixed arbitrarily to a gold standard is not a guarantee for price stability, especially considering that the price of gold itself can fluctuate, and that the ultimate control of its price is with the Federal Reserve Board in Washington. His view is that a stable exchange rate is a consequence, not the result, of domestic price stability. In his pamphlet *The economic Consequences of Mr Churchill* Keynes expressed his views that the decision to fix sterling to the gold standard at $4.65 will intensify unemployment.

Keynes got involved in politics for a short period between 1926 and 1929, when he advised the Lloyd George Liberal Party on its economic policy, in particular to conquer unemployment. His service on the "liberal Industrial Inquiry" in 1927-8 was the high point in his political involvement, and also his means of testing his political philosophy of the "Middle Way", first outlined in his pamphlet *The end of Laissez-Faire* Of 1926.

In 1929, Keynes, in his *Can Lloyd George do it?*, written jointly with Hubert Henderson, argued in favour of spending on public works to produce a "cumulative" wave of prosperity. The timing was not very useful, because the collapse of world economy and business confidence induced people to hold on to "orthodoxy". On 25 August 1931, the state of public finances in Britain necessitating the replacement of the Labour Government by a National Government, and on 21 September, sterling was forced off the gold standard because of serious balance of payments deficit.

Further works appeared: *The Means to Prosperity* in 1933, and his work: *General Theory of Employment, Interest, and Money* in 1936, and other smaller published works. The *General Theory* work was considered revolutionary, but was not actually implemented until after World War II. This will be dealt with later.

In May 1937, at the age of 53, Keynes had a coronary thrombosis, but he recovered, and by 1939 he was restored through the aid of a Hungarian physician, to his old vigour.

Soon after Britain entered the war in 1939, Keynes was made a member of the Consultative Committee set up to advise the Chancellor of the Exchequer on war finances. He was given a room in the Treasury and a secretary, with "no routine duties" and no office hours. This gave him the opportunity and the freedom to involve himself the way he sees fit. He was elevated to the peerage in 1942, becoming Baron Keynes of Tilton He thus acquired the rank that would give him more authority particularly in such events as negotiations in missions to Washington.[126]

Keynes' most important service in the last period of his life was to help build the domestic and international foundations of the managed capitalism to which his theory pointed. During the war there was full employment in Britain as a result of the war effort. To prevent inflation there was a need to absorb surplus money from people and allow it to be spent only by government. He therefore devised a scheme of "deferred pay", whereby excess purchasing power was mopped up by a progressive surcharge on all incomes (with offsets to the poor in the form of family allowances) part of which would be given back in instalments after the war in order to counteract the anticipated post-war slump. This allowed the economy to run at full capacity with only moderate inflation. He hoped that what could be achieved during war can also be done in peacetime.[127]

Keynes then established the **Bretton Wood System** allowing "managed" exchange rates and thus currency stability. In this system, reserve assets were to consist of a mixed package of gold, certain so-called key currencies, primarily the dollar and sterling, and certain credit facilities of which countries could avail themselves, unconditionally or under certain conditions. The International Monetary Fund (IMF) was thus conceptualised. The idea was that, under a full gold standard, payments deficits (and surpluses) led to reserve/gold losses (or inflows) which automatically brought about contraction (or expansion) in the money supply and increases (or decreases) in interest rates, thereby altering relative price levels until international payments balance was restored[128]. The difficulties that arose were a result of the large post-war imbalances, and the social and political repercussions that were to arise as a result of violent swings in domestic policies. Moreover, to work very efficiently, it meant that some countries would have had to surrender "financial" sovereignty to a greater degree than was politically accepted. The IMF, ideally should have developed into an international central bank, operating as a lender of last resort and controlling credit conditions generally. The fact that the system worked for some time was because in difficult situations, other mechanisms were improvised on an ad hoc basis to even out any impending or actual crisis. The Marshall plan of reparations to Europe, was, indeed an important factor in allowing the system to keep on working because of the liquidity sustained by the American dollars funnelled in order to assist in the rejuvenation of Europe's economy and industry.

Keynes had actually introduced in 1942 his famous **Clearing Union** plan, which provided a link between each national currency and a new reserve asset **"bancor"**. Surplus countries would accumulate "bancor" balances in the Union; overdraft facilities would be made available to deficit countries up to the total of the surpluses. This scheme, similar in some respects to the IMF was actually defeated, but in spite of this Keynes worked hard for the alternative arrangements at Bretton Wood.

Keynes' final act of statesmanship was in his negotiations in Washington in September- December 1945 for a loan to cover the British Government war-debts of $ 7bn. He wanted $5bn, but was "rebuffed" and allowed only $3.75bn. from the USA and a further $1.25bn. from Canada, on condition Sterling was allowed to float within one year of the loan. He had to convince the British Government and Parliament that the alternative to this deal would be "Nazism or Communism". He had to swallow his pride and once again visited America for the inauguration of the IMF in March 1946.

Keynes was known to be a person who had many interests, and the last ones he took were positions in Arts & Music forums. He died of a massive heart attack on 21 April 1946, and it is interesting that his father and mother were still alive and attended his funeral.

The Economic Theories of KEYNES

I   Philosophical aspects

Keynes, as was mentioned earlier, was influenced by the philosopher G.E. Moore, who provided him with the thoughts that would allow him to lead a life separate from the family orientated Victorian mores and values. Moore's *Principia Ethica* (published in 1903) was the manifesto of modernism to Keynes' generation: later Keynes described it as "The opening of a new heaven on earth". Keynes, however, did not accept all his views without questioning. The first main philosophy was "The indefinability of Good" But to this Keynes added his own thoughts about the concept of "probability" which appeared in *Treatise on Probability*, published in 1921[129].

Good, Moore said, is the name of a simple non-natural property, intuitively known. Secondly, good and bad states of mind are prior to good and bad actions...good actions were those which brought about good states of mind. Moore attributed personal virtue, private and public duty ... *(as forming)* the rational end of human action and the sole criterion of progress. Keynes felt that there is "no necessary connection" between individual and universal goodness, and that "because we never have the opportunity of direct inspection (of other people's states of mind), it is impossible to tell what kind of action increase the goodness of the Universe as a whole". There were more details to these philosophical stands, but the important point to note is that Keynes, on the one hand takes his stand in economics from an ethical and philosophical platform (in keeping with most other preceding economic thinkers as has been mentioned previously), and on the other hand, looks at these matters from an atheistic viewpoint.

The other strand to Keynes' ethical basis to his thoughts is his study of "Probability", an audacious insight published in his *Treatise on Probability* in 1921. In this line of thought he developed further Moore's concept that "we ought to behave in such a way as to bring about the greatest possible amount of goodness to the universe. But our knowledge of the effects of our actions is bound to be, at best, probabilistic. Since it is impossible to know the probable effects of actions stretching into the remote future, the best we could do in most cases, was to follow moral rules which were generally useful and generally practised". Here Keynes saw that Moore confuses knowledge of probabilities with knowledge of relative frequencies of occurrence. He postulated that all we have to have is *no reason to believe* that any immediate good we achieve would be overturned by distant consequences. Keynes was thus on the "optimists' side of the argument in favour of doing good, and "hoping for the best". This led him to consider the question of choice (of action), i.e. what are the principles of rational choice and action when the future is unknown or uncertain. He claimed that the mind could often "reduce" uncertainty to probability, sanctioning a "degree of belief" in the conclusion, perhaps through intuition or perception.

Keynes was thus optimistic about the power of human reason, and pessimistic about the secrets of the universe. As a result, he looked at the "weight of argument" as a good basis to make a decision which, though not affecting the probability, will nevertheless increase our confidence in the rationality of the decision. The upshot, then, is his "moral risk" consideration, whereby it is more rational to aim for a smaller good that is more probable to be attained, rather than a greater good, that is less probable, when the two actions have equal probable goodness. This thought is probably why Keynes did not favour revolutionary change. It also reveals his idea that individual judgement is necessary at times, rather than following generally accepted rules, because: " Whatever the immediate consequences of a new truth may be, there is a high probability that truth will in the long run lead to better results than falsehood".

Keynes had another influence: that of Edmund Burke and his thoughts on "Conservatism". Applying Burke's thought to his political philosophy, Keynes married two elements of conservatism (ideas of Burke): contentment as the aim and risk avoidance as the method of government, to two key elements in reforming liberalism: a commitment to truth and belief in the possibility of rational individual judgement. This became his "Middle Way" between unthinking (Political) Conservatism and radical Socialism, which reflected the two main elements of political system between the wars. He was thus a sort of "liberal" in his political thought, accepting that the existing social order unfairly or unjustly distributed life chances, but that *laissez-faire* did not protect existing economic and social norms. Injustice to him meant arbitrary changes in settled social arrangements, such as those produced by changes in the value of money. He therefore transferred the problem of justice from the microeconomy to the macroeconomy, and then only as part of the machinery of macroeconomic stabilization, not as a means to an ideal goal such as justice. In his essay "The end of *Laissez-Faire*" (1924), he considered that "the evils of the existing order arose largely from risk, uncertainty, and ignorance" and their remedy required "deliberate control of the currency and of the credit by a central institution", the "collection and dissemination of business facts", a " co-ordinated act of intelligent judgement" concerning the aggregate volume of savings and their distribution between domestic and foreign investment, and a "population policy "which pays attention to innate quality as well as to...numbers"[130]. In the *General Theory* he offered the notion, as a criterion of public intervention, of a service or activity which was "technically social" in the sense that only the State could provide it. In the same spirit, large private corporations and individualistic capitalists would give way to "socialized" capitalism. He was a leveller who wanted to level upwards not downwards. "I want to give encouragement to all exceptional effort, ability, courage, character. I do not want to antagonize the successful, the exceptional" It is interesting that at the time of writing, the recently elected Labour Government in Britain is talking profusely about the "Third Way".

II   Keynes Monetary and Economic Theories

In summary, the principle theoretical features of Keynesian economics are as follows[131]:

1   A shift in method from micro-economics *(those related to individuals and firms and their conduct and behaviour in economic matters, especially relating to prices of goods and services, without necessarily due regard to the overall aggregates of the economy)* to macro-economics *(The branch of economics concerned with the problems of unemployment, economic stability, inflation and economic growth, relying on income and employment analysis)*,

the italics are the author's additions. From the long period to the short period, from real to monetary analysis, and from variations in prices to variations of quantities as central objects of analysis.

2   Both aggregate consumptions and aggregate savings are taken to be stable functions of income but investment is treated at least partly as autonomous, inherently volatile and subject to pervasive uncertainty.

3   Saving and investment are said to be carried out by different people for different reasons and are only brought to equilibrium by changes of income itself.

4   The rate of interest is explained in monetary terms as a function of the stock demand for money interacting with an exogenously determined supply of money.

5   Real wages are treated as determined by the volume of employment rather than the other way round.

The main thrust, therefore, was to establish stability, but to start with, Keynes related his thoughts to the main theory current at the time: "The Quantity Theory of Money", with its two main forms: that of Irving Fisher's "transaction version" or that of Alfred Marshall's "cash balances". The first was laid out in the equation: **MV=PT** (where M is the quantity of money, V, is the velocity of circulation, i.e. the number of times per period a pound or dollar is spent, P is the average price of each transaction, and T is the total number of transactions). In Marshall' cash balance theory, the equation is **M=k PT** (where M,P & T are the same, but *k* is the fraction of the community's wealth or income.

Keynes regarded the two theories are basically the same. In the climate, where as mentioned previously, money was a medium of exchange, and a means of effecting purchases and sales of goods and services, and no other purpose, a change in the quantity (or value) of money could disturb a previous equilibrium only if it produced non-proportionate changes in agents' money stocks. Rising prices, it was typically said, benefit investors and entrepreneurs at the expense of savers and wage earners; falling prices the reverse. Money had no utility other than as a means of effecting transactions. The role of money can act as a temporary abode of purchasing power, a bridge to the "store of value". When, therefore, entrepreneurs increase their borrowings, it is the spending of their new deposits which first causes prices to rise, and this stimulus gradually spreads to all parts of the community, until the new "gold" is needed to finance a volume of real trade no larger...than before. The price level is what equilibrates the "demand for cash" with the "supply of cash". It follows that under the gold standard, the supply of purchasing power depends upon banking and gold jointly.

Keynes moved from these thoughts to the idea that an equilibrium level of income and output need not correspond to a situation of full employment. As the poor have, according to Keynes, a higher propensity to consume than the rich, a "paradox of thrift" could arise, whereby in an economy with unemployment more saving means more, not less, unemployment, and an economy can be stuck in a low-level employment equilibrium trap. To avoid a "social revolution" monetary reform and management with stability of prices, credit and employment was required. Falling prices would injure employment, because money-wages are fixed in the short run, and also because falling prices depress expectations of sales proceeds. "It is worse, in an impoverished world", Keynes wrote," to provoke unemployment than to disappoint the *rentier*".

Keynes presented four points of interest: 1- He was against restoring the gold standard, because he felt that fixed exchange rates will create inflexibility in the domestic prices', and employment levels', ability to adjust. This was especially significant at the time because of the emerging dominance of the USA, which could mean that Britain would end up surrendering some of its power to regulate internal price level and credit cycle to the Federal Reserve Board. Separate dollar and sterling blocks could be established, for steady dollar or sterling price, and gold would act as the ultimate means of settling international debts. 2- He maintained that stable prices could be achieved by monetary policy alone, controlling inflation being mainly a matter of stopping inflationary government finance. 3- He considered it important to "watch and control the creation of credit and to let the creation of currency to follow suit", thus coming out in favour of "broad" rather than "narrow" money *(narrow money being just notes and coins in circulation, and broad money to include bank and savings accounts, and nowadays credit-card balances. Author's italics)*. Thus he was in favour of measuring forward indicators rather than the backward one of quantity of money. 4- Keynes favoured discretionary management, rejecting a money supply rule as unsuitable for controlling the credit cycle. His formula for this is: $n=p(k+rk')$ where n is currency notes and other forms of cash in circulation, p is the index number of the cost of living, k is the real value of cash in hand, k' is the real value of bank deposits including overdrafts, and r the ratio of banking system's reserves to liabilities. Consequently, a change in n will cause an equiproportion movement in p. Double the quantity of money, and you double the price level. "Now in the long *run*" he stated " this is probably true... but in the long *run* it is a misleading guide to current affairs". When price are rising, people reduce their "real balances" (k and K'), when prices are falling they increase them[132]. Central banks vary their reserve requirements to offset gold flows...and they can vary the amount of cash it makes available by buying and selling securities. Keynes's principle novel prediction in his economics is the value of the ***instantaneous multiplier*** which is greater than unity. That is, that any increase in real income and employment could be achieved by a sufficiently large autonomous increase in consumption, or investment, or government expenditure, and that this effect is enhanced because of the multiplier factor, whereby money injected into the system remains flowing between households and business, all the time increasing in size. While in theory this may be indefinite, in practice, it is limited by what is termed "leakages", particularly money set aside as saving. In this way government and central banks, not just supply and demand, will be able to determine the amount of money in circulation, and indeed interest rates. Individuals and businesses will react to interest rates and take it into consideration when deciding on investment, spending, borrowing or saving. However, individuals were less sensitive to interest rate variations, because they are more interested in consumption, and only after satisfying their needs will they consider saving any surplus. The important factor, therefore, is their level of income. The spend on consumption is proportionately higher when income is low, and becomes proportionately less when income grows, when savings are likely to rise both absolutely and as a proportion of income. The effect on employment, therefore, is evidently a factor of interest rates, but indirectly, and "in the *opposite direction* to that usually supposed" whereby reduced rates will stimulate activity and more investment, allowing national income to grow. Higher levels of income, in turn, would produce a larger volume of saving, leading to a new equilibrium at increased levels of investment and income. The causal link is therefore indirect, running from interest rates to investment, from investment to aggregate income, and from aggregate income to actual saving.

The level of economic activity will have a major impact on employment and unemployment. An increase in demand for workers in turn will generate demand (consumption), and the money they spend will contribute to the aggregate money, and aggregate equilibrium. This was later (after Keynes) integrated with his theory as the "acceleration principle". But Keynes was aware that the relationship between national income and the aggregate demand for labour was difficult to establish precisely. Wage cutting, in his views offered no cure for unemployment. It will curtail effective demand still further. Wages tend to rise with increased profits and inflation, but tend to lag behind in going down when profits reduce and inflation goes down. The same with unemployment: it remains "jammed" in a low employment state as a recession turns up.

Another of Keynes' thoughts was that government spending on projects for services and infra-structure would be useful in stimulating economic activity, particularly in depressions, but provided the projects initiated are not those that should, or would have been anyway, undertaken by private enterprise. On the other hand, he also postulated, *laissez-faire* (the unregulated market system) was likely to be chronically unstable and incapable of assuring the full utilisation of productive capacity. Not only was there a need for government intervention in the economy, but that thrift was not necessarily a social virtue. Indeed, when resources were under-employed, thrift was a social vice. Keynes hoped that the essential features of the capitalist system could be preserved. But its virtues could be safeguarded only if the social unrest generated by mass unemployment could be eliminated by appropriate reforms. *Laissez-faire* was essentially a fair weather system, capable of remarkable productive performance when conditions are favourable, but it was inherently unstable. Governments had a major responsibility for regulating the economic climate in ways that would permit the market system to achieve its full potential.

Keynes was pleased to note that his views were being undertaken on the other side of the Atlantic. He went to the USA to study the "New Deal" inaugurating by President Roosevelt, and was impressed. He was not so impressed with the socialism that was exhibited in Nazi Germany, perhaps because he was not impressed by the regime there. After the World War II, the question of employment was, as mentioned above, given top importance in both the USA and Britain, and Keynes found rapport more in the States than in Europe except for Sweden, where the Swedish School was in tune with his thoughts. The adoption of a Keynesian approach by Western Governments has not been least responsible for the high degree of stability exhibited by their economies in the years since the Second World War[133].

Post Keynesian Economics

Keynes had his advocates, as mentioned above on both sides of the Atlantic. His views, however, were not universally accepted. A leading critic was Harvard's Joseph SCHUMPETER, who criticized Keynes vehemently on the basis that Keynes insisted on uniting economic theory with practical policy, and that he was afflicted by the "curse of usefulness". Again, initially, Alvin Harvey Hansen (1887-1975) was a ardent advocate of the market, liberal international trade and the generally self-correcting mechanisms of the classical system. However, after he carefully considering Keynes's *"The general Theory"* he changed his mind and was converted to Keynesian economics, becoming its most effective spokesman in the USA. Keynesians in Washington met regularly, and their convictions were re-enforced by the sharp recession of 1937-38, which, in turn, followed a well publicized drive toward a more conservative fiscal policy -- tax increases, expenditure curtailment and renewed promises of a balanced budget. The great depression of 1939 was seen as a result of the unfair competition which is the basis of the classical theory. Thereafter, maintaining full, or at least, adequate levels of employment became all important to the governments. It was even enshrined in a law (Congress bill S 380) to make it mandatory for the Government of the USA to maintain the policies that would ensure adequate employment. The Federal Reserve's remit is to this day, the regulation of interest rates and the pursuance of monetary policies aimed at maintaining adequate levels of employment.

The conflict between the two aspects of Keynesian economics, whereby deflation and unemployment called for higher public expenditure and lower taxes (politically agreeable), and inflation calling for lower government spending and higher taxes (politically disagreeable), were soon to be proven not easily effective, because of the appearance of the modern "wage-price" inflation, where Keynesian economics proved to be a "one-way" street, easy going down, but difficult and uncertain going up. Inflation began to become the leading political and economic problem since the late 1960's, and was especially significant in the USA where inflation was almost unknown until after the Korean War. The occurrence of wage increases with price rises was partly due to the appearance of large corporations which had a very substantial control over their prices, at the same time that large powerful trade unions wielded substantial power in wage negotiations, and other benefits to their members. This was the recipe for what is now called "the wage-price spiral". Moreover, large corporations were able to influence consumers to a great extent through their advertising and sales, and in their function were able to control the allocations of capital, labour and material. They became the new, but much enlarged, operators of microeconomics. Governments reacted by imposing prices and wages controls, but these efforts proved not really serious or effective. At best, they helped as a stop gap while government macroeconomic measures to control inflation came into effect. In the early 1970's, the unwelcome inflationary effects of international cartels, mainly the oil producing OPEC organisation, became an important factor in raising prices and inflation, together with reducing the control of individual governments over their internal (national) economics. This was a situation where Keynes microeconomics created changes that were beyond the reach of his macroeconomics.

Keynes, a man of his time, spanned what could be described as the most important half century in the history of the world. A period of history that was so full of sea changes, with two world wars consuming the resources of Europe, and dragging, on the two occasions, the USA, rather reluctantly during World War I, but with much less hesitation in World War II where Nazi Germany was seen as a threat to democracy and a thrust to achieve hegemony. Perhaps more cynically, World War II was seen as an opportunity for the two big threats of the time, the Communist Soviet Union and Hitler's Germany to fight it out and relieve the West of some considerable pressure. Entry of Japan into the war, and the disastrous decision to attack the American Naval base at Pearl Harbour in the Pacific served to awaken the American giant to the reality that it and its people cannot anymore cocoon themselves in their "fortress America" and remain isolated and immune from events in the rest of the world.

The effect of all this on world economics was extremely significant, and the role of Keynes in tapping the American economy's resource to assist Britain to finance the war effort, was nothing but crucial to the success and eventual destruction of the German war machine and Nazi "socialism". The war proved also to be the final catalyst that triggered off the dismantling of the two main Empires that up until that time coloured the world map effectively into two colours: the vast expanse of the pink or red colour of the British Colonies, Dominions and overseas protectorates, and the smaller area of blue indicating the

French dominated Territories. Freedom became the watchword and Independence the Right. The political and economic consequences of the ensuing period and to this day provide very interesting and important thought provoking considerations that will merit more mention later in this work.

Keynes, playing that crucial role in that most pregnant phase of history, managed to show his qualities as a man of tremendous and varied talents, as well as a man able to deliver his messages in convincing manner, and, for that period at least, dominate economic thought and method. He started as a philosopher, ethicist and moralist, with distinct atheistic but not overtly rebellious attitude. He moved to academic economics, and finally ended as a statesman with no particular political involvement, a most senior British Government official with sweeping responsibility over the British Government's financial and economic machinery. He brushed briefly with politics, leaning towards the liberal/middle socialist sector of political thought, but stopped short of assuming actual political position or party membership. His interest in Art and Music rounds him up as a man of good all round interests and a balanced worldly outlook. A man who perhaps lived his life to the full, but importantly proved the great place of economics in present day life on all levels of society, and in the management by governments not only nationally, but also with increasing importance, internationally.

The Rise of Monetarism

With the OPEC "oil shocks" accounting for perhaps 10% of the inflationary pressures, and inflation reaching 13.5% in the USA in 1975, President Gerald Ford was alarmed enough to call a conference of leading economists to make recommendations. There was full professional agreement on only one remedy: the review of government regulations with the aim of removing any obvious impediment to market competition. There was, however, one other means that was politically possible: Monetary policy or Monetarism.

Milton Friedman (1912--2006)

Friedman, of the University of Chicago, and later of the Hoover Institute of War, Revolution, and Peace, became the leading exponent of the free market, and indeed, with his views filled the post Keynesian void, especially in the English-speaking countries. Indeed, he is said to have "supplanted" Keynes as the world's most influential economist[134]

His revolutionary theory was in relation to taxes, whereby, he proposed, taxes should reduce to reach zero in the lower income brackets, and then, at the lowest income brackets, should become negative, i.e. return income. This was a radical welfare suggestion to maintain minimum income for all. His major economic theory was in relation to money supply and its effect on the control of prices. Thus, the control of money supply will, after a period of lag, lead to price stabilization. This meant that government function will be reduced significantly, microeconomics orthodoxy and competition will rule, and inflation is controlled through raised interest rates. The objection here is that raised interest rates favour those who have money to lend, or the well to do, and will harm especially those who have to borrow. Taxes were not required to be raised.

This system was adopted first by President Jimmy Carter, Thirty Ninth President of the USA, (1977-1981), and then, more ardently, by Margaret Thatcher, Britain's Prime Minister, from 1979 to 1990 (and to a lesser extent, by the Conservative Prime Minister, John Major, who succeeded her after she was ousted by the Conservative Party). The election of Ronald Reagan to the US Presidency (1981-1989) established a similar reliance on the market and minimum

Government intervention as the policy across the Atlantic. The Keynesian Revolution was folded in, and John Maynard Keynes gave way to Milton Friedman[135].

While some countries were still sceptical, in spite of the new system's early success, inflation, particularly because of oil price increases, combined with stagnation to create a new condition which became known as *Stagflation*. Controlling inflation through the restriction of money supply and record high interest rates had the effect of sharply curtailing economic activity, with markedly reduced housing starts, sales of automobile and other consumer goods, and the general drying up of investment. Naturally, unemployment rocketed. The value of currency, particularly the dollar and sterling rose sharply, sucking in fresh funds from other countries, especially Japan, to capitalise on the high interest rates. With the high exchange value, imports into Britain and the USA became cheaper, and exports more expensive. This resulted in further slowdown of the economy, although on the plus side raw material and new production plants (required for manufacture and consumption) became cheaper. Eventually, in the period 1983/84 there was a sharp reduction in the Consumer Price Index (inflation). In the USA, prices became stable, and this was followed closely by the same reaction in Britain. High unemployment, current at the time, provided an added factor for reducing inflation, as Trade Unions became reluctant to drive hard bargains for their members, seeing that every member out of work is also a member dropped out, not just a personal tragedy. Industries had to slim down, and become more "mean" and efficient, in order to become more competitive. Indeed, the end result, while quite painful at the time the remedy was administered, was a rise in productivity, competitiveness, and therefore earnings to extents far exceeding any previous levels of efficiency and earnings. Unemployment gradually reduced in both the USA and Britain, at the same time as it was rising inexorably in the rest of Europe and latterly in Japan. The experiment, however, is far from over. But like other economic ideas, it may be right for the present, inasmuch as Keynesian economics may have been right for its time. At the time of this revision of the original draft of this work, the world is witnessing the most drastic of financial crises, initially attributed to that newly coined term: "*Sub-prime*" mortgage lending, followed by very serious loss of liquidity within the banking and financial institutions world wide. The effect of this extensive and simultaneous loss of financial activity and confidence led to unprecedented government interventions and "bailing out" as well as partial or full nationalization of some of the institutions. Venerable time honoured names such as Lehman Brothers and "Fanny May" and "Freddie Mac" (both ultimate insurers to the USA mortgage market) all fell victims to serious mismanagement and loss of adequate liquidity to meet their obligations. It is too early to see this upheaval through the prism of future developments or forecasts, but suffice it to say, that apart from market losses counted in trillion of dollars, the legacy in terms of world recession or at least a serious downturn of the economy, will be far reaching and maybe prolonged. Dr. Ben S Bernanke, Chairman of the US "Federal Reserve System" saw it fit to announce that the "downturn is likely to be protracted", and Mervyn King, the Governor of the Bank of England also saw it fit to state that "Not since the First World War has the banking system come so close to collapse"[136].. The repercussions on the USA and the rest of the world can only be viewed with much concern, particularly as Britain and almost the whole of Western Europe and major Asian countries are similarly afflicted, to varying degrees of severity.

While these situations can be temporary, and will most likely be resolved sooner or later, there appears to be a state of "chronic" malaise that has gradually developed in the financial and economic activities worldwide. Recent tragic disclosures of failures within the financial institutions were overcome, mainly because of the financial tools developed to cope, but also because there still are reasonable reserves worldwide to utilise when things go wrong. The question is: how many such failures can the reserves withstand, and whether there is a need to look at better systems, not only based on economic principles, but also encompassing other aspects of human behaviour that would safeguard against such financial misdemeanours as we have witnessed particularly in the latter half of the twentieth century and the first decade of the twenty first. Bearing in mind that the initial foray of both Adam Smith and J.M. Keynes into economics was via the route of ethics and moral considerations, it is appropriate, therefore, to consider some aspects of present economics in more detail, and to look at the future, which, in the light of quite momentous developments at the time of writing this treatise, merits careful consideration and thought.

PART VII

CONTEMPORARY WORLD ECONOMIC:

Considerations And Needs

It would be an obvious statement to say that the present state of the world is one of greater complexity than at any other time in history. If economics as a subject started primordially as a thought exercise in ethics and the needs of the individual and society, and if it later developed into a science with quantitative and qualitative theories, and if it has intertwined with politics and affairs of state, it is easy to appreciate that it has now reached a stage where "globalization" has imposed on it new necessities, and new realities. This, in turn, has prompted all creditable economists to look at the implications of this move into the international arena, its interdependence, its far reaching effects on a greater part of the world and how it affects conditions in any one part of it.

Such a statement may be obvious enough. What may be less so apparent, but nevertheless acknowledged, is the very close dependence of the economic health in any society or country on the social and ethical integrity or otherwise of the individuals, groups, authority and institutions, that together form the so-called society or nation. In the recent past, one is aware of the internal corruption and oligarchic system that has been accused as the underlying cause of the collapse of the Russian economy and its currency, the Rouble, to an extent even defying international efforts at rescue. Other current "collapses" are indicative of other ills, such as "shady" or "risky" financial ventures that have ended in enormous, nay gargantuan losses with great implications on the health of world economies and financial establishments. However, as mentioned above, the reserves available worldwide, and in the case of Russia its natural resources, all made amends to these difficulties and restored more value and trust in the failed currencies. The collapse of the "Bank of International Credit and Commerce" in 1994, the insolvency of that most traditional and time honoured British based bank, "Baring's" allegedly as a result of the excessive and perhaps irresponsible dealings of a so-called "rogue" trader, and, almost literally on the day of writing this, the "Long Term Leasing & Credit Bank" in Japan, and most distressingly, the "Long Term Capital Management, LTCM" of Wall Street, requiring $ 3.5 billion for immediate rescue, with the hope, but not the certainty, that this will be enough to avoid what is described as possible collapse of world finances. These are but examples of the scale of operations in world finance, and the difficulty of regulatory authorities to monitor all operations adequately or to interfere in a timely manner to avoid calamities. Operations and transactions are undertaken, with such rapidity and crossing every border and time zone several times a day, that monitoring, at best, can only be trailing behind, hopefully close enough to keep good tract. Alas! We have seen that this was not robust enough to avoid yet more gargantuan losses recently as mentioned above. Indeed, every major state of collapse seems to eclipse the one before it.

It is in these situations that self monitoring of the responsible individual at every level is paramount. This may be a given and a code of conduct that appears to be prevailing. However, within an erratic ethical environment of pure selfish gain or narrow remit to provide creditable performance for the establishment, it is an understatement to say that this may not be enough. There is a need for a more comprehensive consideration for the good of society or even the world, a more holistic review of world economics and finance.

On local or national levels, the considerations for the economy will once again inevitably cover the most basic of principles: and that is, what society or the country can afford, and what are its priorities. Although every government ends up attributing any failures to the simple fact that the country or budget cannot afford better, it is not difficult to find in any part of the world evidence of failures that will easily point to mismanagement (if we are charitable), or sadly, to downright corruption and misappropriation. However easy it is to lay the blame on the government or authority, it is nevertheless only one side of the story. For the individual, and the community, almost always share a good measure of the blame.

For the above reasons, discussing economics in isolation of the ethical and moral standards that govern or guide the individual, society, or state, will not provide enough and appropriate answers. To look at the difficulties encountered by individuals, families, or communities without consideration of the fabric of society, the structure, and constitution of the principles and tenets that decide their conduct and behaviour, is to put the onus of economic stability and future prosperity simply on the "supply and demand" of material substance, and the use or, as we increasingly see, the misuse of wealth. A good look at the different systems and regimes in the world to-day, and the political ideologies under which various governments operate, will show some common economic principles almost universally agreed upon, and others that differ widely. It is for example, agreed in all but a few very rich (usually small) states that government must collect tax.

This usually constitutes the major source of revenue. The tax schemes will differ in different countries, and the proportion of this source of revenue will also differ from being almost the only source, where natural resources are very poor, to its being a very small part of the total revenue. Countries are assessed for their wealth and/or prosperity by a number of measures, mainly the "Gross Domestic Product or GDP". This is an assessment of the value of all the goods and services produced in a country. There is also the "National Income" of a country, which is the amount of money flowing around the economy in that country. When this figure is divided by the total population of that country the result is the "Per Capita" income estimate of that country. Within this very simple model of understanding, one can add some further measures which effectively explain these raw figures in term of the value of any given wealth. Thus, the balance of payment of the country is calculated, the strength of the currency determines the value of that currency, and (if there are no exchange controls) this currency value is the exchange value of that currency in relation to other currencies. Some currencies are plentiful enough and valued enough to make them so called "Reserve Currencies". At present these are mainly the US Dollar, the Pound Sterling, the "Euro" and the Yen. Other currencies are appearing on then horizon, particularly because of the strength of the reserves available in these currencies, and the strength of the production and trade in the countries they belong to. Examples at present are the Chinese "Yuan" and the Indian "Rupee".

As for commodities, the time honoured precious metals: gold, silver, and platinum, have a significant place as reserves, because of their scarcity and because of new and valuable uses to which they are put, particularly in industry. They appear to be always useful as a hedge during economic downturns or industrial boom. The same applies to the world price of crude oil.

These, therefore, are the main measures of income or wealth. The other side of the equation in considering the economies of the various states, is that of expenditure. There is, in expenditure, an extremely wide variation in emphases. An integral part of the expenditure programme of any government at present falls within the sphere of essential services. These are mainly health, education, law and order, the judiciary, and of course, defence. While the infrastructure, such as transport, utilities, roads etc., in some countries are run as private concerns, most countries still provide these services from within national or "local" government budgets, the latter mostly paid for through local municipal taxes, rents or other sources of local revenue, sometimes subsidized from national budgets. An important item of government spending merits separate mention. That is "Social Welfare". This is the avenue of government expenditure where ideology really matters. In many situations it is not so much what the state can afford that decides how much it will spend on helping those who fall below an agreed "poverty" line, who are unemployed, or disabled or who are in need of housing. It is very often the priorities that each party or regime in power works out, and the attitude of the recipients or potential recipients of such state aid. In this context the issue falls to a great extent into the realm of the conduct and ethics of the governments on the one hand and of the population on the other. This will be explained further in a later section.

The purpose of this preliminary, and admittedly quite simplistic discussion of contemporary economics is to lay the foundation for the subsequent sections, which, as mentioned above, will look at economics from a wider angle in order to see the importance of the structure of society, the attitude of the individual, the paramount need for justice, and the best means of sharing duties and responsibilities between those who are in authority, and those who are governed. The question will not be centred on rights and privileges, important as these are, but also on civic fellowship, appreciation of the communal good, and the sincere and whole-hearted acceptance and that what is good for society will inevitably be also good for self. With this must go, hand in hand, the full probity of those in authority, who will also be a full and fair representation of those who freely and voluntarily put them in custody of their affairs.

Taking this ideal a step further, it will become evident that in this contemporary world of global interdependence, opportunity and wealth should be spread or at least made available equitably to all nations and peoples. The pundits may work all their formulae and formulations, the politicians may cry from the roof-tops with their slogans and "sound-bites", the media will be awash with experts in all disciplines and walks of life explaining, condoning, or even encouraging good and *not so good* practices, and the financiers will exhaust their tricks and wizardry. But the final outcome, almost beholden already, will be the total bankruptcy of thought *and wealth*, unless and until there is a timely appreciation that the source of all real wealth is a combination of material as well as spiritual richness.

The value of combining the spiritual and material basis for a sense of well being and prosperity may have been appreciated in the past, and especially at the early times in the history of any religion. The ideals enunciated in the various religious scriptures may have been followed by the believers sometime, but sadly this was short lived. The Israelites had to be reminded and guided periodically through successive prophets. The Christians needed their Popes and Saints to demonstrate and exemplify aspects of the Christian ideal. And the Moslems were led in the early stages by the Prophet and thereafter by the early Caliphs. Humankind has regrettably been found wanting when it came to maintaining and perpetuating these ideals. The effects were devastating, as opportunity after another was squandered, and peoples or nations reverted to individual or collective greed, strife and dissipation of energy, resources, and life. In the past, however, these misconducts were limited in their effect because of the circumscribed circumstances prevailing, whether it is in relation to the area covered by such misconducts, or the span of time involved. The means of destruction were, in the past, rather limited. In this era, however, the world can ill tolerate this any more. There is an urgent need to look again, and in greater earnestness, at the essential combination required: that of the spiritual overtones combined with the material causes and means, for achieving prosperity and well being. It is essential to consider an upgrade and an update of the spiritual teachings available to us in the light of the prevailing circumstance and conditions in the world to-day. This is best discussed under specific headings.

In the next section reference will be made of the writings and teachings of the Baha'i Faith, the most recent of the revealed Religions, heralded in Persia (now Iran) by the *Báb* in 1844, and established as the full Faith by *Bahá'u'lláh* during the period 1853 to 1892. Following the ascension of Bahá'u'lláh and, as specifically stipulated by Him, His appointed Son **Abdu'l-Bahá** assumed the role of Interpreter and Exemplar of His Father's Teachings, and added valuable detail and insight into the meaning and application of these Teachings. His utterances are accepted by the Baha'is as also inspired and revered. The passing away of Abdu'l Bahá in 1921 revealed His Will and Testament in which He appointed his grandson *Shoghi Effendi* as the *Guardian* of the Baha'i Faith, with the spiritual and infallible authority to further implement and develop the Baha'i Faith. The Faith saw its Institutions and its numerical and geographical expansion grow markedly during the period from 1921 to 1957 when Shoghi Effendi passed away while on a visit to London. His letters, and His messages and writings are valued and revered by the Baha'is, and accepted as extension to the Writings of the Three Principle Figures of the Faith mentioned above, although the Status assumed by Shoghi Effendi is emphatically described by Himself as clearly not to be compared with Them (the *Báb,* Bahá'u'lláh and Abdu'l-Bahá)

The passing away of Shoghi Effendi provided the first opportunity to establish the ***Supreme Spiritual and Administrative Body*** for the Baha'i Faith world-wide, described by Bahá'u'lláh as the ***Universal House of Justice*** with its seat in Haifa (Israel) within the area of the Holy Lands occupied by the Shrines of those Spiritual Figures and Founders of the Faith. With its role as the elected (rather than appointed) body responsible for the affairs of the Faith throughout the world, and with the conferred infallibility (as a body) accepted by the followers of Bahá'u'lláh, there continues the process of enlargement of the Faith and of further understanding of more detail and application of Its teachings, not only through messages of guidance and dissemination of information received by the Baha'i world continuously, but also through the management and administration, in a practical manner, of the affairs of the Faith worldwide. The role of the Universal House of Justice has increasingly become interactive with (non-Baha'i) governmental and non-governmental establishments throughout the world. With this on-going effort, the Baha'i Faith is brought into everyday aspects of life, sharing in the process which the Baha'is firmly believe will ultimately result in the establishment of Universal peace and prosperity.

In the spirit of this need and practicality of interaction between the Baha'i Faith and the highest levels of Human thought and endeavour, the Bahá'í Faith draws on the expertise available in every field, including that of eminent economists. The fusion of such expert knowledge with the spiritual values and Tenets of the Bahá'í Scriptures is gradually taking place. In this manner all worthwhile contributions are acknowledged, valued and made full use of. Economics is no exception. The quotations from the Baha'i writings and teachings of all the above mentioned Founders and the Universal House of Justice that are to follow will be mentioned in the same spirit of inclusion as was quoted earlier on from the teachings of the Three Main Revealed Faiths, Judaism, Christianity and Islam.

The Individual

At the risk of stating the obvious, a reminder at the outset may be worthwhile, and that is that the individual is the cornerstone upon which any system or method relies for success or failure. In no field is this axiom more true than in economics, where, the action of the individual, and the ethos within which the individual thinks and acts, will affect the outcome and effectiveness of any economic theory or practise. In most, if not all, nations the need to allocate resources to counteract the ills of society is perhaps the only growth factor written into their budgets. Whether it is more money or more staff, such resources will only be possible when vired from other services. To give but one example noted at the time of writing this section, the British Government has decided to allocate £ 500 million over a period of time to counteract "truancy and disruptive behaviour" in State schools. This is commendable, but one is forgiven to ponder why there should be such a need for a spend on a problem that should not be there in the first place. Where does the root cause lie? The answer can be argued and discussed endlessly, especially by the pundits, and every sector of the population concerned will concentrate in its argument on its own field of expertise or interest. Accepting therefore that this is a multi-factorial problem, one cannot disregard the one obvious factors that must weigh more heavily than others, and that is the way schoolchildren have been brought up at home, the structure of the family, the realization on the part of the children of the vital need for education, the adequacy of the school atmosphere and environment, and last, but not least, the cleverness, attitude and behaviour of the teachers. Some of these factors could be resolved with money, particularly such aspects as the school premises and environment. Most of the other factors, however, hardly need money to correct.

Personal Qualities

Human behaviour

From time immemorial, Religions and ethical thought have applauded the high moral qualities of human behaviour. All people, with minor variations on emphasis, accept such high moral values as conducive to good human interaction. The world, however, is full of vice, malice, and crime. In economic terms, all this is wasteful of the world's resources, and is directing the Human Race towards increasingly "costly" scenarios or even catastrophes.

In previous religions, the emphasis was on personal salvation, or, as seen above in the case of Islamic nationhood, the mutual commitment of fellow Muslims to the common cause of the "Nation". These two emphases were good enough for the state of the world at the time. Abdu'l-Bahá commends unreservedly the achievements of the Prophet Mohammed in the following passage : *"All praise and honour be to the Dayspring of Divine wisdom, the Dawning Point of Revelation (Muhammad), and to the holy line of His descendants, since, by the widespread rays of His consummate wisdom, His universal knowledge, these savage denizens of Yathrib (Medina) and Batha (Mecca), miraculously, and in so brief a time were drawn out of the depth of their ignorance, rose up to the pinnacles of learning, and became centres of arts and sciences and human perfections, and stars of felicity and true civilization, shining across the horizons of the world."[137]*

The need now is not only to replicate that golden achievement, but to take it further. In the same reference, Abdu'l Baha says : *"We must now highly resolve to arise and lay hold of these instrumentalities that promote the peace and well-being and happiness, the knowledge, the dignity, value and station, of the entire race. Thus, through the restoring waters of pure intention and unselfish effort, the earth of human potentialities will blossom with its own latent excellence and flower into praiseworthy qualities... Then will this become in every sense the focal centre of human perfections, reflecting as if in a mirror the full panoply of world civilisation..."*

To break down this overwhelmingly beautiful picture into the smaller, albeit vital, morsels of individual behaviour, it is necessary to consider but a few of the most important qualities that adorn human behaviour in every day life: The first is ***"Trustworthiness"***. Baha'u'llah says in the fourth "Taraz" (*ornament*)[138], *"The fourth Taraz concerneth trustworthiness. Verily it is the door of security for all that dwell on earth and a token of glory on the part of the All-Merciful. He who partaketh thereof hath indeed partaken of the treasures of wealth and prosperity. Trustworthiness is the greatest portal leading unto tranquillity and security of the people. In truth the stability of every affair hath depended and doth depend upon it. All the domains of power, of grandeur and of wealth are illuminated by its light..."*

It is no exaggeration therefore to consider this one quality as paramount in lifting the burden of cheat, robbery, embezzlement, and every other feature of impropriety that is so prevalent in the world to-day. It is now a serious matter. Not only on an individual basis is this principle becoming so vital. It is indeed on the collective basis where people in privileged position can singly or collectively sap the resources of society. Law alone may be a deterrent, but it is never an absolute guardian. And it is the ordinary people or the underprivileged, going about their life and livelihood, who at the end are the sufferers, although they may be in their turn untrustworthy and dishonest in a more petty way.

We can deduce from the above other qualities that will strengthen this vital attribute of trustworthiness, such as truthfulness, integrity and fairness in people's dealings. These are collective societal behavioural patterns that will only become the norm when the generality of society accept it collectively as the ethos under which it operates. In spite of this, there may still be unwelcome space for some incidences of violation, but such events can be dealt with through the collective abhorrence and shunning, perhaps shaming, of the individual/s concerned, to the extent that eventually these acts will become so rare as to be insignificant,. The Baha'i Faith has in its teachings some mechanisms that would, when implemented, bring about this sea change in Human conduct. But in the context of economics, the loss and squander as a result of dishonesty and untrustworthiness are so great as to be almost unquantifiable.

Human conduct

In earlier sections of this work, the affairs of the world, especially in the early Christian and medieval times, and also in the Greek society of Socrates, Plato and Aristotle, were conducted on the basis that the (ordinary) individuals should not look at worldly or material matters. They were told that these aspects of human life are best left to the ruling elite, the Church establishments, or the landed gentry class of the feudal society, the so called "Squirearchy". The ordinary person's reward is in "heaven".

In economic and socio-economic terms, this is now not enough. Opportunity and assistance must of necessity be available to every member of society, as only in this way can the maximum potential of society as a whole be attained. The days of internecine strife between the possessed and the dispossessed, have regrettably not ended yet. But there is no doubt that this is deeply frowned upon, and no longer tolerated in respectable societies or countries. Baha'u'llah in the first Taraz[139] says: *"The first Taraz and the first effulgence which hath dawned from the horizon of the Mother Book is that man should know his own self and recognize that which leadeth unto loftiness or lowliness, glory or abasement, wealth or poverty. Having attained the stage of fulfilment and reached his maturity, man standeth in need of wealth.."* This is a strong statement which puts the whole matter of human endeavour and aspiration on a footing equal to, and dependent on, the maturity, self recognition, and the use of the correct "balances". Baha'u'llah then indicates some practical aspects to this ideal: " ..such wealth as he acquires through crafts and professions is commendable and praiseworthy in the estimation of men of wisdom, and especially in the eyes of servants..." *and here there is parallel requisite that goes hand in hand with this attitude of the individual: that of the "servants who dedicate themselves to the education of the world and to the edification of the peoples. They are, in truth, the cup-bearers of the life-giving waters of knowledge and guides unto the ideal world..."* [140]. This, therefore is the balance, whereupon it is the duty of every individual to strive and use his/her talent, at the same time as there are the educationalists and other servants whose duty is to assist each with his/her endeavour. The whole society, in this image, is working in harmony and the effort is directed to the betterment of everyone.

In this society the talk is of fairness. In the fifth Taraz Baha'u'llah says:[141] *"The fifth Taraz concerneth the protection and preservation of the station of God's servants...The people of Baha should not deny any soul the reward due to him, and treat craftsmen with deference...In this Day the sun of craftsmanship shineth above the horizon of the occident and the river of arts is flowing out of the sea of that region. One must speak with fairness and appreciate such bounty..."*

To this is added the importance of acquiring knowledge, and the bounty of the flourishing availability of sources of knowledge. Thus:[142] *"The sixth Taraz: Knowledge is one of the wondrous gifts of God. It is incumbent upon everyone to acquire it.* Baha'u'llah made this statement more than a century and a half ago in Persia, one of the darkest societies at the time. He goes on to state: *"In this day the secrets of the earth are laid bare before the eyes of men. The pages of swiftly appearing newspapers are indeed the mirror of the world...This is an amazing and potent phenomenon. However, it behoveth the writers thereof to be purged from the promptings of evil passions and desires and to be attired with the raiment of justice and equity..."* In this way knowledge, arts, crafts and professions all combine to create for the individual the best environment to exercise his/her choice, best effort, and best use of the opportunities, not only to better themselves, but also to contribute to the general well being and prosperity of society in the spirit of justice and equity.

This leads very well to one of the central themes in religion. In the earlier sections the importance of work has been emphasized in Islam, Christianity and Judaism. In the Baha'i Faith, work has been elevated yet further. In the Holy Book, the **Kitab-i-Aqdas** Baha'u'llah states[143]: *"O people of Baha! It is incumbent upon each one of you to engage in some occupation-such as a craft, a trade or the like. We have exalted your engagement in such work to the rank of worship of the one true God... Waste not your hours in idleness and sloth, but occupy yourself with what will profit you and others...The most despised of men in the sight of God are they who sit and beg."* He follows this with the promise:*"Hold ye fast unto the cord of means and place your trust in God, the provider of all means."* Work is necessary even in wealth: *"..The inheritance of wealth cannot make anyone immune from daily work"*[144].

It is interesting that Baha'u'llah asks the people to engage in some "occupation" such as a craft, a trade or the like. Occupation is defined in the dictionary among other meanings as "the state of being employed or occupied" as well as "one's habitual employment, profession, craft or trade".(Chamber's 20th Century Dictionary).It is reasonably therefore to consider Baha'u'llah's Teaching as an indication that taking up an art, craft or trade, is advisable both as a means of earning and livelihood as well as a hobby, a past-time, or a "fall-back" capability or talent that would serve one to earn at least some money and be occupied should that person be out of (regular) work for one reason or another. Moreover, because arts or crafts represent the "creative" aspect of human beings, acquiring any such ability or honing and sharpening an existing talent, is an important factor in the continuing development of society at every level, and all the time, without necessarily the need for an establishment to work within. This is a very personal admonition and advice.

Having established the salient elements relating to the individual in the context of an economic study: essentially the purity and excellence of conduct, and the personal obligation to work, occupy one's time, and aim not only to benefit one's self, but also others, the next level for discussion will, necessarily, be that of society in general, and how these personal elements relate to the proper and fruitful development of the economic system. It will be obvious that by this means, development will start at the grass roots, and work its way from the bottom upwards, and all the way to a world economic system. In this manner, the system, while taking shape, will rely on the wholehearted acceptance and understanding at every level of society. Even where the technicalities may not be understood and appreciated by some people, nevertheless everyone will feel, or be made distinctly aware, that he or she is an integral part of a system that is all embracing and aiming at universal rather than individual gain at the expense of others. Factional, sectarian, narrow nationalistic, or worse of all selfish, attitudes would, to a large extent be reduced to an insignificant extent, not through deterrence, but by consensus.

The Community

In a new "world order", it is important to think of the "Community" not in terms of a diffuse amorphous structure, but rather a live and vibrant organism in which people acquire a sense of belonging to, and ownership of, its affairs. There are at present so many systems around the world that attempt to divide society into practical unitary sizes, usually for administrative reasons. These are the so-called "local" authorities. They are endowed with local budgets and deal with amenities, local services and civic affairs. In most "democratic" systems where voting is the norm, the representatives elected to these local authorities more commonly present themselves along party political affiliations. This is not by all means universal even within one country or locality. But even when not affiliated to a political party, there is quite a lot of "politicking" in the manner that affairs are conducted within the individual unitary administration. One will have to be charitable and not assume that such "politicking" will end up in "horse-trading" of benefits and privileges for certain factions. Whether this represents true democracy in the sense that the individual, no matter how unassuming, has the unhindered access to the mechanism of expression of his/her true feeling and desire, and whether the system is dynamic enough to allow the best and most suitable persons to represent the community, and in turn allow the easing out of unsuitable representatives in a respectful and non embarrassing manner, this must be the real touchstone of the validity of any system.

The context for the above introductory paragraph is the manner in which the economic principles in the Baha'i Faith interact with the administrative system. The latter will be seen as addressing the spiritual and administrative needs of the community represented, but within this lies essentially the economic well-being and health of that community. The individual, the administration, and the economic principles working together under the holistic umbrella of the spiritual qualities expected (and delivered) from all people, will in the fullness of time inevitably create that environment of mutuality in all of the highest qualities of endeavour and practice.

The Baha'i Administrative order is based on at least three levels of elected bodies. Named the *"Houses of Justice"* in the original texts, two tiers are at present called *"Spiritual Assemblies",* each with nine members elected annually through universal franchise of all adult members of the Baha'i community with no partisanship, no electioneering, and no canvassing. Together with secret ballots, the system is probably the best one available that will ensure that only the most suitable persons (men or women) will be elected. The system is based on merit (spirituality and capability) rather than any other consideration. For the immediate concern of the economics within the community, the body concerned will be the *"local"* spiritual Assembly. At present, in the UK this is based on the local borough configuration. This, however, is the most convenient at present, but it may change in future, and naturally, the configuration can be different in different countries, depending on the existing unitary boundaries as determined in each country.

Local (Community) Economics In The Baha'i Faith

The economic principles in the Baha'i Faith are in some respects very exciting and far reaching, and in other respects in need of further development in the light of the evolution of the needs of society and the thoughts of eminent economists, Baha'is or non-Baha'is.

An important underlying principle, however, within the overall Baha'i teachings is the one announced by Abdu'l Bahá[145]: *"It seems as though all creatures can exist singly and alone. For example, a tree can exist solitary and alone...an animal upon a mountain or a bird soaring in the air might live a solitary life. They are not in need of cooperation and solidarity...On the contrary, man cannot live singly and alone...He is need of continuous cooperation and mutual help...He can never singly or alone, provide himself with all the necessities of existence. Therefore, he is in need of cooperation and reciprocity.*

"The mystery of this phenomenon, the cause thereof is this, that mankind has been created from one single origin, has branched off from one family. thus in reality all mankind represents one family...that thus this family might live in perfect happiness and well being.

"Regarding reciprocity and cooperation, each member of the body politic should live in the utmost comfort and welfare because each individual member of humanity is a member of the body politic and if one member of the of the members be in distress or be afflicted with some disease all the other members must necessarily suffer. For example, a member of the human organism is the eye. If the eye is affected that affliction would affect the whole nervous system... hence God has desired that in the body politic of humanity each member shall enjoy perfect welfare and comfort..." The human race may not have accepted or taken to heart this simple, yet very effective, concept. The Islamic Scholar Ibn Khaldun has, as mentioned in previous chapters, shown that humans differ from animals in that they can combine abilities of different animals in a way that can enable them to overcome the massive superiority of certain individual abilities in these animals. It was also noted previously that people have different abilities and no one person can combine all the talents that

he/she or society needs. So while differentiation and specialization had been accepted along the ages, it is for the first time that this is described ***not*** so much in terms of the ***differences***, but in term of the ***interdependence*** and, at an even higher level of human ideal, that the welfare and well-being of the part is essential to the welfare and well-being of the whole. The example of the effect of affliction of one organ, the eye, is apt enough to demonstrate the almost total interconnection of that organ with the rest of the body. Taking this concept to within the economic sphere, Abdu'l Baha goes on further to state in the same reference: *"Although the body politic is one family yet because of lack of harmonious relations some members are comfortable and some are hungry, some members are clothed in most costly garments and some families are in need of food and shelter. Why? Because this family lacks the necessary **reciprocity and symmetry** (author's conversion to bold)...Is it possible for one member of a family to be subjected to the utmost misery and to abject poverty and for the rest of the family to be comfortable? It is impossible unless those members of the family be senseless, atrophied, inhospitable, unkind...His holiness Baha'u'llah has given instructions regarding every one of the questions confronting humanity...Among them are (the teachings) concerning the question of economics that all members of the body politic may enjoy through the working out of the solution the greatest happiness, welfare and comfort without any harm or injury attacking the general order of things."* This last statement is well worth dwelling upon. The world has seen so many upheavals, some quite serious destruction, in the name of economics and the welfare of society. It is apparent to any student of history, and it has been shown in earlier chapters, that many wars were waged in the interest of some country or some faction of society to the detriment of others. While ostensive pretexts may have been given for a particular war or struggle, the ultimate aim has almost inevitably been the gain expected from such strife. Revolutions, the

Bolshevik to give but one example, has had at its core the upturning of the economic (and naturally the political) structure of the vast territories that subsequently became the Soviet Union. Ironically, it almost did not take a shot fired in anger for the system to eventually dismantle. The devastating two world wars that gutted the continent of Europe, and spilled over into other continents, were both essentially for economic reasons, and for hegemony. It is also not difficult to imagine that the Falkland war and most certainly the Gulf war, while outwardly appearing as the product of political and principled reason, are, in fact, inwardly and most essentially tied so neatly with the economics of the region as the ultimate purpose.

However, the purpose of this section concerns the community in a rather local sense. The above digression will hopefully be forgiven, but in the context of the need to take fully to heart the principle that the good of the whole is dependent on the well-being of all the parts, any local community must look at the ways and means for ensuring that these thoughts are implemented and not just accepted as pious hopes. No economic system is capable of ensuring this without the wholehearted acceptance and collaboration of the individual. A spiritual order as mentioned above is also required as a guarantor and as a means of overcoming difficulties and failings that are the hallmarks of human "fallibility". The Baha'i economic system, therefore, has in the same way to be accepted, as mentioned above, as an evolving system. Shoghi Effendi[146] states that: *"The economic teachings of the Cause, though well known in their main outline, have not yet been sufficiently elaborated and systematized to allow anyone to make an exact and thorough application of them on a restricted scale...The writings are not rich on the subject and many issues at present baffling the minds of the world are not even mentioned. The primary consideration is the spirit that has to permeate our economic life, and this will gradually crystallize itself into definite institutions and principles that will help to bring about the ideal condition foretold by Baha'u'llah.....No, Baha'u'llah did not bring a complete system of economics to the world...There are practically no technical teachings on economics in the Cause...The contributions of the Faith to this subject is essentially indirect, as it consists of the application of spiritual principles to our present-day economic system...Social inequality is the inevitable outcome of the natural inequality of man. Human beings are different in ability and should, therefore, be different in their social and economic standing. Extremes of wealth and poverty should, however, be abolished..."*

The above quotations are extracts from the texts, and the extracts chosen here are intended to demonstrate two essential facts: **1-** that the Baha'i Faith recognizes the complexity of the subject of economics, especially in the context of the rapidly evolving society and world needs, and **2-** that the Faith considers economics and its systems as necessarily falling within the spiritual framework, and that its aim is to ensure equity and the avoidance of extremes of wealth and poverty.

Other quotes, however, will eventually be mentioned to show that there are indeed many principles that are to act as guidance for the world to consider when the experts engage in the continuing process of evolving world economics. It will be seen that these principles, though distinctly avant-garde and prophetic in their time, are currently accepted as being essential to the economic and socio-economic well being for the state of the world, and indeed some are being implemented gradually but noticeably.

This matter is re-enforced by the guidance given that Baha'is, individually and collectively, should take an interest in economics as part of their continuing effort to acquaint themselves with important subjects intimately related to the principles of the Faith and its overall thrust. In a letter dated 13 March 1944 to an individual believer, the Guardian advises: "*...concerning what studies you should specialize in* *with a view to teaching in the future: He would suggest either History, Economics or Sociology, as these are not only fields in which Baha'is take a great interest but also cover subjects which our teachings cast an entire new light upon...*" and in a statement in[147] : "*The Guardian has always advised young people to study deeply such subjects as History, Economics and Sociology as they are all related to the teachings and aid in understanding the Faith*", and indeed in the same reference, page 636, the importance of economics among other similarly useful subjects is described: "*When deciding what course of training to follow, youth can consider acquiring skills and professions that will be of benefit in education, rural development, agriculture, economics, technology, health, radio and in many areas of endeavour that are so urgently needed in the developing countries of the world*". This statement is significant in many ways. For a start it is not a comprehensive list of subjects and it can never really be intended as such. But it indicates how necessary it is for youth to consider, when deciding on their careers, those subjects that will be useful to other people especially in the developing world, where the need is greatest. Moreover, and quite importantly, the passage does not limit the need for such interests only in relation to acquiring professions. Individuals can take interest in any of the subjects mentioned, even only as "skills". Thus, whatever may be the individual's job, profession, or pursuit for livelihood, there is also a need to take an interest in one or more of the kind of subjects mentioned. The benefit of this to the individual must be that it adds a dimension to one's outlook to life, and also adds ability to serve humanity with a wider understanding of such matters of importance. Once again, it becomes apparent that the onus is on the individual to assume as full a responsibility and awareness of the world around him/her, as possible, and to do his/her part, however small, towards the betterment of any section of society, and responding to those needs that the person can be help with..

sentences earlier indicates the value of *"knowledge of such sciences ... as can profit the peoples of the earth.."* This then is the general theme: that the individual is enjoined to a participative role in society, and in the process create in himself/herself a sense of esteem and worth.

We have seen above that Baha'u'llah teaches the need to engage in some form of occupation, raising that to the status of worship, and to *"waste not your time in idleness and sloth"*[148]. The two concepts here combine so beautifully to ingrain in each member of society that combination of duty whereby the individual will "take ownership" of his or her destiny and in the process acquire the happiness and self realization. A very interesting expression of this notion is found in the third encyclical (formal policy setting letter to the Roman Catholic Church) issued by Pope John Paul II late September 1981. The document was titled *Laborem Exercens (translated as "On Working")*. He quotes the book of *Genesis* and cites God's command to man to *"subdue the earth"* and interprets this to mean that "work" is "for man" and never "man" "for work". An interpretation of this can probably be that work has been created as a gift for humanity, to be enjoyed, cherished and not shied away from or denied to oneself. How often does one hear the elderly or sick bemoaning their inability to do what they were capable of in previous times. The author has extensive experience dealing medically with physically disabled people. How many or most of them wished their condition allowed them a "normal" life with work, travel, hobbies and other occupational activities. Indeed, an important part of the programme of restoration or rehabilitation is to allow them whatever is possible in terms of engagement and occupation even if it were totally non-remunerative.

The person in poverty therefore, should first look at himself, and take courage and guidance from the teachings mentioned, consider work, in any capacity, as an act of worship, a means of self-fulfilment and maintaining one's dignity and self esteem, and lastly to consider the "gift" of work for self-realization and the benefit of others as well as one's self and his or her dependants. As a principle, this is quite momentous, as it upturns the time honoured concept initially introduced by the Greek Philosophers, that work is in essence "toil", and "burdensome", and should therefore be considered a chore. So the upturn now is for every effort to be made to gain training or education where this is required, and to look at avenues of work, whether self employment in whatever capacity or regular paid employment if that is preferred and available. One must never allow himself to be seen as inept or unwilling as these are self destructive attitudes and liable to create a vicious circuit leading to further loss and failure.

So what if the person is not sloth, incapable or inept? This person needs help, and most probably deserves help. The Baha'i teachings offer several sources for help: Firstly: The person must rise in his/her spiritual qualities, drawing on the strength gained from these two superbly comforting and protective qualities: Prayers and patience: Thus, in Lawh-i-Hikmat (Tablet of Wisdom), Baha'u'llah enjoins us to *"Be generous in your days of plenty, and be patient in the hour of loss. Adversity is followed by success and rejoicings follow woe. Guard against idleness and sloth, and cling unto that which profiteth mankind, whether young or old, whether high or low""*[149] In the Hidden Words (Arabic), Baha'u'llah again says[150]: *"O SON OF BEING! If poverty overtake thee, be not sad, for in time the Lord of wealth shall visit thee..."* It is acknowledged that these Teachings, and indeed others with a similar or related message, are given within a spiritual as well as a material dimension. But it is what the affected person holds on to. It is the "internal mechanism" of self preservation, essentially to desist from misdemeanours or activities of an unlawful nature, detrimental to oneself and possibly to others.. There is no excuse in the Baha'i Faith or indeed in any other religion, for a person to resort to theft, violence, dissension, destructive rebellion or usurpation in order to overcome poverty or need. Naturally, this "internal" mechanism has to be bolstered by more practical and tangible help. This is where the balancing side of this "social" equation comes into play: that the "community" as represented by the locality administrative body mentioned above (the Spiritual Assembly or House of Justice) activates whatever means or mechanisms that have been established for this purpose, so as to look at the best method or service this person requires. Again, this may be education, training, or, if actual lack of ability is identified, financial help. Rich people within this new order have a role to play, and this will be discussed in the next section.

In summary, therefore, this section deals with the individual who finds himself/herself in poverty or need, who sets out first and foremost to look at himself/herself, take courage and strength from the Holy Writings, consider every possible means of righting his/her situation, desisting from hand-outs (State, Communal or begging), take comfort from the attitude of patience and fortitude in adversity, and, when all this is insufficient, feel entirely free and dignified to approach the "community" administrative body for assistance.

The Economics Of Wealth

This section will have three main messages as gleaned from the Baha'i Teachings:

1- That wealth is not only acceptable, but even desirable. Baha'u'llah as previously mentioned states[151]:.. *"Having attained the stage of fulfilment and reached his maturity, man standeth in need of wealth, and such wealth as he acquireth through crafts or professions is commendable and praiseworthy in the estimation of men of wisdom..."*

2- That wealth carries with it a spiritual and a social responsibility. On the spiritual level, Baha'u'llah in the first *"Ishraq"*[152] states: *"They that are possessed of wealth and invested with authority and power must show the profoundest regard for religion".* On the social and humanitarian level, Bah'u'llah states in the Lawh-i-Hikmat[153]: *"..Man's merit lieth in service and virtue, and not in the pageantry of wealth and riches"*

3- That the poor are God's trust to the rich: Baha'u'llah in his *"Proclamation to the Kings"*[154] states: *"Know ye that the poor are the trust of God in your midst".*

So once again, it is the individual, this time the rich one, who carries the responsibility for his/her deeds. When Baha'u'llah also tells the world:[155] *"Dissipate not the wealth of your precious lives in the pursuit of evil and corrupt affection, nor let your endeavours be spent in promoting your personal interest"*... and when He, as mentioned above enjoins the people to be *"generous in your days of plenty"* (Same reference), there appears the initial framework within which the rich will feel that bounty is to be re-cycled rather than amassed. To be enjoyed, but not squandered or abused. The effects of these values in the overall state of economics will be discussed further, but this is the section dealing with the individual. So even before the rich individual would consider obeying the ordinances and bye-laws in the Baha'i Faith, he or she will consider the immediate social and communitarian responsibilities which wealth has placed upon his or her shoulders.

The Principle Of Voluntary Submission To God's Commandments

Before proceeding further, it is important to state this principle and cardinal spiritual requirement expected from each and every individual believer and devout adherent to the Baha'i Faith: This voluntary submission and acceptance is the one cause of happiness and prosperity. In the third *"Ishraq"*[156] Baha'u'llah states: *"It is incumbent upon everyone to observe God's holy commandments, inasmuch as they are the wellspring of life unto the world"*. In the Arabic Hidden Words No. 39 He again states:*" O SON OF MAN! Neglect not My commandments if thou lovest My beauty, and forget not My counsel if thou wouldst attain my good pleasure"*. In the "The Kitab-i-Aqdas*"*[157] the two statements complement each other:*".Know assuredly that My commandments are the lamps of My loving providence among My servants, and the keys of My mercy for My creatures.."* and:*"He who has drunk the choice wine of fairness from the hands of My bountiful favour will circle around My commandments that shine above the Dayspring of My creation. Think not that we have revealed unto you a mere code of laws. Nay, rather, we have unsealed the choice Wine with the fingers of might and power"*. And finally, the crowning statement from Baha'u'llah in this context is that in the *"The Kitab-i-Aqdas"* (p.20,Ln30): *"Observe My commandments for the love of My beauty"*. The choice of these statements is in no way exhaustive, and many similar quotes can be added.

It is in this spirit that the rich person needs to conduct his/her affairs, with full appreciation of the personal commitment to obeying the laws laid down on the very simple yet so weighty an acceptance that one should discharge his/her duty, whether it is financial or otherwise without external imposition or the necessity to await any enforcement. Laws concerning such matters as "tax", tithes, and inheritance will be mentioned later. But the message in this section is twofold: **1-** That the

Baha'i Faith abhors the *amassing* of wealth, and even more so the use of wealth as a means of power and corruption. **2-** That the emphasis is on the *voluntary* rather than *compulsory* discharge of one's duties and obligations.

Finally, the individual has to demonstrate *care* and *.compassion* towards his fellow humans. Baha'u'llah's call:[158] *"O ye rich ones on earth! If ye encounter one who is poor, treat him not disdainfully..."* and :*"O rich ones of the earth! flee not from the face of the poor that lieth in the dust, nay rather befriend him and suffer him to recount the tale of the woes with which God's inscrutable Decree hath caused him to be afflicted. By the righteousness of God! Whilst ye consort with him, the concourse on high will be looking upon you, will be interceding for you, will be extolling your names and glorifying your action"*[159]. There are so many quotes regarding compassion, but one that encapsulates so much in so few words is in the Tablets of Baha'u'llah Pg 73, Ln 2: *"..Under all conditions, whether in adversity or at ease, whether honoured or afflicted, this Wronged One hath directed all men to show forth love, affection, compassion and harmony"*. In the context of economics, this intellectual as well as spiritual quality is just so necessary in dealings between people, and it has such a powerful element of pull away from deranged sentiments or selfish conduct when money or material possession is in the heart of that dealing.

It is easy to see these principles as echoing similar Teachings of other Revealed Faiths. In the Bahá'í Teachings, however, they find an application in individual behaviour within the overall sphere of personal finance and behaviour. It comes through very strongly in the words of Bahá'u'lláh. The difficulty is that this attitude can be the most difficult to adopt, but observing it must count as one of the real touchstones of the individual's faith and submission.

The world is so full of very rich people, individuals, who through cleverness, hard work or talent, have enormous wealth. Many show such courage and sacrifice as to be incredible. At the time or writing this, the news provided a magnificent example: the owner of the "Domino Pizza" chain, who started his business from very humble beginnings, built it up to a world-wide chain worth to him alone more that $600M, and then found himself urged to sell out and donate all the proceeds to the Roman Catholic Church's humanitarian and charity agencies. This is, admittedly, an extreme example. But certainly not unique. Other rich people have decided to donate greater wealth to charity, sometimes leaving a tiny but adequate fraction to their children. Lesser, much lesser, deeds of this nature will also be praiseworthy. Indeed, it is the little deeds exhibited by the many, of meagre or more substantial means, which should, through the spirit of the teachings mentioned above, add up, create a groundswell of "love and compassion" arising from grass-roots, and finally delivering the "universal" new ethos whereby the rich do not allow themselves to amass and become too swollen with their wealth, and the poor do not allow themselves to loose their dignity by relying on begging or hand-outs, do not allow themselves to reach abject states of poverty, but, when their efforts fail, or their capabilities are wanting, graciously and with dignity accept the assistance that will be triggered off by the "system" to which the rich have contributed. This is the basis of the "new" society, upon which the structure of the laws and ordinances related to economics in the Baha'i teachings will be discussed in the next sections which will consider the community, wider national, and finally the international scene.

PART VIII

A SPIRITUALLY BASED SYSTEM OF ECONOMIC PRINCIPLES AND STRUCTURE

The Community

The Village:

In studying the social and administrative teaching of the Baha'i Faith, one is struck by the emphasis on the village on the one hand, and the global picture on the other hand. This emphasis on the "village" will become apparent in the references to be mentioned soon. But first, there is a need to try and define the meaning of the "village" in relation to the Baha'i teachings. There is no doubt that the world has seen an inexorable shift of population in most parts from the rural settings to the town and city conurbations, from the countryside to the "metropolises". The reasons are many, but economics is an important one. Developments, services (State or otherwise) especially education and health, trade and other economic activities, and therefore livelihoods, have mushroomed in town and city, especially capital cities. Resources and investments have been siphoned out, all to the detriment of the countryside and its rural populations. The more such developments take place the more people migrate to the large conurbation seeking work, refuge with family, previous fellow countryside acquaintances, or because of sheer exasperation from the loss of opportunity and quality of life in the smaller settings. This process appears, regrettably to be faster in the underdeveloped countries, but it is a world-wide phenomenon.

Looking at the word "village" from the perspective of the Qur'an, one finds it used over fifty times in different contexts, all not really meaning a village as is nowadays recognised. Indeed, every time the word "village" is translated by J.M. Rodwell, the English word used is city or cities. Thus, to give but a few examples: the Sura *"Ornaments of Gold"* vs,3 :.."*And they said, Had but this Koran been sent down to some great one of the two cities.."* (in Arabic, two villages). The Sura *"Houd"*, vs. 100:.."*such histories of the cities that we relate to thee.."* The Sura *"Al Araf"*:vs. 4:"*How many cities have we destroyed..*", and vs. 96:"*But if that the people of these cities had believed and feared..*". And another example corroborated with the Old Testament:Sura *"Jonah, Peace be unto Him"*: vs.98:"..*Were it otherwise, any city, had it believed, might have found its safety in its faith. But it was so only with the people of JONAS.*" It is, of course known, that the city of Jonah was *"Nineveh"*, described in Chapter 3, vs.3 of the Book of Jonah as *"..an exceeding great city"*. In all these quotes in the Qur'an, the word used is *"Qariah"*, which translated literally would be *"village"*.

However, In the Baha'i Writings the differentiation between *"village"*, *"town"* and *"city"* is made in many texts: Thus, Abdu'l Baha in *"Memorials of the Faithful"*, Pg. 80 says of Jinab-i-Husayn:..*"In every town and village along the way, he ably spread the Faith..."*And in the Tablets of the Divine Plan He Says[160]: *"..In every city and village they must occupy themselves with the diffusion of the divine exhortations and advices.."* And as a confirmatory note the following quote from Baha'u'llah states: *"In future, Baha'i Houses of Worship will be constructed in every town and village"*[161].

When, therefore, Abdu'l Baha speaks of the *"village"* in the context of the economic principles, one is justified to understand it as meaning a town or a city. But it would most probably be more in keeping with the spirit of the Baha'i teachings to understand it as indicating **the smallest viable unit of population**. It may therefore relate to a rural *"village"* or, in terms of the administrative population structure of, say, the United Kingdom, a ward, which is the smallest unit within a *"borough"*. In this way the whole structure, as will be seen later, upon which the "community" aspect of economics will be based is one which can be recognised so easily by the population concerned, and not in any way remote or impersonal. While this may not be practical at this stage, it will most probably become so as the numbers of Bahá'ís increase, and the system become accepted and implemented. It is important to state, however, that any evolution of the administrative, and by implication such activities and responsibilities as economics, will be in accordance with the guidance of the Universal House of Justice, and the thoughts presented here may be partially speculative.

Now the economic activity of the "Community" in the Baha'i Faith, as has been mentioned previously, is based on the Baha'i administrative structure. This in turn starts with the "Local House of Justice" or, as it is at present called: The Local Spiritual Assembly". The starting point of the economic activity is laid on by Abdu'l Baha thus: "..*In every village there must be established a general storehouse which will have a number of revenues*"[162]. In the same reference Pg 40, He says: *Certain trustees will be elected by the people in a given village to look after these transactions*". It will be assumed at this stage that these "trustees" are the members of the local house of justice (or local spiritual assembly) and so as not to keep repeating this statement, let it be assumed that the meanings are interchangeable and are indeed the same. To discuss this further, one has to note a fuller text of Abdu'l Baha's Teachings on this subject, and this is found in the same reference:

The Storehouse:

Abdu'l Baha's pre-amble (same reference) to the subject introduces the humanitarian and practical angles: *"...(The teachings) concerning the question of economics that all members of the body politic may enjoy through the working out of this solution the greatest happiness, welfare and comfort without any harm or injury attacking the general order of things. Thereby no difference or dissension will occur, no contention will take place. This solution is this:*

"First and foremost is the principle that to all the members of the body politic shall be given the greatest achievements of the world of humanity. Each one shall have the utmost welfare and well being. To solve this problem we must begin with the farmer; there will we lay the foundation for system and order because the peasant class and the agricultural class exceeds other classes in the importance of their service. In every village there must be established a general storehouse which will have a number of revenues.

"*The first revenue will be that of the tenths or tithes.*

"*The second revenue (will be derived) from the animals.*

"*The third revenue, , from the minerals, is to say, every mine prospected or discovered, a third thereof will go to this vast storehouse.*

"The fourth is this: whosoever dies without leaving any heirs all his heritage will go to the general storehouse.

"Fifth, if any treasures shall be found on the land they should be devoted to this storehouse.

All these revenues will be assembled in this storehouse

This list is probably not meant to be comprehensive. As will be seen later, there are more details regarding personal (voluntary) contributions, other obligatory (in the religious sense) payments, and the multitudinous sources of business and corporate economic activities, earnings and profits.

Moreover, it is not clear from the above text how the "village" storehouse will relate to such sources of wealth as mining, and treasures. These more often than not cut across boundaries and may involve large swathes of land. Other sources can be very local indeed, such as the example of the intestate death. These are the sort of detail in application that will have to worked out by the experts as mentioned previously, whereby, according to the Universal house of justice (in a letter to a National spiritual assembly dated May 7, 1974:".. *The application... is left to develop in the same way that economics is left to economists*", and in *"The Lights of Guidance"* vol. 2, Pg. 77-78:*" We have the basic principles... The Bahá'í system... has yet to grow and mature"*.

Abdu'l Baha continues in the above discussion giving some details in relation to one faction of society which he regards as most important. In a Tablet addressed to an individual believer in October 4, 1912 (translation corrected in the World Baha'i Centre in December 1985), He states: *"The question of economics must commence with the farmer and then extended to the other classes inasmuch as the number of farmers is greater than all the other classes, many times greater. Therefore it is fitting that the economic problem be first solved with the farmer, for the farmer is the first active agent in the body politic. In brief, from the wise men in every village a board should be organized and the affairs of that village should be under the control of the board...A General Warehouse Will Be Founded which Will Have seven Revenues "...Likewise a general storehouse should be founded with the appointment of a secretary. At the time of the harvest, with the approval of the members of that board, a determined percentage of the entire harvest should be appropriated for the storehouse.*

"*The storehouse will have seven revenues: Tithes, taxes on animals, wealth without inheritors, all things found whose owners cannot be discovered, a third of all treasures (money) found in the earth, a third of the mines, and voluntary contributions*" So here more detail is found, with seven instead of five sources of revenue, and the farmer class is given its due consideration as the major and core active agency in society. There will be further detail later, again exemplified by the farmer class.

But in the same reference (Lights of Guidance) the expenditures the board will deal with are laid out: "*On the other hand, there are seven expenditures:*

1- *General running expenses of the institution-salaries etc., and the administration of public safety, including the department of hygiene.* (author's note: In Arabic, and probably also in Persian, the same word is used for hygiene or health. So this can read as the "department of health".)

2- *Tithes to the general government (State)*

3- *Taxes on animals for the State.*

4- *Support of an orphanage.*

5- *Support of cripples and the incurables.*

6- *Support of educational institutions.*

7- *Supplying any deficiency for the expenses of the poor.*

It would appear, therefore, from this outline, that the function of this (locality) economic activity takes into its remit the essential services required within the (locality) community. But there is a line extended to the "State" or "Central" administration/government which has its own requirements for revenue in order to perform its more widespread functions, and presumably the bigger services, or the long term (strategic) services that can only be economical or even possible when undertaken on a larger scale. Abdu'l Baha also talks of "support" and supplying any "deficiency". He does not specifically say "to provide" these services. How intentional this is, it is not clear. But the implication here probably is to re-enforce the concept of self reliance of the individual and/or the institution. Again, whether this means that, for example, educational institutions are to be run essentially on a fee paying basis, privately or otherwise, is not clear. But the whole thrust of this Guidance is that the storehouse and the board do not appear to be responsible for the detailed services on a day to day basis, as is the case in most countries at present where a State or Local Authority directly run services. It may be that in some parts of the world or in some part of a country there will be a need for directly run services, while in other, perhaps more affluent or more mature parts of the world or a country, such services can be provided on a fee paying basis. No matter which system is adopted, there is no doubt that the spirit of this Guidance is that the board has the responsibility of seeing to it that such services are provided one way or another, are adequate, and that should a shortfall appear, the board has the responsibility of redressing the imbalance in whichever manner or method it sees fit, and according to the prevailing circumstances.

Abdu'l Baha then introduces another principle: That of an equitable income/expenditure/tax or tithe policy. He explains this principles again using the farmer as an example: [163] "*As to the first, the tenths or tithes: we will consider a farmer, one of the peasants. We will look at his income. We will find out, for instance, what is his annual revenue and also what are his expenditures. Now, if his income is equal to his expenditures, from such a farmer nothing whatever will be taken. That is, he will not be subjected to taxation of any sort, needing as he does all his income. Another farmer may have expenses running up to one thousand dollars we will say., and his income is two thousand dollars. From such an one* a tenth will be required, because he has a surplus. But if his income be ten thousand dollars and his expenses one thousand dollars or his income is twenty thousand dollars, he will have to pay as taxes, one fourth. If his income be one hundred thousand dollars and his expenses five thousand, one third will he have to pay because he has still a surplus since…if he pays, say, thirty five thousand dollars, in addition to the expenditure of five thousand dollars he still has sixty thousand left. But if his expenses be ten thousand and his income two hundred thousand then he must give even half because ninety thousand will be in that case remaining. Such a scale as this will determine allotment of taxes. All the income from such a revenue will go to the general storehouse."

"Then there must be considered such emergencies as follows: a certain farmer whose expenses run up to ten thousand dollars and whose income is only five thousand dollars, he will receive necessary expenses from the storehouse. Five thousand will be allotted to him so that he will not be in need."

"Then the orphans will be looked after, all of whose expenses will be taken care of. The cripples in the village-all their expenses will be looked after. The poor in the village-their necessary expenses will be defrayed. And other members who for valid reasons are incapacitated-the blind, the old, the deaf-their comfort must be looked after. In the village no one will remain in need or in want. All will live in the utmost comfort and welfare. Yet no schism will assail the general order of the body politic."

"Hence the expenses or expenditure of the general storehouse are now made clear and its activities manifest. The income of this general storehouse has also been shown. Certain trustees will be elected by the people in a given village to look after these transactions. The farmer will be taken care of and if after all these expenses are defrayed any surplus is found in the storehouse must be transferred to the national treasury."

"The system is thus well ordered so that in the village the very poor will be comfortable, the orphans will live happily and well, in a word, no one will be left destitute. All the individual members of the body politic will thus live comfortably and well...For larger cities, naturally, there will be a system on a larger scale... "

This then is a "rough and ready" system of economic activity, based on local interaction. While the example is that of a farmer, whether in relation to crop or livestock, there is no doubt that the same principle of graduated progressive taxation will be applied to other fields of economic activity such as trade, business or even salaried employment. In the same way, needs have to be satisfied and should there be a shortfall between income and necessary expenditure for an individual or a family, some method will be activated to bridge this gap, not as a handout, but as part of the recognised system of overcoming difficulty in one corner of society at the same time as benefiting from surplus in another corner. The system, if applied in the spirit in which it is described can be very simple to administer. But it also begs several questions. To start with, how can the board of trustees verify the claimed income/expenditure? What can be considered acceptable levels of need, or acceptable measurements of income and expenditure?

The psychologists, philosophers, and ethicists have worked hard and are still working hard to find answers to these questions, all the time appreciating that that it may be difficult or impossible to provide such answers and definitions that will be applicable universally. There must be room for flexibility, and also accepted conventions. To start with, there is the widely accepted hierarchy of human needs, from the lowest to the highest, as formulated by Marlow in 1954: At the most basic level, humans have *"physiological"* needs, those of eating, drinking, shelter etc.. Then there is the *"safety need"* against disasters, dangers, the elements, violence, aggression etc. Once these are satisfied, humans will look at satisfying their need for *"love and belonging"* followed by *"esteem needs"*, both levels being determinants of the relationships within family, friends, and society in general. Having moved on from the physiological to the emotional needs, the next level is bound to be that of the *"cognitive needs"*, which relate to one's intellect, intelligence and knowledge. From that level, two of the highest tiers are reached: that of the *"Aesthetic needs"* of sophistication, eminence, moral judgement, perceptiveness, and similar qualities that elevate the human above empirical understanding, and utility. The highest level to be reached is that of *"self actualization"* at which one attains the spiritual, emotional, and intellectual well-being and achievement[164] . Looking at need from a different angle, and according to Doyal and Gough: there are *"minimal needs"* and *"optimal needs"*, but any of these have to be considered in relation to *"need satisfaction within those sharing the same culture"* [165].

Now, coming back to the farmer, the example Abdu'l Baha gave assumes farming in its simple, rural setting. He did mention, however, that for cities a different arrangement is needed. This is quite apparent in present day farming and agriculture. While the most widespread practice around the world is still the poor peasant who would till a small plot of land and hopes to produce enough to satisfy his and his family's needs, in the developed countries, there are so many settings, from the vast prairielands of the midwest in the USA and Canada, to the small holdings in parts of even western Europe, particularly Germany and France. On the whole, however, agriculture and farming, whether animal, crop, vegetable or fruit in the West is a large industry. And as in any large industry, it is run as a business concern, with management, computerized records and function, and an auditable balance sheet at the end of the year or the season. In addition to being big business these so-called "farmers" are a very powerful group who can bring pressure to bear on policymakers, whether within a State, or, as is occurring currently, in a multi-state community such as the European Union (EU). The irony is that in the EU the world had witnessed such a distortion in the farming activity because of policies aimed at maintaining price levels by controlling production or distribution and marketing. So the policies of "set-aside" whereby farmers are paid in order to stop cultivating a proportion of their land, subsidies, storing of surplus and so on, have had the adverse effect of creating a sense of false security, protectionism from competition, and most significantly, the lack of interaction with the rest of the world where people are in need at the same time as produce or potential produce is destroyed. In spite of all this protection and assistance from the states, the evidence of greed is ever-present. Overactive fishing and depletion of the seas and waters, sometimes using nets that collect elements of sea life that is not even used is well recorded. Attempts at overfeeding to accelerate cattle rearing resulted in such disasters as the "Bovine Spongieform Encephalopathy (BSE or "mad-cow" disease), a condition that was recognised, and farmers and governments officials notified of its dangers, long before farmers stopped feeding their cattle with (affected) animal food.

It is thus quite evident that all these distortions and anomalies will have to be considered in any new system based on the principles stated by Abdu'l Baha. Some of these will probably be amenable to "regulation" on a local basis by the storehouse and the trustees. But others will no doubt have to be dealt with on a larger scale of jurisdiction. In this wider consideration, Abdu'l Baha presents further guidance, but this will be discussed later.

This discussion centring essentially on the individual and the locality is by no means exhaustive or comprehensive. If this section succeeds in providing the "flavour" of the Baha'i teachings in this context, there is plenty of scope for the interested reader to delve deeper. There is a gradual transition in the Baha'i Scriptures from the individual to the locality as outlined above, and in the same way there is a gradual transition from the locality to the wider area of activity. Whether this is considered in relation to a State or a Country, a Region or a large Metropolis, the principles will start to cover aspects of suitably required systems, laws, jurisprudence and regulations. Mention of politics is purposely omitted, because any system of economics within the framework of the Baha'i Teachings has to be governed by the overall thrust of the Faith to look at very novel, world embracing and unifying systems that eliminate the elements of present day factional, adversarial or confrontational politics witnessed even in democracies, or, on an international scale, the aggressive competitiveness between nations.

Economics Of The State

Following on the above paragraph, it would appear easier for the sake of simplicity to talk of the "State" as the wider area of activity in relation to economics. Naturally there are many examples and sizes of such "States" as for example the "City State" of Singapore, or the "Principality" of Liechtenstein on the one hand, to the vastness of the USA or Canada, or Mainland China on the other hand, and until recently, what was the largest country in the world: The USSR. There are other examples of autonomous or semi-autonomous states or regions within countries, linked only in relation to Foreign Affairs and defence, and occasionally also finance. Examples are the Channel Islands and Britain, Hong Kong in relation to China, the States of Sabah and Sarawak in relation to the Federation of Malaysia, and several others.

The Baha'i Faith provides for the extension of the administrative structure from the "locality" board of trustees mentioned above to the "National" or "State" or "Regional" board of trustees to serve such wider areas. At present, these are called National Spiritual Assemblies

(NSA's), but in the Scriptures they are referred to as the "Houses of Justice", again local, national or otherwise. On the National the Guardian states[166]:*"I wish to reaffirm in clear and categorical language, the principle already enunciated upholding the supreme authority of the National Assembly in all matters that affect the interests of the Faith in that land* (the message referring to a particular country, but obviously applicable to any country). *There can be no conflict of authority, no duality under any form or circumstances in any sphere of Baha'i jurisdiction whether local, national or international...It is the trusted guardian and the mainspring of the manifold activities of every national community. It constitutes the sole link that binds these communities to the International House of Justice, the supreme administrative body in the Dispensation of Baha'u'llah"* It is not intended here to discuss at length the functions of the National Assemblies, but it is important to cite a few quotes to throw some light on this. These Assemblies are also formed of nine members, all elected from the entire adult membership of the Baha'i Faith in the country through a secret ballot, and by way of elected delegates to an annual National Convention of these delegates and the incumbent NSA. *"The first condition"* Abdu'l Baha says[167] *"is absolute love and harmony amongst the members of the assembly. They must be wholly free from the estrangement and must manifest in themselves the Unity of God, for they are the waves of one sea , the drops of one river, the stars of one heaven, the rays of one sun, the trees of one orchard, the flowers of one garden".* This then is the spirit in which the members would function. Their remit is encapsulated in the following quote from "Kalimat" (ninth paper)[168]:*"We exhort the men of the House of Justice and command them to ensure the protection and safeguarding of men, women, and children* (Note: safeguarding here refers not only to physical protection, but also spiritual and moral well-being). It is incumbent upon them to have the utmost regard for the interests of the people at all time and under all conditions. Blessed is the ruler who succoureth the captive, and the rich one who careth for the poor, and the just one who secureth from the wrong doer the rights of the downtrodden, and happy the trustee who observeth that which the ordainer, the ancient of days hath prescribed unto him". This then is the "nerve centre" receiving and delivering messages, collecting information, applying the laws and legislating on affairs not specified in the Writings. This matter concerning the law is of particular importance in relation to economics. For Abdu'l Baha says that on the one hand:[169] "*The secrets of the whole economic question is Divine in nature, and are concerned with the world of the heart and spirit.*" but on the other hand: *The Baha'i Cause covers all economic and social questions under the heading and ruling of its laws. The essence of the Baha'i spirit is that in order to establish a better social order and economic condition, there must be allegiance to the laws and principles of government".* This latter exhortation for allegiance to the laws and principles of government is recognised by Baha'is all over the world as paramount, no matter which country and government they live within. What applies now, should just as much apply later when the Bahá'í Faith gains more allegiance and jurisdiction.

It is once more important to mention a cardinal point regarding the Baha'i teachings on economics, as shown in the following quotes[170]: "*No, Baha'u'llah did not bring a complete system of economics to the world...There are practically no technical teachings on economics in the Cause, such as banking, the price system, and others. The Cause is not an economic system, nor its Founders be considered as having been technical economists".* This, however, does not mean that the Cause is bereft of a cohesive set of principles. In the fullness of time, and with the help of the expert economists who will, with their expertise, be able to fill in the details according to the requirements of the time, the world will be presented with a comprehensive schema that can be implemented, with the spirit of acceptance and compliance expected of a world enraptured with and enamoured of the spiritual qualities and edicts that it will eventually experience and cherish. *"The contribution of the Faith to this subject is essentially indirect, as it consists of the application of the spiritual principles which should guide future Baha'i economists in establishing such institutions which will adjust the economic relationships of the world"* *(ibid)*. Some of the principles that will govern these "adjustments" in the relationships of the world will now be outlined.

The starting point in this regard must be in relation to the general ethos within which the following considerations will have to be presented

1- Fairness, Justice And Equity

These three terms are often used in an interchangeable manner. But in fact they indicate three phases intended to achieve a positive and desirable effect or end result. While fairness indicates an *attitude* of reasonableness and impartiality, it is in a sense the pro-active attitude that a person, a system or an institution assumes in any thought process or action. Justice, on the other hand, is the *quality* and *process* of fairness and impartiality. It is the means whereby fairness is put into action. Equity is *the right*. It is the law of nature. It is also the moral justice, and the principle that governs the application of law. It is the expression of fairness, especially of the law. It is therefore the enshrinement of all the virtues of fairness, justice and the law, whether of nature or of human endeavour.

To think of equity it is imperative to think of the body politic of humanity as one family. Thus , Abdu'l Baha states on the one hand that:*"First and foremost is the principle that to all members of the body politic shall be given the greatest achievements of the world of humanity. Each member shall have the utmost welfare and well-being"[171]*, and on the other hand, He also states that : *"Although the body politic is one family yet because of lack of harmonious relations some members are comfortable and some are in direst misery, some members are satisfied and some are hungry, some members are clothed in most costly garments and some families are in need of food and shelter"[172]* This is an obvious discrepancy witnessed in the present state of the world, and one which Abdu'l Baha ascribes in the next sentence of this quotation in answer to His question *"Why? Because this family lacks the necessary reciprocity and symmetry"*.

Abdu'l Baha expands on this same reference on Pg. 41 by repeating and re-affirming similar utterances of Christ and Mohammed: *"God is not partial and is no respecter of persons. He has made provisions for all. The harvest comes forth for everyone. The rain showers upon everybody and the heat of the sun is destined to warm everyone. The verdure of the earth is for everyone. Therefore there should be for all humanity the utmost happiness, the utmost comfort, the utmost well-being.*

But if conditions are such that some are happy and comfortable and some in misery, some are accumulating exorbitant wealth and others are in dire want-under such a system it is impossible for man to be happy and impossible for him to win the good pleasure of God. God is kind to all. The good pleasure of God consists in the welfare of the individual members of mankind". The last sentence here is of particular significance. It is not only that equity, reciprocity and symmetry are the desired state for humanity, but it even surpasses that to become a cause of God's pleasure.

The question of reciprocity and symmetry has been, in one guise or another, expressed in socio-economic studies, and as an example, Will Hutton writes: *"The key to personal well-being, argues Wilkinson, is not absolute but relative position...happiness may mean eating an apple rather than a pear, but if a pear is half the price of an apple, then happiness is gained from eating a pear and using the spare money to buy something else"*[173].This is the intellectual argument that avers that humans can adapt and accept alternate situations if this is not seen as a denial in the midst of plenty. It also shifts the thought from setting uniformity and absolute equality as the standard that society should aim for. For here the talk is not of absolute equality, but of ownership of one's privilege to exercise choice, and to see the value of a situation where choice has to be made, indeed a situation that virtually everyone has to go through so often through a lifetime. It is acceptance without dissent that is the key to happiness and well-being. The other angle to this intellectual exercise is the fact that people cannot all be equal in ability. Roles will differ, and levels of earnings, responsibilities, and contribution to the whole body politic of society will differ within the membership of society. This point is explained by Abdu'l Baha as follows[174]: " *Nevertheless, there will be preservation of degrees because in the world of humanity there needs be degrees. The body politic may well be likened to an army. In the army there must be a general, there must be a sergeant, there must be a marshal, there must be infantry; but all must enjoy the greatest comfort and well-being... The arrangements of the circumstances of the people must be such that poverty shall disappear, that everyone, as far as possible, according to his rank and position shall share in the comfort and well-being.."* So provided one is reconciled to his/her duties for society, and the system within society in turn reciprocates by provided the required levels of livelihood, the result should be a "symmetrical" state of happiness and well-being. Will Hutton mentions the magnificence of this mutual reciprocal endeavour in society by stating that: *"Work is a supremely social act...to engage in work is to employ hand and brain in the exercise of production in association with others"*[175]. The ultimate in this "reciprocity" may well be that in the example described above, the "money saved from eating a pear instead of an apple" may be used not "to buy something else" but indeed to pass on to a more needy person or cause. Provided, that is, this money will not be needed to meet another necessity for the person who saved it.

2- The Law

It may well be that the above state of "Nirvana" can be achieved simply by way of universal acceptance in spirit and in action. This, however, is unlikely. Even with all the good-will and supreme intentions on the part of the vast majority of society, equity cannot be guaranteed. This may be for the simple, indeed even well-intentioned, reason that people will have different understandings and applications of general principles. There can be so many reasons for individuals to fail in their appreciation even if the sinister ones are excluded. But everyone, most especially the well intentioned members of society, will feel so much secure with the knowledge that a law, understood, obeyed and resorted to if required, is available, especially if it in an easy ready-reckonable form.

The world is accustomed to law. Much of it is written. But tradition has its value, and even in tribal societies to this day, the tribal chiefs have the duty of arbitration using the unwritten tribal tradition as "law". Civilizations flourished probably primarily because society was governed by apt and just laws. Religions, while based on spiritual teachings, would not have developed their societies and civilizations except for the fact that the leaders and followers worked at least within the shadows of law. How greater and more gratifying these religious civilizations would have been had they remained under the very umbrella of the law rather than its shadows, is a matter for perceptive historians to elucidate. It is, nevertheless, an acknowledged fact that most modern state laws have their origins and roots in the various Religious texts and teachings, albeit with modifications, additions, and expansions to suit evolving needs.

But it will also be a credible thought that the more compliant society is to a set of principles, the less need there is for law, or at least detailed law. It never ceases to amaze, that no matter how developed and sophisticated society is, new and additional laws are being enacted by governments and parliaments all the time. Every new law comes on to the statute books usually because society was confronted with new problems, some serious.

Economics is no exception. Laws are necessary as is well known, to cover every aspect of economic activity. It is not the purpose of this work to go into the details of the laws governing economic activities, but it is important to state that laws are needed to ensure that fairness is firstly understood, and secondly adhered to or worked towards. This is explained by Abdu'l Baha as follows: " *The Baha'i Cause covers all economic and social questions under the heading and ruling of its laws. The essence of the Baha'i spirit is that, in order to establish a better social order and economic condition, there must be allegiance to the laws and principles of government...The governments will enact these laws, establishing just legislation and economics in order that all humanity may enjoy a full measure of welfare and privilege; but this will always be according to legal protection and procedure. Without legislative administration, rights and demands fail, and the welfare of the commonwealth cannot be realized*"[176].

There will be more on law as the next sections are dealt with, but to what extent will these laws apply locally or on a wider scale depends so much on the shape of the development of the "administrative" structure of the world in future. For the foreseeable future, governments as at present have to be assumed. But the Baha'i Faith has within its concepts different possibilities. For simplicity at this stage, the next section will discuss this matter under the "generic" term of "administration".

3- The Administration

In a generic manner, administration is a term applied to management (in a general sense of the word) as well as to government. The world is used to the term "the American Administration" as a reference to the Presidency and Cabinet in the USA. Governments around the world take an infinite combination of characteristics in their composition, political agendas, method of governing, and extent of interaction with the people governed. The extent of "democracy", means of reaching power or holding on to it, and whether the titular head is a chief minister, president, sultan or, rarely royal, are all examples of modalities. The situation is changing quite noticeably of late, particularly as the era of absolute hold on power in perpetuity is waning, and in its place more elected governments or political parties claim the legitimacy and accountability of attaining power through the ballot box.

While not going into the detail of the subject of government, it is important to state at this stage that the Baha'i Faith accepts the legitimacy and authority of government, and that: *"What mankind needeth in this day is obedience unto them that are in authority, and a faithful adherence to the cord of wisdom. The instruments which are essential to the immediate protection, the security and assurance of the human race has been entrusted to the hands, and lie in the grasp, of the governors of human society"*[177]. Again, in the *"Will and Testament"* of Abdu'l Baha, in His loving tone of *"O ye beloved of the Lord"* goes on to say:*"It is incumbent upon you to be submissive to all monarchs that are just and show your fidelity to every righteous king. Serve ye the sovereigns of the world with utmost truthfulness and loyalty. Show obedience unto them and be their well-wishers. Without their leave and permission do not meddle with political affairs, for disloyalty to the just sovereign is disloyalty to God himself"*[178].

As mentioned previously, the Baha'i "Administration" takes the shape at present of a "local", a secondary or "national" elected body (House of Justice), and at the apex is the "International" or "Universal" House of justice. In the context of this section on Administration, it is the "national" Assembly or House of Justice and its role in the various countries and nations that is being discussed. In this respect, while not functioning at present as a central or National government, it is assumed that in future this may be the case. This therefore will be the backdrop against which the economic principles and role of government will be outlined. The shape of such governance will evolve, and it will be difficult to consider the manner in which it will evolve or the final shape it will take in this work. The brevity of this outline is therefore very definitely apologetic, but hopefully understandable.

The (National) General Storehouse: The National Spiritual Assembly (NSA) formed of nine elected persons, acts on a national scale in comparable manner to the elected board of trustees mentioned previously in relation to locality spiritual and administrative function and overall pastoral care. These functions must of necessity include the economic health and welfare of the community, in this case the nation. No doubt nine members will not be able to undertake all the tasks expected, and the way in which different NSA's will organize their tasks is open to every NSA to work out. From the economic aspect, there will be the expected "General Storehouse", but in this case it will be on a larger scale. As was mentioned, the tax recovered from economic activity as exemplified by the farmer, will also apply at this national level, either through passing on of surplus from the local to the national "storehouse", or from conglomerate establishments, whether industrial, commercial, farming, utilities or mineral extractions. To a large extent it will be the equivalent to national taxation as distinct from, but inter-related with, local taxation. Other forms of voluntary contributions will be discussed later.

NSA Services and Responsibilities: As expected from the above outlines, these will eventually develop as for present day governments. The mode of governance will differ from present day political ideologies and systems at least in some respect, particularly in view of the great important laid on the individual sense of duty and commitment to a common cause of welfare to the whole of society. Friedrich Von Hayek compared two situations which illustrate this point: *"In one army soldiers can only move exactly in the direction and amount they are ordered by some general operating at the centre; in the other army, soldiers are given general objectives and told to respond as fits the situation as it develops. It is clear who will win the battle"*. This translates in the Baha'i world in the manner in which NSA's, other administrative bodies, and individuals will have the leeway to manoeuvre and adapt to situations, but all the time conducting themselves within the general Laws and Bye-laws of the Faith and the guidance of the Universal House of Justice.

This principle will apply to such activities as planning and co-ordinating certain economic decisions, particularly regarding levels of production and consumption, and creating the incentives for people to appreciate and collaborate in the overall schemes so that at least the essentials are available to all the members of the "body politic" at affordable cost. Surpluses are made available to other communities or countries, again in the spirit of attaining well-being and levels of comfort to humans regardless of boundaries or artificial barriers. Naturally all this can operate within a market economy, and within fair competition. Such fair competition will amount to what is termed "perfect competition" whereby the price of any product will equal the "marginal revenue" but not more, or any variant that involves collaboration and "healthy" competition, not with the aim to destroy the competitor. Thus, The Guardian states:*" The call of Baha'u'llah is primarily directed against all forms of provincialism, all insularities and prejudices...For legal standards, political and economical theories are solely designed to safeguard the interests of humanity as a whole, and not humanity to be crucified of the integrity of any particular law or doctrine[179]."* In this context, it is safe to say that the Baha'i Faith is not reconciled to the idea of "Monopoly" and its potential or actual hold on the market be it the locality market or the product market. This opinion is gleaned from what appears to be the only reference to monopoly in the writings: *"Regarding your question concerning Baha'i attitude on various economic problems...the problem of trusts and monopolies... the Teachings of Baha'u'llah and Abdu'l Baha do not provide specific and detailed solutions to all such economic questions which mostly pertain to the domain of technical economics...there are certain guiding principles in Baha'i Sacred Writings on the subject of economics, and are mostly intended to guide further economic writers and technicians to evolve an economic system which would function in full conformity with the spirit and exact provisions of the Cause on this and similar subjects."[180]*. In addition to the principle of *"voluntary sharing"* which will be discussed in more detail later, and *"a new Universal Attitude...to be fostered --based on Spiritual Verities...*(and)*the solution calls for spiritual, moral and practical approaches"*, and, no less significantly, that *"It cannot be overemphasized that venturing into the social and economic development rests upon the fundamental principles enshrined in the Teachings concerning the inter-relationship between the spiritual and material aspects of life, and if the social and economic activity is not placed on a spiritual basis it may well prove counter-productive or even harmful, as without a spiritual base the people are likely to become corrupt and materialistic"[181]* This leads one to consider that monopoly with its usual aim of achieving a stranglehold on a product, a service or a geographical sphere of activity, is the opposite extreme from "perfect competition" and is thus not likely to serve society or humanity in the spirit of the above stated principles. *"Whereas in the case of perfect competition, there are so many individual producers that no one of them has any power whatsoever over the market... in contrast, a monopoly firm has the power to set its market price...will produce less, charge a higher price, and earn greater profits..."* The only let up in a situation like this is that the high profits of a monopoly will act as an incentive for other "firms" to penetrate the market. But this will only be possible if there are no impenetrable barriers to such entries, as such barriers will violate the spirit of the principles mentioned. In effect, a monopoly will neither be attempted, nor its stranglehold maintained if the monopolists adhere to these principles or if the "system" disallows such developments. To a certain extent this will apply also to "Cartels" and "Oligopolies" if, in both situations, an agreement in price fixing and maintaining impenetrable barriers is strongly adhered to. A salient present day example is the stranglehold that De Beers hold on the marketing and pricing of diamonds, partly to maintain artificially higher price, but also to perpetuate the "mystique" and "sentimental value" of that (perhaps not so precious) natural resource. The example also of the sudden and steep price rise of crude oil engineered by OPEC (Organisation of Petroleum Exporting Countries) in the early seventies and early 2000's demonstrates the above mentioned points quite well, in that, as a cartel, it succeeded in delivering a shock to the world and turmoil in its economies. However, as a result, several "new players" found it economical to invest in new explorations, managed to enter the field, and gradually created a glut of oil. This, plus investing in alternative sources of energy, as well as energy saving, resulted in both situations in a drastic reduction in the price of oil. This is a good example of where global cooperation can bring in systems and regulations that would govern use of scarce resources as well as development of alternatives.

If therefore, *"... The elegance of the market economies is that it cuts through...confusing ambiguities...the controlling idea is that the human being a trader, constantly weighing up the advantages and disadvantages of various courses of action: weighing costs and benefits..."[182]* it could be said that within the principles of the Baha'i Faith, these costs and benefits will relate to benefits of others as much as, and perhaps more so, than the benefit of self.

The NSA, in all this will be the "guardian" for all these values, and will provide the spiritual and moral guidance to the Local Spiritual Assemblies (LSA's) and non assembly communities. But it will also be the "guardian" of the law in the country. So while the NSA will consider that *"The fundamentals of the whole economic condition are divine in nature and are associated with the world of heart and spirit,...It is* (also) *neither just nor lawful that we should possess great wealth while there is abject poverty in this community",* and again *"The Baha'is will bring about this improvement not through sedition and appeal to physical force-not through warfare, welfare."[183]* These laws will cover everyday matters such as ownership, property and probity. Abdu'l Baha in 1919 addressing "the Central Organisation for a Durable Peace" accepts the legitimacy of "property", and Baha'u'llah asserts that *"A person hath full jurisdiction over his property"* (Aqdas: Questions and answers, Pg. 127). But Abdu'l Baha further states: *"Among the teachings of Baha'u'llah is voluntary sharing of one's property with others among mankind. The voluntary sharing is greater than* (legally imposed) *equality, and consists in this, that one should not prefer oneself to others but rather should sacrifice one's life and property for others. But this should not be introduced by coercion...nay, rather, man should voluntarily and of his own choice sacrifice his property and life for others, and spend willingly for the poor..[184]. "*

It may well be that reference here to property is rather generalized, meaning any means belonging to an individual. But it must also refer to property as is currently understood. It is thus acceptable to own, among other things, property, but at the same time to be conscious of the needs of others, and to be willingly prepared to share. The law under such prevailing circumstance will be invoked rather rarely, but it will be there should it become required. The same applies to the necessity to maintain courts of law, as well as all other aspects of the framework of government in its role as protective and arbiter.

The NSA (or "government") will adopt a role in harnessing the best in society and extending its "value judgements" derived from the Teachings as well as the particular cultural and other circumstantial conditions prevailing in that society. There will be no "uniformity" in the Baha'i World, but rather "Unity in Diversity".

Other roles and responsibilities of the NSA will not necessarily be directly related to economics, but, it is accepted that economics will figure somehow in practically everything involved in any governing role. Apart from attempts to boost the economy in general, and a guiding and facilitating role in research and development, The NSA will be responsible for social, educational, welfare and health services, the management of disasters, pestilences, and other unforeseen difficulties, and will look at world-wide factors, economic and otherwise, that require collaboration and co-ordination. This will be discussed further in relation to the International scene as envisaged in the new "World Order" called for by Baha'u'llah.

4- The Embodiment Of Highest Aspirations

This heading will be an interesting "interlude" and to taking some breath before resuming the discussion of other matters in economics. To start with, the qualities and the standards expected of the NSA's (and indeed also the LSA's) are gleaned from the following guidance of Abdu'l Baha:*" The prime requisite s for them that take counsel together*(referring to the Assemblies) *are purity of motive, radiance of spirit, detachment from all else save God, attraction to His divine fragrance, humility and lowliness amongst His loved ones, patience and long-suffering in difficulties and servitude to His exalted Threshold. Should they be graciously aided to acquire these attributes, victory from the unseen Kingdom of Baha shall be vouchsafed to them. In this day, Assemblies of consultation are of the greatest importance and a vital necessity. Obedience unto them is essential and obligatory. The members thereof must take counsel together in such wise that no occasion for ill feeling or discord may arise. This may be attained when every members expresses with absolute freedom his own opinion and setteth forth his argument. Should anyone oppose, he must on no account feel hurt, for not until matters are fully discussed can the right way be revealed. The shining spark of truth cometh forth only after the clash of different opinions. If after discussion a decision be carried unanimously, well and good; but if, the Lord forbid, differences of opinion should arise, a majority of voices must prevail.*

"*The first condition is absolute love and harmony amongst the members of the Assembly. They must be wholly free from estrangement and must manifest in themselves the Unity of God, for they are the waves of one sea, the drops of one river, the stars of one heaven, the rays of one sun, the trees of one orchard, and the flowers of one garden. Should harmony of thought and absolute unity be non-existent, that garden shall be dispersed and that Assembly be brought to naught.*

"*The second condition: They must when coming together turn their faces to the Kingdom on high and ask aid from the realm of Glory....Discussions shall be confined to spiritual matters that pertain to the training of souls, the instruction of children, the relief of the poor, the help of the feeble throughout all classes in the world, kindness to all peoples, the diffusion of the fragrances of God and the exaltation of His Holy Word. Should they endeavour to fulfil these conditions the grace of the Holy Spirit shall be vouchsafed unto them and that Assembly shall become the centre of the divine blessings, the hosts of divine confirmation shall come to their aid, and they shall day by day receive a new effusion of spirit*[185]

This then is the template that the assemblies have to forge themselves against in order to achieve the desired aims and aspirations, not only of the assembly, but also that of the community as a whole. Dedication, supreme sincerity, and wholesome consultation are the key elements. If achieved, there is the ultimate "bonus", that of the blessings and aid of God that will assuredly lead to success. To contrast this set of guidance with the workings of administration in any of its forms around the world to-day will immediately demonstrate the inevitable frustrations that the citizens will encounter, the divisive nature of the world of politics, the confrontational postures seen in party politics in particular, but also within the international relationships, and the muting of any voices of expression of opinions regarded to be not, as the buzz word goes these days, "on-message".

The next template presented to the Assemblies is that of the sphere of activity. This is rather vast and, as mentioned previously, covers all functions expected from a government. But one quotation will give the "flavour" of the guidances on this matter. Shoghy Effendi describes it as follows: " *...By no means the only issue which should receive the full attention of these assemblies. A careful study of Baha'u'llah's and Abdu'l Baha's Tablets will reveal that other duties, no less vital to the interests of the cause, devolve around the elected representatives of the friends in every locality.*

" *It is incumbent upon them to be vigilant and cautious, discreet and watchful, and protect at all times the temple of the Cause from the dart of the mischief-maker and the onslaught of the enemy.*

228

"*They must endeavour to promote amity and concord amongst the friends, efface every lingering trace of distrust, coolness and estrangement from every heart, and secure in its stead an active and wholehearted cooperation for the service of the Cause.*

"*They must do their utmost to extend a helping hand to the poor, the sick, the disabled, the orphan, the widow, irrespective of colour, caste or creed.*

"*They must promote by every means in their power the material as well as the spiritual enlightenment of youth, the means of education of children, institute, whenever possible, Bahá'í educational institutes, organize and supervise their work and provide the best means for their progress and development...serve and promote the social, intellectual and spiritual interests of their fellow-men...*"[186]

Within the above two templates, it will be easier to comprehend that *The fundamentals of the whole economic condition are divine in nature and are associated with the world of the heart and spirit...and without knowledge of its principles* (Baha'i teaching) *no improvement in the economic state can be realized...It is neither just nor lawful that we should possess great wealth while there is abject poverty in this community...Strive, therefore, to create love in the hearts in order that they may become glowing and radiant. When love is shining, it will permeate other hearts even as this electric light illumines its surroundings. When the true love of God is established, everything else will be realized. This is the true foundation of all economics....* "*Endeavour to become the cause of attraction of souls rather than to enforce minds. Manifest true economics to the people. Show what love is, what kindness is, what true severance is and generosity...*" [187].

The real success of the "package" can now be envisaged, and it is another example of "reciprocity and symmetry" whereby a pure and benevolent attitude of servitude on the part of the Assembly is reciprocated by understanding and practising of the ideals by the individuals. It is easy to appreciate that such a state of society will create the best opportunity for progress, but it will be difficult to disagree with the view that such idealism is difficult to attain, and that in any way the world has made progress along the ages with hardly any of such high principles underlying common practice. But proof that is the most conducive pathway to real success comes from a totally different angle. For Will Hutton[188] mentions: *"As Robert Axeleod shows in "The Evolution of co-operation", the strategy that works best in hundreds of different simulated games is to be straightforward rather than dishonest, always to reciprocate what is done to you and above all to co-operate. Keeping your integrity and imposing heavy costs on someone who has been dishonest, produces the best results".* The Baha'i teachings do indeed impose heavy cost on those who have been dishonest, but to discuss this further will be an unwarranted digression. However, this finding brings into focus the "Golden Rule" which comes in two main guises: the "passive" one which advocates not doing to others what one would not wish to be done to him (The Talmud, The Mahabharata, The Shayast-na-Shayast, representing respectively the Judaic, Hindu and Zoroastrian Faiths) and the "Pro-active" version which advocates doing to others what you would like done to you as in the Christ's Teaching: *"All things whatsoever ye would that men should do to you, do ye even so to them: for this is the law and the prophets (Matt. 7:12, and Luke 6: 31),* and the Muslim Hadith: *"No one of you is a believer until he desires for his brother that which he desires for himself",* and finally Baha'u'llah's teaching: *"And if thine eyes be turned towards justice, choose for thy neighbour that which thou choosest for thyself*[189] The distinction made here is not in any way intended to say that one version is better than the other, but it is intended to show that even if people may fail to initiate a good deed, it is still meritorious to avoid a harmful one.

The world is certainly ready for what Abdu'l Baha states: *"Old ideas and modes of thought are fast becoming obsolete. Ancient laws and archaic ethical systems will not meet the requirements of modern conditions, for this is the century of a new life, the century of the revelation of the reality and therefore the greatest of centuries"* [187].

Understanding these high ideals will be shown to be the stepping stones upon which humanity will traverse the route towards the glorious aspirations for this century with all that it promises. For the world rulers now appreciate the need to make that quantum leap into the virtuous circuit of good administration reciprocated by the goodwill of the people who are aware of their individual responsibilities to be guardians of the new ethos, and conscious of the need for this sea change in attitudes, at the same time as being fully enfranchised and participatory in the process of change. While not expected to occur overnight, the evolutionary process appears to have already started, with people and governments realizing the futility of pursuing all that brought strife, destruction and desolation in large swathes of the world, particularly during this century of rapidly unfolding history and change.

5- Taxation

It may appear unusual to speak of taxation immediately after the previous section dealing with the high ideals and aspirations. But it is hoped that the Baha'i concepts of taxation, already mentioned in relation to the locality activities and the "farmer" will be understood as not only a necessary contribution to maintain the budgets of the administration (government, NSA, or otherwise) but that it is the interest of the individual and the commercial enterprises to see to it that it is fairly and willingly given. That there is a need for any administration to secure at least the means to sustain its most essential expenditure is of no doubt. Where such means are obtained from other sources than individuals and enterprises, in particular where there is enough income from natural resources, the need for a tax system is negligible or non existent. This is the state of affairs in some rich oil producing countries, although their numbers are dwindling. So, in its extremely simple form, taxation *does not exist!*. Indeed, according to a very good summary review of the question of taxation in Britain, Andrew Roberts in the Sunday Times (10 January 1999, Section 1, page 11) describes "this *month as the bicentenary of the introduction of income tax...introduced by Wiliam Pitt the Younger to help see Britain through the darkest days of the Napoleonic wars...The tax was truly revolutionary. For the first time it shifted the principle of taxation from expenditure...paid on the purchase of land, luxury and imported goods...to income...Having refused to make peace with France in 1796, the war led to a haemorrhaging of treasury funds in order to keep the coalition against France together...At first the taxation rates were modest (1%) then it was raised to 10% for those earning more than £200 per year, thus setting a precedent (of progressive taxation)...Tax was abolished after peace was declared in 1815, but income tax was reintroduced by Sir Robert Peel in 1842...There was a concerted effort to get rid of it in 1874 but this did not happen...The rate was up to 35% in the mid-1970s, rising to 83% later, which, when an additional levy of 15% is added for unearned income, some people were paying a confiscatory 98% in the pound at the top rate".* At present the standard rate of income tax in Britain is 22%, and the top rate is 40%. But there is also the 17 ½ % "Value Added Tax" or VAT on purchases. In another significant development, David Lloyd George, the British Prime Minister found it necessary to appeal in 1917 to the British people in a patriotic rallying cry, to contribute to the war effort (World War I) through a war loan that was established by the government. The public responded enthusiastically and sacrificially and £2.5 billion was collected, equivalent to £120 billion at present. While the loan was undated, thereby not committing the government to a repayment date, the loan incurred interest payable to the holders of the loan certificate. Indeed, the loan is still probably not paid up in its entirety, although there is a distinct government plan to do so soon. The interest payment, thus represented a financial burden on the state for the past 82 years.

This shows the serious impact of any war effort on the finances of any state, a fact still in evidence to the present time, where the expenditure on armament and war is ever increasing in cost and proliferation. The effect of elimination of such expenditure is truly unimaginable in the release of worldwide resources towards the benefit of humankind, and Bah'u'llah's exhortations in this matter will be mentioned later. The possibility, therefore, of income tax reducing to an easily manageable scale is not all that far fetched, if the world's priorities are re-arranged. The voluntary contributions in obedience to the Laws of God in the Baha'i Teachings as well as in most other religions as has been described earlier when adhered to and when offered in the spirit described should more than compensate. At present, however, a situation like this will need a groundswell of belief and concurrence before it can be realistically hoped for. So, for the time being at least, and particularly in developed countries, it is a truism that, as the saying goes (sometimes in rhetorical jest), there are only two certainties in life: taxation and death.

Role of Taxation:

Taxation is not only a means of extracting money for the state. It plays so many important roles both in affecting or maintaining an equilibrium in the national income and expenditure programme, and also in regulating the state of the economy particularly in relation to the levels of consumption, savings, reserves, investment, and services, to mention but a few. In earlier sections the effect on prices, wages, balance of payments and currency exchange value were discussed. In this section the discussion will revolve around the philosophy of taxation, and the manner by which it can be accepted as a participatory effort to enhance the well-being, welfare and prosperity of society, and not, as it is looked upon in most instances at present, as a grudging obligation on the part of the tax-payer.

At present, the tax laws in many of the developed countries are so complex, that the wizardry of the tax consultants and accountants manages to secure for the rich person so many ways of avoiding tax, through so-called "creative accounting", the use of "tax havens", and so on. While tax avoidance can be quite within the law, if not actually within the "spirit" of the law, it is also very costly not least because of hefty consultants' fees. So it can only benefit the rich.

From another angle, there are two main types of taxes: direct and indirect. **Direct** taxes are those that are calculated in relation to income (of an individual) or profit (of an individual or an enterprise) and collected through the tax (Inland Revenue) government department. **Indirect** taxes are those levied on purchases, usually on consumer items, custom, utilities and services, as well as duty on imported merchandise. Both types of taxes serve a common purpose: that of being a source of revenue. But apart from that, they serve, as has been shown in previous sections, quite disparate purposes. So people may be paying taxes even when they are not aware that they are doing so, as when they buy an item in the shops for a price that includes, but not necessarily shows, value added tax (VAT). Everybody knows that there is excise duty on luxury items such as tobacco, alcohol, motor cars and so on. Such duties are a readily available and easily collectable source of revenue that not only helps in the government budgets, but may even be used as means of controlling what is seen as undesirable consumption, simply because of the hike in the "natural" value of the item.

Perhaps the most important source of aggravation, particularly on the part of the individual taxpayer, is the fact that once the tax is collected, the taxpayer almost always loses control of how it is spent. Even in democracies, where the taxpayer is also a voter, the influence an individual has on the expenditure programme of the government is minuscule if it is present at all. Even when considering more localized set-ups such as the local government (sometimes called municipal government, borough council or any other name), the local rates, once collected, say on property, the "rate-payer" loses control.

No one would be unhappy for the money collected to be spent on worthwhile services as will be discussed later. But the sheer complexity of present day Local and Central Government budgets allow these governments to decide and perhaps dictate the spending programmes and the "Agenda" based on political philosophy, ideology, and, more cynically, expediency. The state of the world at present makes such complexities inevitable. And any discussion on a new way to look at taxes, other revenues, and expenditures, must be considered in relation to a total orderly revolutionary appraisal of this state of affairs. Bearing in mind that the Baha'i Faith will not accept any form of violence or sedition, such a "New World Order" must arise from the grass-roots, be built on common consensus and acceptance, and must be based, as mentioned before, on spiritual as well as material principles. Above all, it will only work when there is universal participation based on the principle of even and equal franchise, rights and parallel and equally strong sense of duty and obligations.

From this perspective, a look again at the principles of tax and contributions in the Baha'i teachings become easier to comprehend, and perhaps simpler to manage.

Progressive Taxation, Tax Relief And Subsidy

It was shown in previous quotes that Abdu'l Baha advocates a gradual increase of tax collection as the income of a person (the example given was that of the farmer) increases beyond his/her expenditure. Where the income is matched by an equal level of expenditure, no tax should be due from that person, and where the income falls below the level of income acceptable under the prevailing conditions, a subsidy, which in modern terminology can be called "negative taxation", is allowed. All this is regulated through an elected Board of Trustees, whose other side of function is to ensure that all the income is spent on the welfare of the population under its jurisdiction, and any surplus is sent up the line to the "National" or the "Universal" Board of Trustees or House of Justice. So, as Abdu'l Baha states: *"...A man's capacity for production and his needs will be equalized through taxation... Therefore, taxation will be proportional to capacity and production..."*[91]. A very important principle here announced is that it is the *capacity* of the individual to produce that is the assessment factor. This poses a welcome need for attitudinal and behavioural modification on the part of every worker to do his/her utmost, regardless of the (consequences of) taxation on increased income over expenditure. Producing becomes one's contribution to the overall welfare and prosperity. The equilibrium means that everyone will feel at ease, knowing that whether he pays tax or not, he is still a contributor because he is working within his "capacity", and is certainly not idle.

Details on this sketchy explanation of the system will, no doubt be worked out in future. And while it seems so simple as described here, it is far reaching in its potential essentially because of the mechanism with which it will be operated, and the probity expected when the motivation of the Board of trustees is unsullied by behaviour and conduct unworthy of the trusted body elected according to the principles shown above.

But, from another angle, this simple scheme will be paralleled by enormous reductions in the levels of expenditure. It will also be supplemented by an elaborate system of voluntary contributions over and above this simple tax system. This may perhaps be even more effective, because it will depend on self assessment within one's very personal spiritual strength that makes such a voluntary scheme obligatory to all but the most deviant of followers of Baha'u'llah.

In later sections, the role of rulers, kings, and heads of state will be discussed, and it will shown that Baha'u'llah had exhorted all of them to reduce the burden of expenditure and eliminate extravagance. When these exhortations are heeded, the avenues of expenditure will be limited to the services that will enhance society, in particular health, education and welfare to those who, with no ability to meet their needs in full, can graciously and dignifiedly accept the help and or custody of that elected body. There will inevitably be surplus as a result of this "New World Order", even if just one avenue of expenditure is eliminated, that of armaments and war. But with the social conscience of the generality of people awakened within this spiritual atmosphere, people will manage to avoid so many of the causes of disease and disability, the majority of which are currently the result of abuses and faulty lifestyles. The social ills of society emerging from the dilution of the cohesion cementing institution of marriage especially when not entered into with sound and solid perception, the dwindling deference and respect for authority, knowledge, talent, and other qualities within society, and the sense of disenfranchisement that bewilder especially the youth, and other ills, all impose a grave and intolerable burden on present day budgets for welfare, law and order, and loss of opportunity when individuals are not *"producing within their capacity"*.

Voluntary Contributions:

A- *HUQUQU'LLAH* (Rights of God)

As an introduction to this foremost of the ways by which Baha'is can engage in and enjoy this "voluntary contract" with God, Baha'u'llah's description will serve to orientate: *"Huququ'llah is indeed a great law. It is incumbent upon all to make this offering, because it is the source of grace, abundance, and all good. It is a bounty which shall remain with every soul in every world of the worlds of God, the All-Possessing, the All-Bountiful."* [192]

In the section on the economic content in the religious texts of Judaism, Christianity and Islam, the laws regarding similar contributions were discussed, particularly in relation to Judaism and Islam. In Islam the "Zakat" is an annual contribution on property, livestock or other elements of wealth. This principle was re-introduced during the short dispensation of the Bab (The Herald to Baha'u'llah), and so in announcing Huququ'llah Baha'u'llah confirmed the principle and set it in its definitive form: *"This matter was revealed in the Most Holy Book in conformity with the pronouncement in the Bayan"* He state:*"* *Later, however, as a token of wisdom on Our part, We laid down the ruling whereby the minimum amount of property liable to the payment is fixed at Nineteen. The purpose underlying this is to ensure that the General Treasury is strengthened in the future..."* and further: [193] *"According to that which is revealed in the Most Holy Book, Huququ'llah is fixed at the rate of 19 mithqals out of every 100 mithqals worth of gold. this applies to possessions in gold, silver or other properties... The minimum amount subject to Huququ'llah is reached when one's possessions are worth the number of Vahid;* (A numerical counting convention whereby the Arabic alphabet carries an numerical value. The sum total of the v-a-h-i-d- is 19). *"that is whenever one owneth 19 mithqals of gold, or acquireth possessions attaining this value, after having deducted therefrom the yearly expenses, the Huquq (Rights) become applicable and its payment obligatory*"[194]. Shoghi Effendi explains this further thus: "*Regarding the Huququ'llah... this applies to one's merchandise, property and income. After deducting the necessary expenses, whatever is left as profit, and is an addition to one's capital, such a sum is subject to Huquq. When one has paid Huquq once on a particular sum, that sum is no longer subject to Huquq, unless it should pass from one person to another. One's residence, and the household furnishings are exempt from Huquq... Huququ'llah is paid to the Centre of the Cause*" [195].

So while this is an obligation according to the Law of Baha'u'llah, we will not lose sight of the fact that only the individual can assess himself/or herself. For Baha'u'llah further states: " *The payment of the Right of God is conditional upon one's financial ability. If a person is unable to meet his obligation, God will verily excuse him. He is the All-Forgiving, the All-Generous.... This is the Book of Generosity which hath been revealed by the King*"[196].

There are, as expected, more detail on this contribution. But it will be salutary to ponder on the philosophy behind this Law. First, it is a contribution that has to made only after all other dues are met: "*It is God's Command that the cost of burial take precedence, then the payment of debts, then the Right of God...Well it is with him who ascendeth unto God without any obligation to Huququ'llah and to his servants* ". Second, the discharge of this obligation is a blessing: " *It is clear and evident that the payment of the Right of God is conducive to prosperity, to blessing, and to honour and divine protection. Well is it with them that comprehend and recognize this truth and woe betide them that believe not. **And this is on condition that the individual should observe the injunctions prescribed in the book with the utmost radiance, gladness and willing acquiescence**"[197]* .This is Bah'u'llah's "gift" to the individual if that individual discharges this obligation with full compliance and willingness. But thirdly, and this is the spiritual "balancing" Utterance, again by Baha'u'llah, in total comforting beatitude: *"Say: I swear by God! No one is despised in the sight of the Almighty for being poor. Rather is he exalted, if he is found to be of them who are patient. Blessed are the poor that are steadfast in patience, and woe betide the rich that hold back and fail to observe that which is enjoined upon them in His preserved Tablet... Blessed is the rich man whom earthly possessions have been powerless to hinder from turning unto God, The Gracious, the All-Knowing"*[198]

To summarize, therefore, this contribution, The Rights of God, is voluntary in that no one will be coerced to forward it: *"To demand the Huquq is in no wise permissible.. Therefore, if someone, with utmost pleasure and gladness, nay with insistence, wishest to partake of this blessing, thou mayest accept. Otherwise, acceptance is not permissible."*[199] It is self assessed, and only the person can decide what is surplus (profit) and what is current and needed or spoken for. And last, but not least, it is a source of blessing for both the rich who will not hesitate to discharge this obligation wholeheartedly, and also the poor who, while unable to contribute, can still attract the blessings conferred upon him because of his/her attitude of acceptance and patience.

Once again, it will be seen that this voluntary/obligatory contribution is another means by which, on the one hand, the equilibrium between rich and poor is assisted, and on the other hand, it is a spiritual exercise with all this entails in inner tranquillity, contentment and self fulfilment. In this voluntary/obligatory "top slicing" of one's profits, the real feeling of richness (material as well as moral and spiritual) will become evident, and the apex of wealth, as contrasted with the basement poverty will be blunted.

B- *INHERITANCE TAX*

In the Baha'i Faith, this is a tax or a contribution depending on whether the estate of the deceased is defrayed according to the Law of the Aqdas, or distributed in accordance with an available will. A will is an absolute privilege of the individual, and it has to be executed with all accuracy and faithfulness by the family and/or beneficiaries, in collaboration with the legal authorities of the land and with the assistance of the Spiritual Assembly if deemed necessary. In this respect it can be considered voluntary if a will is available or obligatory according to a system if no will is made during the life of the deceased. The will, naturally has to be written and witnessed. Hearsay is not accepted unless accurately corroborated by the Spiritual assembly.

Baha'ullah stresses the importance of writing a will in verse 109 of the Aqdas:" *Unto everyone hath been enjoined the writing of a will. The testator should head this document with the adornment of the Most Great Name, bear witness therein unto the oneness of God in the Dayspring of His Revelation, and make mention, as he may wish, of that which is praiseworthy, so that it may be a testimony for him in the kingdoms of revelation and Creation and a treasure unto his Lord, the Supreme Protector, the Faithful"* In the Aqdas "Notes", No. 38 Pg. 182, this matter is further explained as follows: " *The Baha'i laws of inheritance apply only in case of intestacy, that is, when the individual dies without leaving a will. In the Kitab-i-Aqdas (Para. 109) Baha'u'llah instructs every believer to write a will. He elsewhere clearly states that the individual has full jurisdiction over his property and is free to determine the manner in which his or her estate is to be divided and to designate, in the will, those, whether Baha'i or non-Baha'i, who should inherit (Q & A 69). In this connection, a letter written on behalf of Shoghi Effendi explains that:*

...even though a Baha'i is permitted in his will to dispose of his wealth in the way he wishes, yet he is morally and conscientiously bound to always bear in mind, while writing his will, the necessity of his upholding the principle of Baha'u'llah regarding the social function of wealth, and the consequent necessity of avoiding its over accumulation and concentration in a few individuals or group of individuals."

So the will is again an obligation to be drawn out in whichever way a person is comfortable with. There is absolute freedom of disposal of the inheritance, but the understanding believer will appreciate the importance of not creating an accumulation of wealth. Baha'is are also enjoined to make use of legal advice where this is appropriate, again so that there can be no ambiguity in the choice of words or the proper and legal formatting of the will, especially if it is involved and complex.

But it is interesting to note that the will serves another purpose. This time purely spiritual: It is a statement of faith and submission and a final "witness" to one's obedience and abidance by God. That the Baha'ís are enjoined to "write" a will, is probably to serve these two cardinal purposes for this exercise: avoidance of ambiguity and reliance on "hearsay", as well as a final opportunity on this planet to testify to God.

In case of Intestacy, *"A system of inheritance which provides for distribution of the deceased's estate among seven categories of heirs"* (Aqdas Notes, Pg 183) works as follows: Based on multiples of the basic number of nine, the estate is configured (in total value) to the sum of 2520 (shares). The seven categories are then worked out as follows:

Children (equal share to male or female): 1080 out of the 2520 total shares.

Husband or wife	390 "	"	"	"	"	"
Father	330 "	"	"	"	"	"
Mother	270 "	"	"	"	"	"
Brother	210 "	"	"	"	"	"
Sister	150 "	"	"	"	"	"
Teacher	90 "	"	"	"	"	"

Where children, or other relatives do not exist, there is a system of devolving the relevant share to the next category or categories.

From the point of view of an economic study, the significance of this configuration is that, once again, it allows wealth to be distributed and spread. The interesting category that will need further guidance from the Universal House of justice is that of the teacher. During the time of Baha'u'llah, teaching was in small groups in what is termed the "Kuttab" or the "Madrassa". The essential feature of the education was the study and memorizing of the Qur'an and acquaintance with the language. There would have been one or only a few "teachers" who would take the group through the entire scholastic career. It was, therefore, easy to identify the "teacher" element of society. There is no doubt the situation has altered throughout the world, even where some similar system to that described may still be found. The category of teacher, therefore, can now be applied to so many disciplines, probably not only those pertaining to education. For teaching and promulgating Faith and Religion may come into it, educational authorities and/or institutions can be considered. Any speculation at this stage is not likely to be fruitful, and will not serve the understanding of the main thrust of this system which is to spread the wealth around, and reduce any tendency to the building of enormous accumulations.

C *Tithes (Zakat)*

This is yet another form of voluntary contribution which at present is ill defined but will become more so when the Universal House of Justice develops the necessary guidance. Baha'u'llah states in the Aqdas, verse, 146:*" It hath been enjoined upon you to purify your means of sustenance and other things through payment of Zakat...We shall, if it be God's will and purpose, set forth erelong the measure of its assessment..."* Further light on this matter is shown in the Notes section of the Book:*" Baha'u'llah states that the Baha'i law of Zakat follows "what hath been revealed in the Qur'an" (Q&A 107). Since such issues as the limits of exemption, the categories of income concerned, the frequency of payments, and the scale of the rates for the various categories of Zakat are not mentioned in the Qur'an, these matters will have to be set forth in the future by the Universal House of Justice. Shoghi Effendi has indicated that pending such legislation the believers should, according to their means and possibilities, make regular contributions to the Baha'i Fund. "* (AQDAS Pg 235)

D- *General Contributions*

This category of voluntary contribution takes its cue from the above section. But in addition, it is important to see the difference between this category and Huququ'llah, both of which are in operation at present. And while this represents the "rough and ready" channel for some money to be made available to the Spiritual Assemblies at every level, and to International "ear-marked" funds for world-wide activities operating under the aegis of the Baha'i World Centre, it will, no doubt, need to be looked at afresh once the system of "Tax", Huququ'llah, and Inheritance as sources of revenue are fully and universally acknowledged and operational. At present there is the need to keep the Baha'i Administration going. This is done through the contributions of the individual Baha'is in amounts that each individual feels comfortable with. It is done privately, although receipts are in most situations given by the Treasurer, but the total flow with most NSA's is quite meagre, and barely sufficient to keep it going. Special capital projects or major activities bring calls for extra sacrifice on the part of the Baha'is, and sacrifice they readily do. Surplus contributions to the LSA's are funnelled to the NSA or to the International Funds according to the decision of the LSA. The same is true of the NSA's as they see to it that, no matter how meagre their resources are, some money is channelled to the Baha'i World Centre and its Agencies.

All this will be re-arranged in the future development of the Baha'i Faith. But on a scale of proportion, it is fair to say that the Baha'is around the world, even in poorest societies in Africa, Asia or Latin America, will always find even the few "pennies" to give, hardly ever to take. If the concept of universal participation in the welfare of society is in need of proof, one should go no further than look a little closer to the workings of the Baha'i finances. When money is given by individuals with absolutely no condition, and sometimes with the full knowledge that it will be used for some other worthwhile cause as distant and as far from the sphere of the giver as possible, a true picture of the sense of global responsibility emerges. It emanates not only from the richer Baha'is, but even from the poorest. This then, may be the first rays of the dawning sun that will, in the fullness of its noon, become so radiant as to spread cheer, warmth, and true life throughout the world.

PART IX

TOWARDS A BLEND OF THE MODERN AND THE SPIRITUAL

Labour And Capital

Relations between those who provide or contribute capital to any project or business, and those who are engaged in the labour services or input within services, enterprises, businesses or industries, have been, as mentioned in previous sections, the subject of intense interest and study, and quite justifiably so. From the very early era of the emergence of labourers from the status of serfdom, slavery or allocation to the lowest strata of society, these relationships altered and evolved in so many different manners, depending on the circumstances prevailing or allowed by the particular society considered. To this day, examples are to be found of very primitive relationships, even those akin to "slavery", although one would be hard put to actually locate somebody who would actually still lay claim on a "servant" as a "slave". Remaining individual "permanent household servants" are few and far between, usually quite elderly folk who had been bought, or their direct descendants, with no where else to go to.

Regrettably, rich, rather immature, societies still manage to attract labourers and domestic servants from poor countries who would accept very mean status and treatment for the pecuniary reward with which they manage to maintain their relatives and family back "home". State laws and safeguards are not always observed scrupulously enough, and severance of the employment by the wage earner is not always easy or straightforward. This, thus, represents the lowest grade of relationship found in the world at present. It is fair to state that governments are aware of such "misconduct" on the part of employers, and would not overtly or consciously allow its persistence.

The next (upward) level or grade of relationship, is usually found in third world countries, and in particular, rural village societies, where the labourer, as often the woman in the family as the man, will provide primitive manual labour to landlords and shopkeepers, or domestic help to salaried employees who can afford it. While such relationships can be very rewarding to both parties, and indeed, very good personal relationships can develop between the helper and the employer or his/her family, the usual situation is one of very obvious dominance of the wage provider, and humble subservience, sometimes total reliance and obsequiousness, on the part of the wage earner. In this situation, the only "negotiating" position is that of the wage earner pleading acceptance of his/her labour and effort from the provider. Loss of the job could prove calamitous to the whole family, and there would be many others to fill the "vacancy". The only "social security" will be found in the collective poverty of the family or the extended family. Nevertheless, even under these circumstances one can find examples of dignity and self esteem, perhaps tagged on to submissiveness to "God's" will, and the strength of holding on to hope.

But there is a flip side to this picture. For it will be wrong to assume that in these societies wage earners are always ready and eager to give their best effort consistently, reliably, and responsibly. Indeed, as often as not, individuals who would perhaps need to be grateful for a job, would easily squander it once they have earned a meagre wage or two, out of an attitude of ignorance or an inability to assess the real value of work and perseverance. The status of subservience and poverty may therefore be self inflicted, albeit not consciously.

To discuss all the alternative conditions that prevail in different societies would be difficult and tedious, and will probably not contribute much to the value of this discussion. A leap to the industrialized developed countries is necessary in order to discuss the subject of labour/capital relations in mature societies, where safeguards have been worked out and laws governing and regulating these relations have evolved.

Labour/capital/management Relationships In Advanced Countries:

An educated trained and responsible labour force buttressed by well appointed and carefully selected Trade Unions should, in theory at least, prove a reliable and tested means of safeguarding the interests of both labour and capital or management.

There are, however, several models of such relationships, among which, until recently, one would consider the Communist model. It would, however, have been difficult to decide whether the largest of the Communist States, the USSR, would have been categorized as an advanced industrial "empire" or, as was often described, a "third world" country with heavy (mainly military) industries, nuclear power and a "Space Agency". Regardless of categorization, the only capital in operation was a State capital, and the "Management" was almost totally intertwined with the Political structure upon which the State was run. This same model was replicated in all the "Satellite" European Communist States, all of which have now dismantled their Communist Regimes, but it remained entrenched in that other vast and most populated country, "The People's Republic of China", as well as perhaps only two other countries still entrenched in Communism: Cuba and North Korea. It is significant that China is gradually and methodically emerging from its strict communist ideology, and is doing that very cautiously, perhaps particularly to avoid the effects that accompanied the sudden collapse of the regimes of the USSR and the European Communist States. It is spurred on in that direction particularly after the handing over of Hong Kong from British control, and the imminent handing over of Macao by the Portuguese.

Cuba also is belatedly starting to veer very carefully and studiously, away from its strict State run enterprise system to one that is opening up to foreign capitalist investment and internal private enterprise. And it appears that the only country still not changing its very repressive totalitarian communist regime is North Korea, and the total collapse of its economy and indeed society is hardly an advertisement for such a model.

Labour Relations In The Communist Regimes:

Labour within the communist ideal or practice was, as discussed in the relevant previous section, reckoned as the major source of power for a rolling economy. That economy was able to deliver certain immediate benefits, such as the development of major basic industries, notably electric power and steel production, as well as other infrastructure projects which will succeed in a highly planned government programme drawing upon the technologies copied from more market-oriented economies[200] Labour in this form of economy was almost totally within the state payroll. Adopting Marx's theory of "surplus value" in relation to labour and wage, whereby a labourer works not only to satisfy his needs, but also a little extra for the benefit of the capitalist, which is the profit, the theory went further so that this little extra might as well be for the benefit of the whole community. Furthermore, it was accepted that, in keeping with Marx's opinion, the capacity of capital to exploit labour, i.e. to realize a surplus value and hence a profit, varies inversely with the degree of mechanization. Capital will therefore tend to flow from the more highly mechanized (and allegedly less profitable) industries, to the less mechanized, and more profitable ones. It would follow that less should be spent on upgrading and thus developing sophisticated productivity. The result was that wages were held down, but at the same time growth and productivity was also held down.

Disregarding the social and political dimensions of this theory and of how Marxism/Communism developed as witnessed in the middle half of the twentieth century, the effect on labour was the acceptance of very modest reward with no private enterprise to create the stimulus and/or competition for a rise of living standards comparable to societies that operated a more free market system. The mixed blessing here was that while on the whole there was a "levelling down" of society's consumerism and freedom of manoeuvre, there was at least the assurance of availability of basic needs in terms of food, shelter and services. The collapse of Communism in the 1980's has revealed not only the very fragile economies of these states, but also the sad appearance of want to an extent never experienced or heard of under communism.

It can be seen, therefore, that labour relationships in the Communist states was rigidly regulated, and the dictum *"from each according to his ability, to each according to his needs"* would sound rather hollow when the channels of negotiation are hardly available and the means of raising one's own standard through hard work or entrepreneurial acumen is almost totally denied. From another angle, the situation that prevailed made the collection of tax a very modest activity of state, and the possibilities for the individual to contribute to the general welfare voluntarily very limited. The *egalitarian* ideal was thus forced upon the nation, and even if one accepts that universal "levelling down" is egalitarian, the prevalence of the privilegentsia, called *"Apparitchnicks"* in the former USSR, was a de facto denial of such egalitarianism. Labour relations therefore were not very happy, and far from ideal. There was neither equal opportunity, nor equality in any meaningful sense.

Labour Relations In Capitalist Countries:

Will Hutton in his book "The state we're in" 1995, Publishers: Jonathan Cape (London), 282/3 sets out the principle features of the four major capitalist systems. It will be useful to set the whole table at this stage, because of its relevance to subsequent sections. In addition, as he states: *"It is not exclusive and merely attempts to isolate the key features of each variant. Each is an interdependent whole, in which the character of one set of institutions interacts with the others; each shapes and is in turn shaped by the whole".*

It will be seen from the section on the Labour market that there are variations in the important aspects of this relationship. But for the full analysis the two subsequent sections need to be taken into consideration. As job security is inversely related to labour mobility, for example, this is reflected in turnover. Where the labour/management is adversarial the pay differential widens, and the profit motive becomes more prominent. Welfare expenditure is proportionately greater in the less "severe" capitalist systems, as in the more "severe" capitalist system the individual bears a greater responsibility for his and his family's health, educational, and financial security.

It would appear from the table that the system in Japan is the closest one would get to the ideal. And indeed, at the time that book was published, there was every indication that this is so. Except that almost at the time the book appeared the *"major faults"* in the Japanese economical system became apparent. A façade of financial and industrial policy/management rectitude and wisdom was soon to be demolished by the capitulation of major financial establishments, the re-entrenchment of major industries, and the acknowledgement that the Japanese tradition of *"a job for life"* will hold no more. The reasons for this new situation was mainly mismanagement, with "cosines" between finance and industry leading to incipient but gradually deepening erosion of profitability and to increasing debt.

The situation within Europe other than Britain is also interesting in that the unions are still rather powerful and are able to influence government policies quite significantly, as exemplified most glaringly in France. State enterprises are running at a loss, and governments are being pressured or even "blackmailed" into increasing their subsidies and support, even at the risk of violating the European Union market rules that would make such intervention illegal. Various excuses and twisted descriptions of these subsidies were accepted by the EU Commissioners of trade, notably in the cases of the Spanish and French National Airlines, *Iberian and Air France,* both of which would have become insolvent otherwise. When the French Government attempted to make a stand and force Air France to reduce its over-manning and introduce efficiency and economy, the reaction of the unions and the workforce was so widespread and aggressive, that in the end it was the Government rather than the Airline that capitulated. Other examples of inefficiency abound.

Labour laws are a means of regulating and safeguarding good work practices, rights, privileges and obligations. While the main thrust of these laws is usually the economical considerations, the additional and quite important value is the social dimension. In the most useful situation they are enacted after full and practical consultation with all concerned. This most commonly means labour unions, business confederations, and government. In practice, however, many of the laws are passed because of political considerations or pressure from vested interests. The recent laws reducing the maximum hours of work permitted within the EU to 35 may not have the interest of the working staff in mind as much as the opportunity to reduce unemployment, and gain some political kudos. But for real benefit, such a law has to be set against the effect it will have on business, which will bear greater overhead expenditures, and on prices, which will reflect this. Add to this the effect on inflation, loss of competitiveness in the global market, and the result could be a reversal of the economic and political benefits. This is only a simplified discussion. The technicalities of this subject are the domain of extensive expertise and exposition. From the workers' angle, the shortened working week is only a means of earning the same amount for less effort. The individual can either use the extra time to enjoy more leisure or other non remunerative pursuits, allowing others the opportunity to work the rest of the hours in his/her place, or that same individual could take up additional employment earning more, thereby denying others the work opportunity. A social conscience issue is hereby presented, but under the prevailing materialistic attitudes, the author is under no illusion as to where the preference of the majority will lie. People will just succumb to their consumerism, perhaps greed, or perhaps the simple ambition to achieve more secure financial status. Whatever the aim, the majority will go for the additional money rewards.

A comparison of four systems

CHARACTERISTICS	AMERICAN CAPITALISM	JAPANESE CAPITALISM	EUROPEAN SOCIAL MARKET	BRITISH CAPITALISM
Basic principles				
Dominant factor Of production	Capital	Labour	Partnership	Capital

CHARACTERISTICS	AMERICAN CAPITALISM	JAPANESE CAPITALISM	EUROPEAN SOCIAL MARKET	BRITISH CAPITALISM
"Public tradition	Medium	High	High	Low
Centralisation	Low	Medium	Medium	High
Reliance on price-mediated markets	High	Low	Medium	High
Financial system				
Market structure	Anonymous Securitised	Personal Committed	Bureaucracy Committed	Uncommitted Marketised
Banking system	Advanced Marketised Regional	Traditional Regulated Concentrated	Traditional regulated regional	Advanced marketised centralised
Stock market	V. important	Unimportant	unimportant	V. important
Required returns	High	Low	Medium	High
Labour market				
Job security	Low	Low	High	Low
Labour mobility	High	High	Medium	Medium
Labour/management	Adversarial	Co-operative	Cooperative	Adversarial
Pay differential	Large	Small	Medium	Large
Turnover	High	Low	Medium	Medium
Skills	Medium	High	High	Poor
Union Structure	Sector-based	Firm-based	Industry-based	Craft
Strength	Low	Low	High	Low
The Firm				
Main Goal	Profits	Market share Stable jobs	Market share Fulfilment	Profits
Role top manager	Boss-king Autocratic	Consensus	Consensus	Boss-king Hierarchy
Social overheads	Low	Low	High	Medium, down

CHARACTERISTICS	AMERICAN CAPITALISM	JAPANESE CAPITALISM	EUROPEAN SOCIAL MARKET	BRITISH CAPITALISM
Welfare System				
Basic principle	Liberal	Corporatist	Corporatist	Mixed
Universal transfer	Low	Medium	High	Medium, down
Means testing	High	Medium	Low	Medium, up
Degree education				
Tiered by class	High	Medium	Medium	High
Private welfare	High	Medium	Medium	Medium, up
Government policies				
Role of government	Limited	Extensive	Encompassing	Strong
Openness to trade	Adversarial	Cooperative		Adversarial
Industrial policy	Quite open	Least Open	Quite Open	Non Existent
Top income tax	Little	High	High	non-existent
	Low	Low	High	Medium

In all this, there is a sort of "tug-of-war" between the pull of the trade unions on the one side, whose main interest is the call for greater remuneration, rights and privileges for their members, and the State or Business management on the other side, whose main aim is to reduce overheads and expenditure and to increase profits. While this may be the simplistic description, it certainly applied starkly in the western world, especially the UK, USA, France and Italy up to perhaps the 1970's. It was only in the 1980's onwards that a social dimension began to emerge in the conduct of this "tug-of-war", whereby the unions saw it as part of their responsibility to their membership to be as reasonable as possible in their demands, and also to look at the wider implications of their members' needs in training or re-training, to allow job and location mobility, and to participate actively and co-operatively in introducing flexible working patterns within their fields. The state and business management also worked towards enhancing the skills of their employees, ensuring as optimum a skill mix as would be of general benefit to their respective concerns. It was recognized that such a policy entailed extra expenditure, but this was fully justified as an investment, which will pay dividends with increasing efficiency and productivity. Social care and recreational activities are more frequently becoming the sign of good and enlightened management, providing pleasant working environment and added feeling of security. Overall, the importance of job satisfaction became increasingly recognized.

It is within the spirit of all these developments, surprisingly recent if looked at historically, that the principles enunciated in the previous religious teachings as mentioned in the relevant sections above, and also the principles announced by the foremost figures of the Bahá'í Faith, that the various threads, apparently so disparate and unrelated, begin to come together to provide the world of the present and, at least the immediate future, with the pattern of labour relationships that is becoming such a necessity. But these teachings and principles need to be analysed and considered in relation to present day essentials with regard to wage setting, employment/unemployment, the "globality" that has been achieved in the market place, and the programmes of social and financial security available in any country, business establishment, or society in general. The term globalisation has been hackneyed well enough in the past few decades, and it is gradually being replaced by the recognition that as a process it has already to a large extent achieved its aim of effective globality. It is therefore essential to look at these issues either with the world situation in mind rather than the narrow requirements of a small section, or to look at the ethical standards that, once accepted on a large scale, locally, nationally or internationally, will set the scene for a new economic order based on the reciprocal contribution of the individual to the system as well as the system to the individual. Indeed there appears to be no conflict between the necessity to consider the global interdependence of the economies, and the full realization of the individual's potential, no matter how minuscule, within this hugely global picture, even though this picture often needs to be broken down into as small sections to suit particular considerations.

Wages

A wage can simply be described as a reward for a service rendered. This can be agreed on an item of service or on a more long-term employment basis. But whichever way it is considered, there are two important elements in setting out such rewards: **1-** The "market forces" of supply and demand, and **2-** The overall level of need as reflected in the cost of living in any particular setting under consideration. These two elements are, however, only the mechanics of wage agreements. They can be so distorted in favour of the wage earner or the wage payer, dependent on several factors. What is quite difficult to achieve, is a fair assessment of what could be regarded as a "just wage". In previous sections, this question was shown to have been the concern of economists and religious teachings. The section on Islam shows the importance of being fair in all transactions, so that a person gives and takes fairly and without meanness, or thrift ("minish"), and the wage earner not to be greedy. Monopoly was "accursed", and especially if used to raise prices. Ibn Khaldun was astute enough to recognize that increasing taxes will only lead to reduced incentives for work and subsequently reduced revenue: *"It should be known that at the beginning of the dynasty, taxation yields a large revenue from small assessments. At the*

end of the dynasty, taxation yields a small revenue from large assessments…"
He thus anticipated by 600 years what was to be known as the **"Laffer curve"** which shows that tax rates beyond a certain level will decrease tax revenue[201]. In the New Testament, in the parable of the *"labourers in the vineyard"* (**Matt. Ch.20, vs. 1-16**) Jesus describes a situation where labourers hired into a vineyard, some early in the morning for a penny wage, others about the third hour (probably meaning midday), and yet others at the end of the day. But all groups were given the same wage, a penny for the day's work. Those who started at the beginning of the day were disappointed that they worked all day for the same wage as those who started so late. His answer to one of them was: *"Friend, I do thee no wrong: didst thou not agree with me for a penny?"* While it should be mentioned that this parable essentially refers to the kingdom of heaven, where *"the last will be first, and the first last"* it does state a principle that an agreement has to be honoured, and accepted even if it appears unfair in a certain aspect. Similar teachings are to be found in the Old Testament.

The thoughts of the early economists on wages, their assessments, and the factors that affect them was also discussed in the relevant sections above, particularly those of Petty, Locke, Cantillon, and Hume in the pre-Adamite era, and the Physiocrats' thinking that wages are to be assessed according to the basic needs of the worker. Marx's thoughts on the exploitation of the workers, which eventually developed in the communist world the centralization of the means of production and distribution, in the hope that an "egalitarian" society is created, had the "revolutionary" germ that grew and flourished and found its expression in that way. History is already judging this experiment unfavourably. And the world has moved on. During this century, and especially the latter half of it, wages appear to be affected by two factors which currently play pivotal roles: **1-** The Trade Unions, and **2-** The falling costs of transport and communication. It is in the light of these factors that the following discussion is undertaken, and it will relate essentially to employment. Item of service wages are a matter for individual negotiations.

The inter-reaction between wages, prices, productivity, inflation, employment and unemployment, and finally, but no less importantly lifestyle preferences, is the subject of continual study not only by economists, but by politicians, government departments, sociologists, not to mention religious leaders and teachers.

The social and lifestyle issues will be discussed in more detail in later sections. But essentially, workers in employment in many situations consider their job in relation to its career structure, security of tenure, job satisfaction, and status value. Relationships within the work environment may have an influence on an individual's happiness with the job. But an important issue is what an individual perceives as the level of reward the wage offered provides, and the cost of losing a particular job. Thus, workers will put in a greater effort, if they feel they are well rewarded, and will try hard to safeguard their employment. On the other hand, an important incentive for work in relation to lifestyle is how much an individual will value that level of earning as a trade-off for leisure and the hours of work put in. If there is a choice, and job security is not an issue, an individual may prefer to work fewer hours so as to enjoy other pursuits or more time with the family. They may wish to earn more, however, if this means affording those expensive luxury or leisure goods and activities, or even to retire at an earlier age. In advanced societies where employment is more freely available, these are considerations that swirl in people's thoughts perhaps all the time. This may not be affordable in the less developed countries where work is hard to obtain, and the matter of luxury may not even be a possibility.

The other side of this discussion is the situation where the wage is perceived by the worker as to be too low, and therefore losing the job is not a significant set back. The decision is made so much easier where a social security system is in operation so that losing a low paid job will only mean receipt of unemployment benefit payments. The decision may be a little more difficult where the level of earning is border-line inasmuch as the job pays approximately the equivalent of the unemployment benefit. The important consideration in this situation is indeed not a financial or economic one, but ethical. If the person believes that unemployment is an unacceptable state if it can be avoided, then that person will prefer work to any other consideration. Political considerations regarding the ideologies of governments and political parties have a bearing on these issues as is well known, but will not be discussed further.

Determination Of Wages:

In economic parlance, the number of people willing to work is called the *"labour force"*. The total number of hours they are willing to work is called the *"supply of effort"* or more simply, the *"supply of labour"*. The proportion of the total population or some sub-group such as men, women, or youngsters that is willing to work is called the *"labour participation rate"*. It will be easy to deduce from the preceding paragraph that the wage rates can influence the labour force, and the number of people generally or those within the subgroups who are working, as well as the number of hours individuals will want to put in. All this depends on how much a person is willing and able to exchange leisure for consumption and for time spent at work. In a freely competitive market and where there is no union involvement, both demanders of labour and suppliers of labour are working competitively, and the wage rate and volume of employment is determined by the forces of supply and demand. This situation may, however, be skewed if there is a single purchaser of labour, called a *"monopsonist"*. A single purchaser or an association of employers working in unison are in a position to dictate the rates of wages. But in doing so they will be aware of the fact that a fair wage will help maintain their productivity and, more importantly, avoid disenchantment of the labour force who have to accept what is on offer, but will discourage new entrants into the profession or trade. The labour force and the expertise will eventually wither away, to the detriment of all concerned. On the whole, however, monopsonists will strive to lower the level of wages, and on the social and ethical level of consideration this will be an unfair deal favourable to the "purchaser". Even outside business and industry similar situations are found, as for example when the state is the single purchaser, usually of services such as health, education, the armed forces and so on.

The Effect Of Unions:

It is outside the scope of this work to go into detailed description of "Trade Unionism" and its various operational philosophies, methods, or remits. Moreover, the activities of the unions will vary according to the type of craft or trade or professional groupings they represent. They can be very wide based with large representation, as for example the miners' union in the heyday of coal mining, when in the UK the union spoke for nearly a million members. Or it can represent a small group of elitist members such as, in the UK, that speaking for the so-called "First Division" or "Top Civil Servants".

Many countries, especially in Western Europe, have seen very ugly examples of serious strife and very damaging strikes. A glaring example is the coal miners strike in the UK in 1973/4. This brought the whole country almost to its knees through such a serious reduction in power supply that the government had to declare a three day week, effectively ordering the country to "shut down" for the rest of the week, In addition, it even brought down the Government of the day, directly and almost single handed..

It is to the relief of all concerned that the situation now is much better in most countries and most unions, as an environment of less aggression and strife, and greater understanding and maturity has set in. Nevertheless, the situation is still one of antagonism and a feeling of belonging to two sides of the proverbial fence. And unions can still decide on "minimum wages", type of job done, demarcations especially in industry, and such methods as "the closed shop". Again, maturity seems to be setting in, and there is a greater understanding that higher wage can only lead to lower levels of employment, or worse still, lower profitability and loss of business as a result of the higher prices and poorer competitiveness resulting. Aggressive bargaining, especially when made possible because of the "closed shop" situation, can, as mentioned previously be detrimental in the long run. But this should not detract from the fact that higher wages, especially if perceived by the workers as fair and rewarding will increase efficiency: the so-called **"Efficiency wages"**.

It will be seen from the above that the important issue is ***fairness,*** whether to the worker or employee, or to the employer or owner of capital, and ultimately but surely, fairness to society in general. A healthy economy, based on fair reward and profit, will be materially, psychologically, and morally of great benefit. If it also operates within the ethical and spiritual principles and fervour, it will have acquired all the safeguards of a system and climate in which there will be no reliance on confrontation and strife, and almost total reliance on dialogue, fruitful consultation, and constructive agreements. This will not lead to *equality* in the sense that was envisaged by Communism. On this subject Abdu'l Baha states: *"In the Bolshevistic principles equality is* *effected through force. The masses who are opposed to the people of rank and to the wealthy class desire to partake of their advantages. But in the divine teachings equality is brought about through a ready willingness to share. It is commanded as regards wealth that the rich among the people, and the aristocrats should, by their own free will and for the sake of their own happiness, concern themselves with and care for the poor. This equality is the result of the lofty characteristics and noble attributes of mankind"[202].*

Any discussion about fairness, therefore, according the Bahá'í principles is based on mutual accord and willingness to share. This leads to the issue of **equality**. This is totally different from fairness, and again Abdu'l-Bahá states[203]: *"Equality is a chimera! It is entirely impracticable! Even if equality could be achieved it could not continue - and if its existence were possible, the whole order of the world would be destroyed. The law of order must always obtain in the world of humanity. Heaven has so decreed in the creation of man.*

" Some are full of intelligence, others have an ordinary amount of it, and others again are devoid of intellect. In these three classes of men there is order but not equality. How could it be possible that wisdom and stupidity should be equal? Humanity, like a great army, requires a general, captains, under-officers in their degree, and soldiers, each with their own appointed duties. Degrees are absolutely necessary to ensure an orderly organization. An army could not be composed of generals alone, or of captains only, or of nothing but soldiers without one in authority. The certain result of such a plan would be that disorder and demoralization would overtake the whole army"... "For the community needs financier, farmer, merchant and laborer just as much as an army must be composed of commander, officers, and privates. All cannot be commanders; all cannot be officers or privates. Each in his station in the social fabric must be competent-each in his function according to ability but with justness of opportunity for all."

`Abdu'l-Baha recounts the following historical experiment:

"*Lycurgus, King of Sparta (and a philosopher) who lived long before Christ, conceived the idea of absolute equality in government,… made a great plan to equalize the subjects of Sparta; with self-sacrifice and wisdom…He proclaimed laws by which all the people of sparta were classified into certain divisions. Each division had its separate rights and function. First, the farmers and tillers of the soil. Second, artisans and merchants. Third, leaders or grandees. Under the laws of Lycurgus, the latter were not required to engage in any labor or vocation, but it was incumbent upon them to defend the country in case of war and invasion. Then he divided Sparta into nine thousand equal parts or provinces, appointing nine thousand leaders or grandees to protect them. In this way the farmers of each province were assured of protection, but each farmer was compelled to pay a tax to support the grandee of that province. The farmers and merchants were not obliged to defend the country. In lieu of labor the grandees received the taxes. Lycurgus, in order to establish this forever as a law, brought (the) nine thousand grandees together, told them he was going on a long journey and wished this form of government to remain effective until his return…He made them and the people swear an oath to protect and preserve his law and maintain the same order of government if he should leave the country, also that nothing should make them alter it until his return. Then the king called the people of his kingdom, and made them swear a great oath to maintain the same order of government if he should leave the country, also that nothing should make them alter it until his return… Having secured this oath, he left his kingdom of Sparta and never returned. Lycurgus abandoned the situation, renouncing his high position, thinking to achieve the permanent good of his country by the equalization of the property and of the conditions of life in his kingdom…No man ever made such a sacrifice to ensure equality among his fellowmen… All the self-sacrifice of the king was in vain…A few years passed, and the whole system of government he had founded collapsed, although established upon such a just and wise basis... The great experiment failed. After a time all was destroyed; his carefully thought out constitution came to an end...*

"*The futility of attempting such a scheme was shown and the impossibility of attaining equal conditions of existence was proclaimed in the ancient kingdom of Sparta. In our day any attempt would be equally doomed to failure...Difference in capacity in human individuals is fundamental. It is impossible for all to be alike, all to be wise. Bahá'u'lláh has revealed principles and laws which will accomplish the adjustment of varying human capacities...*

"*A financier with colossal wealth should not exist whilst near him is a poor man in dire necessity. When we see poverty allowed to reach a condition of starvation it is a sure sign that somewhere we shall find tyranny...It is important to limit riches, as it is also of importance to limit poverty... Men must bestir themselves in this matter, and no longer delay in altering conditions which bring the misery of grinding poverty to a very large number of the people. The rich must give of their abundance, they must soften their hearts and cultivate a compassionate intelligence, taking thought for those sad ones who are suffering from lack of the very necessities of life.*"[204]

These two examples and experiments, one (that of King Lycurgus) in the distant past, and the other, Communism, in the recent past and of contemporary relevance, have proved that equality when imposed will not work. However, what the world needs as an experiment, is to prove the value of voluntary and compassionate relinquishing of extreme wealth. This would be coupled with a distinct endeavour on the part of everyone to use whatever capacity and ability available to oneself in order to avoid extreme poverty and want.

Shoghi Effendi states:[205]

"...Whatever the progress of the machinery may be, man will have always to toil in order to earn his living. Effort is an inseparable part of man's life. It may take different forms with the changing conditions of the world, but it will be always present as a necessary element in our earthly existence. Life is after all a struggle. Progress is attained through struggle, and without such a struggle life ceases to have a meaning; it becomes even extinct. The progress of machinery has not made effort unnecessary. It has given it a new form, a new outlet."

Abdu'l Baha takes this matter further in his talk on 1 July 1912 in New-York, drawing on the Teachings of Christ (probably in relation to Christ's edict that it is more difficult for a rich man to enter the Kingdom of God than it is for the camel to go through the eye of a needle), and adding the changes in attitude required in this age. For he states:[206]

"What could be better before God than thinking of the poor? For the poor are beloved by our heavenly Father. When Christ came upon the earth, those who believed in Him were the poor and lowly, showing that the poor were near to God. When a rich man believes and follows the Manifestation of God, it is proof that his wealth is not an obstacle and does not prevent him from attaining the pathway of salvation. After he has been tested and tried, it will be seen whether his possessions are a hindrance in his religious life. But the poor are specially beloved of God. Their lives are full of difficulties, their trial continual, their hopes are in God alone. Therefore, you must assist the poor as much as possible, even by sacrifice of yourself. No deed is greater before God than helping the poor. Spiritual conditions are not dependent upon the possession of worldly treasures or the absence of them. When one is physically destitute, spiritual thoughts are more likely. Poverty is a stimulus toward God. Each one of you must have great consideration for the poor and render them assistance. Organize in an effort to help them and prevent increase of poverty. The greatest means for the prevention is that whereby the laws of the community will be so framed and enacted that it will be impossible for a few to be millionaires and many destitute...."

It will be seen here, that Abdu'l Baha even in 1912 has envisaged the age of the maturity of humanity so that it is not any more wrong to acquire wealth, and that a rich person can still attain nearness to God. But the onus is on that rich individual to realize his/her responsibility first not to allow the wealth to come in the way of nearness to God, and second to appreciate that this wealth also carries the responsibility towards the poor.

Thus*:" When perfect justice reigns in every country of the Eastern and Western World, then will the earth become a place of beauty. The dignity and equality of every servant of God will be acknowledged; the ideal of the solidarity of the human race, the true brotherhood of man, will be realized; and the glorious light of the Sun of Truth will illumine the souls of all men"*.

For this to be facilitated, there is a need for some laws. As Abdu'l-Bahá states:[207]

"It is impossible for a country to live properly without laws. To solve this problem rigorous laws must be made, so that all the governments of the world will be the protectors thereof"

This legal and administrative framework has been discussed above in relation to the "Houses of Justice" or the "Spiritual Assemblies", but they will need to be discussed further.

Social And Welfare Services

Addressing this subject follows naturally and logically from the above. For while the individual and the relationships between capital and labour were addressed, and the various individual and institutional roles were considered, the next tier of care needs to be discussed in relation to the State and what it can, and perhaps should, organize in order that any failings on the part of the individuals or institutions are either corrected or not allowed to progress to serious detriment.

It was seen above that Abdu'l Baha suggested government laws to regulate the welfare of the community. It was also seen that within the village or the city, the duties of the "Trustees" are essentially to safeguard the welfare of all factions of the community and to provide for the needy, the old, and the infirm.

But the world is now complex. Society has justifiably allowed itself high expectations and ambitions. Advances in Science and Technology have fuelled and continue to energize these ambitions. Whether it is the advances in medicine, or the high levels of education and training requirements, or even the aspiration for a quality of life not previously deemed possible or worthy of even a dream, all, on the one hand impose demands on the "State" system, and on the other hand form legitimate desires of people in every society to be satisfied.

But here again, there is a need to balance out *privilege*, which is the extent to which demand can be satisfied and/or the extent to which the State's capability or limitations can provide, and *responsibility*, which reflects what the individual and society undertake to satisfy perceived or essential desire or demand through their own efforts. At the very least, responsibility should be expected whenever assistance or services from the "Community" or the "State" are offered or accepted.

In any situation, whether it is "State", "Local Authority", the "General Storehouse" or a "Charity", resources are finite. To attain maximum benefit, it is axiomatic that two factors need to be ensured: **1-** Efficiency and **2-** Equity. In the long run, a third factor is also essential: **3-** Growth. Growth is the factor that will increase the resources, and this in turn will not only enable individuals to overcome the need for assistance through improved opportunity, but will also make available increased provision for those who remain in need. As such it is easy to include growth within the overall factor of efficiency, but as a subject, growth is better dealt with separately in a later section. Efficiency and Equity need further consideration here. Efficiency and equity are discussed here in the context of the overall subject of social services and welfare, and that growth will also relate to this, although reference to micro-economics will need to be made.

Efficiency

Efficiency is a general aim in any effort or service. While absolute efficiency in any situation is difficult to quantify, it is also almost impossible to attain. It is a continual process of improvement in effectiveness, and is an accumulation of experience, improved methods and management, and a sincere desire to perform to maximum ability. Above all it reflects a high level of integrity and motivation. With this so-called "allocative efficiency" the "bundles" of goods and services will be optimally utilised and/or delivered.

But efficiency is not only the duty or prerogative of the person or establishment delivering social services or welfare. It is also imperative on the recipient to "take" only as much as is optimally required, and certainly no more than is sufficient for his/her needs. This becomes the unwritten "social contract" between provider and beneficiary. It is also the contract of conscience that is only regulated through a spiritual and moral framework, perhaps punctuated (and only punctuated) by laws and regulations. Such laws and regulations will fulfil part of the essential process of providing information and laying out standards, allowing "informed" decisions and a "social conscience" that accepts an attitude of sharing of finite resources rather than greedily "taking" regardless of others.

Public Goods and Facilities:

The case for the above considerations on social contract and conscience, and of sharing is best exemplified in a brief discussion about public goods and facilities or amenities. It was noted in previous sections that there are certain services that would not, on the grand scheme of things, be of economic interest as an enterprise, and these include the provision of security, education, health, and the judiciary as examples. The same applies to social services and welfare. These have to be provided by Central or Local government and paid for through the tax system or the local rates. But there are variations in the degree and extent to which such amenities or services are used by the individuals. Where, for example, a museum is established, some will frequent it often, and others may not be bothered. A local library may be used by the few who may appreciate the services enormously. But such amenities are paid for by whoever falls within the tax or local rates system regardless of whether they use them or not. The same goes for even more expensive services such as care of the elderly and the disabled, child care, community social or health care and others. All these items are examples of services that are budgeted for and their cost are, within narrow variations, well identified. There are, however, other costs on society at large that are not necessarily so readily identified and quantified. Examples are the effect on the environment of say putting up a large building for public services, or the health hazards of overcrowded so-called low cost residential housing projects, the psychological stresses of dealing with difficult elderly persons within a family, or the marital and family strains resulting from unemployment.

In all these situations, the concept of efficiency can be stretched, and while at any one time one can possibly assess and quantify the so-called *"Static efficiency"* i.e. the efficiency as assessed at a moment in time, whether maximized or otherwise, to quantify the *"Dynamic efficiency"* which takes into account the continuing expansion of welfare that growth provides may be more difficult, but perhaps even more important over time.

Standards of efficiency vary a great deal. It is generally accepted that governments and especially government run public services tend to lack efficiency if compared with similar operations within the commercial (private) sector. Recognizing this fact led some governments to launch programmes of "privatization" of utilities, some public services and even some management roles within government.

Once again, there is a need to harp on the role of the public in ensuring that efficiency is assisted or even augmented by the simple measure of having the social collective and individual conscience to look at ways and means for conserving the finite resources of the "state" or nature. For example: *"Many environmentalists do not like the use of self interest incentives to solve social issues. Economists who point to the voluminous evidence of the importance of self interest incentives are often accused of ignoring higher motives such as social duties, self sacrifice, and compassion. Although such motives are absent from the simple theories that try to explain the every day behaviour of buyers and sellers (because it has not been necessary to introduce such motives into these theories), economists since Adam Smith have been aware that these higher motives often do exert strong influences on human behaviour…Such higher motives are very powerful at some times and in some situations, but they do not govern many people's behaviour in the course of day-to-day living. If we want to understand how people behave in the aftermath of a flood, or an earthquake, or a war, we need motives in addition to self interest; if we want to understand how people behave day after day in their buying and selling, we need little other than a theory of self interested responses to market incentives. Since control of the environment (for example) requires influencing a mass of small, day-to-day decisions, as well as a few large ones, the appeal to self interest is the only currently known way to induce the required behaviour through voluntary actions"*[208]

This brief extract from a more lengthy discussion in the reference mentioned indicates the importance of behaviour in determining how the resources, and by implications, services, can be optimally harnessed, conserved, and utilized. A social conscience is just one step removed from the higher level of overall regard for Human values as enshrined in the Spiritual Teachings of Faiths. These will, if piously adhered to, not only safeguard the best standards available to Humanity at any one time, but will also correct the inevitable deviations that can be promulgated by individuals or societies in their, often misguided, quests for "modernisation" or to introduce variety. Chaos is only a short distance away from anarchy, and although "upgrading" and "renewal" is always necessary, this is most safely and assuredly introduced as Baha'is believe, through progressive Revelations, Divinely inspired, and voluntarily adhered to. *"Should the lamp of Religion be hidden"*, Baha'u'llah declared, *"chaos and confusion will ensue."*[209] And also: *"The Baha'i conception of social life is essentially based on the subordination of the individual will to that of society. It neither suppresses the individual nor does it exalt him to the point of making him an anti-social creature, a menace to society. As in everything, it follows the `golden mean*[210]*'.*

Above all, society and individuals should make it difficult for the so-called *"free rider"* to benefit personally and selfishly because of the motivation of each person to understate the value of a public good to him or herself in the hope that others will end up "paying" for it.

Equity

Following on the discussion on efficiency above, the question of equity must follow as naturally as any cause or effect should. For the "social conscience" mentioned above will be difficult if not impossible to maintain, unless there is a distinct and perceived spirit of equity pervading throughout society. Abdu'l Baha's stipulation that absolute equality is neither possible nor desirable has been mentioned above. A similar argument in economic terms is found in the following: *"On the distribution side, it is clear that growth and equity may come into conflict. It is quite possible to argue, for example, as the famous American philosopher John Rawls has argued, that the only distribution of income that meets strict cannons of equity is absolute equality. Not everyone would agree, but for those who do there is a clear trade-off, since an equal distribution would leave no incentive for the entrepreneurial risk-taking associated with growth-creating innovations"[211]*. Clearly this would be a recipe for stagnation and a fatal deadening of human capacity.

The opposite extreme, already discussed is also seriously flawed, i.e. when there is a large discrepancy between the "haves" and the "have-nots".

Governments all the time "grapple" with this problem in their tax policies, expenditure distribution, and welfare programmes. While in most situations the motivation is political, it is important to acknowledge that even this can be an incentive to improve the lot of the population, especially in intelligent democracies. In its simplest form, government calculation can be done on the basis of individual *"earned"* income i.e. wages or salaries received for services or employment, and *"Unearned"* income i.e. the returns of investments, rents, inheritances etc.. Tax will be calculated on the level of income, and each country will have its minimum allowances, below which no tax is due. Again, all income above certain levels is taxed in a variety of rates, tranches, or schemes.

What is more difficult to work out, is the levels of *"indirect"* taxation, and how that can be pitched so as not to create particular difficulties for some people more than others. The commonest form of indirect taxation is the so-called *"Purchase or Value Added"* tax paid for as part of price of goods or services, with the tax passed on by the vendor or provider to the relevant authority be it local, regional or national treasury. For example: Value Added Tax (VAT) levied on books will raise their prices and may inhibit the poorer individual. The same applies to essential items such as children's needs, domestic fuel, and food. Excess VAT on luxury or potentially harmful items such as leisure, tobacco, and luxury motor vehicles may be more acceptable not only as a source of revenue, but also as a means of re-distribution of the national wealth.

Generalizations in all these considerations will always attract arguments to show aspects of inequality or unfairness. For example, where it can be argued that domestic fuel is essential and therefore should be taxed less or not taxed at all, it will also be shown that those who can afford it, will often squander or misuse it by, say, overusing heating or air-conditioning. Subsidized essential foodstuffs are classically misused, as for example in Egypt when at a time the national loaf was so heavily subsidized that it was cheaper for the people to feed it to their cattle rather than use fodder or silage. The government subsequently had to redress this anomaly. Another situation worth noting is when a job is skilled risky, difficult or unpleasant. Naturally such jobs will be taken only if pay is commensurate with the demands. It can be argued that to treat such incomes for tax purposes on an equal basis to those of less demanding jobs is not only unfair, but possibly unwise, as it will reduce the incentive for people to take up such jobs. The rewards must to a reasonable extent match the demands, risks, hazards or skill.

Tax policies alone cannot therefore be relied upon as an instrument of equity. But that they are useful is beyond doubt. Other policies include:

The distribution of wealth: This is most commonly done at the point of transfer of wealth, mainly in two ways: **a)** At the point of realizing the proceeds of capital appreciation when wealth is transferred between one owner and the other, and **b)** At the point of transfer of wealth as gift or inheritance.

In these and similar situations, tax will act as a suitable instrument for top slicing part of the transferred wealth in order to benefit the general public. But! Inevitably this generates resentment. In the society advocated and envisaged in the Teachings of all Divine Religions, as has been demonstrated above, this is enjoined on all people so that the giving up of stipulated surpluses, whether they be Tithes, Zackat or Huququ'llah, is on a voluntary basis, spurred upon by a sincere and spiritual acceptance of the imperative ethos of not accumulating excessive wealth and also the social conscience towards fellow human beings. The highest degree of such endeavour is demonstrated, again as shown earlier, in the Baha'I Teachings which put the onus entirely on the individual to assess the amount of wealth to be transferred. It can only be assumed that in God's Wisdom, Humankind has attained a level of maturity since the times of the previous Divine Dispensations, that would make such high level of conscious mutuality and reciprocity of well being a matter of individual judgement making use of the "guidelines" stipulated in the Teachings. It is not a reflection of any lack of high ideals on the part of previous Revelations and their Teachings, which had appeared at times when Humanity required more "gentle" egging or urging than at present, and the needs of society were perhaps less complex than at present.

Another form of distribution of wealth relies on the provision of free goods or services. It has been stipulated in Islam as was shown previously that the essential elements of life such as water, air and fire are not to be owned by individuals, but should be common "good/s". Water is available free of charge in some countries now. But this is a rarity. Modern society needs good and reliable sources of water and other essentials, almost always to be delivered at the point of usage, and this inevitably incurs processing, distributing, and maintaining at adequate flow pressures and sanitation. This has a cost. To date, air is still breathed freely!!

Essential services delivered free of charge most commonly include health and education. This is another form of re-distribution of wealth, whether that is because some use the free state services while others choose to pay for parallel private services, or because there is direct government insurance deductions from earning individuals to provide the funding. It may be encouraging that healthy people may go through a good period of their lifetime not needing these services, and yet continue to pay for them.

That these services are almost sacred duties and responsibilities of society and government, or (as in the Baha'i Faith) through the "trustees" is not arguable. The "political" dimension, however, extends to whether the contributions for such services are to be direct and ear-marked, such as special taxes for health care, or that they could be funded from the overall budget. As for the social dimension, this can extend to the level of conscious, voluntary contribution of individuals towards the well being of their fellow human beings, either as part of the voluntary assessments of dues as seen above or indeed as additional charitable contributions.

The concept of the *"Minimum Wage"* as a means of distribution of wealth is a third method enforced legally in some countries. Its value is rather dubious, because there are means of getting round the law if the employer is really eager, and also because it can have an inflationary effect on the economy, and can lead to higher unemployment by killing off some jobs. The point has been discussed previously. Nevertheless, this method may be useful, especially as a means of maintaining a level of revenue to the government, enabling it to invest and create further wealth and employment. Once again, such a measure is best accepted by employers on a voluntary basis, and on the basis that the employee is more effective if satisfied with his/her income. The personal satisfaction of the employer in caring for his/her employee must be a worthy factor which can compensate for any reduced profit. In some situations, especially if imposed on a "monopsonistic" market, a minimum wage can increase both wages and employment in that market.

Growth

Growth is an essential ingredient in raising the standards of living. It creates a dynamism that can be self feeding and perpetuating, and in a society that enjoys growth, there is a "feel good" factor that pervades and has a knock on effect on people's attitudes, behaviour, self confidence, and drive. One is tempted to mention some negative effects resulting from growth, if only to maintain some balance. Thus growth can result in increasing people's appetite for further material gains (greed?), and it can result in a less caring attitude as people find their interests in material and technological acquisitions that end up occupying their sensibilities and eroding their social interactive skills. On the whole, however, growth is healthy and desirable. It is a mixture of macro-economics (total savings and total investments), and micro-economics (entrepreneurial and innovative successes). On its own, it can enhance the effects of efficiency, and indeed, enough growth can occasionally overcome the drag of inefficiency. This latter point is particularly evident in developing countries, where, in spite of inefficiencies, and even corruption, growth patterns in the order of 6-8 percent per annum were, and probably still are, to be seen. Until recently, the so-called *"Tiger economies"* of Asia were a good example of this phenomenon. Set backs do occur, but rebounds also occur.

The role of government in assisting the process of growth will be discussed later, and it is sufficient to mention here that the engines of growth available to governments are many. The main engine is the tax systems. But there are additional means. Enhancing education and the health of the population, providing information, setting standards, maintaining public services and the environment, encouraging mobility and flexibility of labour, all create an environment suitable for enterprise, innovation, and investment. Trade, especially export are also to be facilitated. All this will create wealth and can enable the caring for the vulnerable factions of society and maintaining internal and external security and peace, and a general harmony within society.

Once again, it is reasonable to state, that the best government plans can only succeed if the population is carried along willingly and enthusiastically, and can be most successful when there is an overall atmosphere of mutual trust, integrity, and honesty. These latter qualities have to be demonstrated clearly by the people in authority. The given wisdom is that "the fish starts its putrefaction in its head". The body then follows. This is to a great extent the function and inherent responsibility of the "electorate". A system of government based on competing political factionalism, adversarial in nature, and appealing to part, as distinct from the whole, of society, is bound to result in limited overall benefits, and may not be seen as enjoying the franchise of the total body of the electorate. A system, however, where the person is elected on merit, to represent the *whole body politic* of society, will hopefully demonstrate allegiance to that whole rather than a part or a faction. Only then will *"Reciprocity and Symmetry"* as declared by Abdu'l Baha and mentioned in sections above, become a reality.

Finance

Finance is a general term relating to money, transactions, and the management of wealth. It spans the most meagre of individual resources to the most complex government or even world economy.

One essentially thinks of money, and no doubt money is the expression of finance that is obvious to everyone. But expression is only one part of the variety of means which together constitute the value of resources, wealth, and exchange. Emerging from the primitive method of exchange of value through *"barter"*, the world has developed a complex system of currencies and other units of value with which to measure, not only exchange, but also storage of value, and building quantum and variety of wealth.

As a measure, therefore, money is valued in many ways: **1-** As an intrinsic material the content of which is assessable, e.g. in terms of the weight content of a precious metal. **2-** As a promissory note backed by an individual or authority that can be relied upon to deliver the face value indicated on the note. **3-** A service or commodity which is acceptable and assessable as a means in any transaction.

Metal & Coins:

Gold and silver were the main precious metals used to hold as wealth and for trade. The scramble for these and other precious metals and commodities was at its peak, as was discussed earlier, during the acquisitions of territory in the Americas and Africa. Their value lies in the scarcity, the *"timelessness"* as well as their ability to enter into works of art, treasure, ornament, or industrial products. Carting such commodities around, and cutting them to appropriate sizes and weight to suit so many conceivable transactions, is, quite obviously out of question. The initial way to overcome this was to issue the *"promissory"* note that relates to a certain weight of say gold or silver, and to keep that weight in a safe place ready to exchange it for the promissory note if redemption is sought. Thus, the word *Pound Sterling* originally was a note backed by a pound in weight of (sterling) silver. Later, a *gold or silver coin* became the recognized currency and was handled for transactions. The difficulty arose when new coins disappeared as soon as they were minted and acquired, because people naturally preferred them to old or base metal coins which would have lost part of their face value, no matter how small that loss. This totally reasonable behaviour on the part of people is clearly in keeping with the so called *Gresham law*[212] which indicated that "bad money drives out good". Dealing with coins even in non precious metal ones occasionally created other difficulties as when inflation makes the inherent value of the metal in the coin greater than the face value of the coin itself. This happened in Chile in the 1970's, and is nearly happening at present because of the rise of the price of copper. People may, under the circumstances, benefit from melting the coins to use the metal.

2- Paper Money: Issuing notes is a more practical and convenient way to facilitate trade and exchange. It is easy to carry, and as promissory notes they can be printed in many denominations. While the earliest recorded coinage is attributed to the kings of Lydia around the fourth century BC, one of the earliest issuers of formal bank notes was the *Riksbank* of Sweden, established in 1668[213]. Traditionally, paper money was backed unit for unit by gold. But, allowing for the natural phenomenon that not everyone holding a paper note will wish to redeem it all at the same time, and also that while some are redeeming their paper notes, others are depositing them or their equivalents in gold, the system developed so that there was enough *"cover"* at any one time in a particular bank to satisfy the needs of those wishing to redeem the notes in their possession. And while traditionally again notes were issued by *"Central Banks"* this was, and probably still is to a limited extent, not the only issuing authority. Thus, the various big Banks in Honk Kong issued their *"Banknotes"*, and Scotland has its own Scottish Pound note. The important factor is that such notes are both legal tender, and are backed by a reliable resource and authority. Money declared by government as legal tender, i.e. acceptable in exchange, is known as *Fiat money*.

3- Goods and services: Money, as has been shown above, is an expression of a value. The actual value, however, depends upon what that value can be exchanged for. Thus, a unit of currency could buy an item of clothes or food or a particular service such as a train ticket or a job done by a plumber. In these disparate examples, and the lists can be endless, the value of the unit of currency is expressed in so many different forms, each one of which is an expression that is only relative to the others, and they are so different. Considered in a slightly different way, the value of the currency unit depends on what the individual would like to exchange it for. What can be important for one, for example food, may not be so for the other. Moreover, when one is not in need to exchange this unit at a certain time, it can be "stored", i.e. saved. In so doing it can be drawn upon when required, and may gain in value through interest accruing if put in an interest bearing account or used in another investment capacity. These aspects were discussed in previous sections, but the point to be made here is that money, while nominally carrying a value, that value is in fact only a relative one, and depends on the resources and method of consumption and the relative price or need.

This is important not only in individual small scale situations, but just as much in national wealth and budget considerations. For while one government will lay emphasis on the acquisition of arms and the upkeep of a large armed force, another government may wish to invest more in infrastructure such as roads, education, or health, and another may give more importance to investing in new industry, agriculture or other means of production. In practice all governments do all those things, but it is the emphasis that differs. Again, some government may choose to borrow, from its citizens (bonds, treasury bills etc..), or on the international money market, running an internal or an external budget deficit, in order to meet its commitments or fulfil its investment and development plans. Another may act on the belief that a financial surplus in its coffers is the sure way to maintain or enhance the value of its currency, which in turn would assist indirectly its development plans. In all these situations, it is the relative, rather than the absolute value of money that has the real significance. Relativity here is not only in what the unit of currency can purchase, but also in how this particular unit values against other world currencies. With a freely convertible currency where there is unrestricted exchange this relative value depends on the level at which each currency finds itself according to so many factors that interplay on the international currency valuation and/or speculation. In countries that restrict the convertibility or free exchange of their currencies, the value of currency is dependent on the arbitrary setting laid down by the government in question, whether realistically or otherwise. These valuation settings are usually made in relation to other world accepted currency, and may be tied to a particular currency such as the US dollar. If this arbitrary valuation is not realistic there will be what is termed a "black market", whereby people will endeavour to undertake exchanges on the basis, quite commonly, of the real value as opposed to the artificial one set as described above.

This is quite a complicated situation when considered world-wide. In recent times, the world has seen wild speculations on currencies that were either deemed unrealistic in their declared value, or, in a more sinister way, these speculations were nothing but organised "gambling" on the part of individuals or financial institutions, to create a desired change in the valuation level so as to suit the speculation aim of eventual profit. There is a greater awareness of the dangers inherent in these situations, and governments are working in concert to alter the conditions that allow these speculations, as they can only create or enhance financial, and occasionally general economic and even political instability. The creation of the *Euro* is one bold step taken by the European Community replacing individual member nation currencies. This move was entered into enthusiastically by some members, one of the first being Italy, as it saw this as a means of ridding itself of the weak and small denomination *lira*, or reluctantly, as in Germany, where the general sentiment and the economics made it difficult to get rid of the strong Deutsche Mark it was so proud of. At the time of writing, the attitude of the UK, whose *pound sterling* plays an important role in world currency and financial transactions, is still undecided as to the merits or demerits of entering the *Euro*. At present, therefore, the world is dealing with essentially four major currencies: the US dollar, Sterling, the Euro, and the (Japanese) Yen, with the Swiss Franc not too far behind. Smaller countries who wish to maintain a recognized valuation to their currencies frequently arrange that their currencies "shadow" or get "pegged" to a major currency. Thus, Egypt has for some years now pegged its pound to the US dollar. Argentina very recently declared its desire to do that. Even Cuba has recently started to issue its "export" peso, equivalent to one US dollar, allowing it to be used only in foreign trade and tourism.

4- Barter: This method of exchange was mentioned at the start of this section as a primitive means of exchange long ago superseded by money. The difficulty with barter is very simply. It is unwieldy, and it relies on the inevitability that for the barter to occur, there must be a coincidence of the mutual need of those parties who are undertaking the barter. In its simplest form, the author recalls with interest the situation in the Southern Sudan in the late 1950's when the natives would come to the town with an animal (sheep, goat, chicken etc..) to barter it with the local shopkeeper for a measure of grain (usually sorghum). It can only be assumed that this still does occur in some places around the world. But, it can be seen, that for this barter transaction to be fulfilled, the coincidence of availability of the grain and the need for the animal given in exchange has also to be fulfilled. It is easy to see that this is not a very practical way for present day society.

This is not to say, however, that barter does not occur nowadays. Indeed it often occurs on a very large scale. The most common barter agreements can be in billions of dollars or pounds between the oil producing countries and the major industrial countries. Multi-billion deals agreements for crude oil sold at an agreed price for several years in advance, are struck in exchange for arms, aircraft (civil and military), large development (mostly construction) projects and other trade. The situation can get more complicated when one recognizes that the crude may not actually end up in the country which originally entered into the barter agreement, but may be re-sold several times over and to different countries or concerns. So barter is still alive, and will certainly have its place in world trade for the foreseeable future. Indeed, it may be said that it could be valuable in encouraging countries and people to look at what they are best at, whether a local produce or craft, or industry or service, and develop these further. This would avoid unnecessary duplications and imitations and also discredits a major misapprehension among some people and governments, that it will be in their best interest to achieve so-called *self sufficiency*. Self sufficiency is neither appropriate, nor even possible. And one can easily see that if every country is self sufficient, trade will come to a grinding halt. This notion is mentioned only to be dismissed as unrealistic, unachievable and dangerous to pursue.

Circulation Of Money:

It is natural to consider the next stage of this brief and simplified description of money, in relation to the fact that the essential value of money is in its circulation. Indeed, it is not only money that has to circulate, but also wealth in its wider concept. In previous sections, the wisdom of Francis Bacon that "money is like muck, most useful if spread around" is here worthy of recall. Circulation of money spreads the value so as to create benefits through any channel that happens to have use for an amount of money. It also can enhance the initial value of the money through interest accrued or investment returns. It was not so long ago that an elderly head of a small "sheikhdom" in the Gulf area insisted on keeping all the cash earned through his territory's oil in sackfulls!! The situation was altered only when this Sheikh was deposed by his own family, allowing the development of proper financial and banking systems and many other improvements in the territory's conditions.

The practical means of allowing the efficient and (largely) secure way to utilize money and allow it to circulate is through the system of banking.

Banking:

Discussing banking in detail is outside the scope of this work. The important features to describe revolve around four main categories of banks: **1-** Private banks. **2-** Central (government) banks. **3-** International or Multinational Banks. **4-** The World Bank.

Private Banks: These enterprises started simply as money or precious metal deposit facilities especially for gold. They grew out of at least two other trades. While goldsmiths naturally played an important role in weighing, measuring, and working crude gold ore into coins, ingots and jewellery, they also acted as depositors of gold for people.

The scriveners (scribes) who had writing skills sold their services managing other people's financial affairs. Further developments created the "Merchant Bankers". These would have been individuals or small groups who would trade in commodities but ended up also trading in finance. The Rothschilds started this way and are still referred to as "merchant bankers" today, but the other great name was the Barings Bank, now defunct and taken over[214]. Riksbank of Sweden (1668), mentioned above, started as a private enterprise, but is now the Central Bank of Sweden. In the same way, the Bank of England (Central Bank of the UK), was established in 1694 (26 years after Riksbank) and started also as a private joint-stock company.

Since these early days, numerous banks developed in practically every country as soon as that country developed any form of system for finance or trade. These private banks fall into two main categories: The *Commercial banks.* These deal mainly with taking deposits and making loans. They become household names within one or more countries. Examples are. Barclays Bank and Lloyds Bank. Or they may be *Investment banks* (or *Merchant banks*) which operate at the level of companies, enterprise and business, raising capital, providing loans, and, on a much larger scale, advising on and managing large changeovers, take-overs, mergers and similar large scale activities. These activities in the present climate of globalisation increasingly cut across national boundaries, or parochial interests.

The situation is currently changing so fast that the above distinction is being blurred, and most banks now have themselves merged so as to provide a range of products and services on both the individual, small scale level, as well as the larger corporate and government levels. Moreover, this simple description of the *commercial* banks grossly overlooks specializations developing in the banking systems, whereby some would be more involved with property loans, others with industrial developments, agricultural projects or other financial and investment services. Again, in all these activities, there used to be a distinction between those institutions dealing with the *retail* end of the business (individuals or small businesses), and the *wholesale* activities dealing with large corporate customers, government agencies and financial institutions.

The main feature in all these banking activities is the availability of money through the cumulative accounts that depositors provide, on scales that may be beyond the capacity of individual people or businesses. Depositors expect security for their deposits, as well as interest, and borrowers expect to repay their loans with interest. So the question of interest looms very large and crucial in to-day's world of trade and finance. While the world accepts this fact without challenge, the Islamic world still has to get to grips with it, and to reconcile it with the very clear prohibition of interest as mentioned previously. Various means are being devised to overcome this difficulty, such as considering any "profit" accruing on deposits as a distribution of a proportion of the overall profits of the bank. This may overcome the religious difficulty, but it will not suit the overall means of controlling and regulating such banking activity, which is the responsibility of the Central Bank or other financial "watch dog" authority of the country where such a "religious" bank is registered. Whether it will also create the best environment for such a bank's scope and extent of activity appears to be also in doubt. It would be noted that in this context, Christianity and Judaism include prohibition of interest (usury) among their teachings. So it was God's wisdom for this stage in the evolution of humanity, that a new and clear message concerning this question of interest was revealed by Baha'u'llah:[215] *"...it is lawful and proper to charge interest on money, that the people of the world may, in a spirit of amity and fellowship and with joy and gladness, devotedly engage themselves in magnifying the Name of Him*

Who is the Well-Beloved of all mankind. Verily He ordaineth according to His Own choosing. He hath now made interest on money lawful, even as He had made it unlawful in the past. Within His grasp He holdeth the kingdom of authority. He doeth and ordaineth. He is in truth the Ordainer, the All-Knowing"

In this way has Baha'u'llah spoken with the Authority of the Revealer of a new Divine message, that the previous prohibition on interest is repealed, but that: *"However, this is a matter that should be practised with moderation and fairness. Our Pen of Glory hath, as a token of wisdom and for the convenience of the people, desisted from laying down its limit. Nevertheless We exhort the loved ones of God to observe justice and fairness, and to do that which would prompt the friends of God to evince tender mercy and compassion towards each other. He is in truth the Counsellor, the Compassionate, the All-Bountiful. God grant that all men may be graciously aided to observe that which the Tongue of the One true God hath uttered. And if they put into practice what We have set forth, God - exalted be His glory - will assuredly double their portion through the heaven of His bounty. Verily He is the Generous, the Forgiving, the Compassionate. Praise be unto God, the Most Exalted, the Most Great…Nevertheless the conduct of these affairs hath been entrusted to the men of the House of Justice that they may enforce them according to the exigencies of the time and the dictates of wisdom.…Once again We exhort all believers to observe justice and fairness and to show forth love and contentment. They are indeed the people of Baha, the companions of the Crimson Ark. Upon them be the peace of God, the Lord of all Names, the Creator of the heavens."*

The principle of interest is therefore seen as acceptable to God in this age, and that it should reflect an attitude of compassion, fairness and justice, and that its "regulation" should be entrusted to the (Universal) House of Justice. This will, moreover, avoid the practice referred by Baha'u'llah whereby: "*Many ecclesiastics in Persia have, through innumerable designs and devices, been feeding on illicit gains obtained by usury. They have contrived ways to give its outward form a fair semblance of lawfulness. They make a plaything of the laws and ordinances of God, but they understand not*".

Central Banks:

A Central Bank is an essential part of the financial make up of any country. It can have different names and examples are "The Federal Reserve System" of the USA, The "Bundesbank" of Germany, the "Banque de France", and the "Bank of England". The role is comparable, but they will differ in detail of their remit and the mode of their operation. They all provide the cash to their national economies, maintain reserves as a cover for their respective currencies, regulate and hold reserves for the other banks within its sphere of control, print money on the promise that it will redeem it at pre-supposed values, and act as bankers to their respective governments and "bankers of last resort".

Their role in the macroeconomics of the countries will be discussed in the next section, but it will be useful to state at this stage that the situation is altering appreciably in that they are becoming so interdependent that their individual freedom of manoeuvre is gradually reducing. Europe has seen a major change with the establishment of the **Euro** and the **European Central Bank (ECB)** governing the macroeconomics of the E.U as a single body. Some small countries outside the *Euro-zone* are beginning to tag on to the Euro, the most recent example being Cuba, which, seeing that about 40% of its trade is with Europe, and being almost isolated from the US dollar dealings in its international trade (for political, not commercial or financial reasons), is now finding the Euro a convenient currency and financial environment and medium.

This has been the largest and most significant change in the financial settings since World War II, and it is seen as auguring an inexorably move of the financial world towards a financial system that works in concert and in large blocks. At present, the currency *of last resort* appears to be the US Dollar. But the Euro (which has absorbed the *mighty* Deutschemark), the Japanese Yen, and the Pound Sterling are all sizeable blocks which in one way or another can act as *safe havens* for those individuals, businesses, or even governments who wish to underpin their wealth. These large financial system blocks are not idle. They act as the *power-houses* and *engines* that pull or push world economics forwards, generating growth, through their effect not only as trading blocks and sizeable economies in their own right, but also through their role as *carriages* which the lesser economies or smaller concerns use in their trade and economic activities and developments. They provide a measure of security, and an acceptable range of fluctuating exchange values. A measure of the efficiency with which individual countries can benefit from this situation is reflected on the growth pattern demonstrated in their economies. A good "dynamic efficiency" that is achieved on the back of growth will provide greater resources for such needs of the population as social security and welfare. This should ideally be also accompanied by "static efficiency" by which the usefulness of these resources are maximized.

International or Multi-national Banks:

The banking system has reacted positively to the opportunities made available through the exponential increase in communication, whether through electronics, means of travel, or the more widespread use of English as a language medium. This is maximised through the gradually increasing and continuing abolition of exchange restrictions and controls around the world. The ability to transfer monies across the globe at the press of a button and at any time in the day or night, has become instrumental in facilitating transactions and allowing financial houses to operate regardless of time zones, public days off or time taken for each transaction. The result is the growth of banking across these geographical, political and currency boundaries.

It is not incongruous, therefore to mention the *Globalization* that has encompassed the financial markets. One of the first developments in this movement towards globalization was the growth of the foreign currency markets in Europe in the 1960's. It started with involvement of the US dollar, whereby *Eurodollar* markets were the first to develop. These were markets in bank deposits and loans denominated in US dollars and located outside the United States. Other "Eurocurrency markets" later developed, but the dollar markets dominated. These "markets" acted essentially as the "wholesale" money markets, and were outside the control of the US Federal Reserve. As financial vehicles they were useful as a product of a "window" of opportunity away from Central Bank regulations. They became, however, rather redundant in their usefulness from the 1980's onwards as they were superseded by the fast development of global integration of the financial systems which is now an establish fact.

As the global economy is fast developing, it is imperative that a global financial system is now required which can fulfil the needs as well as the aspirations of the peoples of the world and their leaders. Such a system, however, should operate within all the reasonable safeguards that prevent, detect early, or correct as adequately as possible, the excesses or mishandlings that such a powerful flashpoint system of transactions can generate. Examples of these excesses are in the news all the time, and while many of the catastrophes that have occurred have been the result of "rogue" operator/s, the damages are inevitably grave enough to warrant serious attempts at creating a "fail-safe" system as far as is humanly possible.

Wilful misappropriation is, regrettably, not that difficult. It is, nevertheless, reprehensible. But it is not difficult to see how such misappropriations are so common, given that extraneous or external controls will never, by themselves, be enough. There will be the need for intrinsic, inherent and genuine control exercised by the operators of these systems, and reflected in a real conscience that sees any action in terms of the general good, and devoid of the element of gamble or unacceptable risk taking, let alone greed and avarice. It is natural to allow for the factor of human or system error, but this is different from allowing unacceptable practices, especially the ones similar to what was observed latterly with the big bank failures mentioned recently and in the late 1990's. The material world is probably incapable of providing such safeguards on its own. There is the need for the spiritual dimension provided by religion, and its deep teachings for individual probity, trustworthiness, and honesty. With the development of these qualities in an individual, a further, no less important, faculty develops: that of wisdom. *"The essence of wisdom is the fear of God"*[216]. is an echo of previous teachings, such as those in the book of Proverbs, ch. 3, vs. 13: *"happy is the man that findeth wisdom, and the man that getteth understanding"*, and Ch. 4, vs.5: *"Get wisdom, get understanding: forget it not; neither decline from the words of my mouth"*

The World Bank:

The full name of this organisation is: **"International Bank for Reconstruction and Development (IBRD)**. This is one of the major creations of the United Nations monetary and Financial Conference, (the Bretton Woods Conference) in New Hampshire, USA in 1944. It is based in Washington D.C. and it began its operations officially in 1946, initially receiving capital contributions from (United Nations) member States, each according to its relative economic resources. Only about 10% of each subscriber's contribution is actually paid up. The rest of the money is available and would be called upon if required to meet obligations. The World Bank's loan activities are additionally financed by floating bonds designated in US dollars, against the security of its capital, which has recently been estimated at US $ 200.000 million. Although the first loans were made for World War II reconstruction, by 1949 the emphasis had shifted to loans for the purpose of economic development.

The bank usually makes loans directly to governments, or to private enterprises with their government's guarantee, for specific projects when private capital is not available on reasonable terms. As a prestigious bank it is able to borrow at very competitive interest rates, and in turn can provide its funds at competitive rates. A large part of the bank's portfolio initially consisted of loans to public and private owned utilities for investment in electric power, transportation, and water supply lines, but by the late 20th century, agriculture and rural development had become the most important lending sector. As a matter of general policy, the bank lends only for the cost of the imported material, equipment, and services and disbursements are usually made directly to the supplier. In addition to financial assistance, the bank also provides technical assistance. The project itself must be capable of repaying the interest and the capital over an agreed period.

The bank is administered by a board of governors, executive directors, a president, and staff. The board of governors, composed of representatives from all the member countries, meets once a year; leaving policy matters to be carried out by the 21 executive directors, who approve all loans.

After the initial prestigious capital-intensive projects, the Bank turned to sponsoring more "grass roots" projects in developing countries, such as establishing basic training programmes, population control schemes, and improvements in basic agriculture. Each project is preceded by adequate background research to ascertain its feasibility and its value in the overall development of the economy in the country it is proposed for, as well as the ability to repay the loan[217] &[218].

Three other bodies supervise activities in less developed countries (LDCs) and play a more direct part than the IBRD, although they are part of the World Bank Group: These are:

a- **The IFC (International Finance Corporation)**. The field of activity of this corporation is in relation to the private sector within the LDCs. It helps to develop and encourage private enterprise and business. It takes a share in the equity capital of the companies, securing finance for them and acting as adviser.

b- **The IDA (International Development Association)**. This association is active in the poorest countries, lending funds for approved projects, at heavily subsidized interest rates and with repayment periods as long as 50 years. Many of its projects are for developing the infrastructure of the developing nation— mainly roads, waterways, ports, airports, power supplies, irrigation, and telecommunications.

c- **MIGA. (The Multilateral Investment Guarantee Agency)**. This agency guarantees eligible investments against losses resulting from non-commercial risks such as expropriation of assets by host country, or repudiation of official contracts, or armed conflict and civil unrest. It is reasonable to look at this activity as a form of insurance.

No doubt there would be other vehicles constituted to offer comparable services, but the above mentioned ones are the salient examples.

The above examples also indicate that on a national and international scale, the whole system of finance depends on the factor of interest, whether to the lender or the borrower. But, in addition, the factor of insurance is also in operation. This latter factor is, in some theological opinion, particularly in Islam, unacceptable, as it violates a basic belief that God is the provider, and that true believers must accept the *"Will of God"*. A disaster is considered a will of God, and to ensure against it is tantamount to interference with that "Will", and the consequences resulting. It is fair to say, however, that this viewpoint is only of academic interest at present, and hardly any government or organisation upholds it or acts upon it.

Macroeconomics

Macroeconomics ("Macro" being the Greek word "Makro" meaning "large", as compared with "Mikro" or "Micro" meaning small) is the aspect of economics that deals with the whole of the economy from a national point of view. Inflation, Unemployment, and Growth are the big macroeconomic issues of our time. The three are inter-related, because essentially, as was discussed previously, the measure of prosperity depends on the growth in the economy, which in turn is a factor of increased real wealth (wealth that is not just an expression of inflation) and its effect on the population's employment opportunities and actual earning capabilities. Indeed, the *"central problem of economics in the second half of the twentieth century is the management of **prosperity** to maximize individual and general welfare"*. The term prosperity is highlighted and underlined because it will constitute the central theme of the next section of this work. At present the world tends to think of prosperity in terms of **national income.** This is described by Alfred Marshall (1842-1924), the English economists mentioned previously as : *The aggregate net product of, and the sole source of payment for, all the agents of production".* Thus, the factors that create and then enjoy or consume national income, or the aggregate net production of goods and services, taking into account depreciation, wear and tear, replacements and so on (hence the emphasis on *net*), all contribute to, and constitute all the earnings of individuals, society, and government, that, in turn allow all these their expenditures (*payments* for goods and services). The important factor here, surely, must be fairness in distribution of this *net source of payment.*

It is interesting that Marshall stated that: Prosperity alone—growth in national income—was necessary, but not sufficient to eliminate poverty. This opinion is also agreed by another eminent scholar, Henry George.[219] They also agree that poverty is both debasing to the individual and a serious hindrance to progress and further prosperity. Indeed Marshall also invokes the necessity to consider the reciprocal relationship of prosperity and spirituality, both aspects of human life that mutually enhance each other.

National incomes have grown very significantly over the past century in spite of the two World Wars and so many other wars and manmade catastrophes. As an example, Britain's government budget in early Victorian times was only £30 million. Even by 1881, it was only £69 million. This is compared with more than £600 billion in recent years. This is increased wealth in every way even allowing for inflationary factors on the increased figures. The situation is replicated in most advanced economies with some variations, but in the case of lesser advanced countries the increase is not so significant, and the inflation is more often than not greater in magnitude.

There will be many factors to account for this increase in genuine prosperity, but they fall into four main categories: **1-** Greater exploitation of the ***natural resources*** of the world, including better utilisation of the existing soil for agriculture, increase development of sources of energy, and scientific means of rearing livestock and fish-stock for food. **2-** The increase in population around the world, increased education and sophistication of people, and the greater skills they develop, all add up to an increasing wealth within the ***human resources***. **3-** The world had learned to develop and maintain its ***capital resources***, a term here that embraces better financial management and conservation, as well as the development and maintenance of tools, plant and machinery, and including elements of the infrastructure of society such as houses, public buildings, schools, hospitals, roads, ports, airports and railways. **4-** ***Trade and foreign investments.*** Included in this would be the "multiplier" factor that increases, *and spreads,* wealth around the world. Self sufficiency may have its exponents, but, as mentioned, previously, it can hardly ever be achieved in the complex world today, and its place in modern economics can only be entertained within the overall concept of efficiency and good management of the resources available to geographical or demographic areas of the world, rather than countries as circumscribed within political boundaries. In this manner, consumption is achieved at as maximum efficiency and economy as acceptable within the overall enjoyment of prosperity, and all surplus is made available to other areas of the world in good and fair exchange. The situation at present where the USA consumes an estimated one fifth of the world resources while constituting only about 1% of the world's population, is both unacceptable and unsustainable.

Determinant Forces Within Macroeconomics

A detailed discussion of macroeconomics is beyond the scope of this work. But it is important to note that the factors that determine the three essentials mentioned above, *inflation, employment/unemployment, and growth* revolve around the supply and demand for money, the prevailing interest rates and the influences that affect their changes, the rate of exchange of any currency in relation to other currencies, and the balance of payments as an indication of net growth and/or prosperity. Individual government budgets, internal budget deficits or surpluses, state of employment, and business cycles (national, regional or global) are all reflections of the management techniques, and perhaps the economic philosophies or ideologies, that prevail at any one time within a country, a region or the world. The salient ideologies of recent times have been the *Keynesian, the New Classical, the Monetarist, and the Supply Side* schools of thought.

The Supply And Demand Of Money:

Money, as mentioned previously is either in the form of cash or assets. Both have a value, but one can say that holding cash is least risky but also least profitable, while assets can be more profitable, but also more risky. In whichever form it is, money carries a value, and as such, the value can be an appreciating or a depreciating one. Money not earning interest will depreciate in value, while any interest earned will either maintain or increase its value depending on that rate of interest in relation to the prevailing rate of inflation. As for assets, they will also depreciate if they suffer loss of value, deterioration, or misjudged risk. They will appreciate in value if they provide income or respond to a positive supply and demand situation. In its simplest form, an asset can be seen as a "bond", which carries a nominal value, and provides a predetermined return. As such, it can be kept or traded, and its value will depend the rate of return. This is a simplified description which will suffice the needs of this discussion.

The other simplified point is that of the equilibrium of supply and demand of money. In theory, an amount of money may be available to satisfy a state of demand exactly. Normally, however, money is (or bonds are) in circulation, creating transaction balances of receipts and payments (or disbursements). As a safeguard against a mismatch in time between receipts and disbursements, or to safeguard against eventualities or unforeseen circumstances, individuals or organisations will retain some spare money or assets. This is termed **precautionary balances**. This produces two effects: the determinant of the *quantity* of money, and the *velocity of circulation* of money. The quantity of money is defined as: **M0** which is the cash in circulation. It is a term used only in the UK. **M1** which is M0 plus demand deposits. **M2** which includes deposits in banks and financial institutions, such as mutual funds. **M3,** again only used in the UK, **and it is** M1 plus the public and private sector time deposits. **M4** used in the USA comprises M1 plus negotiable cash deposits, that is the wholesale bank deposits by institutions.

However, money does not normally stand idle, and within annual transactions every pound, on average, is used 5 times each year. This "work" that money does can end up with each pound creating up to 4 times its value, thereby becoming a means for enhancement of the *national income.*

Monetary equilibrium, therefore, is in need of something to maintain it. This adjustment factor is the interest rate. As the quantity of money and "bonds" is fixed, individuals or institutions who may need more money than they have available, may wish to sell some of their "bonds". Within small scale changes, this will have minimal effect on the overall "fixed" mix of money and "bonds". But on larger scale disposal of bonds, their price will fall, interest rates will rise, making it more profitable to increase money balances. A (new) state of equilibrium then arises when the supply of "bonds" dries up and their prices start to rise. Interest rates will then start to reduce and people will dispose of some of their cash to start buying again. At some point the demand for money will equal the supply. *"Monetary equilibrium occurs when the rate of interest is such that the demand for money equals its supply, and hence the demand for bonds equals their supply"*. Similarly: *"Monetary disturbances which can arise from changes in either the demand or the supply of money,* (will) *cause changes in the interest rate"*[220]. Governments use these effects when determining their fiscal (budgetary) and monetary (money supply) policies. In national terms, therefore, an increase in money supply by the government (or Central Bank) will result in lowering of interest rates. In an international economy with no currency restrictions, depreciation of value of the currency involved will result, and sale of assets in order to invest in foreign assets will produce a higher return. A state of equilibrium may occur when exports in that currency become more competitive, and imports more expensive, investments expenditure increases, leading to increased national income. If this process is extended, the value of the currency in question will rise because of increased aggregate demand and wealth, expenditure or desired expenditure may exceed actual output in the economy, and an *"inflationary gap"* is created. Central Banks (or governments) will resort in these situations to raising interest rates if the situation warrants intervention.

Attempts at "managing" the economy were, until the 1930's hardly significant. While Keynesian policies proved quite successful in dealing with states of economic depression, prosperity created a climate more in tune with the monetarists' (neo classicists') policies of *laissez-faire*, allowing the forces of supply and demand to interact and arrive at suitable prices. The added benefit in this situation is that almost full employment can be achieved, apart from the proportion of "unemployables" within any society. The whole economy is looked upon in terms of the *aggregate demand-aggregate supply* **(AD-AS)** which in the context of macroeconomics, analyses fluctuations in the aggregate price level (i.e. inflation and deflation) and aggregate output (booms and slumps). There is a connection here between macroeconomics, which relates to government policy, whether it is (Keynesian) interventionist, or *laissez-faire*, and the microeconomics of the operation of individuals and firms within the market forces. This connection is part of the so-called **"Supply-side"** economics, which, though usually government inspired, depends on the premise that growth in the economy is achieved not by increasing demand, but by increasing productivity and therefore the supply of goods and services. By removing hindrances, people are encouraged to work harder and to demonstrate a spirit of enterprise, responding to change with agility and cleverness. The result can be that overall the markets (with their market factors of land, labour, capital, and enterprise) will work better.

The *supply-side* economics has been the basis of the policies in recent years of the Reagan era of the USA presidency, as well as the Thatcher era of administration in the UK. In the UK there was a need to re-enforce these policies by removing the restriction imposed on and by the vast businesses, services, and industries that formed the nationalized infra-structure of the economy in the Britain, and hence the robust programme of **privatization** that characterized Prime Minister Margaret Thatcher policies during the 1980's and 1990's. The other measures that form the core policies devoted to increasing growth and prosperity through the supply–side principles can be summarized as follows:

1- **The Labour market:** Freedom of mobility is an essential factor in gaining more out of the available labour force in any society. The British Government assisted in this by introducing policies to release tenancies in "Council" houses and making these available for purchase by the tenants with concessions. Owner-occupiers of property have a greater freedom to move from one part of the country to another in search of work. Pension rights have been freed so that they can be carried with the employee from one job to another without loss of their cumulative benefits. Social security benefits have had their thresholds raised so that people will accept employment at lower pay levels, and the burden on employers has been reduced through adjustments to their National Insurance charges. Loss of extravagant demands for wages or minimum wages by Trade and professional Unions, restraint on public sector pay levels, to discourage excessive demands within the private sector, provided additional and cumulatively beneficial effects.

2- **The Capital market:** With the capital market there is an interplay of several factors. The main ones are: freeing of exchange controls on currency, tax changes that make it profitable for businesses to invest and raise capital through the issue of rights (extra share) rather than loans, facilitating the functions of the stock exchanges to make them more competitive, abolishing dividend controls, hire-purchase restrictions, and tax incentives for the individuals, and in general encouraging incentives and harder working by allowing people to keep more of their earnings.

3- **The Release of Land:** The major release occurred as result of privatization of the nationalized industries, The sale of surplus land led to other forms of use of the land or use of released asset value and all this created opportunity for developments that would contribute to the overall growth in the economy.

4- **Encouragement of Enterprise:** By allowing individuals and small businesses greater access to "start-up" capital, "tax holidays" for the first few years, easier credit, greater value in self employment, share holding schemes for employees as part of their package of earnings, and other measures, have encouraged people, especially young starters, to develop ventures, and take some risk at least initially. Dependence solely on paid employment became less critical as an option.

To re-iterate the salient factors operating within the macroeconomic policies, which are in relation to employment/unemployment, inflation, and growth, the main threads of such government policies can be summarized as follows:

i-   To maintain a high and stable level of employment.

ii- To secure continuous economic growth.

iii- To keep inflation at a low level, and

iv- To avoid balance of payments difficulties.

The implications of these policies, and the changing environment, has meant that macro models have had to evolve to accommodate openness to trade and the globalization of finance[221], and this will have its relevance in later sections, in particular as they affect the inter-relations between the larger, stronger, economies of developed countries, the free markets that have developed in recent decades, and the effects of all this on those weaker (dependent) economies of the lesser developed world

PART X

WORLD ECONOMICS AND THE PROSPERITY OF HUMANKIND

The Future

In this section the intention is to discuss some of the challenges that are likely to face the world in its evolving and exciting trends. Addressing the issues relating to such matters as the fluctuations that are all the time expected, and that produce changes of a national, regional or international scale in the economic fortunes of the world is best left aside as it is the basis and subject matter for comments and forecasts by economists, politicians and business leaders. These comments and forecasts are quite important, and indeed require the enormous expertise and acumen that characterize the pundits and experts in the field to chart the way ahead for short and medium term decisions by governments, and by financial and business policy makers. The needs of ordinary people vary from one part of the world to the other, but they have to be addressed. Political stability is a sure pre-requisite for economic development and prosperity. But social and spiritual tranquillity and harmony are certainly prime requirements for society to feel fulfilled and for it to appreciate the full value of such prosperity. That state of society (tranquil and harmonious), in turn, is attained only with the feeling that equity and fairness are at the heart of the policies implemented, and equal opportunity the operative mode. In such an environment, the destructive forces of adverse human emotion, and in particular envy, jealousy, and "hegemony" will be hard to find their place in the expressions of individual or factional behaviours and attitudes. Moreover, with compassion and strict adherence to principle, such expressions will be more easily de-fused because of the credibility that can be truthfully demonstrated, and because of the compassionate, but firm, manner by which the elders of society, and indeed the arbitration procedures available, can deal with these situations as they arise.

Historical

In a very well studied book, *"The Wealth and Poverty of Nations"* (1999, Norton Publishers) the eminent historian David S Landes, sets the theme of his book by this quote from a letter by Malthus to Ricardo (26 Jan. 1817):*"the cause of the wealth and poverty of the nations—the grand object of all enquiries in political Economy".* He then surveys in a fairly sweeping introduction the advances achieved in the world in recent times, and the differences that are emerging. Until the late nineteenth century, there was little appreciation of simple measures to avoid infection, such as general cleanliness, clean water, disposal of waste, and better nutrition. Indeed, the commoners of the late nineteenth century and early twentieth century often lived cleaner than the kings and queens of a century earlier. As late as the World War I, the Turks who fought the British expeditionary force in Gallipoli were struck by the difference in height between the steak-and-mutton fed troops from Australia and New Zealand and the stunted youth of British mill towns. Similarly, the children of immigrant populations from poor countries into rich will note that their children grow up taller and better knit than their parents. Life expectancy is improving in developed countries, and the causes of death are shifting from infections to the degenerative and pathological conditions associated with old age or self imposed defective lifestyles.

Diversity around the world is regrettably tainted with inequality, and one can discern three kinds of nations:

those whose people spend lots of money to keep their weight down

those whose people eat just to maintain their lives

and those whose people do not know where the next meal is coming from.

The difference between the rich and poor countries is increasing. Thus, the difference in income per head between one of the richest countries, say Switzerland and one of the poorest non-industrialized countries, say Mozambique, is 400 to 1. Two hundred and fifty years ago, this gap between the richest and poorest was perhaps 5 to 1, and the difference between Europe and, say, East or South Asia (China or India) was around 1.5 or 2 to 1.

In an editorial article by Kamran Abbasi, the Assistant editor to the prestigious "British Medical Journal"(BMJ volume 318, 12 June 1999, pages 1568/9), the following facts emerge: *"Jubilee 2000 estimates that there are 52 heavily indebted countries that need urgent debt relief, and most of these are in sub-Saharan Africa, Latin America and Asia. Their total debt burden amounts to around US$ 371bn…if, for example, Britain were to cancel the debts owed to it by the poorest countries, British taxpayers would be worse off by just £2 ($3) a year each. Cancelling all the debts from these countries would still only amount to a cost, from the creditor countries, of £12 ($20) per taxpayer. Shifting the burden of debt may make little difference to the lives of the people in richer countries, but it would emancipate the world's poor. The World Bank estimates that 1.3 billion people live in absolute poverty, earning less than $1 a day. For the poorest* *countries debt repayment are mostly double the amount of earnings from exports, far exceed expenditure on health care, and outstrip what is received in aid or loans. For example Uganda spends $2.50 per head annually on health, while $15 per head is spent on debt servicing. The net drain from the poorest countries to the richest countries is around $150bn a year (for every pound sent in grants to developing countries, £9 come back in debt repayment, claim Jubilee 2000. The poverty gap has also widened by 30% over the past decade. Many experts argue that disparity has accentuated the scarcity of resources, hunger, and death rates in the poorest countries— describes as the "pathology of poverty".*

The world is now, apparently, awake to these injustices, and the G8 (richest 8 countries in the world, USA, Canada, Japan, Germany, France, Switzerland, Italy, Britain,) meeting is currently addressing this problem, and there is a distinct and serious desire to cancel large chunks of these debts. This is commendable, and will not only benefit the poor countries, but eventually will be an instrument in the increasing prosperity of humankind in general.

Reasons For Inequalities:

An exhaustive outline of reasons that are or have been mentioned as leading to, or even, justifying the inequalities seen in the world in recent times is neither possible nor perhaps desirable. But a brief glimpse into innate, natural, human behaviour may be salutary as an opening statement in this section. That human beings are by nature sociable, kind, generous, and equitable is perhaps difficult to entertain. That they are innately peaceful and non aggressive will also raise at least some objection. All these attributes are nowadays so masked by the so-called progress of society and "civilization", that any mention of them in the context of real human nature is only accepted as wistful, unfounded, and certainly unimaginable. Even if the author would aver that in his experience while a young doctor, he had witnessed all these qualities in the tribes of southern Sudan, mainly the *"Dinkas"* the largest tribe in the three southern provinces of that country, as well as the people known as the *"Upper Nubians"* in the western provinces, it may not be enough to satisfy the cynicism of our generation. What hopefully would, may be a quote from Landes' book (page 74/5), describing Columbus' first encounter with the inhabitants of the Islands he discovered, presumably Cuba, as follows: *"Nakedness was not a trivial consideration: it was construed in the beginning as a sign of edenic innocence. Columbus, for example, was initially enraptured. 'They go naked as the day they were born,' he wrote, 'the women as well as the men'. And: 'We Christians said they were remarkably beautiful, the men as well as the women'. And: This beauty was moral as well as physical....they are the most pleasant and peaceful people in the world'.*

"Along with the beauty went innocence. 'The Admiral said he could not believe that a man could have ever beheld people so good of heart, so generous and timid, because they all gave away everything they had as soon as they saw us'. And: 'In exchange for anything you give them, no matter how trifling, they immediately give you all their possessions.' And: 'They do not covet other people's property...Whatever you ask for that belongs to them, they never refuse. On the contrary, they ask you to help yourself, and show so much love that you give them your heart.' And: 'They are very gentle and know nothing of evil. They know nothing of killing one another...One thing these generous people were not ready to give away, and that was their women". This last sentence of the quote is particularly poignant, in that there was a moral code so complete, that everything but the most sacred of possessions, that emblem of human society's integrity, the sacred relationship of man and woman, has been so much in evidence. Sadly! Pascal Bruckner (*"The tears of the white man, page 10"*), "argues

persuasively in the context of the above quote, that the Indian was *"condemned from the beginning because he had been declared perfect"*.

The story of Adam and eve, figurative as it may be, seems to be a true reflection of the state of the human being as his Creator had intended prior to the lapse in judgement and fall from the edenic state to one of endeavour, compromise, and ultimately loss of innocence. While these sentiments may be seen as diversion, perhaps they will indicate the baseline structure of humanity, where equality and mutual support was the order of the day, to the later conditions, where other factors set in, and which explain how inequality was allowed to develop, to the benefit of some, but the disadvantage of many.

Factors Relating To Nature:

<u>Geography:</u> In the present day spread of wealth in various parts of the world, one cannot ignore the fact that most of the lesser developed countries lie within the tropical and semi-tropical zones. Climatic conditions prevailing in these areas, particularly heat, humidity, storms, and the prevalence of disease may play a part in reducing the ability to perform. It is easier to retain heat in a cold climate, either by generating more heat through the energy of work, or by increasing insulation through shelter or more clothing, or, within reason, use external heat. To work in the heat and sun, with or without humidity is more difficult. Shedding clothes is of limited value, and external cooling is useful only in confined places.

Lack of rain in desert areas increases the need to invest so as to secure water, or rely on utilizing the limited areas provided by oases. Even then, the variety and all year availability will at best be limited.

Infestations and disease, are these tropical conditions that were the scourge of the inhabitants and the immigrants (or colonialist settlers), are all too well known, and are the material of a complete and separate medical speciality.

All this may have provided some excuse for slavery, which was a means of using labour for the cost of upkeep, and easing any work on the proprietor. There was even a thought that people from the tropics can function better in hot climates than those from temperate climates. This alleged variation in human physiology and the ability of anyone to adapt has been challenged by some. Blaut in *"The colonizer's model"*[222] is ideologically opposed to the notion that the favours of nature may be unequally distributed. So while one's thoughts about slavery would naturally go towards the American scene, where the sugar, cotton and maize plantations of the southern states of the USA required the hard intensive labour of the imported Africans, one should not lose sight of the fact that slavery is almost as old as the emergence of the human society from base-line primitiveness, and perhaps reached its zenith when the Arabs established their footholds in Africa, both because they made use of slaves themselves, and because they were very active procurers of slaves as a thriving trade. To this day, in the experience of the author, the natives of the Southern Sudan apply the term in Arabic equivalent to "procurer" when they refer to the (Northern Sudanese) shop keeper just because the forebears of these shopkeepers were engaged in slave trade in addition to the more conventional trade in foods and other necessities of life.

Whether this factor of geography can be upheld, and to what extent, can lead to extensive discussion, and perhaps argument. It is interesting to note that while *"Global warming" was not an expression people used at the first millennium, it was nevertheless, an experience they shared with us. The Year 1000', a scholarly, lucid and lively account by Robert Lacey and Danny Danziger of life 999 years ago, based on Julius Work Calendar of Canterbury Cathedral .Between about 950 and 1300 AD Edinburgh, we are told, enjoyed the climate of London today, and London that of the Loire valley. (In the midst of this period the Cistercians, a splinter group of Benedictine monks, founded their order and set about perfecting the wines of Burgundy-in conditions considerably more benign, it seems, than those of today...I was also fascinated to learn from this admirable little book that the 'hungry gap' before the harvest in August, when that of the previous year was either used up or growing mouldy, drove the poor to eat whatever they could forage. Their bread, such as it was, could include poppies and hemp, and rye on which the flowering ergot had produced LSD. The result was the sort of spaced out village fetes painted in such detail by Brueghel the Elder...It helps to bring into focus the revolutionary importance of the potato, when it arrived from America 500 years later, to remember that our ancestors had to wait until after midsummer to bring in an edible harvest*[223].

In recent times, with the advance of medicine, disease (at least those related to the prevailing climate) is to a large extent controllable, and some diseases have actually been eliminated, particularly smallpox. Other diseases can be controlled more effectively than at present, particularly Malaria, but for this to happen, the will, education, and money spent, has to be of a magnitude commensurate with the serious effects of this one condition that is recognized to be the cause of the greatest waste in health, vigour and life in most tropical areas. Schistosomiasis (Bilharziasis) is another scourge of areas such as the Nile valley in Egypt the Nilotic regions of African and indeed some regions in Japan. This again is a parasitic infestation of a very destructive nature whether to the urinary systems or the liver, depending on the variety, but one which can be controlled through a mixture of health style education and the introduction of potable water and good waste disposal. These are only two examples, of a list that can be too exhaustive. Suffice it to say that improving health has been shown to improve important statistics, such as the fall in infant mortality from 146 per thousand in 1965 in the poorest countries (114 in China and India) to 91 in 1992 (79 in India, 31 in China)

Apart form the "given" condition of nature that may contribute to the reduced productivity and capability of the individual, there are other factors that would contribute to the well being of the inhabitants of these regions. Tropical produce (fruit and vegetable, condiments and spices, tea, coffee and cocoa) is recognized as exotic and plentiful. The seas and waterways are source of immense bounties. Elevated sections of the topographical landscape are temperate and may even be cold, because of the altitude. The variety is thus enormous. If the inventions and discoveries and recent technologies are now added to the equation, it will not be difficult to accept that whatever conditions may have applied in the past and may have been considered as reasons for the lesser development in these parts of the world, will not hold now. The important consideration, though not exclusively, is the transfer of this technology and of funds (capital), so that the benefit, where the will and the integrity is secured, will become available. Recent examples have shown that this can be achieved. In recent years, India has become the most prolific centre for the computer and chip industry and is now a major supplier to the rest of the world, notably the USA and Western Europe. And history does confirm that the lesser developed geographical areas of the world of today were indeed the advanced nations of yesteryear. The civilizations of Egypt, Sumeria, China, and India are all so much older than the current civilization based on Western science and technology. Technology has made it possible for humankind to tap into and harness nature in temperate and even cold climates where hardly any useful life was possible until as recently as the last century. Europe knew famine and pestilence, epidemics and pandemics. The Steppes of Poland and Russia were for a long time uninhabitable, and certainly inhospitable. Had it not been for technology and science, a lot of it transferred from the Ancient Egyptians, Indians, and more recently the Muslim seats of knowledge in Southern Europe, the situation referred to by Edmund Burke[224] when contrasting the Indians and the English: *"a people for ages civilized and cultivated...while we were yet in the woods"*. would perhaps have prevailed in Northern Europe, and the non-discovered parts of the world.

History: Europe and the Europeans are rightly seen to be the fountain source of advanced society built on a wealth of scientific, technological, philosophic, political, literary and artistic achievements. The Americas have owed their developments to the settlers and colonialists, and the transfer of technology since the early part of this century to Japan and the Far East, all have the greater part of their origin from within Europe. It is, however, important to note that Europe was at its darkest not so long ago in historical terms and scale. *"In the tenth century, Europe was just coming out of a long torment of invasion, plunder, and rapine, by enemies from all sides. From what we know as Scandinavia, the Norsemen or Vikings, marine bandits whose light boats could handle the roughest seas and yet sail up shallow rivers to raid and pillage far inland, struck along the Atlantic coast as far as Italy and Sicily. Others went into Slavic lands, established themselves as a new ruling class (the Rus, who gave their name to Russia and ruled that sombre land for seven hundred years), and eventually penetrating almost to the walls of Constantinople...Also coming from the sea, across the Mediterranean, were the Saracens (Moors), who set up mountain bases in the Alps and on the Cote d'Azur, and went out from these to raid the trade routes between northern and southern Europe...linked to Muslim lands...and folk legend has it that to this day some villagers in the high Alps carry the colour and appearance of their Maghrebin origins...Finally from the east overland, but highly mobile for all that, rode the Magyars or Hungarians, one more wave of invaders from*

Asia, pagans speaking a Ural-Altaic language (a distant cousin of Turkish)
sweeping in year after year...enough to move in a single campaign from
their Danubian bases into eastern France or the foot of Italy..."

"...*The Europeans learned to counter these thrusts...It has been*
suggested that this danger from without launched Europe on the path of
growth and development...[225].

All this is but a glimpse of the factors of history that has assisted in
shaping Europe. Not to be underestimated also, should be the effects of
the Greek civilization, philosophy and politics (the word deriving from
Polis meaning the free city), and the Roman Empire with its power to
fuse together large swathes of land and peoples into a coherent mosaic
of dependencies and governorates. *"A long period of population increase*
and economic growth, up to the middle of the fourteenth century, when
Europeans were smitten by the Plague (the 'Black Death')...and a third
or more of its population died... That was a jolt, but not a full stop... This
long multicentennial maturation (1000-1500) rested on an economic
revolution, a transformation of the entire process of making, getting, and
spending such as the world has never seen since the so-called Neolithic
revolution. That (c. –8000 to –3000) had taken thousands of years to
work itself out. Its focus has been the invention of agriculture and the
domestication of livestock, both of which had enormously augmented the
energy available for work." [226]. Medieval Europe managed to innovate
on the "technology" of the plough, to cultivate more intensely, to use
the labour of women and children, developing early specialization of
labour, and starting the agricultural revolution, and more trade between
nations. All this provided, in turn, the launching pad for the industrial
revolution.

History therefore, allows for the flow of knowledge and transfer
of whatever technology, no matter how primitive, from one part of
the world to the other. The circumstances leading to this flow may

have been triggered off by social events, migrations for livelihood, hegemony, or simple banditry. But the effects have universally been of mutual benefit when history is judged over a length of time, and analysed intelligently and objectively. Even colonialism, with all its reported horrors and injustices, can be seen to have provided some benefit to large areas of the world, previously closed off to sources of knowledge. With the "winds of change" that swept these territories eventually, the effect lead to emancipation and emergence from under the rule of the colonial powers, and thereafter assuming their rightful place in the family of civilized nations. For sure, events of history could have taken a more benign and benevolent course. But for the purpose of this work, it is reasonably to state that history indicates the value of movement: whether it be the movement of peoples, knowledge, trade, or ideology. It is this movement, as contrasted with stagnation and isolation, that creates the friction, which in turn results in sparks, light, or further movement. A "rolling stone gathers no moss" can be contrasted with a stagnant one covered with moss. A further indication of the value of movement and transfer will be seen in looking at the value of inventions.

INVENTIONS:

Europe of the middle ages, rather than being simply a dark interlude between the grandeur of Rome and the brilliance of the Renaissance, has been one of the most inventive societies that history has ever known. The following examples are useful:[227]

1- *The water wheel*: This facility was known to the Romans, and it probably survived on Church estates where it freed clerics for prayer. It was revived in the tenth and eleventh centuries, multiplying easily in a region of wide rainfall and ubiquitous watercourses. In England, at the time nothing but a peripheral, backward island, the Doomsday census of 1086 AD showed some 5,600 of these mills; the continent had many more. The technique advanced, and the invention was enhanced through dams and ponds, and put to a variation of uses through adding cranks, toothed gears, reciprocating motion and other means for maximising their usefulness, and multiple applications, some at a distance, were some of the benefits. Significantly, the power generated led to easier production of paper, and was used in rolling and drawing sheet metal. This meant that Europe, as nowhere else became a power-based civilization in the making.

2- *Eyeglasses:* Taken for granted at present, eyeglasses were singly responsible for almost doubling the working lifetime and capability of skilled craftsmen, especially those engaged in precision instruments, fine jobs, reading, and scribing. The invention started with the simple magnifying lens useful for compensating older people losing their ability to focus. The industry and physics of this invention progressed to the more complex requirements of people with short sightedness and other refractive difficulties. Man's abilities multiplied inexorably as a result of this invention, making it possible to invent other finer instruments, and indeed creating a totally new science of optics, lenses, magnifiers, telescopes, microscopes and others. Whole new fields of discovery and creativeness became possible.

3- *The mechanical clock:* Another of the instruments taken at present for granted, the clock revolutionized the way society worked, and established a method to set in some rhythm and order to a life that was based on vague appreciation of time as demonstrated by the unreliable instruments. Sundials will be ineffective in cloudy weather, and water clocks will not work when there is a freeze. The clock was invented probably simultaneously in England and Italy. The effects led to enormous changes in the way people appreciated the time to work, and the time to rest. More importantly it benefited the church authorities as it eliminated the need to control people's prayer times. New discussions on such theological time concepts as the "end of the world", and the orderly celestial movements of the sun and the planets became the exciting new past-time exercises. More critically, people gained the ability to make order of their lives without the need to heed the dictates of the clergy in everyday activities.

4- **Printing:** Printing was invented in China in the ninth century and found general use by the tenth. The Chinese had also invented paper, and so printing on paper was the right answer for the Chinese whose writing is in the form of drawings. Printing on paper was therefore so obviously easier than carving in blocks. Its use in China was, however, to a certain extent suppressed because the mandarins discouraged dissent and new ideas, and these would have been easier through writing. Europe came to printing centuries after China, and for a long time it remained in block form rather than the more practical movable type. The first Western book to be printed in movable type, and one of the most beautiful, was the Bible, first published as such in Gutenberg in 1452-55. Jews and Christians had presses in Istanbul, but the Muslims resisted on religious grounds, as printing the Qur'an was unacceptable. The world has since seen the benefits of this invention, a potent means of expression and diffusion of knowledge.

5- *Gunpowder:* Europe probably got this invention from the Chinese in the early fourteenth, possibly the late thirteenth century. The Chinese knew gun powder in the eleventh century and used it at first as an incendiary device, both in fireworks and in war, the latter often in the form of tube flame lances. The Europeans managed to use gunpowder in "corned" form rather than simple powder form. The effect was more rapid ignition, and more complete and powerful explosion. Casting in metal (a technology derived from the bell industry) provided Europe with the cannon and the military supremacy that went with it.[228]

This fascinating interaction of geography, history and human ability and creativity, whereby humans interacted with nature and in between themselves, provides a mosaic of human endeavour characterised by inventiveness and adaptations, acceptances or refusals of new ideas, reliance on authority or rebelliousness, hegemony or absorption, all within "melting pots" which history and geography can only explain with the benefit of hindsight, study and research. The time has probably come when the same world, enormously more sophisticated and wise, chastened by the worse excesses of conflict and war, aware of the resentment, reaction and loss of dynamism resulting from inequality and injustice, should take a fresh look at the present and the future. To consider the interest of the many rather than the few, and to heed the lessons of history which have shown time and again that the seeds of one conflict may have been sown in the field of a previous one through ignorance, arrogance, or shear stupidity. The seeds of World War II are recognized as having been sown in the aftermath of World War I and the treaty of Versailles, essentially because of the injustice meted to the Germans. The seeds of one recent conflict in the Republics of what was Yugoslavia, have been sown in previous conflicts in the same region, perhaps much earlier on in history when "balkanization" became synonymous with factionalism and strife. The rise of internecine conflicts in Africa may have their origins in the manner in which colonial powers had drawn territories arbitrarily with no due consideration to the tribal mix.

In general, the underlying factor in most of the twentieth and twenty first centuries in particular, were predominantly the result of hegemony and injustice, which in its most depraved form is manifested in all the atrocities of that abhorrent phenomenon of "Ethnic Cleansing".

Considered even from the economic aspects, the recent decision of the G8 to "wipe out" $70bn of debt (£43bn) owed by the world's poorest countries (Times of London, 19 June 1999, page 27) to the G8, the IMF, and the World Bank is a recognition that this debt burden, regardless of why or how it has accumulated along the years, is an injustice worthy of sacrifice on the part of those countries (and people) who can afford to be so magnanimous, now that prosperity is so evident in these rich nations.

Where history shows that people were denied the benefits of these advances and opportunities, or more importantly, where people were reluctant to accept them, there was decline and loss. Two examples from history are mentioned by David Landes and are worth noting:

"The first, Islam, initially absorbed and developed the knowledge and ways of conquered peoples. By our period (roughly 1000-1500), Muslim rule went from the western end of the Mediterranean to the Indies. Before this, from about 750 to 1100, Islamic science and technology far surpassed those of Europe, which needed to recover its heritage and did so to some extent through contacts with Muslims in such frontier areas as Spain. Islam was Europe's teacher.

Then something went wrong. Islamic science, denounced as heresy by religious zealots, bent under theological pressures for spiritual conformity. (For thinkers and searchers, this could be a matter if life or death.) For militant Islam, the truth had already been revealed. What led 'back' to the truth was useful and permissible; all the rest was error and deceit. The historian Ibn Khaldun, conservative in religious matters, was nonetheless dismayed by Muslim hostility to learning:

When the Muslims conquered Persia (637-642) and came upon an indescribably large number of books and scientific papers, Sa'ad bin Abi Waqqas wrote to Umar bin al-Khattab asking him for permission to take them and distribute them among the Muslims. On that occasion, Umar wrote back to him:' Throw them in the water. If what they contain is right guidance, God has given us better guidance. If it is error, God has protected us against it'.

Remember here that Islam does not, as Christianity does, separate the religious from the secular. The two constitute an integral whole. The ideal state would be a theocracy; and in the absence of such fulfilment, a good ruler leaves matters of the spirit and mind (in the widest sense) to the doctors of the faith. This can be hard on scientists.

As for technology, Islam knew areas of change and advance: one thinks of the adoption of paper; or the introduction and diffusion of new crops such as coffee and sugar; or the Ottoman Turkish's readiness to learn the use (but not the making) of cannon and clocks. But all this came from outside and continued to depend on outside support. Native springs of invention seems to have dried up. Even in the golden age (750-1100), speculation disconnected from practice: 'For nearly five hundred years the world's greatest scientists wrote in Arabic, yet a flourishing science contributed nothing to the slow advance of technology in Islam.'

"The one civilization that might have surpassed the European achievement was China. At least that is what the record seems to show.

Witness the long list of Chinese inventions: the wheelbarrow, the stirrup, the rigid horse collar (to prevent choking), the compass, paper, printing, gunpowder, porcelain. And yet in matters of science and technology, China remains a mystery—and this in spite of a monumental effort by the late Joseph Needham and others to collect the facts and clarify the issues. The specialists tell us, for example, that Chinese industry long anticipated European. In textiles, the Chinese had a water driven machine for spinning hemp in the twelfth century, some five hundred years before the England of the Industrial Revolution knew water frames and mules. In iron manufacture, the Chinese learned early to use coal and coke in blast furnaces for smelting iron (or so we are told) and were turning out as many as 125,000 tons of pig iron by the late eleventh century—a figure reached by Britain seven hundred years later.

The mystery lies in China's failure to realize its potential…the Chinese industrial history offers examples of technological oblivion and regression… None of the conventional explanations tells us in convincing fashion why technical progress was absent in the Chinese economy during a period that was, on the whole, one of prosperity and expansion…Only Galilean-Newtonian science was missing…The reasons given were many, including lack of a free market,… the quasi confinement of women in homes,… totalitarian control…and others, all pointing to the effect of reducing incentive and stifling initiative[228].

Events throughout history will provide many such examples, but recent history deserves brief mention. Colonialism, in most situations starting in territories opened up through trade, as in India, Java, Sumatra, and East and South Africa, would have been an enormous opportunity for the transfer of knowledge and technology. Indeed, the present lasting effect of language, literature and culture is a testimony to how powerful the influence was of the interaction between two societies, one advance and civilized, the other primitive, poor and backward.

Anyone looking at a map of the world up until the beginning of World War II would not have failed to notice the vast expanse of two colours: red or pink indicating the territories under British rule, and blue indicating those under French rule. To this day, the world is essentially divide into the English speaking people and the "Francophone" people of ex-French dominated territories. The USA had itself settled, prior to independence, under the British rule following the failed attempts by the French to retain hold on such states as Louisiana.. Just as importantly, and probably more significantly, is the prevalence of the two cultures throughout, with names of salient philosophers, artists, playwrights and others tripping over tongues in the thickets and deserts of Africa or the jungles and mountains of Asia.

What has regrettably failed to materialize, was a conscious, planned, and well executed effort on the part of the colonial powers to ready their territories for the inevitable handing over of independence. The scramble for independence which gathered pace in the aftermath of World War II, had seen countries suddenly in charge of their destinies with only a handful of university educated citizens, no tarmac roads, and pathetically rudimentary infrastructure. It is not the purpose of this work to discuss the causes or overall effects of the wars or of colonialism. The main purpose of this brief discussion is to highlight the effects of unfairly leaving large areas of population so underprivileged and so bereft of the means of sustaining a decent standard of living, or at least having a credible base from which to re-launch themselves and catch up with their previous "masters". To be sure, the leaders of some of these countries, probably most of them, have conducted themselves appallingly once power was handed over to them. Mismanagement, despotism, nepotism (amounting often to tribal hegemony), corruption, violence, flamboyancy, internecine conflicts, racial and religious based rivalries, and many other sorrowful conduct have exerted their toll on these people in terms not only of economic hardship, but more seriously that of loss of life and limb.

But in all this, there was that theme, that common thread, which of necessity is herewith unashamedly repeated. That is the thread of *"Injustice"*. Whether it is through oppression, omission, denial, political or military dominance, or suppression, the result is injustice. This had to be endured by the generality who were, and many still are, unable to unshackle themselves from these yolks, and would probably continue to be so helpless, unless there is a sea change in attitude throughout the world, and unless the world develops the means and mechanisms to deal with the residual problems that still fester in so many areas. Recent developments provide us with the pointers in that direction. The fall of the communist regimes is at last ridding the world of the presence of two powerful blocks, which in their efforts to sustain their "cold war" power bases supported their respective "client" states or factions. The world is fast arriving at conclusions that co-operation in this field of overturning or resisting injustice, is preferred to confrontation, and that if force is necessary to deal with aggression, such force has to be co-ordinated and well planned and executed. The United Nations, the Security Council, and the combined forces of Nato (North Atlantic Treaty Organisation) and the (now defunct) Warsaw pact have been seen to work together. This must be the beginning, perhaps after earlier false starts, of the fulfilment of Baha'u'llah's call to the world through the rulers of America, to be instruments for the establishment of justice and the crushing of oppression:

"   *Hearken ye, O Rulers of America and the Presidents of the Republics therein, unto that which the Dove is warbling on the Branch of Eternity: "There is none other God but Me, the Ever-Abiding, the Forgiving, the All-Bountiful." Adorn ye the temple of dominion with the ornament of justice and of the fear of God, and its head with the crown of the remembrance of your Lord, the Creator of the heavens… O concourse of rulers! Give ear unto that which hath been raised from the Dayspring of Grandeur: "Verily, there is none other God but Me, the Lord of Utterance, the All-Knowing." Bind ye the broken with the hands of justice, and crush the oppressor who flourisheth with the rod of the commandments of your Lord, the Ordainer, the All-Wise. "[229]*

The world may be about to reach its rightful glorious destiny , but to achieve this it needs to adopt the principles which all civilized people would wish to see, and all religions, thinkers and wise leaders longed for and worked for. Justice is a major element.

It may have taken the world over fifty years to look back at 1945, with its mixed emotions of triumph and defeat, relief and despair, revelation and ruin, joy and sorrow [230], to appreciate that the atrocities and cruelties, the 55 million dead, 35 million wounded and 3 million lost, that fill the ledgers of cost of that one truly world-wide conflict, may at last have given birth to a true feeling that war and injustice need to be phased out and replace by a "New World Order".

This has not been easy. It will still require much sincere toil and sacrifice. But, as Niall Ferguson, author of *"Virtual History"* says in his comment on David Landes' book: *"Not since Max Weber has the relationship between collective mentality and economic divergence, been so subtly explored and explained".* Max Weber (1864-1920) is considered one of the founders of sociology and its relationship with administration as well as "the rationalization sociology of Religion and Government". Collective mentality therefore is key to any change. Circumstances in many countries, even in Europe, since the early part of this century have shown the truth in this statement. It is hard to believe that France in 1948 was but a *"tired version of France-1900..hardly any cars, no street lights, petrol pumps hand cranked, a mere 3 ampere electric supply to most homes, shared privies, iceboxes rather than refrigerators",* and the list goes on. *"In the next three decades—what came to be known as the* trente glorieuses *(the thirty wonderful years from 1945 to 1975), France moved in with alacrity"..* France became one of the richest countries in the world, with a standard of living that at times surpassed Britain. A government directed economic revival (*dirigisme, etatisme*) reminiscent of Colbertism (mentioned in earlier sections), engineered this great leap forwards.

The German comeback after almost total debilitation as a result of the savage conduct of the war by its troops and by the attacking "allies" and Russia, is another feat of remarkable ability to regenerate, to rejuvenate, nay, to even surpass almost every other country and nation in Europe, and at some stage even posing a real threat to overtake the USA in productivity and per capita income. While suffering humiliation and bankruptcy immediately after the war, it managed to restart its industries, replace its Reichsmark with what became the "mighty" Deutsche Mark (1 DM for 10 RM), and was considered for some time to be the "economic locomotive" of the world. That position was to be weakened relatively when the "miracle" of unification of East and West Germany finally materialised. The economic burden taken by the West was certainly too onerous, but at least it was done with that spirit of sacrifice that was demonstrated by the fact that the East Germans received one DM for every for every one of the almost worthless Mark they possessed. That shock of re-unification and the burden of reconstruction (especially of Berlin) has now faded, and the world has to face the economic might of a unified German population of over eighty million highly industrious and disciplined people, and the motoring engine of the E.U. This is certainly an impressive example of "collective mentality" working towards a good end.

The same will be said of Japan, which may have presented an even more spectacular economic miracle. Having grudgingly surrendered, and only after two atomic bombs were dropped, it faced its future with one salient lesson learnt. That was that in its quest for raw material, which was the main driving passion that led to its entry into the war, it is much easier to buy them than to fight for territories in order to acquire them. To be sure, this was helped by the emergence of freer markets and greater access to raw material than pre-war. Nevertheless, it is this "collective" mindset after the war that led Japan to look at every aspect of manufacture and production, to study all the products on offer, from toys to electronics to precision instruments to cars and other heavy industry. Its genius was, and still is, providing products that people want to buy, and to provide them at a price people can afford and a reliability people can trust.

What is just as important, is that Japan, the USA, and western Europe, "discovered" that by "outsourcing" items of production, from components to whole goods, they were able to reduce cost and become more competitive. Manufacturing plants were thus set up in countries where labour was cheaper, and possibly raw material more readily available. Japan used the adjoining countries like Southern Korea, Singapore, Indonesia, and Malaysia. The USA used some European countries, notably Spain, where labour was relatively cheaper. Europe, especially Britain, used India and Africa. The emergence of China brought this whole aspect of world trade into true perspective.

That is laudable in so many aspects. But one cannot fail to add another important shift that had occurred. Thus, "migration" of manufacture actually proved to be also a "Technology Transfer". Korea made use of this "with a vengeance", especially through investments from the USA, most notably in the car industry. It was an effort to face the competition from Japan, but Korea managed to become perceived in its own right now as a threat by the Japanese and other industrial countries. Singapore and Hong Kong, both developing in separate and different ways, have proved formidable financial and high technology bases. They moreover, have shown the value of the return of the "City State" unitary identity reminiscent of Venice and late medieval Italy, but now on a global scale of influence. The work ethics and values of the Chinese race have never been in greater evidence than in these states, and in neighbouring countries such as Thailand, Indonesia and Malaysia, and more recently, in Australia. While most people "work to live" the Chinese appear to "live to work". The author has witnessed his hospital staff (mostly of Chinese descent, some even first or second generation immigrants from mainland China) doing their shopping at 4.30 am, then having breakfast and starting work at 8.00 am. There was never any evidence of tiredness or inefficiency. Indeed, there was no such thing as even reluctance to perform beyond the call of duty.

Again it is worth noting in this context, that these advances were made possible not only through the power of Technology Transfer, but also through the enormous benefits of the free flow of Capital, and foreign direct investment (FDI), which has been growing even faster than world trade.

The Far East is a prominent beneficiary of this global investment, and the so-called "Tiger economies" mainly of Indonesia, Thailand, Malaysia and S. Korea, have all had their success, perhaps punctuated with a few "downturns". The future of Hong Kong and Taiwan is rather difficult to predict, because of the political uncertainty, especially with Taiwan. Hong Kong appears to maintain its leading financial and trade position as well as its level of activity and is benefitting form the Chinese Government's policy of "Two systems, one country".

In many of the situations mentioned above, the transfer of technology made fast progress easier than in other situations where new inventions are made. It is also to be noted that only a handful of countries are responsible for the vast bulk of industrial patents.

The accumulation of such inventive, or more likely, research and development capabilities, means that the well endowed economies, mainly those of the USA and western Europe, will maintain for the foreseeable future their commanding position in new technological advances. No better an example of this would be the personal wealth of Bill Gates, the initiator/owner of *"Microsoft"* computer programmes and the richest or second richest human being in the world. In one of his interviews, he candidly stated that his continuing strength lies in his ability to "hire" the best brains money can buy. No one can quibble with that. But if this state of affairs is perpetuated in other inventions and developments, all concentrated within a circle that will likely get closer and closer, the difference between the rich and poor will grow even to a greater extent than it is now. More importantly, it will reduce the pool of inventiveness, which in the natural process of human capabilities is not the preserve of one people or one nation or a group of nations. It is rather the common attribute and aptitude of all humanity in varying degrees, provided the full potential of the individual is given a chance to develop, thrive, and thus eventually be achieved. The rewards will be immense. For the whole world will appreciate to a much greater extent the value of each invention, and just as importantly, will appreciate the interaction between the utility value of the invention with the effects on other aspects of life, such as the environment. The fast growth of some economies, based on simple "absorption" of technology, has resulted in gross disruption of quality life, both in ethical aspects where society was unable to adjust in time to the growth of such inventions as the motor car, the television, the cinema/video industry and more recently, the computer and internet, and also the environmental issues with their knock-on effects on health, pollution, and loss of natural beauty, to name but a few examples. "Haste makes waste" may be a dictum the world could and perhaps should take to heart. Sadly, even with significant advances in economy, inequalities appear, or even become exaggerated. An example is Thailand, one of the Asian "tiger" economies. Only 2% of Bangkok's population is tied to proper sewage disposal, and the annual income in 1995 for the Bangkok metropolitan area was estimated at 2.5 times the average for the entire kingdom[231]. This is socially and politically unacceptable. Indeed, disappointment in spite of some (relative) prosperity is one of the underlying factors in present as well as historic unease, unrest and even conflict. Religious, especially Muslim, fundamentalism has some roots in this feeling of disenfranchisement by the many, in the midst of affluence and profligacy of the few. Islam, as has been mentioned previously, is essentially an advocate of egalitarianism, not only in worldly material acquisitions and opportunity, but also in spirituality and commonality in basic religious/social activities such as *"Salat"* or prayer, especially the Friday noon prayer. The affluent profligates are seen not only as violators of this egalitarianism, but also the perpetuators of a sinful way of life "imported" from these non-Muslim "infidels" of the western world. The solution, in their view, is therefore to re-institute Islam by fair means or otherwise, and regardless of whether Islam is shapeable and adaptable enough to fit the present times without losing so much of its essentials as to be irreconcilable with its original intent. An example of a historical relic that still lingers is the famous or infamous "potato famine" of Ireland. All blame for a long time has been laid at the doorsteps of the British, who are said to have artificially created the shortage in order to raise price. This led to massive emigration from Ireland, mainly to the USA, who, in spite of eventually prospering, remained, like their relatives who stayed in Ireland, resentful and aggrieved. Recent information coming to light, however, shows that many in Ireland were also profiteering, and had a vested interest in maintaining the shortage.

Wise And Intelligent Use Of Technology Transfer

It will not take too much effort to find examples where technology was used inadequately or ineptly. One of the earliest significant industrial revolutions outside Europe in recent history was started in Egypt in the early nineteenth century by the Khedive Muhammad Ali, who was initially the representative of the Sultan of Turkey, but later assumed sovereignty over Egypt and its independence from the Ottoman rule. An intelligently constructed dam on the Nile River just north of Cairo was instrumental in a vast expansion of irrigation and thus agriculture. Among other things it helped expand the area growing the Egyptian cotton, known for its long staple (fibre). For about a hundred years, there was good cooperation between the cotton production in Egypt and the cotton industry in Lancashire, England. After World War II Egypt decided to add value to its cotton by investing in cotton-spinning mills. This triggered off the inevitable competition from other cotton growers and weavers, ending with a poorer, non-competitive cotton products made in Egypt, shrinking the export market and the ability to invest further. Another tragedy befalling the Egyptian cotton occurred in the early second half of the twentieth century, when the Government forced the cotton growers (through its grants and subsidy system) to forgo the long-fibre seeds year on year and use instead imported varieties, probably American, allegedly because of greater resistance to parasites. The result was deterioration in yield as well as quality, in spite of the noted ingenuity of the Egyptians technicians.

The direction taken by the communist states in Europe and elsewhere provides another example of the mishandling of "imported" technology. While developing the nuclear, space and arms sections to world beating levels of excellence, the remainder of industry and economy languished in the lower end of technical specifications and in reliability. The legendary "Trabant" motor car, beloved to the East German authorities, was only legendary in its primitiveness and unreliability. The "Skoda" car of Czechoslovakia was the butt of ridicule until taken over by VW of Germany. People were led to believe through the propaganda machinery that they were en par with a world quality and productivity, and were lulled into obeisance. To man these failing industries hundreds of thousands of labourers were carted from one end of the country (in Russia especially) as so-called "white coal" to work in projects in far off and inhospitable parts of the land. The most vivid, and perhaps the worse example, of misuse of technology is the damage done to the Aral Sea, once the fourth largest body of fresh water on the face of the earth. Today, it is a dying patch of water shrinking over a fetid stinky area strewn with corpses of rusty dilapidated boats that once plied the sea for trade or pleasure. There is hardly any useful fish or marine life remaining. This regrettably is a man made disaster resulting from ill conceived projects of diversion and reversal of waterways feeding that once thriving inland sea. Similar, but not so drastic criticisms are currently expressed regarding the most major development project of the sixties and seventies in Egypt, The High Dam, built on the southern reaches of the Nile in Upper Egypt. Some ecological implications are beginning to appear, although the hope is that they will not prove so severe as not to be taken care of.

Some disasters are probably inevitable, such as the Three Mile Nuclear generator near tragedy outside New York, the chemical leak in Bhopal (India) in 1984, and the Chernobil disaster in the Ukraine in 1986. But one wonders whether these and others could not have been averted had more care and respect for human life and health and for the environment not been subordinated to shoddy workmanship, lack of diligence, and maximizing of profit. In other situations, not even these excuses can be entertained. Some oil producing countries have shown such disregard to the bounty of oil that was to become the main source of their wealth. Drawing on foreign technology, expertise, and manning to produce, refine, and market the oil, the rulers and governments then squandered the proceeds in acts of personal aggrandisement and/ or political or military adventurism, leaving minimal reward for the common people of their countries.

Other situations demonstrate disregard for the applicability of transferred technology. A salutary example is the project launched by the British in Tanganyika over the period 1946-54 *"intended to demonstrate what the state was capable of…when it harnessed modern Western technology and expertise…A plan submitted by United Africa Company, a subsidiary of Unilever, and vetted and approved at British cabinet level, aimed at producing enough groundnuts (peanuts) to satisfy the British need for the nut and its oil. It would save valuable dollars and 'raise the standard of living of the African peasant*[232]. The machinery failed, there was no maintenance facilities, the soil eroded, and the so-called experts had no better clue than guesswork. Another example is Algeria, in the immediate aftermath of the French rule, and the discovery of oil and natural gas. It was flush with ideas of becoming the next Japan as a miracle economic performer. Haste and total disregard for adequate planning led to one disaster after the other. Encouraging bigger families to increase the population and consequently the ability to mobilize large armed forces only resulted in bigger families requiring vast resources for education, health and other services. The young generation found themselves hopelessly bereft of opportunity for work or wealth and became the so-called "wall people", because they had nothing to do but lean against the wall and watch the world go by.

The moral of all this is surely not to denounce the transfer of technology, nor to denigrate its value, but rather to re-iterate the earlier part of this section and re-enforce the notion that an essential part of creating fairness is on the one hand to make available all possible opportunity to the peoples of the earth without fear or favours, and on the other hand to ensure a sound moral and spiritual base within people, especially those in authority or command of affairs, so that all such availability is utilized with the best intentions, and greatest diligence in the interest of the people, and for the good of all. Only then will mistakes (which inevitably will occur because of human fallibility) be tolerated and adequately amended.

Human Behaviour And Attitude

The effects of nature, geography, history and the flow of inventions which have been briefly analysed in the preceding sections, have demonstrated the fact that humankind in the past has achieved a lot, and varying peoples have made use of opportunity to a varying extent. The fact that it was the European's good fortune to discover the Americas and tap into its natural and human resources, is an echo of the expansion of the Muslims into Persia, Africa, the Far East and part of Europe, again benefiting from the knowledge, science, philosophy, and history they found among the peoples in these lands, and allowing them to develop a civilization unique in its time. The further back one goes into history, the more such examples can be cited and identified, perhaps more limited in their scale or effects. Moreover, the older the parts of history we delve into, the more blurred they become.

The important consideration in this pre-amble is the fact that the world, in spite of having been rather disjointed and separated through lack of sophisticated means of transport and communication, nevertheless showed the unique human quality of seeing the values that others may have, whether scientific, ideological, practical or even just functionally convenient. However, it is also an important consideration to be noted, that along the lengthy history and relative isolation of peoples, esoteric ways of thinking developed, biases took shape and prejudices took hold. To this day, the average Chinese would call any non Chinese as some sort of "devil". Thus, a European is a "white devil", an African is a "black devil" and so on. They may not assume the same connotation as is common in today's ordinary speech when they use the word devil in this context. So, in a charitable spirit, one should assume that by this they mean essentially "alien" or "foreign". Nevertheless, it indicates the common feeling that a non-Chinese is an alien. This is not an unusual attitude, and it is certainly not confined to the Chinese. Apartheid in S. Africa was an extreme example, but the world now and during its history is full of similar examples of a greater or lesser degree of bias and prejudice.

Is it therefore time to draw a line under these attitudes? Is the world ready for such a sea change? Difficult questions, and ones that will certainly not be answered in a humble work of this kind. That they have to be addressed is, however, not in doubt. That they <u>are</u> being addressed is also not in doubt. The world community is extremely conscious of the need to do away with many of these existing attitudes, relics and "baggage" in the hope that gradually but inexorably, a "New World Order" (a term and concept adopted publicly by the USA President George Bush in 1995 in the immediate aftermath of the Iraq campaign to roll back Saddam Hussein's occupation of neighbouring Kuwait), is established. The Bahá'í Faith contributes to this effort, in quite a practical and effective manner, by creating the right Universal environment within its burgeoning community of adherents world-wide, so that the systematic development of this "World Order" becomes evident at least within its network of communicating communities, currently totalling over 300,000, spread over every corner of the earth, and embracing nearly every ethnic contingent there is. It may well be worth considering the offer given by the Universal House of Justice to the world, in its Message: "The Promise for World Peace", 1985", section IV[233], to examine this system, the "Bahá'í Model" where:

"The experience of the Bahá'í community may be seen as an example of this enlarged unity. It is a community of some three to four million people (currently more than six million) *drawn from many nations, cultures, classes and creeds, engaged in a wide range of activities serving the spiritual, social and economic needs of the peoples of many lands. It is a single social organism, representative of the diversity of the human family, conducting its affairs through a system of commonly accepted consultative principles, and cherishing equally all the great outpourings of divine guidance in human history…another evidence that humanity can live as one global society, equal to whatever challenges its coming of age may entail. If the Bahá'í experience can contribute in whatever measure to reinforcing hope in the unity of the human race, we are happy to offer it as a model for study… We reaffirm the belief that the* 'potentialities inherent in the station of man, the full measure of his destiny on earth, the innate excellence of his reality, must all be manifested in this promised Day of God' "

This is not just pious hope. The fact that nations and peoples benefited from advances in knowledge and inventions in the past is all the time being echoed in the present, and will no doubt continue to do so in the future. In an article under the heading *"World wealth is waiting on the phone line"* by David Smith, the economic editor to the London Sunday Times Newspaper, published on page 5, section 5, dated 11 July 1999, some very interesting insights are noted: He quotes David Landes ("The wealth and poverty of Nations") perceptively in the following passage: *"Landes account of why some countries are richer than others, and why some are better placed to benefit from new technology and globalisation than others, stresses the role of culture. 'If we learn anything from the history of economic development, it is that culture makes all the difference,' he writes. 'Witness the enterprise of expatriate minorities---the*

Chinese in east and south-east Asia, Lebanese in west Africa, Jews and Calvinists through much of Europe---and so on' " David Smith's article starts by some disturbing statements about the state of the world which, he says reflects the *"Gullivers"* of Gulliver's Travels, rich and towering, and the *"Liiliputians"* scurrying around at ground level and scratching a living. The world's three richest billionaires, Bill Gates, Robson Walton, of the American Wal-Mart family, and the Sultan of Brunei---have assets worth more than the combined gross domestic products of all the least developed countries, and the hundreds of millions of people who live in them. With particular reference to the globalising effect of the internet, he then states that the world's richest 20% not only have nearly 90% of the wealth but also 75% of its telephone lines… *"Humanity is living through its greatest technological decade ever… Thurrow calls it the third industrial revolution, the first being the shift from agriculture to manufacture at the end of the 18th century, the second the huge changes brought about by electrification and mass production 100 years ago. And: 'These technological opportunities creating fortunes faster than they have ever been created. The United States in the last 15 years has created more billionaires than ever in its history---even correcting for inflation and changes in average per capita gross domestic products.'* " David Smith then states reassuringly that these inequalities need not be seen as incorrectible. Describing the so-called "robber barons" J D Rockefeller, J P Morgan and Andrew Carnegie of 19th century America as having been in relative terms even richer than Bill gates, he then states that these empire situations do not last. Techniques are copied, new entrants appear, and the old monopolies lose the drive and ruthlessness that got them there in the first place. He ends the article by describing the possible rewards of the present optimistically noting the ability of all people to benefit from this "round" of wealth creating revolution thus: *"The third industrial revolution offers more opportunities* to the Third World than its predecessors. No longer need economies be held back by climate, lack of natural resources or location. The internet---electronic globalisation---is already creating new opportunities. Accounting and back office work for western financial businesses is done in Bombay. The West Indies has a thriving processing industry. The opportunities will multiply…"

The scene is thus set for the realisation of that concept of "Equal Opportunity" much touted in the context of employment and social welfare in the western World. It is, however, so much more needed now than ever before. It is needed, and is indeed available at present, and only requires the re-structuring of people's thoughts and attitudes, to deliver at the end that much vaunted prize of justice and equity. That ultimate objective must surely be the creating of the template upon which the whole of humanity gains access to the bounties and resources of the world, combining the best of world knowledge, expertise and energies. The challenges that face humanity in trying to achieve this harmonious state will be discussed in the final section of this work.

ADDITIONAL ECONOMIC FACTORS required for World stability, peace and an equitable progressive prosperity

At the time of writing this section, the world has come to realize that on the statistical basis of information available, it has probably witnessed the birth of the six billionth member of its population. An exponential rise in this population count has been seen in the last hundred years, with the curve rising particularly steep in the last 20 to 30 years. In spite of the continuing bloody conflicts in practically all corners of the globe, the combined effect of education, health care, good nutrition and overall prosperity, has produced a resultant net gain in populations in all but a few West European countries, notably

Norway and Sweden. Other countries in Western Europe have almost plateau'ed in their population growth, while countries with a strong adherence to religion, particularly Roman Catholicism and Islam find it hard to reconcile their beliefs with methods of contraception or with abortion. Moreover, most people living in under-developed countries tend towards as large a family as they can have simply as a means of increasing family strength and support, or even as a status symbol. Naturally, ignorance, lack of education, especially of the womenfolk, and lack of government or subsidized schemes for providing contraception and advice, are other factors.

On the face of it, therefore, it would be worrying to see a world with apparently finite resources being consumed (to annihilation?) by inexorable demographic growth. Science and technology, as well as schemes well thought out and executed, mainly by governments, have until now succeeded in maintaining a "managed" balance within this equation. The increased yields in agriculture, increased mobility of people in search of "greener pastures", and perhaps the appreciation of the environmental issues at stake, have all helped. Some Government efforts have been successful. For example, the average family in Egypt which used to be about 5.5, has reduced to 3.6 within about two decades. Further reductions are anticipated. Other government programmes have been disastrous, such as that implemented by Indira Ghandi in India, which had forced male sterilisation as its main element. On the whole, though, the main failures in government efforts have been the result of lack of real care or commitment. The political and personal interests have often led politicians and governments to squander their countries' energy and resources in political and military strife, corruption, and often sheer incompetence.

To achieve a balance, therefore, is something that can be "managed", given the will, and the co-operation. Channelling adequate proportions of national income towards eliminating the causes of imbalance, and a serious attempt to reconcile and draw on the combined strengths of science and religion, at least with regards to contraception and (medically indicated) abortion, in particularly now that more scientifically reliable methods of avoiding or preventing conception are available, may answer at least one religious prohibition, that of effectively "killing" a fertilized ovum through certain hormonal or mechanical contraceptives or through abortion. The world's resources can possibly then last much longer than many alarmists consider possible. But even the most ardent optimists will wish to see such a world-wide and sincere effort enthusiastically undertaken, if they are to be confident that their optimism will be self fulfilling.

Supplementing all this, the world must see, and in fact is already seeing, an unprecedented growth of trade. It is trade in commodities, in manufactured goods, in services and, perhaps most significantly, in talent, that is the critical requisite for the most optimum utilisation of world resources, and, again importantly, their equitable distribution.

International Trade:

In earlier sections of this work, trade was described when it was in its infancy, and thereafter when it developed in theoretical and in practical terms. That trade has taken an international dimension in this and the last century beyond all that was undertaken or even considered in the past, is easily understood. The obvious reasons for international trade now and in the past has been the unequal distribution of natural resources, the development of particular skills in some country or some part of the world, and the propensity for people to acquire taste for needs in response to availability. Thus, in primitive societies, people knew little else than what was immediately seen and available. These were usually the bare necessities for subsistence and shelter, in addition to primitive tools. Immediately accessible raw material such as hide, timber, stone, and perhaps accessible minerals such as copper (and bronze), and iron were the mainstay of circumscribed parochial economies.

Interaction and travel, have changed that. Nature has been seen to endow different parts of the world with different resources. While some countries like Britain may be sitting on a grand mass of coal, (which sadly now is not worth mining to the same extent as half a century ago), and has large crude oils reserves on shore, but more so, off-shore, it does not have copper. The vast oils reserves of Kuwait also tell a story of virtually no other as yet identified natural resource, except the coastline and sea. Example abound.

But nature also means different climates, altitudes, humidity, and other variables, which in isolation or in combination produce unique conditions suitable for certain produce. The Mediterranean and its capacity for citrus fruit, olives and wheat, the tropics for timbre and exotic fruit, and the Far East, especially Burma for rice, are all examples of parts of the world that are capable of enough surplus to satisfy needs in nearby countries or further afield. Even when a country has enough supply of a particular resource to satisfy its needs, the expediency of trade in quality and for other than just exchange come into play. The crude oil produced in the UK is of such quality that it may be more profitable to sell some of it and have it replaced by a lesser quality for home use. The USA has a "strategic reserve" of crude oil, either stored or left in the ground, at the same time as it continues to import the majority of the oil it needs for on-going consumption. This reserve is variable in extent, but usually satisfies around 3 months supply, and is intended for use in an emergency (especially during the era of the "cold war") should the lines of supply be interrupted.

More recent developments of these "quirks" of international exchange is seen in the multi-nationals, as they find it easier to use different countries for there productions in part or in toto, usually to tap into local expertise or lower production cost. The laws governing all these considerations are based on the principle of ***comparative advantage (or least comparative disadvantage),*** or the principle of ***Comparative cost.***[234] In both principles, the cost of producing an item is considered in relation to the effort and expertise available, and whether that effort or expertise is better deployed in one situation or another. An everyday example is where a person can do a job at home with his knowledge in DIY rather than give it to another person more expert in this job. Will this person do a good or better job than the more expert person can, or will he calculate that he can earn more in the time it takes him to do it than he would pay the more expert person for the job. This is the sort of decision that can decide comparative cost or comparative advantage. The same considerations will apply within the international scene, naturally in a more sophisticated and complex manner. The cost of producing a motor car in one country may be compared with the cost of producing a quantity of wheat in the same country or in a different one, and this harps back to Adam Smith, and his principle that no one should produce something that he can buy more cheaply elsewhere.

In all this one assumes that nations will act not only in self interest as indeed individuals tend to do, but in the interest of the rest of the world as well. If the latter is the driving principle in the decision making, it is easy to see a very significant increase in world trade and in world prosperity. Protectionist measures such as embargoes, quotas, tariffs, currency restrictions, "prior to import" deposits, and "technical specifications" are among the many "tricks" resorted to in order to "engineer" an advantage or a disadvantage, whichever happens to be the desired effect. "Dumping" and subsidized exports are other measures which work in the opposite direction, and can be just as harmful. In relation to the concept of fairness, the following quote is worth noting[235]: *"If world trade is not restricted in any way, countries will specialise in those industries where they have a comparative advantage and as a result of this specialisation output will increase. The world will be richer, and production will take place in the most economic location. The volume of world trade will rise, and the whole world will be wealthier; but this will not necessarily mean that all the people of the world will benefit equally. The terms of trade will decide who gets the lion's share of the increased wealth."* This, then is the nub of it. The world can get wealthier, but it must learn to share as equitably as possible.

For this to happen, the world needs to undergo a fundamental shift in many of its long held assumptions, assumptions that have their roots in "tribalism" even of a modern nature. As William Greider writes in his book[236]: *"Grasping the meaning of this new order requires one to set aside reflexive national loyalties in order to see the system as a whole. I have at least tried to do that..'Universality means taking a risk in order to go beyond the easy certainties provided us by our background, language, nationality, which so often shield us from the reality of others', Edward W. Said, the Palestinian-American scholar, has written, 'It also means looking for and trying to uphold a single standard human behaviour when it comes to such matters as foreign and social policy'"..* "When all the larger economic and political questions are exhausted, the heaviest legacy of this "new World", may be the psychological blow to national arrogance...Tribal assumptions of inherited superiority are embedded in the cultures of the French and Chinese and Muslims, among many others. These false illusions are now under vigorous assault..."*

History shows the economic centres of gravity in an ever flowing manner, sometimes labyrinthine, and at others serpentine. Indeed one has only to witness a simple act of nature, that of a flowing trickle or stream of water to see that it will flow in whichever direction provides least resistance. If resistance does occur, the flow will accept temporary arrest of movement until enough water has accumulated to allow the flow to proceed above the obstruction. A historical example is given by Greider (pages 29-31): *"The modern Industrial world's first great centre for iron and steel making was located in several villages in South Wales. Starting in the late 1700s, the Welsh industry expanded to a production peak in 1830 and then fell back, surpassed by the larger mills of England in places like Sheffield and Leeds. A generation or so later, steel moved again, this time to the United States, where, after the Civil War, Pittsburgh emerged as the vital centre of the world's steel production. The younger steel industries rising in America and Germany borrowed the technology first devised by an Englishman, Henry Bessemer, and perfected its application. By World War I, British steel making was eclipsed by both.*

"Steel moved after the devastations of World War II. This time Japan borrowed some American ideas and built new, more efficient integrated rolling mills that by the 1970s were able to outproduce and underprice Pittsburgh. South Korea followed along the same path, and its massive works at Pohang became the largest steel mills in the non-communist world.

"The centre of steel making may be on the move again. The Shanghai No.5 steelworks is said to be as efficient as the most advanced mills in the world and is one of the largest, able to turn out eight million tons a year. With help from German engineering, China's steel output has been expanding rapidly, growing by 50% in a recent five-year period. The world leader, Japan, is steadily declining in size. South Wales, meanwhile, has settled into marginal status as an outpost for low wage, light-assembly factories, most of them owned by foreign companies.

"The pattern of industrial migration, based on borrowed technology and investments in what the modern planners call 'greenfield' production sites, are as old as capitalism. The great French historian Fernand Braudel, author of an epic three-volume history of capitalism, describes how the productive dominance moved around Europe in the centuries before it migrated to the United States.

"Venice was the centre in 1380, until a gigantic shift in 1500 that favoured Antwerp. Economic dominance then returned briefly to the Mediterranean around 1560, this time to Genoa. When the Northern countries of Europe gained ascendancy, Amsterdam became the new capital of commerce and held it for nearly two centuries. By 1815, invigorated by the English industrial revolution, the centre moved to London. In 1929, when Britain's fading hegemony was conclusively destroyed by the great crash, the capital of capitalism moved decisively to New-York..."

At present, the pull is in various directions, shared by New-York, London, Frankfurt, Tokyo, Hong Kong and others. *"The emergence of new economic rivals, resembles a kind of inverted food chain in which the little fish try to eat the big fish and sometimes succeeds".*

But what is certainly not required at this critical juncture for the stability, sanity, and equity of the world to be maintained or regained, is this concept of any fish feasting on another, regardless of which way such feasting occurs. The world must have matured enough to appreciate this simple fact, and the indications, as will be described later, are that this new understanding and appreciation is being given serious consideration at every level of decision making.

World Currency

The evolution of currency has been discussed in previous sections of this work, and the idea of a means of evaluating transactions in terms that can be accepted by the majority of the world's population, whether on an individual basis or on a more widespread scale, almost goes back to the earliest stages of "civilization" and will remain as long as there is a need for exchange of goods and services. Starting with the simple barter of necessary or desired items, and proceeding to the use of precious metal, silver then gold, it reached the present process of exchange through currencies that hold a value. That value, as described earlier, can be based on the underlying support for the currency, the ease of exchange or the need to acquire that particular currency. The word "Sterling" and the "Bank of England" were synonymous with absolute guarantee of value and safety, and arguably still are. But in recent times, and in particular since the end of World War II, the term "Dollar is King" is frequently heard, and the "Fed." or Federal Reserve of the USA is looked upon as the "Gold Standard" and "Bell-weather" of world finance. The dollar was the stabilizing anchor for the world currencies, and from World War II until 1973 the United States guaranteed the fixed exchange-rate system with its own gold reserves. An ounce of gold was worth \$35, and nations or people could cash in dollars for gold, if they wished. This imposed financial discipline on the US as well as other governments. However, the situation became difficult to sustain as inflation eroded the value of the currency, and in 1971 the value of the dollar was "diluted" in relation to other currencies, with the final decision of the US Government to de-couple the dollar from gold taken two year later, effectively cancelling the Bretton Woods agreement. Money was now free to find its own level in the marketplace. Gold soared in price reaching the dizzy heights of \$800 to the ounce in the late 70's/ early 80's, and again recently. But it tends to settle down to average levels most of the time. As readers might know, gold has always found its level in monetary value depending on a variety of circumstances and world conditions. The tendency is for it to be used as a hedge against currency fluctuation, economic recession, or world security disturbances. Its price also may reflect the inherent value and availability for industry or burgeoning jewellery trade. Governments tend to hold gold as part of their reserves, but may divest themselves of large holdings to suit particular currency or economic situations.

There are as many currencies around the world as there are sovereign nations, except for examples such as the "Euro" currency coverage the E.U. member states. Some national currencies are happy to lie in the shadow of one of the stronger currencies. While in the past there were recognizable currency blocks such as the Sterling block and the French Franc block, it is now increasingly the case that the US Dollar is the recognized "Umbrella" under which other currencies huddle, especially in "rainy" times. This is the case with the Egyptian Pound, the Mexican Dollar and the Israel Shekel, to give but a small selection. Indeed, in many such countries the US Dollar is transacted in the streets in even the most mundane affairs. The dollar is more readily understood and accepted in downtown Istanbul by the street hawker than the Turkish Lira.

So has the world actually moved to a "World Currency" and not noticed? Well, this may be, but probably not quite yet. What is not in doubt, however, is the fact that the world is looking for some means to rationalize its financial conditions. It is obvious that the big currencies now are the Dollar, the Yen, Sterling, and the *"Euro"*. Sterling is hovering around wondering whether to join the Euro or keep away. With the "Euro-dollar", the "Petro-dollar", and the "Special Drawing Rights" of the IMF (calculated in US Dollars), the field is already narrowing to three or three and a half currencies, depending on whether Sterling joins or not.

Currency has always been considered an emblem of sovereignty, and when strong, it became also an expression of National "virility", giving the nation it belongs to a sense of potency and strength, and acting as a source of pride. This may be rightly so if the reason for its strength is the industriousness of its people, their resourcefulness or inventive ability. It is difficult to justify when the only reason for such strength happens to be a natural resource discovered and exploited by some foreign technology, as in the small oil producing countries or where the tropical forests are cut down by the acres.

Yet, even the strongest of currencies are today vulnerable to the stresses and strains of intense competition in world markets. This competitiveness, until the electronic revolution of the last two or three decades, was to all intents and purposes the determining factor in deciding on the value of the currency. Currency dealings on a world-wide scale was too slow to impact as decisively as now on the exchange rates, and governments or central banks had time to intervene. Freedom of exchange was much more restricted in most countries, perhaps apart from the USA. Even in Britain, full freedom of exchange was only lifted in the late sixties.

With the development of electronic dealings and the freedom of exchange, the situation altered significantly. Dealings are happening every minute of every hour in almost every currency around the world, and as the currencies are circulating around the clock as a means of feeding these transaction dealings and to maximize the return on capital, the situation is easily open to exploitation. Individuals with large capital reserves, and more so large financial institutions, have the means of forcing the hands of central banks to create artificial and short term exchange rate fluctuations to their advantage, naturally accepting that occasionally they may lose. They are the ultimate "gamblers" who are able in some instances to dictate their luck, and will have no scruples about doing so regardless of the implications on the fortunes of other people. Memories of George Soros' two salient global currencies games must be still in many people's minds, and it is well to quote William Greider[237] who describes the two incidences vividly.

He writes: "*Late one afternoon in July 1993, I happened by chance to telephone an old friend in New York, Robert A. Johnson, just as he was in the middle of another storm of global finance. Rob Johnson was a Ph.D. economist educated at MIT and Princeton, an alumnus of the Federal Reserve's research staff and the Senate's budget and banking committees. He was then working in the highest ranks of global finance traders, as a partner to George Soros whose strategic speculation were famed and feared across continents.*

"*When he came on the phone, Rob's voice was supercharged with adrenaline, fairly cracking with electrical intensity as he spoke in a rapid rush of words.*

"'*What a day' he said. 'I bought more bonds today than in any other single day I've worked with Soros. We probably bought $4 billion in bond today—government bonds from France, Denmark, Portugal, Spain, everywhere we could. Europe just stood there while we shovelled in bonds. We probably did another billion and a half in equities.*

"'*We were paying ten basis points (a tenth of one percent) over the market price, when, usually, if you pay two or three points premium, people think they are really cleaning up on you. This time, if we were going to nickel and dime it, we wouldn't be able to get all the bonds we wanted. So we went for it.*

"'*People on the other end couldn't figure out what we were doing, but the price was so good they sold to us. Sometimes I wonder why these people take such short-term view. They might figure: if Soros wants these bonds so badly, maybe I ought to hold on to them. The smart ones do.'*

"*None of this made much sense to me until Johnson explained the play. George Soros was staking out another bold market position, two steps ahead of other traders but also ahead of governments and central banks. A new currency crisis had been triggered in Europe that morning when the Bundesbank, Germany's central bank, failed to cut German interest rates, as others had hoped. That non event inspired major market players to launch a heavy speculation against the French Franc and other weakening currencies in Europe, betting that they would fall in value.*

"The Soros partners decided to play for the second-day bounce: instead of shorting the currencies, they bought bonds and stocks from across Europe, financial assets that should surge in value once the governments surrendered to speculators, cut interest rates and devalued their currencies. The logic was like a three-cushion shot in billiards.("shorting" a currency or bonds, stocks or any other commodity, is the trader's technique of borrowing the asset from another holder and selling at the current price—gambling that the price will fall and the asset can be bought back later for less. The trader satisfies the loan and pockets the price difference. In massive volumes, shorting itself helped drive down the price.)

"Either way the financial traders were playing off the political crisis ignited by the Bundesbank's inaction that morning in Frankfurt. From the Spanish Peseta to the Dutch Guilder, the continent's major currencies were linked to Germany's Deutschemark through Europe's Exchange rate Mechanism—a formal commitment to maintain currency values within a fixed band of relationships. Since the D-mark was the strongest currency and the anchor for the system, the Bundesbank essentially set monetary policy for all of Europe. When the Bundesbank raised interest rates or persisted in holding rates at a high level, the others had no choice but to follow. Otherwise, their currencies would be rapidly sold off by investors, depreciate in value—and fall below the ERM's required floor.

"The French Franc and several other currencies were already trading close to the ERM margins. But their governments were also desperate for relief from high interest rates because every nation was stuck in recession, with unemployment rates at 10 to 13 percent. Another interest rate increase will only flatten their economies further. Should the governments hang tough and stay in step with the D-mark, even raising interest rates to do

so? Or would they accept the humiliation of dropping out of the exchange rate system in order to reduce domestic economic pain? If the ERM broke up, that would postpone—if not destroy—Europe's vision of achieving a unified currency and economic union by 1997. Soros and the speculators were betting, in different ways, that the governments would fold.

"'The French have to cut rates,' Rob Johnson predicted. 'Realistically, French interest rates should be about four percent on long bonds and they are at seven percent. If they break out of the system, their interest rates will collapse and you'll get a huge bond rally. When the Bundesbank refused to cut rates, it created a French political crisis. The French put all their faith in the Germans and the Germans stuck a boot in their face today. France sticks with the Germans to show its faith in a unified Europe— they envisaged the EC as run by a French-German alliance at the core of Europe. Now they are getting screwed.....

"Europe's central banks fought vigorously, collectively defending the weak currencies by buying up huge quantities of francs, pesetas and the others with the D-marks stored in their foreign-exchange reserves. By selling more deutschemarks into the markets, the central banks softened the D-mark's value while simultaneously boosting the price of weaker currencies by mopping up the market's supply of them. That was the intention anyway. In a few hours, the central banks expended 15 billion D-marks (about $8.7billion) to defeat speculators.

The central banks lost. The Bundesbank stood its ground against the market pressures and did not cut rates, but the ERM blew apart. Four days later the governments sheepishly announced that they were adopting a new, much wider band of currency relationships for the ERM—a de facto surrender that allowed the weak currencies to decline and their interest rates to subside. The crisis was resolved, papered over with stout declarations that the ERM had survived and European Union would not be derailed. But every party understood the real meaning: finance capital has once again bested major governments, forced them to retreat from their own economic policies. A heavy shadow was cast over Europe's vision of unification

"*George Soros—an urbane, brilliant fabulously wealthy—was the arrogant symbol of this worldly power….Soros was attacked, nonetheless. French politicians and press assailed the "Anglo-Saxon speculators" profiting on international discord, undermining European community….*

"*'George Soros calls the bluff of governments', Rob Johnson explained. 'Their job is to pretend that they are in control and he represents a force that blows away that illusion…George Soros is not dangerous if your country is doing sound economic policy.'*

"*Ten months earlier Soros' fund had earned $950 million in one brief exercise by demonstrating that the British government was defending 'unsound policy'. The British press called it Black Wednesday and dubbed Soros 'the man who broke the Bank of England'. In September 1992, the pound sterling was trading around 2.85 to the D-mark, perilously close to the bottom of the ERM band of 2.77. To stay in the band, the venerable central bank had to keep raising interest rates despite the recessionary conditions at home, in order to attract foreign money to its currency. Soros, meanwhile sold sterling short massively, betting $10 billion. Britain could not stay the course.*

"*At noon on Black Wednesday, the Chancellor of the Exchequer, Norman Lamont, bravely announced that Britain would never yield and raised interest rates by an additional 2 percent. The government, he said, intended to borrow $15 billion to defend sterling. 'We were amused,' Soros wrote afterwards, 'because that was about how much we wanted to sell.' By nightfall, the UK government caved and dropped the pound out of the exchange rate system. Italy had already given up the fight for the lira. Soros, counting other coordinating currency plays, figured he realized $2 billion profit from about two weeks of investment.*

"What did George Soros know to be so bold? As he repeatedly explained over the years, his basic investment strategy involved identifying the fundamental misalignments in market perceptions—prices or political\ judgements that were out of line with the underlying realities of economics and politics that were sharply reversed once markets or governments were compelled to recognize them... 'The result is a theoretical construction of great elegance that resembles natural science but does not resemble reality'..."

During the sterling crisis Soros got a hint of this "Realpolitic" in a conversation with Bundesbank President Helmut Schlesinger, who remarked that he liked the concept of a single currency for Europe, but would prefer it to be called the mark. For Soros, the quip was a signal that the Bundesbank was not going to sacrifice its own national priorities in order to hold the ERM system together. His speculative attack followed."

To be sure, not even George Soros always gets it right. Recently he speculated on the Japanese Yen and had his fingers burnt to the tune of over $3 billion. He acknowledged the failed speculation, but not, obviously the scale of the loss.

The world has reached a stage where rationality can be in short supply. The whims and fancies of politicians or their ideologies will often dictate courses of action at the same time that other forces, as powerful and often more powerful, will upset all their calculations if it is in their personal, sometimes selfish, interests to do so. The world of finance has quite evidently moved on to the stage where the speed and colossal size of transactions can be undertaken on many occasions, with no more motivation than self-interest, self-propagation, and often the mere feeding of the dealer's ego or his/her gambling drive. The case of Nick Leeson, the Singapore based dealer for the UK based Barings Bank appeared at the end to be nothing but the classical gambler's attitude that the next throw of the proverbial dice will bring back all that was lost. Sadly, it only brought forwards the demise of the whole bank, the oldest and most traditional of British banks, and a jail sentence for him.

Global Shifts Or Global Instability

As a result of the two main factors mentioned in the previous sections, namely the shift in trade balances and the fast movements of money, the world is witnessing significant gyrations which, while acceptable as necessary in the fast moving global financial affairs, are also a source of constant vigilance and probably worry on the part of all concerned, whether governments or businesses. The accumulation of vast reserves in the new trading countries especially in the Middle and Far East is estimated recently to be around US$ 3.3 Trillion, with seven nations being prominent (Abu Dhabi, Norway, Singapore with two separate accounts, Kuwait, China and Russia). There is a further 5.5 Trillion US dollars additionally accumulated in investment funds, and other smaller countries. This is far greater than any reserve funds that are available to developed industrialised countries with leading manufacture, production and trading activities, namely the USA and Western Europe. These figures are not to be confused with "Gross Domestic Product" which would be quite vast in for example the USA, Japan, and Germany, as well as Britain and France. These countries together are still leading that field. However, this situation is creating a sort of imbalance because it means that smaller countries are gaining greater clout and can, should they wish to do so, dictate their policies or wishes on the "old world" countries. One can argue that used responsibly, such clout can be put to good effect. But "responsibly" here must of necessity be accepted only as "an act of faith". For within the existing system of nation states, leaderships are so disparate in political ideology, so varied in the degree of democracy that brings them to the seats of power, and often so wanting in ethical and moral standards in the conduct of the affairs of their states, even where accountable. This was evident in the surfacing of the degrees of corruption that covered up bad management of governments and their financial policies in such countries as Japan and South Korea, which until recently were looked upon as paradigms of probity and surefootedness in their policies. It was easy, also for other leaders to blame outside factors for their financial woes, as did Prime Minister Mahathir of Malaysia when he intimated that it was George Soros and his likes that precipitated the sudden and severe depreciation of the Malaysian *Ringit (dollar)* in 1998/99. All this, plus the fact that governments are not stable entities at the best of times, any change almost always leads to policy changes, sometimes dramatic. It will not be difficult to see that a new system has to emerge that would both calm these gyrations, and also put in place some order acceptable voluntarily and willingly by all, or at least the major, players in the field. And where players in the field get mention, the proverbial, but crucial requirement of a "level playing field" is not far off.

Cataclysmically, such a new system can grow out of a "global disintegration" that some people, including George Soros, warn about. And while not inconceivable, one sincerely hopes that those in the commanding heights of world powers will be savvy enough not to allow it to happen. The omens are good, for we only have to imagine that the world was in serious threat of a nuclear holocaust not so long ago, and while the threat may not have disappeared entirely, it is certainly most unlikely, save for a faint possibility of a rogue minor occurrence. It is not too optimistic, therefore, to cherish a sincere hope that global financial "meltdown" can be averted.

A gradual transformation is thus more likely. It may happen by putting together the new system piece by piece, ending up with the jigsaw picture of a new financial order, based on equity, soundness and, more importantly, simplicity.

Suggestions are all the time available. Widening of the authority of the IMF so that it can "discipline" individual governments, may be impalatable to these governments or their citizens. Nevertheless, especially in recent years, such advice, commonly administered to poorer (developing) countries, is also given to advanced economies. A well publicised incidences occurred in 1975 when the British Chancellor of the Exchequer, Dennis Healey had to return from Heathrow airport where he was to board a plane to attend a meeting of the IMF. Instead, he had to go back to office to implement urgent requirements imposed upon him by this same IMF in order to meet the needs of a Sterling financial crisis. This is an example of a situation where a respectable nation with all the history of its position as a foremost player in world economics has had to swallow a lot of pride and abide by the wishes of the international financial community as represented by the IMF in order to put its house in order. The IMF may continue to be able to nudge other economies with a combination of advice and financial assistance. It may even manage to "bully" smaller nations or economies. But only, with the submissive acceptance of all countries, and only given that this institution works with scrupulous fairness, and adroit professionalism, will such a regulatory system be plausible and able to stand a chance to succeed. Success, however, in this context, relates mainly to financial regulation. It will not cover political ideology or practice, and will have very little effect on large powerful financial institutions, which, as has been shown above, can reek havoc if it is their immediate interest to do so.

Surrendering control to a free for all financial management through the workings of the market-place is not really a viable proposition. There must be some control on the propensity of humans to go beyond their better judgements in acquiring and accumulating regardless of the effect on the people at large. And while not being too cynical of people's motivations, one can't help feeling that individuals, and for all that, institutions, will easily allow their instincts to overtake their judgements.

Targeted controls, such as the simple reform that governments can take and which[238] *"Yale economist James Tobin more than fifteen years ago, proposed: To impose a very slight transaction tax on all cross-border flows of capital. Applied to major foreign-exchange centres, a small exit-and-entry toll would slow down the furious pace of global finance by taking a nick out of the quick profits (at present volumes, and infinitesimal levy on capital's cross-border movements would yield hundreds of billions in new revenue).."* This may have been plausible fifteen years ago. It is very doubtful as a practical measure at present. The financial worlds have moved on, and any such system will have to be applied on a global basis with all governments in step completely, faithfully and assiduously. Even so, it will at today's pace be almost impossible to implement.

Indeed controls have to come from within (the human organism) first. Abiding thereafter by external controls will be for the purpose of being "in-step" and knowing how to remain so without loss of volition, and without curtailment of those two unique human quality: resourcefulness and ingenuity. Such qualities, will, within a system adhered to out of conscientious submission, will release the most precious and constructive forces and potentials inherent in humans. That such a system may exist, is part of the next discussion.

PART XI

PEACE

Money is The Sinews Of War

This is an age old adage, and it rings true now as it did at all time. It may even be more true now. For in the past war needed the strong sinews of men, in addition to the money. But it was the strength and stamina of the fighting soldier that at the end of the day, won the battle or the war. And while strength and stamina are still the mainstay of modern warfare, whether it is on land, sea or sky, the more effective sinews are those of brain and technological training. Money, however, is now of greater importance than ever before. It can buy the advantages of higher technological capability, with, albeit, a rising cost, and a level of expenditure that is consuming a higher proportion of national incomes than ever before, especially with the lesser developed countries.

In the past, preparation for war could go on quite discreetly for some time before it is noticed. But at present, it is much easier to realize that something sinister is going on before anything really happens. This is because the traffic and flow of moneys is easily monitored as it flows through the financial institutions. And where large amounts are involved with either obscure explanation as to its transaction purposes, or if it involves participants well suspected for possible preparation for war, together with other forms of intelligence gathering, it will not be too taxing an effort to anticipate and work out what is going on.

The burden on national budgets for defence was, and to great extent still is, enormous. But during the height of the so-called "Cold War", the state of readiness on the part of the Communist and the Western Alliances to confront each, which at one time was worked out on the basis of the concept of "MAD" (Mutual Assured Destruction), proved to be so costly that it became a major factor in the collapse of the Communist regimes under its weight during that historically fateful year of 1989. The speed and totality of the domino like collapse of all the Communist states unfolded a vision, which was known to a certain extent previously, and its true scale was guessed at through indirect intelligence. However, what really emerged must be seen in the context of the inevitability of the march of history. It would be a mistake to ignore the lessons related to the bankruptcy that signalled the real underlying cause for the collapse. True, that bankruptcy was ideological. But the economic consequences were dire, and made it easy for the people to discard it at the first opportunity without shedding a single tear. What was East Germany, boasting at the height of the "Cold War" era of being the 11th largest industrial state in the world, proved to be utterly run down in most, if not all, its industries. The symbol was that curiosity of a car they called the "Trabant" and which was endearingly named the "Trabbie". Nothing could have been more embarrassing. There was, however, no doubting the military might that that State possessed. The fact that it did not have to be deployed "in anger" at any time, was only a mercifully conceived act of Providence. Its intelligence and security services were legendary. The ill fated and utterly reprehensible "Stasi" had pervaded almost every household and spread suspicion and fear into every relationship, even the most intimate and close of kin.

In the initial euphoria of the ending of the "Cold War", the world talked of the "Peace Dividend" when the level of preparedness became less acute or severe. And true, the likelihood of a nuclear holocaust between the then super-powers (essentially the former USSR and the USA) has reduced enormously. But the initial sighs of relief may have been a little premature. For in the wake of the new situation, there appeared so many causes for concern emanating from smaller nations and factions strewn across the globe, with much less of the predictability, control, and channels of communication that at least were available between the two super-powers, who, after-all had fairly good control of the weaponry and deployment within their "client" states. The world witnessed major conflicts, such as the "Gulf war" against Iraq in the wake of Saddam Hussein's invasion of the neighbouring small but rich state of Kuwait. Then there were the conflicts within the six Balkan states that were held together by the late Marshall Tito to form his Communist State of Yugoslavia. The implosion that followed his demise demonstrated how tenuous that federation was. At the time of writing, the cinders are still glowing in the Balkan area, and other fires are still raging or are started, particularly in Africa, in the newly formed republics that were once within the USSR, and in the giant State of Indonesia in the Far East. The world is at present heavily engaged in the current two big conflicts in Iraq and Afghanistan.

So much highly sophisticated expertise has been allowed to go loose from the former Soviet Union, and which has become available to whoever will pay, that a worry is now not so much what weaponry and technology is available, but where is it available and with whom. How responsible are the hands they have fallen into. There is thus no alternative to maintaining vigilance and preparedness. The real situation is that now the outlay for arms and defence has not abated to any extent originally hoped for. I hesitate to hazard that it may actually have increased.

But the purpose of this discussion is not to prove how costly war and weaponry are, because this is a well known fact. The purpose is to look at the value of peace as an important factor in stimulating trade, and the development of peaceful resources that can benefit the generality of human world. People with capital will tend to go on in the pursuit of higher returns to their capital, and such pursuit may well, if unbridled by principle or ethical considerations, develop into a state of frenzy. This in turn will eventually face a corrective event that unfortunately may be cataclysmic, such as a great depression or a war. *"... These events will destroy financial capital on a massive scale...and produces vast human suffering... The longer an expansionary era continues without the disastrous interruptions of war or depression, the larger the gross pool of accumulated savings will become in relation to the productive economy. In other words, a period of long running peace and prosperity inevitably feeds the imbalance by piling a greater and greater store of 'accumulated labour'. This should be a cause of celebration, not gloom..."[239]*. Accumulated labour, in this context, is another term for "capital".

Peace is not the absence of war

It is more than that. It is even more than the absence of conflict. It is a mindset. To be pervasive and lastingly effective, this mindset has to be accepted as the basis for avoidance of conflict and for resorting to non-violent means for resolving any conflict should it arise. In a message Statement by the Universal House of Justice, the supreme governing body of the Baha'i Faith, two points are emphasized[240]: *"One is that the abolition of war is not simply a matter of signing treaties and protocols; it is a complex task requiring a new level of commitment to resolving issues not customarily associated with the pursuit of peace...the other is that the primary challenge in dealing with issues of peace is to raise the context to the level of principle, as distinct from pure pragmatism. For in essence, peace stems from an inner state supported by a spiritual or moral attitude, and it is chiefly in evoking this attitude that the possibility of enduring solutions can be found..."*

In the context of economics, these two elements of stability and internalised understanding are essential if the world is to formulate a new "economic" world order, in which the expense, anxiety and uncertainty would be factored in, at least initially, only at the low levels within the overall equations. With the endurance and continued adherence, the element of uncertainty could well disappear, the anxiety will be tolerated to the extent that it provides an incentive for all concerned to remain on their guards and to avoid as far as possible the pitfalls, and the expense or expenditure will be calculated so that :"...*Arms and armaments will, then, be no more needed beyond that which is necessary to insure the internal security of (the) respective countries...(and) the nations of the world will no longer require any armaments, except for the purpose of preserving the security of their realms and of maintaining internal order within their territories. This will ensure the peace and composure of every people, government and nation..."*[241]

In the Statement mentioned above, a further enlightening passage (p.1) discusses the fact that :"*Among the favourable signs are the steadily growing strength of the steps towards world order taken initially near the beginning of this century in the creation of the League of Nations, succeeded by the more broadly based United Nations Organisation; the achievement since the Second World War of independence by the majority of all the nations on earth, indicating the completion of the process of nation building, and the involvement of these fledgling nations with older ones in matter of mutual concern; the consequent vast increase in co-operation among hitherto isolated and antagonistic peoples and groups in international undertakings in the scientific, legal, economic and cultural fields...The scientific and technological advances occurring in this unusually blessed century portend a great surge forward in the social evolution of the planet..."* This is an interesting concept. It is a statement that the stage in the evolution of the world's structure has reached the completion of the *"nation-state"* phase, and is now poised to proceed in the evolutionary process of this planet *"to the next stage, (*which is) *in the words of one great thinker, 'the planetization of mankind"* This thought would fit well with that of ***economic globalization***, and will act as the solid base upon which the latter can operate effectively and appropriately, and, very importantly, with propriety. It is conceptually sound, were it not for the fact that the fast movement of events has almost already turned it from concept to reality. Indeed, the mechanisms are almost all in place for the world to make so much use of this emerging reality. With all the "Agencies" that are now in operation, dealing with the co-ordination of all aspects of international relationships, and all the goodwill demonstrated by the people involved and the governments concerned, there appears to be one lacking element that may not be insurmountable, provided the will is there and the realization of its need is fully and wholeheartedly appreciated. This element is nothing more and nothing less than a credible consultation process and method that is based, not on political, factional, sectarian or self interests, but on the "spiritual" basis that creates the atmosphere of decision making with the detachment, love for the whole of humanity, and the interest of all, small or large, powerful or weak, rich or poor, an atmosphere conducive to the ultimate feeling of all nations, peoples and regions that each and every are the beneficiaries of the best that humanity can offer, and these needs best addressed. "Spiritual" in this context may relate to the time honoured and indeed timeless teachings and wisdoms of the world's religions. But it will also mean that individual quality whereby, with a "spiritual" attitude, people individually and collectively have a greater insight into the affairs they deal with, so that they are better able to invest them with "value" and "meaning". It is that blend of intellectuality and benevolent emotion that results in rationality with compassion and with appreciation.

Dispassionate and Cordial Consultation:

This title is an extract of a passage from the "Promise of World Peace" (p.20), highlighted because of its telling significance and headline value. The context, which will give it added understanding, is : *"The courage, the resolution, the pure motive, the selfless love of one people for another—all the spiritual and moral qualities required for effecting this momentous step towards peace are focussed on the **will to act*** (author's highlighting in bold). *And it is towards arousing the necessary* **volition** *that earnest consideration must be given to the reality of man, namely, his thought. To understand the relevance of this potent reality is also to appreciate the social necessity of actualising its unique value through candid,* **dispassionate and cordial consultation,** *and of* **acting upon the results of this process***. Baha'u'llah insistently drew attention to the virtues and indispensability of consultation for ordering human affairs. He said:' Consultation bestows greater awareness and transmutes conjecture into certitude. It is a shining light which, in a dark world, leads the way and guideth. For everything there is and will continue to be a station of perfection and maturity. The maturity of the gift of understanding is made manifest through consultation.' The very attempt to achieve peace through the consultative action he proposed can release a salutary spirit among the peoples of the earth that no power could resist the final, triumphant outcome.* "[242]

To say that the world is not ready for this new spirit and greater reliance on the all-important principle of dispassionate and cordial consultation, is to deny what the world has succeeded in achieving to-date, and it would be too pessimistic an evaluation of mankind's desire and motivation. For: *"The army of men and women, drawn from virtually every culture, race and nation on earth, who serve the multifarious agencies of the United Nations, represent a planetary "civil service" whose impressive accomplishments are indicative of the degree of co-operation that can be attained under even discouraging conditions"*[243].

However, to think that the world has attained the lasting solutions that it deserves, will be a denial of the need to work hard to overcome so many of the fundamental difficulties that remain. For: *"Our world has entered the dark heart of an age of fundamental change beyond anything in all of its tumultuous history. Its peoples, of whatever race, nation, or religion, are being challenged to subordinate all lesser loyalties and limiting identities to their oneness as citizens of a single planetary homeland.* And *"The well-being of mankind, its peace and security"* are, in Baha'u'llah's words: *"unattainable unless and until its unity is firmly established."* (THE UNIVERSAL HOUSE OF JUSTICE (Baha'u'llah: Aqdas: Other Sections, Page: 11)

Such a unity must be based, not on political expediency, hegemony, colonialism, or any form of economic, numerical, or other power tool or means of subordination or intimidation. It must be based on the willingness, as mentioned above to see this goal as the only means of salvation for a world that has learned to speak of differences rather than similarities, and self interest rather than communal interest. That this should be based on total so-called "egalitarianism" including any form of communism, has been shown as a demonstrable failure. That this would be part of the "hedonistic" communal lifestyle adopted by the so-called "flower" people in different countries, mainly the western "democracies", a lifestyle that allows such people to pretend that they are free and in tune with nature while drawing on the security systems available to them through hard working taxpayers is also false, if not downright dishonest and lacking in moral fibre, purposefulness and benefit to the rest of society. That this unity should be based on groupings of people sharing ethnicity, class, gender, or a particular Faith is effectively the height of disunity. It is a recipe for discrimination, prejudice, and yet greater yawning of any chasms, and more widening of any fault lines within society, nationally, regionally or internationally.

To pursue this subject further will not serve the purpose of this work to any greater extent, as it is enough to highlight the need for unity and for this unity to be on a stable, lasting, and sound basis. From the point of view of economics, such a unity of purpose and solidarity of edifice can only be achieved through the relentless pursuit of prosperity for people, especially those who have been disenfranchised or dispossessed, and that relentless pursuit should be governed by the cardinal principal of **"JUSTICE".** *No light can compare with the light of justice"*[244] says Baha'u'llah, going on to say*: "The establishment of order in the world and the tranquillity of the nations depend upon it."* And further, in addressing the then Shah Persia, He advised him*:" We hope that thou wilt cause the light of justice to shine more brightly. By the righteousness of God! Justice is a powerful force. It is, above all else, the conqueror of the citadels of the hearts and souls of men, and the revealer of the secrets of the world of being, and the standard-bearer of love and bounty."*[245]

PART XII

A LOOK TO THE FUTURE

Prosperity with Tranquillity

Humanity has found it difficult up until now to achieve these two objectives simultaneously. It was either prosperity of one country or nation, or region, at the expense of another, or the tranquillity that reflects an attitude of "anything for a quiet life" by some country or some people. The latter example is not easy to achieve, if at all. A remote independent Island, say in the Pacific, could possible aspire to a lower economic "growth rate" if it can be allowed to remain outside the arenas of large power or a neighbouring "big brother" country's attempts to influence its status or people. For some thirty years or more, the Cuban people appeared to have accepted the regime established in it by its erstwhile President Fidel Castro. While knowing very well that they have fallen well behind in their economic standards, they appeared content at the thought that they had some order within their society, and managed to achieve such successes in international and Olympic sports as to perhaps give them a sense of identity and satisfaction which in turn compensated for the low economic standard and obvious deprivation. Those who felt the urge to improve their lot were "allowed" to take the risk of fleeing by sea to nearby Florida in the USA. Some did not make it, but others did, and many of those prospered, and indeed added to their homeland's wealth through their remittances to family and folks back home. The situation changed, not from within, in spite of some attempts by dissidents to overthrow the regime, but because of the fall-out in the aftermath of the collapse of the USSR. Nevertheless, any change is slow and measured.

In general, therefore, the ruler of such a geographical or political unit will not easily be left alone, if only for the reason that some of his people will feel they can do better for their "Island" and its people.

In other situations, smaller units of this kind can remain outside such "big brother" influence. Examples of this situation are easy to describe. The rich financial (tax) "Haven" status of some islands or principalities, whose people have prospered greatly because of the small population and large wealth, or small countries with rich natural resources, such as oil, are all examples that readily come to mind. Whether such units can enjoy tranquillity at the same time depends more often on external factors than internal ones, as, for example, the case of the Gulf States during the recent wars in that area, or the situation of Hong Kong after its handing over by Britain. City States, on the whole, can manage these pressures more successfully, and particular examples are Singapore and Monaco.

Looking around for other, more telling, examples is not always fruitful as such examples are   more difficult to find. Even after World War II—which ostensibly started mainly because of the need to enhance prosperity through hegemony by one side, with the other side counteracting this in order to maintain markets and fight off aggression—the increasing prosperity of the Western World was achieved within an atmosphere of continuing anxiety and stress. We have witnessed the "Cold War", the innumerable small wars and local strife, the terrorist groups out to further particular aims, such as the

Red Brigade, the Irish Republican Army (IRA) and others. Mention should also be made of the stresses and strains of immigration policies, extremists' activities, and racial and ethnic convulsions. Indeed, the situation may be getting worse by the day, as the conflict now is not between recognized antagonistic or monolithic blocks, but between order and disorder, between a political and territorially recognizable entity, and amorphous, shifty, shadowy bodies, loosely connected, yet often autonomous and outside the confines of political or institutional entities. The motivations, aims and objectives of any destructive or disruptive activities can almost be seen as developing a momentum of its own, and it is easy to see the advent of total collapse of any reason or objectivity.

In all this turmoil, it is still possible to discern that the stage may be about to be set for a fundamental change. To understand why the world is now ready for these changes, it is appropriate to analyse in summary the factors that on the one hand prevail at present, and on the other hand the very factors (among others) that throw a very promising prospective for the future, creating the means that will achieve further prosperity together with the blessings of overhanging tranquillity.

In his book, Global Shift[246], Prof. Dickens shows a diagram which he then describes in the text, expressing his idea of "putting things together", and how *"When we try to understand the impact of globalisation (The Global Economy), on particular places, and on businesses, governments, and people in such places we need to have some understanding of how the individual parts fit together"...He then goes into further details as follows:*

☒ *The substantial global shift in the sphere of production of goods and services...are manifested in the emergence of new centres of production outside the formerly dominant core areas of the*

371

> *industrial world…the East and Southeast Asia. The global*
> *economic map has increased vastly in its complexity and is now*
> *a multipolar multiscale structure; a mosaic of unevenness in a*
> *continuous of flux…*

☒ The emergence of a new global financial system which is not only far more volatile than the one put in place at Bretton Woods immediately after the Second World War, but which is now, in the opinion of many, disarticulated from the sphere of production of 'real ' goods and services. The volume of flows in this new international financial system are not only of unprecedented—and mind-boggling—magnitude but also they are increasingly diversified.

Dickens then speaks of three other forces that are especially relevant:

☒ The highly differentiated and dynamic activities of transnational corporate activity.

☒ The continuing significance of the nation-state as a major influence in the global economy…though with the continuous attempts to regulate within and across its territorial boundaries.

☒ The role of technology as a fundamental enabling force in the internationalization and globalization of economic activity… The cumulative effect of small, incremental periodic creation of entirely new techno-economic paradigms which drastically shape and reshape both economy and society"

In all this fast and furious development, it is inevitable that discrepancies and inequalities develop. The cries from the developing countries may be more loudly heard, but it is the developed industrialized countries that are running as fast as they can in order to fend off the threat from the emerging economies of at least the two giants: China and India, not to mention Brazil, Mexico and others. The serious situations lie with those countries that are "left behind", notably the continent of Africa. Ones' mind boggles when it is stated that the richest three individuals in the world are wealthier than the combined Gross Domestic Product of the 43 poorest nations, and that: *"In 1960, the richest 20% of the world's population had incomes 30 times greater than the poorest 20%. By 1990, the richest 20% were getting 60 times more. And this comparison is based on the distribution between rich and poor countries. When we add the mal-distribution within countries, the richest 20% of the world's 'people' get at least 150 times more than the poorest 20%". (UNDP, 1992, P.1)*

This situation is not getting better. All the aid money that poured into the developing countries over the past 25 years or more have resulted in greater poverty and deprivation. More seriously is the fact that the chasm between the rich and poor is growing, both within individual countries where the rich cliques are getting richer while the ordinary people get poorer, and also between nations. The affluent so called first world are getting more affluent, while the developing countries are getting poorer. Passive infusions of aid does not appear to have greater value than a short and largely ineffective placebo effect. Indeed, it is interesting to note the title of Andrew Sullivan's article in London's Sunday Time (*19 Sept.99, P.(5)99):" The rich are richer, so why aren't the poor revolting?"* The reasoning he gives is even more interesting. While applicable to the USA, it is nevertheless so useful as an analysis in that people will accept gain and affluence if it is justifiably earned. He says:

"The United States has always been a more unequal society than, say, Britain; and far more unequal than most continental European countries. But in the past 20 years, what was once an income gap has become an income chasm...Since 1977, according to a report issued last week, the after-tax income of the richest 1% of Americans has grown by 115%. In the same period, the income of the poorest has fallen by 9%, and the vast middle has clawed up only 8%...It is that Americans, by and large, resent the moneyed elite only when it seems rigid, inherited, and closed to outsiders. And in the 1990's this has seemed to be decreasingly the case...It matters less to Americans that Bill Gates is richer than most countries. What matters is whether he earned it or not..."

This inevitably leads naturally to the next question: **What is happiness: Sunday Times, 06.02.05,quoting "Making Happy People"** by Paul Martin (Fourth Estate, 21.02.05)

Paul Martin discusses this topic as follows:

> *"The Ancient Greeks developed a concept called eudaimonia. This is often translated simply as happiness but it means something more subtle. A more literal translation would be something like: "feelings accompanying behaviour consistent with your daimon or true self"*

> *Your daimon is a state of excellence for which you strive and which gives you meaning and direction to your life. So eudaimonia is a state in which you are expressing your true self, striving to realize your own potential, and thereby living the most fulfilling life of which you are capable.*

> *The Greek philosopher Epicurus, now mistakingly associated with mindless "epicurean" pleasure seeking, taught that all the person requires in order to be happy are the basic necessities of life: food, water, shelter and warmth—plus friendship, freedom and*

thought.

He advocated a simple life, arguing that although each of us has the capacity to be happy, many people poison their lives with needless desires, anxieties and fears.

He espoused a four-part cure for anxiety and unhappiness: do not fear gods; there is no afterlife, so don't worry about death; what actually we need is easy to get; and what makes us suffer is easy to endure.

It was another Greek, Aristotle, who pointed out that people pursue money, power, material possessions, beauty or fame because they believe these will bring them happiness. But nobody seeks happiness in the belief that it will bring them some even higher benefit. Therefore, Aristotle concluded, happiness must be the ultimate goal in life

Indeed it should be, but it is obvious from the whole thrust of this work, that disregarding the spirituality that goes with Faith in the Divine Entity of God, there must be a built-in ingredient for this happiness to be on a solid foundation. Anyone who witnessed the poor people of some parts of the world would easily witness this attitude of utter acceptance of whatever meagre means life has made available to them, to wit: almost the bare survival essentials. Acceptance, however, is not necessarily happiness. A resentment of deprivation can easily develop with the slightest "provocation", usually, the realization that their state of affairs is not fair, and is not shared by those in the immediate surrounds. *"The disposition to admire, and almost to worship, the rich and the powerful, and to despise, or at least, to neglect, persons of poor and mean condition"* is *"the great and most universal cause of the corruption of our moral sentiments"*[247]

Happiness therefore is a shared sentiment and indeed, an emotion. And it is not reliant on material wealth or acquisition, although that can certainly be an important factor.

Happiness, however, is also imparted. The Zoroastrian Faith teaches its followers that they should strive to create happiness for others, as this results in happiness all round. This is but one example of a vast array of religious teachings that enjoin their faithful to look beyond their personal happiness and welfare and engage in efforts to impart these on to others as well.

The End Justifies The Means

This is not a Machiavellian statement. Far from it. It is a statement intended to lead towards finding the factors, avenues, and means in order to achieve the ultimate aims of **prosperity, tranquillity, and above all, happiness.**

That the world is full of resources, is not in question. That the world resources are not evenly distributed, is also not in question. That science and technology is moving at a bewildering speed, needs no elaboration. That the world is in turmoil and nowhere appears to be secure, is beyond doubt. That the social fabric of society is fast eroding, is not in need of affirmation. That morals, ethics and behaviour, are fast descending towards criminality, loss of integrity, honesty and trustworthiness, almost tells its story within people's daily lives.

These, therefore, would be the building blocks that can be used to achieve the ends, and these ends must be the reversing of the above stated ills. A major root and branch reform is needed. The resourcefulness of the world intelligentsia is capable of addressing the material aspects by evolving and developing the economic structures and modalities required for different situations. It will continue to discover and invent. It will create programmes, theories, systems and methods.

What the intelligentsia will not be able to do is to create a worldwide consensus, or to appeal to the highest faculties of the Human individual. For these, we need the spiritual and moral dimension. We need this era's Religious blueprint. A blueprint, which would build on those of the past that, repeatedly and successfully guided the world from the stage of tribalism, through to nationhood, but would now have to cater for the new world order of universality and unity. Such a blueprint would evoke the loftiest manners embedded in every Human from birth, as well as the bringing to the forefront the greatest potentials inherent in individuals and societies and awaiting realization.

This **"New World Order"** has been announced by Baha'u'llah. It is a world order of practical principles enclosed within a very strongly developed spiritual framework, propelled and supported by a practical and fair vehicle of an administrative order delivering the principles of universal participation and enfranchisement, as well as the safeguards against corruption and misuse, especially those resulting from permanent positions of (religious) authorities exemplified by clerics within the different religious orders as witnessed around the world.

It is not the intention of this treatise to elaborate on a presentation of the Bahá'í Faith or its administrative or economic system, but the intention is to offer enough information to demonstrate the need for these two aspects of reform, consultation within a framework of universal participation and enfranchisement, for such a "New World Order", and to allow the reader the opportunity to enquire further for a more rewarding detail of information.

Principles of a New World Order

To speak of a "new world order" these days is so much more comprehensible than it ever was even two decades away. The world has gone beyond the stage when patching up is enough to remedy its ills. The aim is to sweep so much of the established modalities of governance in general and administrative ethics in particular, so as to build in their places such foundations as would be seen to be veritably novel and fit for purpose. On the other hand, there must be a realization that the world has achieved so much progress in the past century or so. Progress in the field of communication, medicine, space, technology, to mention but a few, and all this must be seen as the infrastructure upon which the foundations of governance mentioned above can and should be placed. One cannot disregard all these advances in human achievement or underestimate the power of human inventiveness and creativity. But one is also in need of the guiding principles that would maximise the benefits of these human abilities and minimize the unintended consequences of rampant progress that would disregard the safeguards, checks and balances that are more needed, indeed most needed, when progress is so spectacular.

A "New World Order" thus needs a new "Governance" structure, the emphasis being on the term governance rather than government. A framework of governing bodies of individuals, truly representative of the will and the wish of people, accountable to those people and to their own consciences with no inherent permanence in the system that would create a hierarchy and quasi theocracy, faked democracy, or, God forbid, an autocracy.

Such a "New World Order" was announced by Bahá'u'lláh, the Founder of the Bahá'í Faith in the 19th. Century, the following quote being indicative:

"The world's equilibrium hath been upset through the vibrating influence of this most great, this new World Order. Mankind's ordered life hath been revolutionized through the agency of this unique, this wondrous System - the like of which mortal eyes have never witnessed[248]

While the above words demonstrate a seismic change inherent in the announcement of this world order, Shoghi Effendi (the Guardian of the Bahá'í Faith) identifies this "Order" with the System Baha'u'llah envisages in His Book of Revelation "Al Aqdas", in which He testifies to its revolutionizing effect on the life of humanity and reveals the laws and principles which govern its operation. Beginning with the individual, Shoghi Effendi states:

"Let us also remember that at the very root of the Cause lies the principle of the undoubted right of the individual to self-expression, his freedom to declare his conscience and set forth his views.... Let us also bear in mind that the keynote of the Cause of God is not dictatorial authority but humble fellowship, not arbitrary power, but the spirit of frank and loving consultation. Nothing short of the spirit of a true Baha'i can hope to reconcile the principles of mercy and justice, of freedom and submission, of the sanctity of the right of the individual and of self-surrender, of vigilance, discretion and prudence on the one hand, and fellowship, candor, and courage on the other."[249]

Building in these personal quality requisites puts the onus on the individual who is elected as well as on the person who voted for the elected bodies. Both parties should be working in unison through the process of free and candid consultation, and all should be guided by the principle of abiding by the decisions taken whether unanimously or through majority vote. The next quote from the Guardian of the Bahá'í Faith, Shoghi Effendi then describes the attitude expected from those elected to the governing bodies:

"The duties of those whom the friends have freely and conscientiously elected as their representatives are no less vital and binding than the

obligations of those who have chosen them. Their function is not to dictate, but to consult, and consult not only among themselves, but as much as possible with the friends whom they represent. They must regard themselves in no other light but that of chosen instruments for a more efficient and dignified presentation of the Cause of God. They should never be led to suppose that they are the central ornaments of the body of the Cause, intrinsically superior to others in capacity or merit, and sole promoters of its teachings and principles. They should approach their task with extreme humility, and endeavor, by their open-mindedness, their high sense of justice and duty, their candor, their modesty, their entire devotion to the welfare and interests of the friends, the Cause, and humanity, to win, not only the confidence and the genuine support and respect of those whom they serve, but also their esteem and real affection. They must, at all times, avoid the spirit of exclusiveness, the atmosphere of secrecy, free themselves from a domineering attitude, and banish all forms of prejudice and passion from their deliberations. They should, within the limits of wise discretion, take the friends into their confidence, acquaint them with their plans, share with them their problems and anxieties, and seek their advice and counsel. And, when they are called upon to arrive at a certain decision, they should, after dispassionate, anxious and cordial consultation, turn to God in prayer, and with earnestness and conviction and courage record their vote and abide by the voice of the majority, which we are told by our Master to be the voice of truth, never to be challenged, and always to be whole-heartedly enforced. To this voice the friends must heartily respond, and regard it as the only means that can insure the protection and advancement of the Cause."[250]

This system is at present fully functioning throughout the Bahá'í world, and is based on local representative bodies *(Local Spiritual Assemblies, or **LSA**)* of 9 people, male or female, over the age of 21 and who are fully fledged Bahá'ís. The distribution is at present based on the presence of 9 or more Bahá'ís within an administrative area in keeping with the civic configuration of a particular country. They may thus represent a city, town, borough, village or fit into any unitary configuration available, the width of the area under jurisdiction being dependent on the development of the Bahá'í Faith in that country or part of the world. The more numbers and spread of believers there are, the smaller the area served by this LSA.

While the jurisdiction of these LSA's remain at present confined to dealing with the affairs of the Bahá'í Faith and the Bahá'í communities, it is envisaged that in future they will address all civic issues as well.

The next tier of representative bodies, again elected by universal franchise from within the Bahá'í community on a national scale, is the *"National Spiritual Assembly, or **NSA"**. This is the level of governance that embraces a whole country or a large part of a country that enjoys some separate recognition of independence. All this structure is capped by the ***"Universal House of Justice"*** which is the Body with jurisdiction over the whole Bahá'í world and possesses the special dispensation of right to legislate on matters that are not specifically addressed in any of the Scriptures revealed by the founders of the Bahá'í Faith, The Bab, Bahá'u'lláh, or Abdu'l-Bahá, or have not been expressly explained by the Guardian of the Bahá'í Faith, Shoghi Effendi.

The following quote could usefully encapsulate the essence of this system:

> *"The various Assemblies, local and national, constitute today the bedrock upon the strength of which the Universal House is ... It devolves upon us whose dearest wish is to see the Cause enter upon that promised era of universal recognition and world achievements, to do all in our power to consolidate the foundations of these Assemblies, promoting at the same time a fuller understanding of their purpose and more harmonious*

cooperation for their maintenance and success."[251]

The *"Universal House of Justice"* mentioned above was established in 1963 and is re-elected by members of NSA's all over the world every five years, by secret ballot, and freedom to vote for any fully fledged Bahá'í living anywhere in the world. There are no pre-requisites in term of position, eminence or otherwise, other than the inherent quality of the person and his ability to serve in this capacity. The procedure is again without any electioneering or canvassing, and is undertaken with all the serenity, dignity and spirituality commensurate with the enormity of the responsibility that lies upon the shoulders of those who vote and those nine people who receive the most votes and are thus elected.

It is not the purpose of this work to elaborate in more details on the administrative order of the Bahá'í Faith. Suffice it to say, that it is in operation world-wide, and can be witnessed and studied further. It is specifically mentioned here, because, together with the spiritual qualities required by all Bahá'ís, this administrative will form the basis of the economic order envisaged in the Bahá'í Scriptures and Statements.

Economic Principles As Abstracted From The Bahá'í Faith:

As the title applies, it is only the principles of economics within the overall Scriptures and statements in the Bahá'í texts that can, in this work, be extracted, abstracted and presented. In addition to the need for brevity, there are two main reasons for that: the first is that these principles are, within the Bahá'í "Writings", expressed mainly as principles to guide the world into developing them according to need and circumstances as the "New World Order" unfolds. The guidance/s are clearly there, as well as the most salient headline statements. The second is that these Bahá'í economic principles should not be taken in isolation from the spiritual, moral and ethical principles enshrined within the Bahá'í Scriptures.

Thus, economics rooted in nationalism or nationalistic interest alone, will, from now on not work. The same will apply to economic solutions aimed at increasing the material and/or financial wealth of a country, nation, community, or any group, without due regards to individual responsibility for shared care and without the elimination of the factors of human greed and selfishness. Thus in his article, Dahl opens his discussion on "The Distribution of Wealth" with the statement: *"One of the most critical problems of our time is the increasing tension developing between the growing forces of egalitarianism and equal opportunity, on the one hand, and the traditional forces of economic and political power vested in a privileged few, on the other hand........By contrast, Bahá'ís believe that in the end human social welfare can only rest on cooperation, the recognition of harmony of interests, and the rule of legitimate law and political process."*[252]

The balanced development of the twin factors of increased material prosperity adjoined to such aspects of human life as *"insight and art, human relations, the building of family life, psychological health, joys and sorrows, and spiritual and moral progress"* is essential. Such adjoinment can best be achieved in a world that has adopted the least level of "Peace" agreement: that of ***"relinguishing the use of arms as a means of resolving conflict"***. In the Bahá'í Faith, the term used by Bahá'u'lláh is : ***"The Lesser Peace"*** when arms will be kept at the minimum level require to maintain local order and policing. With time, Bahá'u'lláh

Predicts the advent of the ultimate, the ***"Greater Peace"***, when people will live in real harmony within a unifying global world order. This , according to Shoghi Effendi will be the fulfilment of all the prophecies of old, from Isaiah when alluding to the "Glory of the Lord", the "Everlasting Father" and the "Prince of Peace", to the "Day of the

Lord" as mentioned by Ezekiel and Daniel. That day will also fulfil the prophecy of Zoroaster wherein the World-Saviour, the Sha Bahram will triumph over Ahriman and thus usher an era of blessedness and peace, and is the time when "a Buddha named Maitreye, the Buddha of universal fellowship" should….reveal "His boundless glory". Again, in the Bhagavad-Gita of the Hindus, there is reference to the "Most Great Spirit," the "Tenth Avatar," the "Immaculate Manifestation of Krishna.", and in the New Testament we read about the "New Jerusalem, and the "Day of God", and in the Qur'an the prophecies are so plentiful that it suffices to mention just the greatness of what shall be the "Great Announcement," the "Day of God," and the Day "when the earth shall shine with the light of her Lord.[253]

Furthermore, Shoghi Effendi states:

"The long ages of infancy and childhood, through which the human race had to pass, have receded into the background. Humanity is now experiencing the commotions invariably associated with the most turbulent stage of its evolution, the stage of adolescence, when the impetuosity of youth and its vehemence reach their climax, and must gradually be superseded by the calmness, the wisdom, and the maturity that characterize the stage of manhood. Then will the human race reach that stature of ripeness which will enable it to acquire all the powers and capacities upon which its ultimate development must depend"[254]

What is the ultimate goal? It is non other than:

World Unity Is The Goal

Unification of the whole of mankind is the hall-mark of the stage which human society is now approaching. Unity of family, of tribe, of city-state, and nation have been successively attempted and fully established. World unity is the goal towards which a harassed humanity is striving. Nation-building has come to an end. The anarchy inherent in state sovereignty is moving towards a climax. A world, growing to maturity, must abandon this fetish, recognize the oneness and wholeness of human relationships, and establish once and for all the machinery that can best incarnate this fundamental principle of its life.

"A new life," Baha'u'llah proclaims, "is, in this age, stirring within all the peoples of the earth; and yet none hath discovered its cause, or perceived its motive." "O ye children of men," He thus addresses His generation, "the fundamental purpose animating the Faith of God and His Religion is to safeguard the interests and promote the unity of the human race... This is the straight path, the fixed and immovable foundation. Whatsoever is raised on this foundation, the changes and chances of the world can never impair its strength, nor will the revolution of countless centuries undermine its structure." "The well-being of mankind," He declares, "its peace and security are unattainable unless and until its unity is firmly established." "So powerful is the light of unity," is His further testimony, "that it can illuminate the whole earth. The one true God, He Who knoweth all things, Himself testifieth to the truth of these words... This goal excelleth every other goal, and this aspiration is the monarch of all aspirations." "He Who is your Lord, the All-Merciful," He, moreover, has written, "cherisheth in His heart the desire of beholding the entire human race as one soul and one body. Haste ye to win your share of God's good grace and mercy in this Day that eclipseth all other created days."

The unity of the human race, as envisaged by Baha'u'llah, implies the establishment of *a world commonwealth* in which all nations, races, creeds and classes are closely and permanently united, and in which the autonomy of its state members and the personal freedom and initiative of the individuals that compose them are definitely and completely safeguarded. This commonwealth must, as far as we can visualize it, consist of *a world legislature*, whose members will, as the ***trustees of the whole of mankind***, ultimately control ***the entire resources*** of all the component nations, and will enact such laws as shall be required to regulate the life, ***satisfy the needs and adjust the relationships of all races and peoples***. *A world executive*, backed by ***an international Force***, will carry out the decisions arrived at, and apply the laws enacted by, this world legislature, and will safeguard the organic unity of the whole commonwealth. *A world tribunal* will adjudicate and deliver its compulsory and final verdict in all and any disputes that may arise between the various elements constituting this universal system. A mechanism of world inter-communication will be devised, embracing the whole planet, freed from national hindrances and restrictions, and functioning with marvellous swiftness and perfect regularity. A world metropolis will act as the nerve center of a world civilization, the focus towards which the unifying forces of life will converge and from which its energizing influences will radiate. *A world language will either be invented or chosen* from among the existing languages and will be taught in the schools of all the federated nations as an auxiliary to their mother tongue. *A world script, a world literature, a uniform and universal system of currency, of weights and measures*, will simplify and facilitate intercourse and understanding among the nations and races of mankind. In such a world society, ***science and religion, the two most potent forces in human life, will be reconciled, will cooperate, and will harmoniously develop.*** The press will, under such a system, while giving full scope to the expression of the diversified views and convictions of mankind, cease to be mischievously manipulated by vested interests, whether private or public, and will be liberated from the influence of contending governments and peoples. The economic resources of the world will be organized, its sources of raw materials will be tapped and fully utilized, its markets will be coordinated and developed, and the distribution of its products will be equitably regulated.

National rivalries, hatreds, and intrigues will cease, and racial animosity and prejudice will be replaced by racial amity, understanding and cooperation. The causes of religious strife will be permanently removed, *economic barriers and restrictions will be completely abolished*, and the *inordinate distinction between classes will be obliterated*. Destitution on the one hand, and gross accumulation of ownership on the other, will disappear. The enormous energy dissipated and wasted on war, whether economic or political, will be consecrated to such ends as will extend the range of human inventions and technical development, to the increase of the productivity of mankind, to the extermination of disease, to the *extension of scientific research*, to the *raising of the standard of physical health*, to the sharpening and refinement of the human brain, to the exploitation of the unused and unsuspected resources of the planet, to *the prolongation of human life*, and to the furtherance of any other agency that can *stimulate the intellectual, the moral, and spiritual life of the entire human race*.

A world federal system, ruling the whole earth and exercising unchallengeable authority over its unimaginably vast resources, blending and embodying the ideals of both the East and the West, liberated from the curse of war and its miseries, and bent on the exploitation of all the available sources of energy on the surface of the planet, a system in which *Force is made the servant of Justice*, whose life is sustained by its universal recognition of one God and by its allegiance to one common Revelation - such is the goal towards which humanity, impelled by the unifying forces of life, is moving.

Who can doubt that such a consummation - the coming of age of the human race - must signalize, in its turn, *the inauguration of a*

world civilization such as no mortal eye hath ever beheld or human mind conceived? Who is it that can imagine the lofty standard which such a civilization, as it unfolds itself, is destined to attain? Who can measure the heights to which human intelligence, liberated from its shackles, will soar? Who can visualize the realms which the human spirit, vitalized by the outpouring light of Baha'u'llah, shining in the plenitude of its glory, will discover?

What more fitting conclusion to this theme than these words of Baha'u'llah, written in anticipation of the golden age of His Faith - the age in which the face of the earth, from pole to pole, will mirror the ineffable splendors of the Abha Paradise? "This is the Day whereon naught can be seen except the splendors of the Light that shineth from the face of thy Lord, the Gracious, the Most Bountiful. Verily, We have caused every soul to expire by virtue of Our irresistible and all-subduing sovereignty. We have then called into being a new creation, as a token of Our grace unto men. I am, verily, the All-Bountiful, the Ancient of Days. This is the Day whereon the unseen world crieth out: `Great is thy blessedness, O earth, for thou hast been made the foot-stool of thy God, and been chosen as the seat of His mighty throne!' The realm of glory exclaimeth: `Would that my life could be sacrificed for thee, for He Who is the Beloved of the All-Merciful hath established His sovereignty upon thee, through the power of His name that hath been promised unto all things, whether of the past or of the future.'" [255]

Within the above framework, the basic principles of the economics envisaged in the Bahá'í Faith can be discussed briefly. A good way of summarizing the principles would be to look at the different components of society or the world, from the individual to the family to the community, the nation and finally the world.

The Individual:

Greed has already been identified as the vicious driving emotion that needs to be curbed or, preferably eliminated. There are several balances here that need to be valued. On the one hand, a person should have the incentive to strive, improve his (his will always imply also her) standing in life and earn according to his ability. The proviso here is that such earning is made within the highest spiritual and moral values, and in no way at the expense of others.

Private ownership is accepted, and must be safeguarded. The accumulation of wealth, however, should always be accompanied by a sense of social and humanitarian responsibility and the obligation (freely flowing) to use any undue surplus towards the betterment of others or of society at large.

While any taxation by governing establishments could legitimately be raised so as to fund services on a scale not possible by any one individual, such as policing, education, and health, such taxation must be seen by the rich as a the baseline of their social conscience, and not a clearing of conscience that allows extravagant or misuse of the rest of one's wealth. It should be seen as the necessary obligation to society that leaves more space for voluntary contributions according to one's surplus means and according to one's feeling of obligation to society.

A one-off deduction is envisaged in the Bahá'í Faith whereby a certain percentage is deducted from surplus wealth (estimated in monetary terms) as *"The Rights of God"*. While entirely voluntary both in the way in which such wealth is calculated and indeed whether the person feels the spiritual and moral obligation to offer such a deduction, the Bahá'í teachings impress upon the believers the "cleansing and purifying" effect of this contribution on the remaining wealth. What is surplus for one could be essential or needed for another, and so the entire obligation is a pure and personal, confidential and voluntary assessment.

On the other hand, there is an obligation on every Bahá'í to avail himself of every means of earning and satisfying the needs for himself and his family and whoever would be under his care. There is no place for *begging* in the Bahá'í Faith. There is no place for laggardness or laziness. Indeed, work in the Bahá'í Teachings is equated with Prayer.

Acquiring the skills and the education, as well as making use of any talent, artistic or otherwise, is the duty of every individual. In case of illness, lack of ability, or natural disasters, aid will in whatever form will be allowed, indeed encouraged, provided the individual's dignity is safeguarded and maintained, and the recipient graciously accepting. Such aid should cease as soon as the cause of initiating it has ceased. Such is the balance of rights, obligations and responsibilities between society and every individual, almost a "spiritual" contract.

Working conditions:

It follows from the above that the individual's relationship in employment is one that needs further consideration. The preferred ethos is that the employee and the employer are in fact engaged in a sharing collaborative. Thus, while the employee expects adequate rewards for good and effective and conscientious labour, the employer should be conscious of these needs within the contract of employment, and should, in turn, provide the optimum conditions for his employees and should pursue such behavioural attitudes as would bring out the best from his employees. A social conscience enwrapping such relationships would produce the best results. However, it is probably most useful to put in a system of ***Profit sharing*** as this will be seen as an equitable way to enhance productivity as well as goodwill, and on the other hand establish the important principle of ***mutual interdependence***

Personal taxation as imposed by the governing authority should be levied on the basis of *Progressive* taxation of some sort. The aim is to ensure an equitable burden shifting from the richer in order to relieve the burden of the more needy. Taxation should never be punitive, and must be seen by the government as a necessary means for meeting its commitments with no favours and as equitable and as conscientiously as possible. Bearing in mind that the "New World Order" described above will not be based on party political set up but on a unifying structure, one would easily envisage that such expenditure will not be made according to particular favours or bias.

Social engineering may be one of the needs to consider by any government if there is excessive wealth and abject poverty, the aim is for any such social shift to be the shared responsibility of the rich as well as the government, with the former giving freely and not necessarily only through taxation. This is not unheard of; as the world has always been, and will always be, full of philanthropists. What should be new is that philanthropy should not be the preserve of the very rich.

The personal skills of those not so well off should be improved. The following statistics indicate such need:

John Smith, Business Editor to the Sunday Times: 22.07.07, "our real poverty is lack of skills": In 1923 1% of the population of UK owned 61% of "marketable" wealth, halved to 30% in 1970, and the latest figure in 2003, it is 21%.... The corresponding figures for the top 5% of the population are: 82%, 54% & 40%.

One assumes, therefore, that there is a moral base for the individual and his conduct within an ethos of diligent pursuit of wealth creation and wealth utilisation, even if it were not for his immediate benefit or for his sole benefit. In this respect, the value of **Education** is stressed:

"Abdu'l-Baha, in His Tablets, not only calls attention to the responsibility of parents to educate all their children, but He also clearly specifies that the "training and culture of daughters is more necessary than that of sons", for girls will one day be mothers, and mothers are the first educators of the new generation. If it is not possible, therefore, for a family to educate all the children, preference is to be accorded to daughters since, through educated mothers, the benefits of knowledge can be most effectively and rapidly diffused throughout society[256].

Bahá'u'lláh furthermore affirms this in His verse on: *"exhorting the people of God to educate their children. Should a father neglect this most weighty commandment laid down in the*

Kitab-i-Aqdas by the Pen of the Eternal King, he shall forfeit rights of fatherhood, and be accounted guilty before God"[257].

And in turn, the children have a duty to avail themselves of this privilege:

"God hath prescribed unto every father to educate his children, both boys and girls, in the sciences and in morals, and in crafts and professions....

6. It is incumbent upon the children to exert themselves to the utmost in acquiring the art of reading and writing.... Writing skills that will provide for urgent needs will be enough for some; and then it is better and more fitting that they should spend their time in studying those branches of knowledge which are of use[258]*".*

In addition, the Bahá'í Faith asks everyone to have a craft or an art. As Bahá'u'lláh says:

"When anyone occupieth himself in a craft or trade, such occupation itself is regarded in the estimation of God as an act of worship; and this is naught but a token of His infinite and all-pervasive bounty."[260]

This principle is emphasised by Abdu'l-Bahá thus:

"While the children are yet in their infancy feed them from the breast of heavenly grace, foster them in the cradle of all excellence, rear them in the embrace of bounty. Give them the advantage of every useful kind of knowledge. Let them share in every new and rare and wondrous craft and art. Bring them up to work and strive, and accustom them to hardship."[261]

While this is not an exhaustive description of the part of the individual to be played within the economy of the "New World Order", it is hope that it gives a distinct flavour of the adjustments and ethos that is to develop. All this, as the reader would have gathered, is within the framework of a society based on the *family unit*, which is regarding in the Bahá'í Faith as the bedrock upon which the social fabric can be weaved, and generations develop in a balanced and relatively secure manner.

World Economic Resources:

The above account relating to the principles of economic conduct within the sphere of the individual are in need of further developments, and will no doubt have further input from the economists. Such input will derive from past economic thought, present ones, and probably most importantly, those of the future. For the economic scheme within the Bahá'í Faith is open to accepting, even soliciting, the best economic minds of the age. This is the requisite set by the Founders of the Bahá'í Faith, allowing the Universal House of Justice in particular to seek the best advice and programmes from the best that Human thought can offer, in order to maintain a vibrant, ever evolving civilisation based on the best of that Human thought and coupled with the best that Divine Guidance can confer.

Thus, the principles regarding the individual as described above require the support of a system that the "collective", or the "Community" can provide. The scope of this collective can be a small community or the whole International Arena.

A good initial example is consideration of the world's resources:

Shoghi Effendi states *"The economic resources of the world will be organized, its sources of raw materials will be tapped and fully utilized, its markets will be coordinated and developed, and the distribution of its products will be equitably regulated....Destitution on the one hand, and gross accumulation of ownership on the other, will disappear..."*[262]

Contrast this with the present, where a statistic in 2007 showed that the 1000 richest people on the Sunday Times Rich List—Richistanis as Robert Frank calls them—account for £360 billion between them. That's up from £99 billion 10 years ago (1997). The USA, making up only 1% of world population consumes about 25% of the world resources. These are but two ready reckoners showing inequality on a personal and on a national (inter-national) levels.

The conventional measure of income inequality is the Gini coefficient. A gini of zero would be perfect equality, and a Gini 90 of 1 would be the perfect inequality (one household would have all the income). The UK's Institute of Fiscal Studies (IFS) database shows the Gini was 0.261 in 1961, fell to 0.239 in 1976, before rising during the 1980's to 0.339 by 1990. It remains roughly at that level—the figure for 2005-6 was 0.346—below the high of 0.353 in 2000-1

Another useful measure of inequality is the 90:10 ratio, the incomes of the 90th. Percentile of the income distribution (people 10% from the top), compared with the 10th percentile, those 10% from the bottom.

This has the virtue of excluding those at the very top or very bottom of the income distribution from the comparison, a virtue because in neither case are the statistics entirely reliable.

In 1961 the 90:10 ratio was 3.207, falling to 2.947 by 1978. It, too, rose in the 1980's, reaching a high on 4.44 in 1991. I 1996-7 it was 4.130, slipping to 4.055 in 2005-6. On this measure, inequality is still historically high, but has fallen roughly 10% in the early 1990's

This fall is quite interesting. The world seems to be moving in the right direction, although one would wish to await similar statistics ten years later. However, could the following statements enhance one's optimism?:

"With great wealth comes great responsibility. We've got to take care of these things if wealth creation is still going to be seen as a positive force for the rest of the population" Sir Tom Hunter, the first "home grown" Scottish Billionaire. Quoted in "The Sunday Times", Review page 1, July 22, 2007.

"Has conspicuous consumption given way to conspicuous altruism?"....If so, the result would be a massive increase in the amount of "giving while living", to use the philanthropists' jargon. Andrew Carnegie, the great Scottish-American Philanthropist, would approve. "He who dies rich, dies in disgrace", he once said.

One of the aspects straddling the individual and the communal economics is that of **Inheritance"**. This is one aspect in which wealth can be distributed or re-distributed so as to enhance equity and fairness within society. Once again, The Bahá'í Faith allows the individual to take control of this, and leaving a clear and verified will is obligatory. However, should a will not be available the distribution of the wealth in case of "Intestacy" covers, as was mentioned in the section on religions earlier, not only family and relatives in various proportions, but also requests the "Rights of God " to be deducted first (to be used for the communal services) as well as such recipients as the teacher (probably the school) and this could contribute in future to the educational establishments which must thus feel particular interest in maintaining their services at top level in order to contribute to the upbringing of generation after generation. Naturally, in the will, the deceased is encouraged to follow the principle, and ensure adequate and equitable distribution and avoid accumulation. However, yet again, this is voluntary, and will only work within a prevailing ethos of humanitarianism and spirituality.

International Economics:

Much has already been said on this subject. But it is worth re-iterating the value of reduction on the expenditure on war as a result of adherence to Bahá'u'lláh's guidance, maintaining such expenditure within the level needed for local "policing" services only. Thus the need for taxation would be markedly reduced. Other expenditures will be needed for health, welfare, education, redevelopment, research and technology to mention but a few. In all this, the ethos of conscientious work of all involved added to the principle of equity in distribution of obligations and benefits, is bound to create an atmosphere of real and tangible advance. A system of **International arbitration** is designed to deal with any aberrances that may, and inevitably will, occur from time to time.

A **World Currency** and **World system of measures** will ease and streamline the flow of trade and wealth, and add transparency to discrepancies that could arise, and make **Free trade** a feasible reality.

Happiness

This may seem an aberration in a discussion of economic issues, but the end result of any system in the understanding of the Bahá'í Faith, is that such a system should bring happiness to the world and its people. Optimism is the over-riding emotion that permeates the Bahá'í Scriptures, and an example of Bahá'u'lláh's writing on hope are the following:

Rest thou assured in the gracious favour of thy Lord. The eye of His loving-kindness shall everlastingly be directed towards thee. The day is approaching when thy agitation will have been transmuted into peace and quiet calm. Thus hath it been decreed in the wondrous Book. [263]

We pray God - exalted be His glory - and cherish the hope that He may graciously assist the manifestations of affluence and power and the daysprings of sovereignty and glory, the kings of the earth - may God aid them through His strengthening grace - to establish the Lesser Peace. This, indeed, is the greatest means for insuring the tranquillity of the nations. It is incumbent upon the Sovereigns of the world - may God assist them - unitedly to hold fast unto this Peace, which is the chief instrument for the protection of all mankind. It is Our hope that they will arise to achieve what will be conducive to the well-being of man. It is their duty to convene an all-inclusive assembly, which either they themselves or their ministers will attend, and to enforce whatever measures are required to establish unity and concord amongst men. They must put away the weapons of war, and turn to the instruments of universal reconstruction. Should one king rise up against another, all the other kings must arise to deter him. Arms and armaments will, then, be no more needed beyond that which is necessary to insure the internal security of their respective countries. If they attain unto this all-surpassing blessing, the people of each nation will pursue, with tranquillity and contentment, their own occupations, and the groanings and lamentations of most men would be silenced. We beseech God to aid them to do His will and pleasure. He, verily, is the Lord of the throne on high and of earth below, and the Lord of this world and of the world to come. It would be preferable and more fitting that the highly-honored kings themselves should attend such an assembly, and proclaim their edicts. Any king who will arise and carry out this task, he, verily will, in the sight of God, become the cynosure of all kings. Happy is he, and great is his blessedness!

In this land, every time men are conscripted for the army, a great terror seizeth the people. Every nation augmenteth, each year, its forces, for their ministers of war are insatiable in their desire to add fresh recruits to their battalions. ... We hope that thou wilt cause the light of justice to shine more brightly. By the righteousness of God! Justice is a powerful force. It is, above all else, the conqueror of the citadels of the hearts and souls of men, and the revealer of the secrets of the world of being, and the standard-bearer of love and bounty[264].

The Guardian of the Bahá'í Faith adds:

Ours is then the duty and privilege to labor, by day and by night, amidst the storm and stress of these troublous days, that we may quicken the zeal of our fellow-men, rekindle their hopes, stimulate their interest, open their eyes to the true Faith of God and enlist their active support in the carrying out of our common task for the peace and regeneration of the world[265].

An the final responsibility is on Man, as Abdu'l-Bahá states:

'*If man were to care for himself only he would be nothing but an animal for only the animals are thus egoistic. If you bring a thousand sheep to a well to kill nine hundred and ninety-nine the*'

one remaining sheep would go on grazing, not thinking of the others and worrying not at all about the lost, never bothering that its own kind had passed away, or had perished or been killed. To look after one's self only is therefore an animal propensity. It is the animal propensity to live solitary and alone. It is the animal proclivity to look after one's own comfort. But man was created to be a man -- to be fair, to be just, to be merciful, to be kind to all his species, never to be willing that he himself be well off while others are in misery and distress -- this is an attribute of the animal and not of man. Nay, rather, man should be willing to accept hardships for himself in order that others may enjoy wealth; he should enjoy trouble for himself that others may enjoy happiness and well-being. This is the attribute of man. This is becoming of man.

Otherwise man is not man -- he is less than the animal.'[266]

To see the joy of divine gladness on your faces is the cause of my happiness, for when I see you happy, I am happy also.[267]

THE END

END NOTES

[1] Heimann,E: History of Economic Doctrines, 1951, Oxford University Press, p.22

[2] Ditto, p.3

[3] Raphael, DD: Three great economists, page 8. OUP 1997

[4] Ditto

[5] Abbas A. History of Economic Thought, chapter 1, p 12: Universite de Garyounis, Benghazi, 1991.

[6] Aristotle: "Politics", Book 1, in "Early Economic Thought". Page 10, quoted in Galbraith, J.K.,: "A History of Economics", Page 11, Penguin Books, 1991

[7] Gray A: "The Development of Economic Doctrine", Longman Green 1948

[8] Ditto

[9] Ditto

[10] Heiman,E: History of Economic Doctrines, 1952 OUP, p.23

[11] Aristotle: "Politics", Book 1, in "Early Economic Thought". Page 10, quoted in Galbraith, J.K.,: "A History of Economics", Page 11, Penguin Books, 1991

[12] Ditto

[13] Aristotle: "Politics", Book 1, in "Early Economic Thought". Page 10, quoted in Galbraith, J.K.,: "A History of Economics", Page 12, Penguin Books, 1991

[14] Heiman,E: History of Economic Doctrines, 1952 OUP, p.13

[15] Aristotle: "Politics", Book 1, in "Early Economic Thought". Page 10, quoted in Galbraith, J.K.,: "A History of Economics", Page 15, Penguin Books, 1991

[16] Abbas A. History of Economic Thought, chapter 1, p 12: Universite de Garyounis, Benghazi, 1991

[17] Gray A: "The Development of Economic Doctrine", Longman Green 1948, p.26

[18] Ditto. P. 26/27

[19] Ditto. P. 28

[20] Meir, Asher, 2009: The Jewish Ethicist, Ktav Publishers,

      & "the Ninth Candle" http://www.aish.com/chanukahbasics/chanukahbasicsdefault/

[21] Sharrock P: "Pilgrim's Progress" 1987. Penguin Books: Introduction, P.IX

[22] Raphael, DD: Three great economists, OUP 1997, p. 27

[23] Badran (Aboul Fottouh): "The Shari'a Law, its history and the theory of property and contract". Alexandria, Egypt. Page 86, quoted in Abbas A. History of Economic Thought, chapter 1, p 12: Universite de Garyounis, Benghazi, 1991, page 28)

[24] Ali Abdel Rassoul: "The economic principles in Islam" 1968

[25] Ahmad Amin: "The Dawn of Islam"

[26] Al Maqrizi: Amna'a Al Asma'a, vol. 1 page 66

[27] "The Cow" (Qur'an) Verse 17

[28] "Taha" " " 3

[29] "Surat Al Hadidi" " " 7

[30] "The Cow" " " 188

[31] "Al Tawbah" " " 153

[32] "Al Nessa'" " " 32

[33] "Al Thirayat" " " 11

[34] "Al Nessa'" " " 2

[35] Raphael, DD: Three great economists, OUP 1997, p.39

[36] "Al Imran" (Qur'an) verse 130

[37] Raphael, DD: Three great economists, OUP 1997, p.42

[38] (the "Umra" is the term applied to the *Lesser Pilgrimage",i.e.* visits to the Holy Places at times of the year other than those designated. Such a visit constitutes in Islam a second tier of endeavour for those unable to achieve Pilgrimage as prescribed)

[39] "Qur'an, Al Sho'ara, the poets, verse 181-3

[40] Raphael, DD: Three great economists, OUP 1997, p.47

[41] Raphael, DD: Three great economists, OUP 1997, p.48

[42] Qur;an, "The Cow", vs.270-280

[43] Shepherd, William E., "Sayyid Qutb & Islamic Activism", Brill

[44] "Abu Obeid Ibn Sallam, 1353 A.H. Al Amwal

[45] Abbas A. History of Economic Thought, Universite de Garyounis, Benghazi, 1991, p.35-51

[46] Abbas A. History of Economic Thought, Universite de Garyounis, Benghazi, 1991, p. 55-71:. Reference to "Ibn Khaldoun: The Introduction."

[47] Ebada Koheila:"Al 'Aqd Al Thameen fe tareekh Al Muslimeen, I.S.B.N 977-19-1552-5, p 99-106

[48] J.J. Saunders: "A History of Medieval Islam", Routledge, UK ISBN 0-415-05914-3

[49] Abbas A. History of Economic Thought, Universite de Garyounis, Benghazi, 1991, 54-55

[50] Encycl. Britt. Macropaedia, 1990, vol. 22, page 124).

[51] Abbas A. History of Economic Thought, Universite de Garyounis, Benghazi, 1991, p 56/7

[52] "Muslim Scientists & Scholars, compiled by Muzir Ahmed

[53] Abbas A. History of Economic Thought, Universite de Garyounis, Benghazi, 1991, p. 55-71

[54] The Muqaddimah: An Introduction to History. (Abridged Edition): An Introduction to History (Bollingen Series (General)), Amazon.co.uk

[55] Ebada Koheila:"Al 'Aqd Al Thameen fe tareekh Al Muslimeen, I.S.B.N 977-19-1552-5, p. 134/5

[56] All quotations of the Old and the New Testament in this work are extracted from the Authorised King James Bible.

[57] Aristotle: "Politics", Book 1, in "Early Economic Thought". Page 10, quoted in Galbraith, J.K.,: "A History of Economics", Page 12, Penguin Books, 1991, p. 21

[58] Roll E: "History of Economic Thought" 1968, p. 28

[59] Aristotle: "Politics", Book 1, in "Early Economic Thought". Page 10, quoted in Galbraith, J.K.,: "A History of Economics", Page 15, Penguin Books, 1991 pp 12,21,22

[60] Blaug, M:"Economic Theory in retrospect" 1997, 5th Ed. Cambridge University Press, p. 10

[61] Blaug, M:"Economic Theory in retrospect" 1997, 5th Ed. Cambridge University Press. P. 11

[62] Heiman,E: History of Economic Doctrines, 1952 OUP, p.27,35

[63] Roll E: "History of Economic Thought" 1968, p. 47, 66, 68

[64] Ditto, p. 118

[65] Blaug, M:"Economic Theory in retrospect" 1997, 5th Ed. Cambridge University Press. P. 12, 13

[66] Heiman,E: History of Economic Doctrines, 1952 OUP, p.42

[67] Roll E: "History of Economic Thought" 1968, 47

[68] Galbraith, J.K.,: "A History of Economics", Penguin Books, 1991, p 143

[69] Galbraith, J.K.,: "A History of Economics", Penguin Books, 1991, p. 68

[70] Heiman,E: History of Economic Doctrines, 1952 OUP, p.36-41

[71] Roll E: "History of Economic Thought" 1968, p. 84-96

[72] Blaug, M:"Economic Theory in retrospect" 1997, 5th Ed. Cambridge University Press., p. 18,19

[73] Heiman,E: History of Economic Doctrines, 1952 OUP, p.39

[74] Ditto

[75] Heiman,E: History of Economic Doctrines, 1952 OUP, p.41

[76] Roll E: "History of Economic Thought" 1968, pp 105-111

[77] Abbas A. History of Economic Thought, chapter 1, p 12: Universite de Garyounis, Benghazi, 1991, pp 114-120

[78] Heiman,E: History of Economic Doctrines, 1952 OUP, pp 44-47

[79] Blaug, M:"Economic Theory in retrospect" 1997, 5th Ed. Cambridge University Press.p. 25

[80] Galbraith, J.K.,: "A History of Economics", Penguin Books, 1991, p 49-50

[81] Ditto

[82] Galbraith, J.K.,: "A History of Economics", Penguin Books, 1991, p52

[83] Blaug, M:"Economic Theory in retrospect" 1997, 5th Ed. Cambridge University Press. P 27

[84] Roll E: "History of Economic Thought" 1968, p 112-114

[85] Blaug, M:"Economic Theory in retrospect" 1997, 5th Ed. Cambridge University Press, p.27-41 for diagrams and numerical descriptive equations.

[86] Galbraith, J.K.,: "A History of Economics", Penguin Books, 1991. p.56

[87] John Maynard Keynes, "The General Theory of Employment, Interest and Money" (New York: Harcourt, Brace, 1936, p.4

[88] Galbraith, J.K.,: "A History of Economics", Penguin Books, 1991: (Wealth of Nations, book 1, Ch, 1, quoted on page 59)

[89] Winch,D. Malthus: in "Three Great Economists", Oxford. 1997

[90] Raphael, DD: Three Great Economists, OUP 1997, p. 17

[91] Roll E: "History of Economic Thought" 1968, pp 131-140
And Blaug, M:"Economic Theory in retrospect" 1997, 5th Ed. Cambridge University Press.p.27-29

[92] Raphael, DD: Three great Economists, OUP 1997, pp 25-26

[93] Raphael, DD: Three great Economists, OUP 1997, p 29

[94] Much of the material may be studied in more details in the references already mentioned, especially Raphael & Blaug

[95] Galbraith, J.K.,: "A History of Economics", Penguin Books, 1991, p.39, quoting John Rae: "Life of Adam Smith, McMillan & Co, 1895) .

[96] Galbraith, J.K.,: "A History of Economics", Penguin Books, 1991, p. 64

[97] Adam Smith gives the example of a "Alma Goodheart" who helps a lame lady across the road, and we, as spectators approve and would have does the same. On the other hand we see "Ira Grumpy" kick a cat that has got in her way. We disapprove and develop antipathy to Ira, and sympathy to the cat.

[98] Raphael, DD: Three great economists, OUP 1997, p 39

[99] "The Wealth of Nations", Book 1, Ch. 2: "Division of Labour"

[100]"   , Book 4, System of Political Economy.

[101] Raphael, DD: Three great Economists, OUP 1997, p. 74

[102] Galbraith, J.K.,: "A History of Economics", Penguin Books, 1991, p. 72

[103] Donald Winch: Three Great Economists, OUP 1997

[104] Raphael, DD: Three Great Economists, OUP 1997, pp. 121-125

[105] Galbraith, J.K.,: "A History of Economics", Penguin Books, 1991, p. 75

[106] Blaug, M:"Economic Theory in retrospect" 1997, 5th Ed. Cambridge University Press.p.70

[107] Galbraith, J.K.,: "A History of Economics", Penguin Books, 1991, p. 80

[108] Galbraith, J.K.,: "A History of Economics", Penguin Books, 1991. p.81

[109] Malthus' Second Essay: "An Essay on the Principle of Population", edited by P James, p. 102

[110] Heiman,E: History of Economic Doctrines, 1952 OUP, pp.91-101

[111] Galbraith, J.K.,: "A History of Economics", Penguin Books, 1991, 82

[112] Blaug, M:"Economic Theory in retrospect" 1997, 5th Ed. Cambridge University Press., Ch.4

[113] Blaug, M:"Economic Theory in retrospect" 1997, 5th Ed. Cambridge University Press. P.85

[114] Galbraith, J.K.,: "A History of Economics", Penguin Books, 1991. p. 86

[115] Blaug, M:"Economic Theory in retrospect" 1997, 5th Ed. Cambridge University Press.p.119-124

[116] Galbraith, J.K.,: "A History of Economics", Penguin Books, 1991, p. 127-129

[117] Barber, William J. "A History of Economic Thought" 1991, Penguin Books, p 127

[118] Galbraith, J.K.,: "A History of Economics", Penguin Books, 1991, p.132

[119] Karl Marx: "Capital", Vol. 1, p.106

[120] Karl Marx: "Capital", Vol. 1, p. 554

[121] Karl Marx: "Capital", Vol. 1, pp 836-7

[122] Barber, William J. "A History of Economic Thought" 1991, Penguin Books, p. 151

[123] Böhm-Bawerk, Theory of Interest and Theory of Capital, 1989

[124] Robert Skidelsky in, Three Great Economists, OUP 1997, pp 225-237

[125] Galbraith, J.K.,: "A History of Economics", Penguin Books, 1991, p.230

[126] Robert Skidelsky in, Three Great Economists, OUP 1997, p.258

[127] Robert Skidelsky in, Three Great Economists, OUP 1997, p 259

[128] Roll E: "History of Economic Thought" 1968, p 522

[129] Robert Skidelsky in Three Great Economists, OUP 1997, p. 241-3

[130] Robert Skidelsky in Three Great Economists, OUP 1997, p. 274-276

[131] Blaug, M:"Economic Theory in retrospect" 1997, 5th Ed. Cambridge University Press., p. 646

[132] Robert Skidelsky in Three Great Economists, OUP 1997, p 284-287

[133] Barber, William J. "A History of Economic Thought" 1991, Penguin Books, p. 251

[134] Times Online obituary, 17 Nov.2006

[135] Galbraith, J.K.,: "A History of Economics", Penguin Books, 1991. p. 274

[136] Speech to the CBI, Institute of Directors, Leeds Chamber of Commerce and Yorkshire Forward at the Royal Armouries, Leeds, on Tuesday 21 October 2008

[137] `Abdu'l-Baha: Secret of Divine Civilization, Page: 5

[138] Baha'u'llah: Tablets of Baha'u'llah :p.37, The Fourth "Taraz" or (Ornament)

[139] Bahá'u'lláh : Tablets of Bahá'u'lláh, p. 34/35

[140] Baha'u'llah: Tablets of Baha'u'llah, Page: 35

[141] Baha'u'llah: Tablets of Baha'u'llah, Page: 38

[142] Baha'u'llah: Tablets of Baha'u'llah, Page: 39

[143] Baha'u'llah: The Kitab-i-Aqdas, Page: 30

[144] Baha'u'llah: Aqdas: Notes, Page: 192

[145] `Abdu'l-Baha: Foundations of World Unity*, Page: 38

[146] Shoghi Effendi: Foundations of World Unity*, Page: 19-20

[147] Shoghi Effendi: Youth, Page: 432

[148] Baha'u'llah: The Kitab-i-Aqdas, Page: 30

[149] Baha'u'llah: Epistle to the Son of the Wolf, Page: 93

[150] Baha'u'llah: Arabic Hidden Words, Page: 53

[151] Baha'u'llah: Tablets of Baha'u'llah, Page: 35

[152] Baha'u'llah: Tablets of Baha'u'llah, Page: 125

[153] Baha'u'llah: Tablets of Baha'u'llah, Page: 138

[154] Baha'u'llah: Gleanings, Page: 251

[155] Baha'u'llah: Tablets of Baha'u'llah, Page: 138

[156] Baha'u'llah: Tablets of Baha'u'llah, Page: 126

[157] Baha'u'llah: The Kitab-i-Aqdas, Page: 20

[158] Baha'u'llah, Epistle to the Son of Wolf, p 55

[159] Baha'u'llah: Persian Hidden Words, p 54

[160] `Abdu'l-Baha: Tablets of the Divine Plan, Page: 80

[161] Baha'u'llah: Aqdas: Notes, Page: 191

[162] `Abdu'l-Baha: Foundations of World Unity*, Page: 39

[163] `Abdu'l-Baha: Foundations of World Unity*, Page: 30-40

[164] Gross, Richard: "Psychology" 3rd ed. 1998, Hodder & Sloughton

[165] Doyal, L & Gough, I: "A Theory of Human Need" 1991, Macmillan Education Ltd, pp 92-99

[166] Shoghi Effendi: Directives of the Guardian, Page: 50

[167] `Abdu'l-Baha: Selections ... `Abdu'l-Baha, Page: 87

[168] Baha'u'llah: Tablets of Baha'u'llah, Page: 69

[169] `Abdu'l-Baha: Promulgation of Universal Peace*, Page: 238

[170] Shoghi Effendi: Directives of the Guardian, Page: 20

[171] `Abdu'l-Baha: Foundations of World Unity*, Page: 39

[172] `Abdu'l-Baha: Foundations of World Unity*, Page: 38

[173] Doyal, L & Gough, I: "A Theory of Human Need" 1991, Macmillan Education Ltd. P. 224

[174] `Abdu'l-Baha: Foundations of World Unity*, Page: 41

175 Hutton, Will: "The State We're In", 1995. Jonathan Cape

176 `Abdu'l-Baha: Promulgation of Universal Peace*, Page: 238

177 `Abdu'l-Baha: Promulgation of Universal Peace*, Page: 86

178 Shoghi Effendi: Baha'i Administration, Page: 10

179 Shoghi Effendi: World Order of Baha'u'llah, Page: 42

180 Multiple Authors: Lights of Guidance, Page: 550

181 Multiple Authors: Lights of Guidance, Page: 552 & 554

182 Hutton, Will: "The State We're In", 1995. Jonathan Cape, p. 224

183 `Abdu'l-Baha: Promulgation of Universal Peace*, Page: 238

184 `Abdu'l-Baha: Selections ... `Abdu'l-Baha, Page: 115

185 `Abdu'l-Baha: Selections ... `Abdu'l-Baha, Page: 89

186 Shoghi Effendi: Baha'i Administration, Page: 38

187 `Abdu'l-Baha: Promulgation of Universal Peace*, Page: 239

188 Hutton, Will: "The State We're In", 1995. Jonathan Cape. P. 262

189 Baha'u'llah: Epistle to the Son of the Wolf, Page: 30

190 Abdul Baha: Promulgation of Universal Peace, p.140

191 `Abdu'l-Baha: Promulgation of Universal Peace*, Page: 217

192 Baha'u'llah: Huququ'llah, Page: 490

193 Baha'u'llah: Huququ'llah, Page: 495

194 Baha'u'llah: Aqdas: Notes, Page: 209

195 Shoghi Effendi: Huququ'llah, Page: 515

196 Baha'u'llah: Huququ'llah, Page: 496

197 Baha'u'llah: Huququ'llah, Page: 490

198 Baha'u'llah: Huququ'llah, Page: 496

199 Baha'u'llah: Huququ'llah, Pages: 491-494

200 Lipsey, RG & Chrystal, KA: "Positive Economics" 1995, Oxford University Press. P. 655-656

201 Lipsey, RG & Chrystal, KA: "Positive Economics" 1995, Oxford University Press, p 432

202 `Abdu'l-Baha: Foundations of World Unity*, Page: 44

[203] `Abdu'l-Baha: Foundations of World Unity*, Page: 44-51

[204] `Abdu'l-Baha: Paris Talks*, Page: 152

[205] Lights of guidance page 551

[206] Promulgation of Universal Peace, p. 171

[207] Abdu'l-Baha: Foundations of World Unity*, Page: 44

[208] Lipsey, RG & Chrystal, KA: "Positive Economics" 1995, Oxford University Press, p. 449

[209] Shoghi Effendi: Letters to Aust. and New Zealand, Pages: 1-2

[210] Shoghi Effendi: Directives of the Guardian, p. 53

[211] Lipsey, RG & Chrystal, KA: "Positive Economics" 1995, Oxford University Press, 440

[212] Sir Thomas Gresham (1519-1579), financial agent to Queen Elizabeth I made this observation in 1558. H.D. MacCleod coined the term "Gresham's Law" in the 19th Century.

[213] Lipsey, RG & Chrystal, KA: "Positive Economics" 1995, Oxford University Press, pp 673-677

[214] Lipsey, RG & Chrystal, KA: "Positive Economics" 1995, Oxford University Press, p 677

[215] Bahá'u'lláh Tablets of Baha'u'llah, Pages: 133-134

[216] *Baha'u'llah: Tablets of Baha'u'llah, Page: 155*

[217] Greider, W : "One World, Ready or not" The manic logic of Global Capitalism 1997, Penguin Books, p.347.

[218] Dickens, P : "Global Shift" 3rd ed. 1998, part IV(Introduction, A Summary perspective), Paul Chapman Publishing Limited, p.292-3

[219] Henry George - Alfred Marshall American Journal of Economics and Sociology, The, Dec, 2001 by Nahid Aslanbeigui, Adele Wigk

[220] Lipsey, RG & Chrystal, KA: "Positive Economics" 1995, Oxford University Press, p. 701

[221] Lipsey, RG & Chrystal, KA: "Positive Economics" 1995, Oxford University Press, p. 870

[222] J.M. Blaut: The Colonizer's Model of the World: Geographical Diffusion and Eurocentric History, The Guildford Press 1993, p. 7 footnote

[223] Trade scent's Diary, The Garden, Journal of the Royal Horticultural Society of Gt. Britain, volume 124, part 6, June 1999, Page 413

[224] Speech on Mr Fox's East India Bill, 1 December 1783

[225] J.M. Blaut: The Colonizer's Model of the World: Geographical Diffusion and Eurocentric History, The Guildford Press 1993, pp 29-31

[226] J.M. Blaut: The Colonizer's Model of the World: Geographical Diffusion and Eurocentric History, The Guildford Press 1993, 40-41

[227] Ditto, Ch. 4

[228] J.M. Blaut: The Colonizer's Model of the World: Geographical Diffusion and Eurocentric History, The Guildford Press 1993 Pages 45-59. (paraphrased)

[229] David S Landes: The Wealth and Poverty of Nations, 1999, Norton Publishers, Ch. 21

[230] Baha'u'llah: The Kitab-i-Aqdas, Page: 52

[231] J.M. Blaut: The Colonizer's Model of the World: Geographical Diffusion and Eurocentric History, The Guildford Press 1993, 467-8

[232] J.M. Blaut: The Colonizer's Model of the World: Geographical Diffusion and Eurocentric History, The Guildford Press 1993, p.480

[233] J.M. Blaut: The Colonizer's Model of the World: Geographical Diffusion and Eurocentric History, The Guildford Press 1993, p. 501-3

[234] Bahá'í World Centre Publications

[235] Greider, W : "One World, Ready or not" The manic logic of Global Capitalism 1997, Penguin Books, p. 241-3

[236] Greider, W : "One World, Ready or not" The manic logic of Global Capitalism 1997, Penguin Books, p. 253

[237] Ditto, p 17

[238] Greider, W : "One World, Ready or not" The manic logic of Global Capitalism 1997, Penguin Books, p.238-243

239 Greider, W : "One World, Ready or not" The manic logic of Global Capitalism 1997, Penguin Books, p.257

240 Greider, W : "One World, Ready or not" The manic logic of Global Capitalism 1997, Penguin Books, p. 227

241 "The Promise for World Peace", 1985", Bahá'í World Centre Publications.

242 Baha'u'llah: Gleanings, Page: 249

243 Baha'u'llah: Consultation, Page: 93

244 Promulgation of Universal Peace, p. 24

245 Baha'u'llah: Epistle to the Son of the Wolf, Page: 28

246 Ditto, p.31-32

247 Peter Dickens: Global Shift, 3rd edition, PCP Publisher, 1999, p.25

248 Adam Smith: The Theory of Moral sentiments; 1976, Indianapolis,IN, Liberty Press, p. 126

249 Baha'u'llah: The Kitab-i-Aqdas, Page: 85

250 Shoghi Effendi: Baha'i Administration, Page: 64

251 Shoghi Effendi: Baha'i Administration, Pages: 62-64

252 Shoghi Effendi: Baha'i Administration, Page: 63

253 Economics for a World Commonwealth. Essays on economic theory from the Bahá'í Perspective, Gregory C Dahl, : European Bahá'í Business Forum

254 Shoghi Effendi: God Passes By, Pages: 94-96

255 Shoghi Effendi: World Order of Baha'u'llah, Page: 202

256 Shoghi. Haifa, Palestine, March 11, 1936 (Shoghi Effendi: World Order of Baha'u'llah, Pages: 202-206)

257 Baha'u'llah: Aqdas: Questions and Answers, Page: 138

258 Baha'u'llah: Aqdas: Questions and Answers, Page: 199-200

259 Baha'u'llah: The Arts, Pages: 1-2

260 Baha'u'llah: Tablets of Baha'u'llah revealed after the Kitab-i-Aqdas, p. 26
Baha'u'llah: Tablets of Baha'u'llah revealed after the Kitab-i-Aqdas, p. 26

261 Abdu'l-Baha: Selections from the Writings of Abdu'l-Baha, 1982 ed., p. 129:

262 Shoghi Effendi: World Order of Baha'u'llah, Page: 204

[263] Baha'u'llah: The Kitab-i-Aqdas, Page: 54

[264] Baha'u'llah: Epistle to the Son of the Wolf, Pages: 30-32

[265] Shoghi Effendi: Baha'i Administration, Page: 51

[266] Abdu'l-Baha, Foundations of World Unity, p. 42

[267] Abdu'l-Baha, Divine Philosophy, p. 69

Printed in the United Kingdom by
Lightning Source UK Ltd., Milton Keynes
141581UK00001B/2/P